IRELAND INC

A HISTORY OF
IRISH BUSINESS

IRELAND INC
A HISTORY OF
IRISH BUSINESS

*"Someone's sitting in the shade today
because someone planted a tree
a long time ago."*

-Warren Buffett

Ink Publishing
Unit 1A
Water's Edge
Charlotte Quay
Dublin 4

© Ink Publishing, 2017

978-1-5272-0574-1

Publisher: Ian Hyland (ian.hyland@businessandfinance.com)
Designer: Keith Dalton
Commissioning editors: John Walsh, Ruraidh Conlon O'Reilly
Project manager: Ruraidh Conlon O'Reilly
Contributors: Ruraidh Conlon O'Reilly, Tara Cunningham, Kyran Fitzgerald,
Conor Forrest, Constantin Gurdgiev, Brendan Keenan, Ian Maleney, Tom McEnaney,
Liz McHugh, Ed Micheau, Brian O'Connor, Fearghal O'Connor, David O'Sullivan,
Aileen O'Toole, Ian Parker, Gabi Thesing, John Walsh, Dan White,
Stephen Wynne Jones
Commercial director: Neil Butler
Government affairs: Ben English

Printed and bound by Scandbook, Falun, Sweden.

This book is dedicated to the spirit and memory of those who have shaped
Ireland Inc including TK Whitaker, Paddy Moriarty, Tony Ryan, Gillian Bowler,
Don Keough, Edward Haughey, Hugh Cooney, Oonagh Keogh, Joe McGough,
PV Doyle, Paddy Fitzpatrick, Ivor Kenny, Tom Roche, Jefferson Smurfit,
Tim Mahony, PJ Mara, Michael Killeen, Albert Reynolds, Donal Geaney
and many more who in very their very different ways are wonderful examples of
business trailblazers and public servants – and while not on their own, have made
such an outstanding contribution to Ireland in both a domestic and global context.

Special thanks is due to a very many others – far too many to mention
individually, but they know who they are.

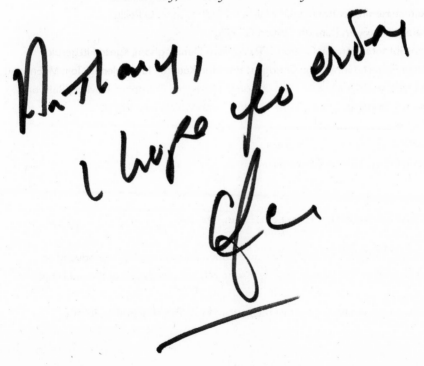

CONTENTS

SECTION 2
INTERVIEWS 2013-2017

SECTION 3
ARCHIVES

PUBLISHED WITH THE SUPPORT OF

KPMG

Aer Lingus

Bank of Ireland

Smurfit Kappa Group

Norbrook Laboratories

Primark

IDA

Enterprise Ireland

IBEC

CPL

Glen Dimplex

Independent News & Media

Maples & Calder (legal partner)

Connolly Capital

BOWING TO THE PAST, SHAPING THE FUTURE

IAN HYLAND, PUBLISHER OF BUSINESS & FINANCE, REFLECTS ON THE EBB AND FLOW OF IRISH BUSINESS LIFE – AND HOW WE CAN BUILD UPON THE ACHIEVEMENTS AND LESSONS OF THOSE WHO HAVE COME BEFORE US.

As the Charles Dickens adage goes: "It was the best of times, it was the worst of times." The same can be also be said for the Irish business climate over the last six decades.

Ireland INC: A History of Irish Business arrives at a time when the country is particularly mindful of its past, commemorating a series of dramatic set-pieces that began in 1912 and ended with Irish independence in 1922 – so, too the evolution of Irish business has seen the acorn grow to a global oak tree.

This book is testament to the great Irish companies, individuals and the teams behind them who have made Ireland's reputation as one of the best places to grow a domestic and global business what it is today. *Ireland INC: A History of Irish Business* presents an opportunity to reflect on where we've come from, where we are, and where we're going as a business community, and provide a unique source of reference for the business leaders and teachers of today and tomorrow.

Via such milestones as the Lemass/Whitaker First Programme for Economic Expansion in 1958, joining the EEC in 1973, Ireland becoming the rising star of Europe, the development of the IFSC and our outstanding

FDI success, along with the challenging times of the Seventies and Eighties, the boom of the late Nineties and 2000s, the global financial crash, recovery, Brexit and the surprise election of President Trump, Ireland's evolutions and revolutions have taken place against the backdrop of an ever-changing global geopolitical and economic landscape. *Ireland INC – A History of Irish Business* provides a first chronology of the evolution of Irish business and Ireland as an economy in both a domestic and global context.

Stories are nothing without storytellers, and much credit is due to the individuals, institutions and media owners who have chronicled the evolution of Irish business over the nearly six decades of dedicated business reporting. This book has drawn on the knowledge and stories of some of our best journalists across Irish and international media owners.

As we reflect, Irish business has been a colourful and energetic scene throughout our lifetime. Fascinating personalities, engaging narratives, impressive achievements and failures abound – all played out in an environment where businesspeople are very often public figures, and their deeds frequently now become front-page news. However, this was not always the case.

As we know, the only place where success comes before work is in the dictionary – and equally, there is little point in studying the past if we don't learn from it. This book shares lessons both cautionary and encouraging from some of Ireland's greatest business innovators.

Among the positives, it is hard not to be struck by the drive and ambition of various eras' business leaders, by their vision, and by our ability as a nation to collectively recognise economic reform as a solution to and opportunity arising from that long-standing Irish curse, emigration. Meanwhile, so many of those surnames who have left Ireland would take leadership roles in the boardrooms of many of the world's best known businesses.

The publication of this book comes after nearly five years of research and writing by so many wonderful business journalists.

On personal note, during my time working with and latterly acquiring *Business & Finance*, I have had the great honour to work with so many outstanding business writers and editors. In addition, this unique platform has allowed me to host and engage with some of the world's most outstanding business and political leaders. So after nearly five years of a journey, to finally publish *A History of Irish Business* and document some of those experiences, including an exclusive series of interviews conducted between 2013 and 2017, is an incredibly proud milestone for all who worked and contributed to this unique chronology.

In 2005, I had the great pleasure of hosting a dinner for Tony Ryan in Dublin along with his peers and friends to honour one of our most unique business leaders and a truly outstanding Irishmen. Tony very kindly recognised the importance of what was a wonderful occasion by sending me a gift of a bottle of his family's 1996 Margaux.

I have never had the right opportunity to open that bottle but on publication of this book I think it only fitting to finally open it and toast all those who have contributed to Ireland INC, its business leaders, pro-business political leaders, public servants, teachers, commentators and the many husbands, wives, partners, parents and children who support that rare breed of business person and entrepreneur who, through their innovation and achievements have played a vital role to put Ireland on the global map and in boardrooms across the world.

I hope this book will be as captivating to the reader as it was to its writers and all who have worked on it – but most importantly, that it forms a fitting salute to all of those who have created, risked and built so much, and to light a torch that can be carried into the future.

I look forward to Volume Two.

Fortis fortuna adiuvat!

Ian Hyland
Publisher

IN THE BEGINNING...

FOUNDING EDITOR **NICHOLAS LEONARD** REFLECTS
ON THE ORIGINS OF BUSINESS & FINANCE.

When the first issue of *Business and Finance* appeared on September 18th 1964, most people doubted whether it would survive 50 days let alone 50 years. The sceptics were confounded but there were some difficult moments in the early history of the magazine when it looked alarmingly likely that they would be proved right.

The Irish economy was far smaller then. Agriculture was still a major contributor and, while industry and commerce were growing, most people believed that the scope for a specialist weekly magazine was small to non-existent.

The man who thought they were wrong was called Hugh McLaughlin, an entrepreneurial and ever-optimistic magazine publisher, whose titles included the fashion monthly *Creation*.

Its editor was his wife, Nuala, whom I met for the first time on a promotional trip for journalists to relaunch the Dromoland Castle Hotel in April 1964. I was financial editor of *The Irish Times* and she urged me to interview her husband about the growth of his publishing company, the Creation group.

I met Hugh for the first time over lunch in the Stephen's Green Club. After chatting for about a half an hour, he said to me: "I have always wanted to start a business weekly magazine in Ireland and I would like you to be the editor of it."

Looking back, it seems extraordinary to me that *Business and Finance* ever got going as our total staff – editorial, secretarial and advertising – was only five people. We started work at the beginning of August, and in early September we printed a dummy edition with numerous blank pages optimistically headed 'Property' and 'Stock Market Report' and a few articles to indicate the kind of coverage we intended to provide.

This was distributed to several hundred senior company executives at a launch party in the Shelbourne Hotel early in September, and less than a fortnight later the first real issue was being printed and had gone on sale.

The first year was very difficult but two crucial developments came to our rescue in 1965. Firstly, in June Hugh McLaughlin recruited an extremely effective advertising manager named George Harman who had previously worked in London. Secondly, the three national newspapers (*Irish Times*, *Independent* and *Press*) were all closed that summer for about four months by an industrial dispute. This gave a considerable boost to our circulation and advertising revenue.

With the invaluable help of Jim Milton and Joe O'Malley as associate editors, *Business and Finance* had become a firmly established media presence by the time I left at the end of 1969.

PART

1

ESSAYS

CHAPTER 1

Economic nadir: the 1950s
By Brendan Keenan

AMID RECORD EMIGRATION AND A SLUGGISH ECONOMY, THE ONLY THING POLICYMAKERS AGREED ON WAS THAT A CHANGE WAS NEEDED – AND THE LEMASS/WHITAKER REFORMS PROVIDED IT.

History does not run in ten-year cycles, but surprisingly often it comes close. The '1950s' can be said to begin in 1948, with the defeat of Fianna Fáil, the election of an inter-party coalition government, and one of the strangest decisions in Irish politics. The decade ended, by common consent, with the publication in 1958 of the famous strategy document *Economic Development*, authored by TK Whitaker.

The strange decision, by modern standards, was the new government's sale of five large aircraft and the cancellation of the transatlantic route planned by Aerlínte Éireann/Aer Lingus. Not only had the previous government acquired the Constellation aircraft, Ireland had been given landing rights in several US cities. It was to be ten years before passengers could fly the Atlantic on an Irish aircraft, by which time probably the best chance of creating a major international airline had gone.

The sale was a potent symbol of the cultural, financial and economic attitudes that bedevilled what is still regarded as the worst decade in the history of the State. True, the aircraft were expensive and public finances, as always, were tight. Spending on housing and health services was seen as more important. It was later claimed that the Labour Party refused to join the coalition unless the planes were sold, on the grounds that transatlantic travel was a luxury for rich people.

One can see the argument. It may be a mistake to regard the 1950s as just ancient history. The issue of investment and savings versus current consumption and public spending is still with us. Ireland is one of those countries where consumption, and acquiring the income necessary to provide it, gets a particularly strong political preference.

In the 1950s, such attitudes were more extreme. There was a failure to imagine the future in any realistic way, or to understand that income ultimately depends on productivity, which requires initial investment. The attitude extended to roads and telephone services, where investment was also cut, on the grounds that these were luxuries for the well-to-do and of no interest to ordinary people.

The origins of that failure of vision go back much further, to the nature of British rule in Ireland and, most of all, to the absence of major industrialisation outside of the greater Belfast area. By 1948 it was already clear that the bold Fianna Fáil programme, led by Seán Lemass, of industrialisation behind tariff walls had failed – but there was little idea of what could replace it.

The Free State economy was caricatured as "beef, beer and biscuits", reflecting the importance of the cattle business and the fact that the only major industrial exporters were Guinness and Jacob's. Along with very conservative banks, with their attachment to the London money market, and the protected Irish manufacturers, these represented the major political forces in the country. There was little pressure for long-term investment or technical progress.

Some economists, especially on the left, believed that the importance of beef farming was to the detriment of economic development. It certainly comes as a shock to see how small the dairy sector was in comparison, while tillage, poultry and pig farming contributed even less.

Frank Aiken, minister for finance at the start of the decade – when Fianna Fáil returned to office – and later minister for agriculture, pointed out that Ireland had lost its ability to compete in butter, bacon and oats. Farmers were abandoning milk production even though, as he pointed out, the country was well suited to it. A later argument held that the dominance of cattle-rearing inhibited the engineering and technological developments seen in other European countries, especially Denmark.

But it is a mistake to think – as many probably do – that things changed only in 1958. The Free State itself ceased to exist with the surprise declaration of a republic by Taoiseach John A Costello in 1949. Some see that as giving birth to new ways of thinking, but it could also be argued that it reflected them.

The election manifesto of one of the smaller coalition parties, Clann na Poblachta, proposed a national monetary authority "to create currency and credit for the economic needs of full employment and full production". Department of Finance opposition saw off any such ideas but the old order was failing, under threat from external forces and criticism at home.

That same year Dr Whitaker, then a middle-ranking civil servant, pointed out in a Department of Finance minute that the desire for British standards of social services and wages (the latter were often actually higher in Ireland) hampered economic development, since Britain was so much more developed. Today, we would call it a lack of competitiveness.

Competitiveness was not a concept in 1950s Ireland. The thinking of Lemass and the Department of Industry and Commerce was that output in the protected industries would just match demand. Firms would not compete with each other and demand for consumer goods itself was not meant to increase rapidly. There was no attempt to create an export sector. Nor was it clear how this could be done.

It has been characterised as the difference between the 'tide' and the 'pie'. Later in the decade, Lemass, who had recognised that faster growth was essential, would famously say that a rising tide lifts all boats. The other view of the economy, still in vogue until quite recently, was of the pie, where the only question is who gets which share.

By 1950 the economy's poor performance was a political issue to an extent that it had not been immediately after independence, in the depressed 1930s or, naturally, during the war years. National income (GNP) had averaged only 1% growth since 1940, half the workforce was employed in agriculture, 90% of exports went to Britain – of which only 7% were manufactured goods. Emigration had already reached a peacetime peak of 35,000, although worse was to come.

There is evidence that the comparative success of Northern Ireland spurred the feeling south of the Border that a wrong turning had been taken somewhere. If the newly-minted Republic was falling so far behind, what had been the point of winning independence in the first place? Some historians focus attention on a speech in March 1957 by Charles Carter, professor of economics at Queen's

University Belfast. Strangely for such an address to the Irish Association, his paper was circulated to cabinet ministers within a fortnight. Professor Carter noted that income per head in the Republic was now about half that of the UK, and the gap was widening. He stressed the point – so alien in the 1950s and not extinct yet – that income must be generated by productive activity, not just distributed.

The Republic was falling behind, "not only in income, but in the technical progress which creates the promise of further income. Though endowed with the great national advantages of closeness to wealthy markets, the absence of substantial defence expenditure and large external assets, the Republic achieves her close progress only by a prodigal dissipation of external assets, occasionally restrained by emergency measures," he said.

Professor Carter explicitly urged the attraction of foreign companies with tax breaks, not just for their capital but for the badly needed technical and management skills that they could bring. He dismissed as illusions the widely-held beliefs that Irish-owned firms were better than foreign ones, and that small firms were better than large ones.

The outside world was crowding in on Ireland, in ways that have largely been glossed over outside academic circles. The US Marshall Plan to rebuild Europe after the war was undoubtedly generous and far-sighted: by 1950, Ireland had received almost £150 million in grants and loans under the plan – but it was not a free lunch and the American conditions posed great problems for Irish policy-makers. They required domestic policies that would promote growth and open the country more to foreign capital and goods (essentially American).

One of the most important results is also one of the least well-known: the creation of the Industrial Development Authority (IDA) in 1949. Most people have a vague idea that it was part of the Lemass/Whitaker reforms at the end of the decade. It played a crucial role in them, but pre-dated them by a decade and its existence owed as much to American demands as Irish ideas.

Some Irish ideas were deeply hostile. The departments of Finance and Industry and Commerce spent most of the decade fighting each other over economic and industrial policy. The latter department was in favour of accepting the Marshall Plan aid, but Finance was opposed on the grounds that the dangers to Irish industry would outweigh the economic benefits.

But both were in agreement in opposing the creation of the IDA. The Industry ministry still hankered after import substitution provided by Irish companies but Finance, backed by British opposition, blocked the establishment of a Foreign Trade Corporation to help with the policy, while the Federation of Irish Manufacturers was against any easing of restrictions on foreign capital to finance such developments. Ironically, much of the protected Irish industry was actually owned by foreign companies, which enjoyed healthy margins, no competition and little need for investment in their Irish operations.

The surprising decision that the board of the IDA be independent of government ran counter to attitudes across the whole civil service – attitudes that persist to this day. Alexis FitzGerald, Costello's son-in-law and economic adviser, claimed that the idea came to him from Eustace Shott, a partner in the accountancy firm Craig Gardner. There was also the establishment of the Export Board, Córas Tráchtála, which is now absorbed in Enterprise Ireland.

Finance insisted that the IDA be confined to seeking foreign investment and give no support to domestic industry. Problems with this distinction continue to this day. At the time, other problems were much more pressing. Under the Marshall Plan, Ireland had to join the OEEC organisation of recipient countries. It insisted on a major reduction in import quotas; 50% in 1949 and 75% by 1951. These measures helped growth but created a problem with which we are once again familiar: how to deal with a trade deficit when the currency is fixed.

As with the modern eurozone, deflation seemed the only option. A record balance of payments deficit in 1951 triggered corrective action from Finance and the Central Bank, leading to recession the following year. With no engines of growth, the problem arose even more intensely in 1955 – the year that the OEEC required the end of 90% of import quotas. The economy was deflated again. The 1956 recession is still remembered as the worst on record, at least until 2008. It remains the worst for emigration. In 1957 almost 60,000 people, or 2% of the population, fled the country.

Over the course of the decade growth averaged 1.7% a year, one-third less than the growth in Northern Ireland, where the fifties were a decade of prosperity. The contrast with the small continental countries enjoying the spin-off from the German 'economic miracle' was even greater, with their economies growing by 36%. One in ten people emigrated – proportions not seen since the 1880s.

In 1956 Clann na Poblachta's leader, Seán MacBride, who had been chief of staff of the socialist remnant of the IRA in the 1930s and foreign minister in the first inter-party government, delivered an influential analysis from the Dáil backbenches to the second such government. It showed that the fastest-growing economy in the previous three years had been Austria, even though it was still partitioned between the western Allies and the Soviet Union. Ireland was the worst performer, growing more slowly than Greece.

Of course, most of these countries were recovering from the ground zero of wartime destruction but neutral Sweden's output had increased by 8% and victorious Britain's by 7%. Ireland had managed to grow by only 4%. With hindsight, one can see that Irish neutrality, while it protected the country physically, isolated it from technological and international developments in the post-war years, while preserving the 1930s political system that was swept away elsewhere, whether in the British and French democracies or the defeated dictatorships.

One exchange between civil servants in the wake of the publication of *Economic Development* shows the difficulties faced by modernisers. Commenting on the idea of more investment in the telephone system, one of the old guard wrote that this would mean diverting capital "to something that is mainly a convenience". The moderniser replied that in a modern economy "an efficient telephone network is an essential basis for progress" but it was the late 1980s before serious money was spent on telecommunications.

Perhaps we should not scoff too much. To many at the time there seemed no way out of the difficulties. Leaving the OEEC risked complete isolation. There were already plans to launch what became the European Free Trade Association (EFTA), but this would formalise the 90% dependence on the British market. The ending of quotas might be followed by reductions in tariffs, leaving no hope that Irish industry could compete at home or export abroad. In the meantime, the balance of payments deficit and the resulting shortage of foreign currency meant that domestic consumption had to be reined in to reduce imports, but harmed domestic production as well.

Yet it was in the despair of 1956 that the first tax relief for exports was introduced. This gave tax breaks on profits earned from exports: 50% at the beginning, but increased to 100% in 1958. It was not aimed at attracting foreign companies, but rather encouraging Irish companies to export. In the event it proved much more successful in the unintended aim than the intentional.

Seán Lemass deserves much of the political credit for the changes that occurred during the decade – but not all of it, as sometimes seems the case. Costello's second government pushed through the export tax relief in the face of Department of Finance opposition, although in defence of the department it must be conceded that the reliefs, along with grants, were a heavy drain on the public finances.

As Whitaker himself put it in a memo about a particular proposal (and which may seem prescient in light of today's monstrous tax avoidance industry): "Nothing we can do will relieve the Danes of all tax on their income. A double taxation agreement would secure that they paid only one tax – and that tax to the Irish Exchequer. The exports tax concession will secure that they pay one tax – but to the Danish Exchequer."

Although the fifties were, on the face of it, a decade of political instability with four different administrations, the new economic ideas continued to develop despite changes in government. With Fianna Fáil back in office from 1951-54, Lemass continued to stress import substitution when he returned as industry minister, asking the IDA "to concentrate all their activities" on examining the possibilities. But the authority used its unprecedented independence to ignore his request and instead pursue ways of attracting foreign industry to establish in Ireland.

The decision to establish an export board was taken by the inter-party government but implemented by Lemass on his return. This body joined the IDA in calling for export profits tax relief. Finance and the Revenue Commissioners had good cause to worry about the effects on government revenues, even when they believed that policy must change. There is always some scheme whose success, it is claimed, will generate more revenue than it would cost, but most are fantasies.

The one certainty shared by all the political parties was that things could not go on as before. This was signalled by Lemass, when the great proponent of protected industry put forward the abolition of import tariffs and a State-funded capital programme, designed to increase productivity rather than, as before, improving living standards.

The unexpected factor was that the new secretary of the Department of Finance, Ken Whitaker, had been working on a whole new set of economic policies. He had also been exploring Irish membership of the World Bank and IMF, which could provide both financial support and technical assistance for economic development.

He had certainly come to the belief that things could not go on as before. This led him to the further conclusion that Finance must keep a firm grip on the changes that had to come. In 1953 he wrote: "Our function is not to select the most meritorious proposals and clap them on the taxpayer's back but, rather, to see that as few as possible emerge as new burdens on the community." This view has never entirely left Merrion Street, but Whitaker concluded that while control of the public finances was essential, it was not enough on its own.

On Fianna Fáil's first day in office after the 1957 election, Whitaker presented James Ryan, the new finance minister, with a blunt assessment of the country's position. It was designed to cut Fianna Fáil to the quick, saying: "Without a sound and progressive economy, political independence would be a crumbling facade." Rather than being upset at such comments from a civil servant, it became clear that Lemass needed no persuading, and nor did Ryan.

The government accepted the proposal for World Bank and IMF membership. The implication was that Ireland was going to embrace open markets and the flow of capital. At this stage, though, the politicians did not know that Whitaker was also leading a team to produce what became the famous *Economic Development*. Among them were three later secretaries of Finance, Maurice Doyle, Tomás Ó Cofaigh and Seán Cromien.

At the end of 1957, Whitaker told his minister what was afoot. Ryan was supportive and began the delicate business of bringing cabinet colleagues on board. Many of their departments, especially Finance's old rival, Industry and Commerce, had little or no inkling of the work that had been done.

But Lemass, the industry minister, was supportive. That left the ageing Taoiseach Éamon de Valera, whose vision of Ireland had been very different. However, he was becoming increasingly detached from day-to-day politics. In his biography, Whitaker recalled that de Valera claimed free trade had really been his policy all along.

In May 1958 the government received a draft of the 249-page document. It is probably a measure of the desperation felt by everyone that the very next day the cabinet decided that all State and semi-State bodies examine it and make their observations within three weeks. Whitaker himself sent copies to the World Bank, IMF and OEEC and got their endorsement of the plan. The World Bank made implementation of the policies a condition for future financial assistance to Ireland.

In July, a committee chaired by Lemass began to prepare a government white paper based on what was still just a civil servant's document, however significant. Politics had not been entirely abolished and the white paper was a mere 50 pages long when it was published in November, and a shadow of the Whitaker brief. But politics had been sufficiently abolished by the crisis for the full document to be published later – unprecedentedly, for a civil servant, under Whitaker's own name, because no-one could agree on its exact status.

The white paper did make some politically-inspired changes to the Whitaker document, which became known as the Grey Book for want of a better description. The latter saw more commercial production of cattle as the future for Irish agriculture and called for a review of financial assistance to farming, but the white paper was more circumspect. If this sounds familiar, there is even more modern relevance in the dispute over whether new industry should be established in large urban centres or whether – as was traditional Fianna Fáil policy – it should be decentralised as much as possible.

Old-school politics may also have inadvertently led Ireland along the road of incentivising exports by foreign companies. By 1958, Lemass was determined to grasp the nettle of repeal of the Control of Manufactures Act, the protectionist measures that he himself had presided over in the 1930s – but partly because of that protection, many Irish manufacturers were supporters of Fianna Fáil.

The wily politician abolished the provisions only for the minority of firms that exported most of their production and, instead of calling it the repeal of the Manufactures Act, christened it 'An Act for the Encouragement of Exports'. In the end, the policy of encouraging exports, especially by foreign companies, became the cornerstone of the successes of the 1960s – and of every decade since.

CHAPTER 2

Rising tide: the 1960s
By Brendan Keenan

AN ECONOMIC AND SOCIAL REVOLUTION GRIPPED THE COUNTRY AS POLICY
OPENED UP TO FREE TRADE AND GLOBAL CO-OPERATION – BUT THE SIXTIES WERE
FAR FROM PLAIN SAILING.

O ver the past 50 years, the people of Ireland have become used to the remarkable ups and downs of the economy: what one economic historian called the biblical "seven lean and seven fat years" pattern. But 60 years ago, no-one could have anticipated the extraordinary achievements of the 1960s, which propelled Ireland to new levels of prosperity and social change. In Ireland, as elsewhere, the pre-war world gave way to the post-war one of consumerism and personal freedom; somewhere, as the British poet Philip Larkin said, between the *Lady Chatterley* obscenity trial and the Beatles' first LP.

Far from those developments, even in Ireland's Department of Finance pessimistic frugality began to give way to optimistic fiscal expansion and a better understanding of the benefits of public investment. This coincided with a general change of attitude among policymakers and the public about Ireland's place in the world, and the ways in which it could emulate more successful economies and integrate with them.

The figures are indeed startling. For the 30 years to 1960, economic growth averaged just 1.3% a year. In the 1960s this jumped more than threefold to 4.4% For the first time since the great industrial depression of the 1930s, the South's economy grew faster than the North's. By

1970 it was the fastest-growing in Europe. By the end of the decade net emigration had ceased, having peaked at 60,000 in 1958. The population grew by 100,000, the first such increase since the Famine. Many of the building blocks of this success had been put in place in the previous decade but the speed of construction of the new economy was still astonishing.

As always with a small open economy, international conditions had to be favourable. The 1960s were years of steady global growth, without serious disruptions such as the Korean War and the Suez crisis in the previous decade. Just as important for Ireland – although rarely recognised – was an improvement in the terms of trade, with a fall in import costs and a rise in export prices. One calculation is that these improved by a third over the course of the decade.

The difference from the past was that Ireland was able to make more of these favourable conditions. This reflected changes in domestic policy and the opening of the economy to foreign trade that accelerated in the 1960s. In terms of income per head, Ireland did not begin to overtake the successful continental economies until the heady days of the 1990s, but at least it kept pace. Looked at in this way, the 1960s were perhaps the last chance for independent Ireland to become a success.

It was also the decade of social revolution. Had the economy continued to flounder while the world outside prospered and abandoned the old social mores, it is hard to know what would have become of the country. Instead, society changed just as much, if not more, than the economy, from debates about the ban on contraceptives to the craze for rock and roll. RTÉ began television broadcasting in 1961. The ageing President de Valera made his concerns about this new medium clear in his broadcast inaugurating the service. But so too did the man who is seen as the architect of the new economy, Taoiseach Seán Lemass.

In a remarkable 1961 interview with the late distinguished journalist Des Fisher, Lemass accurately predicted that contraception and divorce would be legalised by the end of the century but feared, like de Valera, that many of the good qualities of the Irish people would be lost.

As for the economy, this was the decade when US multinational companies began to bestride the globe; a development actively encouraged by the US government with tax incentives that continue to this day, even if they are now a source of considerable controversy.

The arrival of such companies in Ireland in the 1960s is often seen as the entire explanation for the successes of the decade. It was certainly the main source of the increase in industrial output, in contrast to the limited improvements from native manufacturing. Some 350 foreign companies were established during the decade, accounting for 80% of investment. They provided just 2% of total output in 1960 but 13% by 1970 (eventually peaking at more than 40%). Employment in foreign companies assisted by the IDA provided one in five manufacturing jobs by the end of the decade and an even higher proportion of exports.

The irony is that this was not particularly the intention of government policy. The idea had been to encourage domestic firms to export, but as foreign firms showed more and more interest in Ireland's incentives, the incentives were improved. The main attraction was complete tax relief on exports, established in 1958, with the period of the tax break extended to 15 years in 1960. Four years later, the remaining restrictions on foreign ownership and control of companies were removed and full repatriation of profits was allowed – a policy that astonished other European countries for many years.

Foreign investment

There has often been some doubt about the wisdom of these policies. The cost of grants and taxes foregone has been estimated at almost a third of value added in manufacturing. Since the 1960s all corporate profits, not just export or manufacturing earnings, have been levied at low rates – first at 10% and then 12.5% – to comply with EU rules. This further complicates any calculations of cost and benefit but the memory of the transformation throughout the decade may well have embedded an uncritical attitude to the attraction of foreign firms as the centrepiece of Irish industrial policy.

There were no such doubts in the 1960s, as people saw the obvious benefits of foreign investment. One issue did arise, and continues to be a source of contention: how to spread new industry beyond the large urban centres, particularly Dublin and Cork. The well-known War of Independence veteran and Fianna Fáil TD Martin Corry wanted the government to compel industrialists to locate where it wanted. Ministers had to admit that unlike the earlier quota-protected companies, they could not decide where the new operations were to go.

In the end, the IDA had considerable success in decentralising foreign firms, such as the Liebherr crane factory in Kerry, with judicious mixtures of grant aid. As far back as 1952, legislation provided extra financial incentives for companies setting up in the west and midlands. The IDA was also moving into the business of choosing sectors likely to provide fast-growing companies that would be attracted by the Irish tax reliefs and labour force. In what turned out to be an inspired choice, electronics and pharmaceuticals were among the first favoured industries, with Abbott and IBM among big names that set up operations in the 1960s.

The IDA was central to the 1960s' success. It had been around for more than ten years, but was established essentially as a research body to deal with an admitted national lack of knowledge on economic development, or even the structures of industry. To further improve matters, in 1960 Ken Whitaker, the Department of Finance secretary whose 1958 development paper laid the basis for the new policies, secured a grant of $280,000 (€1 million in today's money) from the Ford Foundation to establish the Economic and Social Research Institute (ESRI).

The National Economic and Social Council, now called the NESC, was established in 1963 and became the 'think tank' of the social partners. The origins of social partnership itself may perhaps be traced to the establishment of the Committee of Industrial Organisation, in which government, industry and the trade unions carried out a review of Irish industry.

The IDA was specifically tasked with promoting new investment, although initially there was a separate body, An Foras Tionscal, which assessed projects and decided on grants. Nothing succeeds like success, and in 1970 the authority was able to break the remaining links with the civil service and establish its own recruitment and employment terms, as well as grant allocation, although civil service influence appears to have grown again in recent years.

The other fundamental change, besides the opening of the economy to investment and trade, was the decision to make free secondary school education available to all. Famously, it was announced without warning in 1966 – to an audience of journalists, of all people – by Education Minister Donogh O'Malley.

He was standing on the shoulders of others. His predecessor (later to be president) Patrick Hillery had launched a pilot plan for what became community schools in remote areas, noting that "certain vested interests" – code for the Catholic Church – might not like the scheme but could hardly complain since no other secondary education had been provided for these places. This was part of a wider plan devised in 1963 on the basis of recommendations from the OECD, which has always had a strong emphasis on education research.

O'Malley's coup caught Taoiseach Seán Lemass, the cabinet and the civil service by surprise. His motive seems to have been to create a reality that the church could not overturn. In the Seanad the following year, in a dramatic example of changing sixties attitudes, O'Malley launched a full-frontal attack. In tones not heard again until Enda Kenny's speech on clerical child abuse, O'Malley told senators: "It was our Divine Lord who said, 'Suffer little children to come unto me' [...] Christian charity how are you!" A few years earlier though, in his typically understated way, Jack Lynch as education minister had also ignored church objections by recognising the Federation of Lay Catholic Secondary Schools.

For all its courage, O'Malley's bombshell was not perhaps the ideal way of doing things. It was also part of an uncomfortable pattern of behaviour associated with the sharp-suited trio of O'Malley, Neil Blaney and CJ Haughey.

Referring to the new political breed, Seán T O'Kelly, later to become de Valera's successor at the Áras, wrote: "I hope the bold-as-brass young fellows will do as well for the country as the old brigade." Professor Tom Garvan, in his book *Preventing the Future*, quotes another Old IRA veteran, Cavan TD Patrick Smith: "There are worse ways of entering politics than with a rope round your neck." Even though we have arrived in a new century, those debates continue.

Even supporters of change, including Whitaker, thought that O'Malley's shock announcement caused the free schools scheme to be poorly implemented and cost more than it needed to. The opportunity to shift Irish education from traditional 'academic' studies to more vocational and technical approaches was blunted and has never been fully realised. The history of Irish politics suggests, however, that a more conventional approach would have taken many years. It takes only five to lose a generation of secondary school-age children.

In 1960 there were only some 2,000 engineers in the Republic and three quarters of them were employed in the public sector. In 1968 the National Apprenticeship Board was established to address the problem, but the absence of 19th-century industrial innovation in southern Ireland, especially compared to small European countries like Denmark or Sweden, cast a long shadow over economic development and curtailed the expansion of indigenous private industry in the good times of the 1960s.

Commentators since have noted that native industry also received a double-blow from the removal of both tariffs and quotas on imports, unlike the later Asian tigers that were able to develop export potential while being sheltered on their home markets. However, Japan, and those who followed, also made industrial education and training a central part of their strategy. Ireland never did, and arguably never has.

To a large extent, domestic industrial expansion was confined to the semi-state companies, for whom this was a golden decade never to be repeated. Their role was not just the provision of goods and services, but the development of the management, technical and business skills so obviously absent in private business. In various ways the ESB, Bord na Móna and Bord Fáilte became world leaders in their fields. Tourism earnings – mostly American – topped £80m a year, or 5% of GNP, in the late 1960s.

Lack of expertise alone cannot explain the decline of the semi-states in later years into feather-bedding, inefficiency and excessive costs, but the skills weakness is evident in contrast with the technically advanced Finns, who studied Bord na Móna methods of peat extraction and went on to become successful global exporters of extraction machinery.

But old attitudes die hard and must carry some, perhaps most, of the blame. Ken Whitaker recalled how he had to "gently rein in" Lt General Michael J Costello, the ambitious chief executive of the now defunct Irish Sugar Company. Costello did not find the experience quite so gentle. In more recent times the ESB and Bord na Móna experienced similar pulls on their bridles.

Finance continues to harbour doubts about the wisdom of public commercial investment, and the trade unions about commercial competition. On the other side, the companies succumbed to the old Irish problem of putting income, whether for staff or government, before investment and profitable expansion.

Indigenous private industry did not enjoy even the advantages of skill and scale possessed by the semi-states. The export-driven newcomers posed little direct threat, although they may have pushed up wages and attracted the better local workers and managers.

But native industry could not cope with the direct competition from abroad, first from the Anglo-Irish Free Trade Agreement of 1965, and then membership of the European Economic Community in the following decade. Unemployment remained high, leading to comments on the phenomenon of 'jobless growth', as redundancies in traditional industries and agriculture, along with the growing labour force, offset the gains in employment elsewhere.

Yet Ireland's room for manoeuvre was strictly limited. The 1960s were when Europe first became an issue, and it caused problems from the beginning. Lemass in particular had always seen Ireland's destiny as being in a uniting Europe and was prepared to compromise military neutrality in return. But events set their own agenda in ways over which Ireland had little control.

Towards Europe

The European Economic Community (EEC) had been established in 1958 with the original 'Six,' West Germany, France, Italy, Belgium, the Netherlands and Luxembourg. Britain stayed aloof and in 1960 formed EFTA, the European Free Trade Association, with Austria, Denmark,

Finland, Norway, Portugal and Sweden. The problem for Ireland was that EFTA, unlike the EEC, had no supports for agriculture but would expose industry to more competition in the all-important British market. The temptation to restore tariff protection, despite its obvious failures, was strong.

Instead, prompted strongly by Whitaker, the government decided to go the other way – not joining EFTA, but nevertheless removing remaining trade and investment barriers with Britain. The British were not particularly keen, given the concerns of agriculture and Northern Ireland's industry, but a limited agreement was signed in 1960 giving preferred status to some Irish farm products in return for a review of Irish tariffs on British goods.

The battle over free trade continued over the early part of the decade with divisions in cabinet, the political parties and the civil service, where Industry and Commerce fretted about the threat to Irish industry and Finance, under Whitaker, argued that free trade was inevitable. We can now see that both were right. Free trade in Europe was inevitable, but very little of the Irish industry of 1960 survived the experience.

The government also considered membership of the international trade organisation GATT. But increasingly its interest turned to joining the EEC or, as it was universally known, the Common Market. The evolving Common Agricultural Policy looked like it could solve the problems for Irish agriculture selling at artificially low prices in the subsidised British market, while the threat to industry was no greater than the existing ones.

But the British had still shown no interest in joining the EEC and membership without the UK risked the market to which 90% of Irish exports still went. That changed the following year, when Britain did apply. Ireland did so hours beforehand, but there was a real danger that the UK would be accepted while the Irish economy would be considered too undeveloped for membership.

While full negotiations were open with Britain and Denmark, the EEC requested further discussion of "the special problems" raised by Irish membership. This was despite intensive lobbying in EEC capitals by Whitaker and the secretary of the Department of External (now Foreign) Affairs, Con Cremin, whose efforts included an audience with Pope John XXIII. The Pope is reported to have said to Cremin: "Christian faith can purify even economic matters."

At the beginning of 1962 Lemass and industry minister Jack Lynch made Ireland's case to EEC ministers but the Irish application was not formally presented to the governing Council of Ministers partly, it would seem, because of Ireland's non-membership of NATO. More diplomacy followed, including an official visit by Lemass to West Germany, and in October the EEC agreed to open full negotiations. Then at the beginning of 1963 French president General de Gaulle dramatically vetoed British membership. This was probably to Ireland's benefit, giving it another ten years to dismantle industrial protection and modernise the economy. The impetus already achieved paved the way for the much wider Anglo-Irish Free Trade Agreement in 1965.

Complex relationship

The agreement was the culmination of a decade-long move towards free trade. It had an unlikely beginning, with the decision by Britain's new Labour government under Harold Wilson to impose a 15% duty on all manufactured imports as a way of reducing the balance of payments deficit. This was a serious threat to the Irish economy, affecting a fifth of the country's exports. Yet, in another sign of the strangely complex relationship between the two countries, after a year's hard bargaining the Free Trade Agreement was signed on terms that looked favourable to Ireland.

British duties on Irish imports were removed immediately, while Ireland was given ten years to abolish tariffs on UK imports. Most importantly at the time, agricultural products were granted free access to the UK market. Negotiations were prolonged by the concerns of Northern Irish farmers over this new competition. In just a few years, farmers on both sides of the Border would benefit from the guaranteed prices under EEC membership, although the benefits were greater for the less-subsidised farmers of the Republic.

Yet, looking back on this wonder decade it is possible to detect the seeds of future economic and political problems. Despite the economic growth and expansion of foreign companies, Ireland was again running into balance of payments difficulties – the great problem of the 1950s. Generous bank credit was funding the consumption of imports, while wage rises ahead of productivity growth were putting competitive pressures on exports.

As always with a fixed currency, deflation was the only apparent solution – in this case substantial cuts to the government capital programme. But the new Young Turks of Fianna Fáil, Charles Haughey, Neil Blaney and Donogh O'Malley, largely ignored the directions from finance minister Jack Lynch. Anne Chambers, in her biography of Whitaker, reports how one of his contacts in the Bank of England told him that Blaney was looking for funds from London investment banks to pay for the housing programme that had been cancelled in the budget cutbacks.

The second half of the decade was marked by industrial unrest, which continued on and off for 20 years until pacified by the apparently endless sums of money available from the 1990s. It was proving difficult to control public spending, and in 1966 Ireland made use of a $22m loan from the IMF. The establishment of Fianna Fáil's fund-raising organisation Taca to solicit contributions from business was also a sign of things to come.

In 1966 the remarkable Seán Lemass finally retired. With a bitter rivalry already apparent between the two leading contenders to succeed him, Charles Haughey and George Colley, Jack Lynch emerged as a compromise candidate and became Taoiseach, while Haughey took over as minister of finance.

Haughey began as he would continue, with increases in borrowing to fund higher government spending, both current and capital. The Central Bank expressed its concern in correspondence with the Department of Finance in 1967 and 1968. The department shared the concerns but even Ken Whitaker could not rein in Haughey's free-spending expansionary policies. Ultimately, ministers decide policy and the only man who could have applied the brake, Taoiseach Jack Lynch, seemed unable to do so.

A stage was being set. As Taoiseach himself ten years later, Haughey would make Finance subservient to his will and his successors would do the same to the Central Bank. The 1960s were when Ireland finally got things right – and, some might say, began the process of getting them spectacularly wrong.

CHAPTER 3

Taking stock: Irish PLCs grow up
By Kyran Fitzgerald

AS SOCIETY AND THE ECONOMY EVOLVED FROM THE 1960S ONWARDS, SO TOO DID IRELAND'S BUSINESS CULTURE – WITH THE IRISH STOCK EXCHANGE AND ITS LISTED COMPANIES TO THE FOREFRONT.

In 1964, *Business & Finance* was launched – and in the same year 22 year-old Brian Davy joined the Irish Stock Exchange. Some 50 years later he was still working at Davy Stockbrokers, a symbol of continuity at the firm.

Elsewhere, the changes experienced in the Dublin capital markets have been dramatic. Fifty years ago Davys operated out of premises on Grafton Street. The firm was still run by its founder James and his brother Eugene, the former Irish rugby international. Dick Dennis, a future president of the exchange, had come on board some years earlier with the aim of bridging the gap between the generations within the Davy family. Joe Davy would follow his cousin Brian into the company in 1966.

Early in his career, Brian Davy would spend two hours a day on the floor of the exchange. It was important to get to know and become friendly with his fellow stockbrokers. Davys was expanding its share of the pie; one must not be seen to tread on people's toes. Appear arrogant and business quite simply would not come your way. Stockbrokers in those days played golf together. While they fought over bargains, Brian recalls that the atmosphere was "great". He insists, however, that business standards were high.

The capital market in Dublin was not that well developed in 1964. Stockbrokers were interested in dealing in British stocks on the London Stock

Exchange. The brokers handled, in the main, old family money and the brokers as a group reflected this reality. The main Irish stocks being traded were bank shares, along with Dublin market stalwarts such as Cement Ltd and the department store Arnotts, owned for generations by the Nesbitt family.

The stockbroking firms were large in number but small individually, congregated in elderly office premises close to the HQ of the Irish Stock Exchange in Anglesea Street, Temple Bar. Davys, founded in the 1920s on the back of profits from the family's publican business, was something of a young upstart when compared with its peers. The largest firm at the time was Dudgeon and Co, followed by Goodbody and Webb: one of its principals, Donald Goodbody, served as a director of the Bank of Ireland.

The firm of Butler and Briscoe served as Government broker; in fact it fulfilled this function in an exclusive capacity. Other important players included Solomons, O'Reillys, Tunneys (led by John Tunney), O'Donnell and FitzGerald, and Wilkinson and Falkner. Many of the names would not have been out of place in one of the stock exchanges that still survived in Britain's leading provincial cities. These included Charles Judd, Jobson, Bruce Symes and Wilson, McCaw Fleming, Richard Pim and Co, AH Hinds and Co, and TA Brindley.

The main shareholder in Dillon and Co, TV Murphy, was the son of William Martin Murphy, the leading Dublin businessman who led efforts to break the strike led by Jim Larkin during the Dublin Lockout in 1913. The Murphy family controlled Independent Newspapers until its sale to Tony O'Reilly in 1973. M Dillon and Co, later Dillon and Waldron following a merger with Lawrence Waldron, would eventually be taken over by businessman Dermot Desmond. Senator, later deputy Shane Ross began his career at Dillon Waldron in the 1970s. Other names to conjure with included Stone Doak, Stokes and Kelly and O'Brien and Toole. Colm Ó Briain, partner in O'Brien and Toole, remained an important figure in Irish stockbroking for many years. Many of the firms would be absorbed by Bloxham Toole and Co, later Bloxhams, a firm that survived until 2012 before being wound up. Most of these firms have disappeared. However, one independent firm, Campbell O'Connor, is still in existence.

But change was in the air by the mid-1960s. In a new year editorial in 1965, *Business & Finance* editor Nicholas Leonard pointed out that it had been another good year for the Irish economy and that the Second Programme for Economic Expansion, initiated by Taoiseach Seán Lemass and top official TK Whitaker, "had begun its course".

During the preceding five years interest in the Dublin Stock Exchange had mushroomed, and during 1964 a record £9m was raised by private enterprise through the issue of equity stocks. As Leonard pointed out, this was still small when compared with the £20m to £25m raised each year by the Irish State. "If private enterprise is to be fully supplied with the capital it needs, the Dublin Stock Exchange must be prepared to adjust itself," he wrote. "Investors need more advice and the people who should give it are the stockbrokers. Up until recently, there was too little business to justify brokers involving them in research, but this is no longer so."

And he added, in a swipe at the then-prevailing standards of entry to the stockbroking profession: "There is little justification, in the mid-1960s, for exam-free entry to any profession. Few ambitious young men thought of joining the Stock Exchange unless they had good connections and the Stock Exchange is still about as closed a shop as some of those professions."

During this era mergers were all the rage, and by the end of the 1960s the Irish banking, distilling, paper and packaging and cement sectors would be among the industries transformed through acquisition or corporate marriage. There were a few sceptics. In 1965 a future foreign minister, Cork businessman Peter Barry, wrote to the editor in response to a *Business & Finance* editorial calling for an acceleration in the process of mergers of small tea firms in order to meet the challenge of rising stars Brooke Bond and Lyons.

Barry's response to the advice was terse: "We are a small company (in fact, a very small company), but we manage to stay competitive by concentrating on quality and are now the second-largest tea firm in Cork." Barry, who died in 2016, spent his retirement as chairman of Ireland's largest tea firm having long since been proved correct.

The resurgent economy was also throwing up a new generation of fast-growing Irish firms, many of which tended to gravitate towards Davy

Stockbrokers. By the mid-sixties there was growing demand for shares in Jefferson Smurfit Group, which merited the description "fast-growing paper and packaging firm". The steady expansion of Smurfit along with the rapid emergence of Michael Smurfit, the eldest son of the founder, would be one of the interesting sub-plots of the late 1960s and early 1970s.

At the time the government and its main driving force, Seán Lemass, were engaged in a major restructuring of the economy. In January 1963, Lemass used words that would have puzzled his younger self: "Free competition in conditions of full supply is a far more efficient regulator of prices than any system of official controls yet devised."

The tendency to imitate practices on the larger island across the Irish Sea was being more closely questioned at a time when the UK trade gap was growing and the pound sterling was coming under attack. Across the economy, restructuring and reorganisation efforts sped up. Established grocers like Findlaters buckled under the assault of upstarts such as Dunnes Stores and Quinnsworth.

In the mid-sixties, firms were faced with a credit crunch. As Brian Davy recalls, this did not affect the local stock market: "Stockbroking does not run on debt. Investors do not trade shares on debt the way they trade property. Investors, here, are a conservative bunch."

But listed firms inevitably were impacted by an external environment. Concerns about rising wage inflation and industrial disruption were raised regularly by company chairmen in their reports to shareholders. The signing of the Anglo-Irish Free Trade Agreement in 1965 opened up new markets to exporters, but the gradual lowering of tariff barriers exposed a whole generation of Irish firms to competition in sectors such as clothing and textiles.

ICC and the tariff companies

Many of these were small quoted companies that emerged from the 1930s. In July 1933 the Industrial Credit Company was launched with £500,000 in issued capital. Its establishment was intended as a means of providing greater start-up support for new companies than was available from the commercial banks. The ICC's former chief executive Frank Casey has written in con-siderable detail on the role played by the company in the evolution of the stock market here. In 1933, just 24 industrial companies were quoted on the exchange. These had a combined value of £5m (around €300m in today's terms). By 2000, the combined market capitalisation of companies listed on the exchange stood at IR£56 billion.

Over the period 1933 to 1968 the ICC would be responsible for underwriting 54% of capital raised by way of flotations on the exchange. Between 1922 and 1930 there was only one public issue, with £15,000 being raised. Between 1934 and 1938 the ICC sponsored 27 new issues, raising nearly £5m. According to Casey, "the number and value of quoted shares listed on the ISE approximately doubled as a result of the ICC's early underwriting and issuing house activities". ICC was the only Irish issuing house at the time, apart from Guinness Mahon and Co, which "in accordance with the best City of London practice sponsored flotations only for established companies".

Its efforts were assisted by a provision in the 1932 Finance Act providing for a 20% abatement on tax on interest and dividends in respect of the shares in question: "The flotations were often of brand new industries trying to make their way in a hostile environment where there was no tradition of industrial skill and limited commercial expertise."

ICC underwrote the first issue for the flour miller Ranks (Ireland) in March 1934. Butler and Briscoe were one of the stockbrokers involved. Two weeks later a second issue, for the Irish Sugar Company, was launched. By the year's end the ICC had underwritten four more issues: for Arklow Pottery, Irish Tanners of Portlaw, Irish Aluminium, and a second issue for the Sugar Company. A notable feature was the geographical spread of the firms involved.

In 1935 there were nine issues, including Newbridge Cutlery and Irish Wire Products. Between 1936 and 1939 came 14 more including Irish Worsted Mills and General Textiles; firms involved in import substitution. Many footwear and textile firms launched in this period would eventually cease operations as the economy opened up after 1960.

The regulatory environment was changing too. In 1938 the Banking Commission report led to the establishment of the Irish Central Bank. The report's authors sought to rein in the ICC, concluding that "the scope for future activity in underwriting is likely to be more limited than heretofore as the most obvious openings have been filled". The ICC, however, resisted efforts to clamp down on its activities.

During wartime the ICC, however, sponsored just one flotation, for supplier Williams and Woods. In the immediate post-war environment the old pattern resumed with issues for Athlone-based General Textiles, Irish Ropes and the Irish Wallboard Company.

In 1947 6,000 investors applied for shares in Gypsum Industries in what was one of the most heavily subscribed post-war flotations. In 1949 Clondalkin Concrete raised further funds. In the 1950s the ICC sponsored 13 issues, underwriting one of them: Roadstone Holdings, the building supplies firm established by Tom Roche. The issue bellyflopped. Just 273 people applied for the shares: the ICC was left with more than 110,000 unsold shares.

However, Roadstone would turn out to be a good investment. Its founder would eventually take charge of the ISE's largest industrial quoted company, CRH, following a merger between Cement Ltd and Roadstone. Roadstone later expanded through the acquisition of Clondalkin Concrete and the Liverpool-based Forticrete, in a rare foray outside the island for an Irish PLC. In 1970 Tom Roche masterminded the merger with Cement Ltd in what amounted to a reverse takeover: CRH was to follow a similar growth path to that of Jefferson Smurfit, combining tight management with strategic acquisition.

In 1952 the ICC sponsored an issue on behalf of Irish Glass Bottle, the McGrath family vehicle. Waterford Glass was eventually spun off from Irish Glass Bottle, becoming one of the leading Irish-quoted stocks by the late 1960s. In the sixties the ICC changed tack, focusing more on lending directly to industry. This part of its book experienced a fourfold increase during the decade.

Impact of the upturn

In July 1966 the Anglo-Irish Free Trade Agreement came into force. However, it took some time for the penny to drop as far as the City of London was concerned: Ireland remained a small offshore place of little interest in the eyes of many of its key players.

That August, the Irish government sought to interest the market in some of its debt. Some 80% of this 'London loan' was left with the underwriters, causing *Business & Finance* to lament the "mammoth ignorance of Ireland in Britain, particularly in the financial world".

In the editor's view, the marketing of the loan was conducted in a cack-handed fashion: "Why did the Irish embassy – or Ministry of Finance – not invite the financial editors of the influential London papers to a press conference? The Irish government's advertising looked antediluvian at a time when Britain's unit trusts are employing highly sophisticated PR and advertising firms to pull in money for their sophisticated offers."

At this stage, while the economy had begun to grow, the country's wealth base remained shallow. This in itself would help to explain the backward state of the financial sector. In the tax year 1964/65 only 331 people were assessed by the Revenue Commissioners as having income in excess of £10,000 a year, according to a publication issued by the Irish Congress of Trade Unions. As *Business & Finance* noted, "it is little wonder that the majority of Ireland's most potentially able businessmen find their way to top jobs outside the country".

Nevertheless, change was in the air. By 1967, Bank of Ireland and AIB would emerge in their current form following a process of merger and acquisition driven by concern that leading Irish banks could be taken over by foreigners. Bank of Ireland absorbed three established institutions, the National Bank, the Hibernian Bank and the National City Bank, while Allied Irish Banks emerged in 1966 as a result of a merger of the Munster and Leinster, Royal and Provincial Banks. The three banks retained their separate identities for a period before eventually being subsumed into the AIB brand.

Bank of Ireland proceeded to launch the Investment Bank of Ireland, while AIB established AIIB. Figures such as Kevin Wylie, Richard Hooper and Martin Rafferty helped to initiate a transformation in the way that expanding firms were funded. The restructuring of the country's banking system was driven by the conclusion of the Anglo-Irish Free Trade Agreement and by the emerging prospect of Irish membership of the European Economic Community.

As the businessman Don Carroll, a former chairman of the Bank of Ireland, recalled in a 1987 interview with Ivor Kenny, "we were concerned about the ability of so many small Irish banks to adapt". He recalled meeting with TK Whitaker, secretary of the Department of Finance, and telling him that he did not see how the banking system could bring itself into the latter part of the 20th century with small banks competing with each other. As he put it, "riding economic trends is a very much easier course than trying to prevent them".

It was anticipated, at the time, that the formation of the two banking groups would foster the creation of a Dublin money market. According to Hugh Clark, then chairman of Ulster Bank, this would enable the government's short-term financing needs to be met more effectively while allowing the banks themselves to use their capital more efficiently.

From the mid-sixties, while the domestic banking sector became more concentrated, new competition for corporate business was stimulated by the arrival in Dublin of North American-based banks. The new generation of merchant banks and overseas banks offered alternative forms of funding to those provided within the traditional stock market context.

As Kevin Wylie, MD of the Investment Bank of Ireland (IBI) noted at the time, "a large proportion of Irish industrial companies are not quoted on the Stock Exchange... this does not mean that they have to rely solely on their overdraft facilities for outside finance. The merchant banks have brought to Ireland the full range of fundraising techniques."

In April 1971 Bank of Ireland announced the establishment of three overseas branches, one in New York and two in London, with indications that the continent of Europe would be the next focal point for expansion. The aim, according to managing director Ian Morrison, was that the New York branch would be used to help win custom from some of the new US companies that were beginning to set up operations in Ireland.

In January of that year *Business & Finance* had reported on what it described as the second phase of industrial expansion in Ireland with the arrival of firms such as Snia, Mitsui and Pfizer – the latter firm was engaged in constructing a £14m plant at Ringaskiddy.

A new form of PLC

The rather stagnant, if gentlemanly world of the Irish Stock Exchange was coming under pressure. A new breed of company was emerging. In November 1968, *Business & Finance* reported how Ireland's family-controlled firms had received a "stock market jolt" when the "fast expanding" Jefferson Smurfit and Sons put in a £325,000 takeover bid for the loss-making Temple Press.

The IBI was engaged to help put together a deal, which was strongly backed by the magazine. "The bid is in every sense a test case. If the directors of Temple succeed in blocking the bid without doing anything to justify rejection, the Dublin Stock Exchange will be making a mockery of the takeover code to which it plays lip service." Temple Press was advised by the other newcomer Irish merchant bank, AIIB.

Just as Ireland's banks were joining force, many traditional Irish manu-facturers were also noticing the writing appearing on the wall. By the end of 1970, Cement Ltd would have joined forces with Roadstone to form CRH, while Irish Distillers had also emerged. That year, ambitious efforts were driven by Don Carroll to form an Irish conglomerate consisting of his family cigarette-making business PJ Carroll, Waterford Glass and Irish Glass Bottle, and Irish Distillers Group. The idea was that PJ Carroll's cash resources and marketing expertise would be accessed and used to promote the sale of Irish whiskey and Waterford Crystal products overseas. The plan, however, came to nothing.

Irish Distillers has been a great Irish success story, operating as part of the Pernod Ricard Group since 1988. In an interview with Ivor Kenny for his 1987 book *In Good Company: Conversations with Irish Business Leaders*, the first chairman of United Distillers of Ireland (the entity soon to be renamed Irish Distillers), Frank O'Reilly, recalled the background to the merger that shook up the Irish drinks industry: "In the early 1960s, we were looking around and deciding that Irish distilleries on their own were too small to make the major export drive required for themselves and the country."

The main players at the time were John Power and Son, Jameson's and Cork Distilleries. O'Reilly was a member of the Power family, becoming joint MD in the early fifties before also succeeding his uncle, Bertie O'Reilly, as chairman in 1955. Power's was a quoted company. Both Power's and Cork

Distilleries had branded products, while Jameson's was mainly in the bulk trade. The talks took two years. News of the discussions did not leak into the market. The merger was signed, sealed and delivered in 1966. RTÉ director general Kevin McCourt came on board the new merged entity, United Distilleries, as chairman two years later.

Mergers were all the rage at the time. The minister for education, Donogh O'Malley – best remembered for engineering the launch of free secondary education – was pushing hard for a plan to merge UCD and Trinity College prior to his sudden death in March 1968. The plan was soon abandoned. But the whiskey merger plan was based on much stronger foundations: the industry was preparing for July 1971 when import barriers in the sector would be lowered.

Kevin McCourt had a much more positive vision, as he told Joe O'Malley of *Business & Finance* in early 1969. In his view, Irish whiskey was punching way below its weight, selling just 30,000 cases in Britain – this compared with 6.5 million cases of scotch. In a somewhat counterintuitive move, one of the first acts of the company's new UK head of sales, Donald Mackay, was to put up the price of a glass of Irish so as to "draw a price distinction between it and scotch". The new strategy appeared to be working. In January 1971 United Distilleries was able to report a rise in turnover from £15m to almost £19m in 1970. Between May 1970 and April 1971 the group presided over the launch of Huzzar Vodka, Midleton Reserve Whiskey, Commodore Gin and Kiskadee.

By 1971 a new figure was active on the stock exchange. Tony O'Reilly was chairman of Fitzwilliam Securities, a holding company controlling PLCs Crowe Wilson and Dockrells, both of which had just returned record results – Dockrells boosted by a buoyant construction sector. Its key executives were former *Business & Finance* editor Nicholas Leonard and accountant Vincent Ferguson. Fitzwilliam Securities evolved into Fitzwilton Holdings, merging with well-known fertiliser group Gouldings PLC, in what amounted in effect to a reverse takeover.

Former rugby international Tony O'Reilly had made his name in business in charge at Erin Foods and as boss of Bord Bainne in the early 1960s, establishing the hugely successful Kerrygold brand. In 1973 he gained control of Independent Newspapers. By the late 1980s O'Reilly could talk of Irish corporate success in global markets and of the much greater mobility of capital within the country.

Fitzwilton would never quite live up to the goals of its founders, and the fashion for conglomerates would eventually fade. However, the key trend – the move in the direction of an open pan-European economy – would be sustained, and within a decade or so corporate Ireland would be unrecognisable. As Tony O'Reilly put it in 1987, in an interview with Ivor Kenny: "The days of the fusty conservative old-style bank board which dominated a town, or a province or the whole country, are gone."

He then sounded a somewhat more reflective note: "I suppose that in some strange and perverse way, the influence of *Dallas* and *Dynasty* and the global village of McLuhan have pulled us all together to share common vanities, greeds and ambitions. I sense that Ireland is a fully integrated paid-up member of a rather vulgar, interesting, fast-moving and exceedingly bracing western society..."

Getting left behind

Many firms struggled to adapt to the new reality, and many of these were associated with the Irish Stock Exchange. Examine the list of companies quoted on the stock exchange in the mid-sixties and one will encounter many names that are familiar – and many that have long passed into history.

Whatever happened to Irish Cinemas, or Irish Tanners, Irish Worsted Mills or Dubtex? As for Pye Ireland, it recalls an era when TV sets were box-like, took ages to light up and were typically rented out. Some mid-sized entities have enjoyed a pretty good run: think Heiton Holdings. Some live on as part of a larger global entity, notably Arthur Guinness.

Glen Abbey prospered on the back of tariff barriers. Run by Rory and Colm Barnes, it was viewed as a go-ahead fashion and textiles business. In October 1968 it came under attack from *Business & Finance* over its decision not to give details of the profits earned by its latest acquisition, the Dublin Hosiery Group. Chairman Colm Barnes explained that the reason for the secrecy was that the company did not wish to prejudice its bargaining position when making future acquisitions.

According to *B&F*, such secrecy set a dangerous precedent: "The Dublin Stock Exchange is notorious for its laxity in forcing companies to give relevant information about themselves, but this time it has excelled itself."

The magazine also hit out on other occasions at the delay in releasing profit figures into the market. In November 1967 it noted that it had taken considerable pressure from the stock exchange for Seafield Gentex to release its latest figures. According to the editor, "the exchange must take far more of an initiative in getting quoted companies to provide the vital information on which to base investment decisions".

At that point trade was good at Glen Dimplex, with pre-tax profits almost doubling to £75,000 in the first half of 1968, but as the sixties gave way to the seventies many quoted companies involved in import substitution faced an uphill struggle to survive amid growing competition from overseas and against a background of industrial unrest and soaring domestic inflation. A warning note was sounded in 1968 with the collapse of the empire of 'tufted carpet king' Cyril Lord with the loss of 1,700 jobs, many of them in Northern Ireland.

In the late sixties, however, firms like Youghal Carpets and Sunbeam Wolsey continued to prosper, bringing welcome wage packets to many an Irish provincial town. But by 1971 *Business & Finance* was referring to the 'ailing Offaly jute manufacturer' J&LF Goodbody, which was "gloomily bracing itself for further trading losses". Meanwhile, management at Sunbeam Wolsey in Cork were expressing anger at the "large-scale dumping by British competitors during the closing months of 1970".

The Irish Stock Exchange itself had reason to be concerned about its future. In March 1972, the 101 members of the exchange were voting on whether to become members of a British Isles-wide United Stock Exchange. The Irish government was concerned that the trading floor in government stocks would be transferred from Dublin to London and that it would lose control over the issue of gilts. Smaller stockbrokers quaked at the prospect of London brokers setting up in competition. However, there were fears that if they did not vote to join in, the Irish exchange would be left as a backwater with most of the large investor business going direct to London.

Business & Finance endorsed Irish membership of the planned United Stock Exchange, predicting that it would speed up rationalisation while squeezing a number of brokers out of business. The formal amalgamation of 11 British and Irish regional exchanges went ahead, but the Irish Stock Exchange later split away. Outside London, it is the only stock exchange to survive – though in a much-changed form.

A shake-up close to home

A new generation of investors had begun to spot stock-picking opportunities. John Teeling remains a prominent figure in Irish business through his many investments in exploration and in the whiskey business. A graduate of Harvard University and the Wharton School, Teeling was one of a group of bright young academics coaxed back to Ireland by Professor Michael MacCormac of UCD.

Having established himself as a lecturer in the commerce department, he used some of his spare time to build up investments in Irish-quoted companies such as Seafield Gentex, Glen Abbey, Irish Wire Products and Irish Oil and Cake Mills. "I identified 11 companies which met the Ben Graham (value investment) model. I went after seven of the 11. In each case, the net cash available exceeded the market price of each share.

"The Irish Stock Exchange, at the time, was absolutely somnolent," he recalls. "There was a small clique, strongly Anglo-Irish." In his view, many of the quoted companies were going nowhere. Many had grown up behind tariff barriers, making basic products. With the advent of free trade they had little future. "In 1970, Seafield Gentex (a textiles PLC) had 17 factories. Within a few years, there were five left. One of them, Sanderson Fabric, produced high-quality goods, but it could not compete with the Pakistanis. The Irish Stock Exchange was a small appendage of the London Stock Exchange. The stockbroking firms were one-room, gentlemanly operations. In one case, the office was literally in the attic."

Teeling and fellow spirits such as the businessman Donal Kinsella scouted for opportunities far and wide. Teeling recalls visiting the head office of Irish Oil and Cake Mills in Drogheda with Kinsella, who was sporting a red rose on his lapel and smoking a big cigar when they met with the directors.

Kinsella joked that they would repaint the boardroom when they took the company over. The meeting ended soon after.

Derided as an asset stripper, Teeling believes that he and his kind were really engaged in a cleaning-up operation. He distinguishes his role from that of Michael Smurfit, or Tom Roche, founder of Roadstone and the driving force behind the establishment of CRH. "Tom Roche bought brains. He would only interview the top people in the engineering class, each year. I was cleaning up while they were building things up." Teeling defends his role in the shake-up of the exchange: "There has to be new blood. Every farm has to burn the stubble."

An unconventional chairman

Basil Goulding presided over the board of W&H Goulding Ltd for many years. An unconventional figure known to wear rollerskates to meetings, his chairman's reports were famously entertaining yet not a little windy. His fertiliser company would eventually be swallowed up by Tony O'Reilly's Fitzwilton outfit. In some respects Sir Basil was an anachronism, but in other respects he was quite forward-thinking.

He was fond of referring to the profit and loss account as the 'scoreboard' while describing the company balance sheet as the 'strongroom'. In an address to shareholders in 1967 he suggested that the recorded profit, "after filling up a horrid hole in the ground, displays only a modest mound above it". He had this to say about the threat from importers: "It is time to compose some practical thoughts on the ways wherein Irish production can parry whatever landings may be made by foreign invaders. We hold the inner lines. Manning them by efficiency of production is within our powers and this defence will be good provided reasonably fair rules of trading are upheld by the government and not a declension to free style wrestling."

In 1971 the company showed its innovative side when it commissioned an opinion survey of its shareholders, the first such exercise by an Irish quoted company. The findings provide an interesting insight into the small shareholders of that era.

Some 99 shareholders were interviewed in some depth; 62 were men, 37 women. Almost 60% were aged over 55. Two thirds felt that they had been "let down by the company", concerned that the "value of their capital had depreciated". Some 56% did not know what the company's turnover was. "Women were the least accurate," according to *Business & Finance*.

"Shareholders were equally confused about the trend of return on capital, puzzled or ignorant of the Gouldings-ICI relationship (with the UK's top chemicals group) [...] Younger shareholders tended to know more about the company's diversifications into jewellery, building materials, landscaping [...] Three quarters, when asked, said more information from the company was not required!

"The implication of this would seem to be that the average shareholder accepts the opinion of his stockbroker, of financial journalists, friends, his banker – as a substitute for real knowledge." For information on the company 67% of shareholders relied on the annual report, 56% on the financial pages of the newspapers, and 55% on the chairman's statement.

The survey also revealed some interesting facts about other investments held by the shareholders in question. Some 31% had shares each in Guinness and in Roadstone, 27% in AIB, 26% in ICI, 18% in Imperial Tobacco, 17% in Sunbeam Wolsey (a Cork textiles firm), and 13% in United Distillers (Irish Distillers). Some 55% had land, 48% held gilts, while just 29% had life assurance.

The Stock Exchange in 1972

1972 was the year in which Ireland was getting ready to vote on membership of the European Community, and from May that year was getting ready to join it. Stockbrokers and investors enjoyed bumper returns that year. In January 1973 they little expected what lay ahead: the Yom Kippur War of October 1973 and a long period of stagflation.

In December 1972 *B&F*'s Bill Ambrose reported on that year's share boom, which brought overall capital gains of 80% in industrial shares. The "erosion of earlier years" (in share prices) had been offset. As Ambrose noted, "the dominant feature of 1972 was the emergence of the shell companies". Five of the top ten performing companies fitted into this category. The Mooneys pub chain was involved in a takeover tussle generating plenty of controversy, while the fashion firm Doreen gobbled up Jack Toohey. The

Central Bank governor, TK Whitaker, had expressed misgivings about the rise of the 'shells', some of which were shared by *B&F*'s young reporter. He observed how share prices had "spurted ahead simply on the announcement that an acquisition campaign was planned".

"It reflects little credit on the Irish Stock Exchange that at no time during the year did it make any concerted effort to rectify the situation. The 'caveat emptor' principle (let the buyer beware) does not absolve the exchange of its requirements. Because such a radical transformation is required, these shells should be treated as new companies and should have to conform to the requirements on companies going public for the first time.

"From next year, our stock exchange will be a member of the United Stock Exchange of Britain and Ireland and it must be hoped that higher standards in operation there will be rigidly applied here." Ambrose suggested that PLC company directors should be required to disclose their holdings in the accounts each year (he did not go as far as to suggest that each share deal should be disclosed). Elsewhere, the magazine also proposed that the names of those making quick profits in transactions where shares in a company have unexpectedly jumped should be published as part of an effort to combat insider dealing.

While 1972 was a year notable for the emergence of a new breed of Irish managers and entrepreneurs, and for the seminal political debates that gave the go-ahead to Irish entry to the EEC, it was also a year in which the Irish business world was marked – indeed scarred –by the tragedy of the Staines air crash.

A dozen talented executives died in the crash, including high-profile businessmen Con Smith, Michael Rigby Jones and Guy Jackson, along with Ned Gray, director of the Confederation of Irish Industry and CII colleague Michael Sweetman, who had masterminded the campaign in favour of EEC entry as director of the Irish Council of the European Movement. In a valedictory editorial, the magazine observed that the lost men "were greater than their achievements to date and would, like the rising tide, have lifted all boats. Without really trying, Ned Gray had become the Confederation of Irish Industry... his forthright and obviously sincere manner gave Irish industry a fresh acceptability.

"Con Smith developed Smith Group from a family garage in Cavan into the most profitable motor company in Ireland. In the past week, he had arranged a merger with Gouldings which would have put him at the helm of the second-largest industrial complex in Ireland." (The deal soon collapsed.)

Guy Jackson, then president of the CII, was recalled as the "next managing director of Guinness, who had taken on the task of restructuring the Dublin brewery". Michael Sweetman was remembered as a "social democrat who took an independent view on many issues".

The toll was especially high at a time when the country's core of managers capable of operating in international markets was necessarily meagre given the long period of economic backwardness and isolation that had marked the Republic up to this point.

Many Irish firms would struggle to adapt to the unexpectedly harsh conditions of the 1970s and many leading stock market names would soon recede into history – or re-emerge in almost unrecognisable form.

CHAPTER 4

Into Europe
By Kyran FitzGerald

SOVEREIGNTY, SUBSIDIES, INVESTMENT AND TAXATION DOMINATED 1972'S HARD-FOUGHT EEC REFERENDUM CAMPAIGN IN A HOTLY CONTESTED BATTLE – WITH BUSINESS LARGELY IN FAVOUR OF ENTRY.

On May 10th 1972, the Irish people voted to join the European Economic Community (EEC) by a majority of five to one. Just over 70% of the electorate cast their votes. This was an era of strong political engagement on the part of the citizenry.

The vote came at the end of a hard-fought campaign during which the Irish people were forced to re-examine their own sense of identity: citizens were called on to throw the dice in determining the future direction of the country. The campaign in favour of entry was led by the Minister of External Affairs, Patrick Hillery, an experienced politician who previously served as minister of education and minister of labour. Hillery's task was complicated by the requirement on the government to negotiate terms of entry with the European Commission and with the putative partner countries already established within the EEC.

It was a hotly contested battle. In the run up to the vote it was by no means clear that the supporters of entry to the Community would be able to push the proposition over the line. The trade union leadership came out against membership and the Labour Party was also opposed. Traditional nationalists were concerned about the threat posed to Irish sovereignty.

The powerful head of the Irish Transport and General Workers' Union, Michael Mullen, told a meeting in Cork that he believed "without hesitation" that EEC entry "would whittle away our sovereignty and identity as a nation". Writing in *Business & Finance* in December 1971, Brendan Clarke, the head of communications and information with the ITGWU, noted the unfortunate previous experience of Fianna Fáil governments when it came to pushing through proposals by referenda, with two efforts to alter the Constitution and abolish the proportional representation voting system having been rejected by the voters.

Clarke referred to what in his view was "the outstanding reason for opposition to entry among trade unionists: the fear of redundancies". As he observed, many trade unionists feared with good reason that their jobs were on the line.

The signing of the Anglo-Irish Free Trade Agreement, in 1965, may have prepared the ground for accession. However, it also set in train a sometimes painful process of restructuring, as Irish industries previously operating securely behind tariff barriers were exposed to competitive forces right on their doorstep. As the ITGWU spokesman put it: "This has been the most frightening year for Irish workers since the mid-1950s. Unprecedented loss of jobs in large, traditional manufacturing sectors such as textiles, food processing and the shoe leather trade has dominated the trade union mind for most of the year [1972]."

At the time, Labour came under fire from the journalist Bruce Arnold, a regular contributor to *Business & Finance*, over its stonewall opposition to the Community market which he considered "as bad in its way as the equally slavish commitment of Fianna Fáil about entry." The trade unions warned of the prospect of 35,000 redundancies, in contrast to projections contained in a government white paper of 50,000 additional jobs following entry. Privately, some trade union leaders were supportive of entry or at least broadly neutral.

But plenty of opposition was to be found beyond the walls of the labour movement. Professor Raymond Crotty, a longtime eurosceptic, provided plenty of fodder for the opposition, predicting that accession to the EEC would result in a "swing to cattle and sheep" and an increase in farm size. On this basis, he foresaw a drop in employment in Irish agriculture from around 300,000 to just 45,000, with the number of farms plummeting from 283,000 to around 36,000. As a result many small villages and towns would not survive, while industry would not be able to expand quickly enough to absorb all of those people forced to leave the land.

Justin Keating, a Labour TD soon to become minister of industry and commerce in the Fine Gael/Labour 'National Coalition' formed after the February 1973 general election, also predicted that the small farmer would be squeezed out. Keating was an active farmer whose own profile had been boosted by a farming series that he presented on RTÉ.

Michael Sweetman, the director of the campaign in favour of entry, countered such arguments, insisting that Irish industry would endure within the EEC, even if it encountered difficulty along the way. In his view farming would become a much more attractive option, resulting in a big reduction in the numbers leaving the sector. The Crotty arguments were also countered by research from UCD produced by two academics, including Seamus Sheehy, later a professor of agriculture at the university. The academics predicted that milk prices would rise by up to 50% in the summer, and by just over one quarter in the winter. It was also their assumption that the total acreage under tillage would not drop.

The Irish Farmers' Association leader TJ Maher calculated at the time that around one quarter of the population was directly employed on the land, while another 76,000 people were engaged in industries with a close connection to agriculture. He estimated that farmers and their families accounted for one eighth of spending across the country on goods and services and that agriculture accounted for 42% of total exports. Maher pointed to the country's enormous agricultural potential: "There is reliable evidence that Irish grassland can carry twice as much stock as it now supports." The IFA in particular was in the vanguard of a campaign in which a land of milk and honey was promised to cultivators.

Garret FitzGerald, by then a prominent Fine Gael frontbencher and leading economist, was among a few to put forward more of a philosophical argument in favour of entry. In his view, membership of the EEC would amount to a 'psychological liberation'. The liberation, in this case, would take the form of a loosening in the chains of dependence on the former colonial power, Britain. The transformation in relations between Ireland and Britain would indeed be facilitated, if not enabled, by Irish membership of the EEC, with the Anglo-Irish Agreement of November 1985, a high point of FitzGerald's period in office, serving as a key staging post further down the road.

The idea that Ireland could serve as a magnet for foreign direct investment did not form a central part of the 1972 referendum campaign, though already the Industrial Development Authority was enjoying considerable success in attracting investment from overseas – not just from the US, but also from countries such as Germany.

In the debate on the economic consequences of entry the focus was on the threat to existing jobs in agriculture and industry, and on the opportunities for job creation in rural Ireland. By 1971 it was clear that the hopes raised by the Anglo-Irish Free Trade Agreement that exports to the UK would receive a timely boost would not be fulfilled, at least in the short run. In February 1971, *Business & Finance* concluded in an editorial that the agreement "has proved to be little short of disastrous". The editor pointed to a rise in imports from Britain to Ireland of almost 80% in the preceding five years, with the trade deficit surging from £35m to £72m. The government came under pressure to secure a renego-tiation of the agreement.

Such arguments amounted to an over-egging of the pudding. If anything, freeing up the flows of trade across the Irish Sea provided the domestic Irish economy with a timely shock. Many local industrialists had grown a bit soft after decades of shelter behind tariff ramparts. It is to the credit of people like Ned Gray, the director of the Confederation of Irish Industry at the time, that they did not listen too closely to the nervous clucking of some of their membership.

The organisation played a central role in the campaign, though it would soon be rocked by tragedy in the form of the Staines air crash shortly after the announcement of the referendum result. Katherine Meenan, a young Confeder-ation executive in the run up to entry – later a close adviser of Taoiseach Garret FitzGerald – recalls the late Ned Gray, a victim in the crash, as one of the most powerful people she ever met: "The whole room would turn when he slipped in."

Whereas Gray was an unusually effective operator, Michael Sweetman, who also died near Heathrow, was "more articulate... the intellectual driving force". She recalls attending lively town hall campaigns all around the country, with high levels of voter engagement.

The opponents of entry were not above dragging issues such as abortion into the debate, although Meenan retains particular respect for Micheál Ó Loingsigh, one of the leaders of the opposition to entry, as a person who presented the facts with all honesty, refusing to resort to the darker arts of political campaigning, in her view.

The EIB intervenes

Just weeks ahead of the vote, the political and business establishment in Ireland received some powerful backing from overseas. The president of the European Investment Bank, Yves le Portz, visited Dublin with a team of specialists to introduce himself to the finance minister, George Colley – the minister himself was slated to join the bank's board of governors in the event of a vote in favour of entry.

The president had come to the city bearing gifts, or at least a promise of gifts, but with important strings attached. The bank would be more than willing to assist a small country like Ireland should it opt for membership. Carrots were being dangled. As le Portz made clear, the EIB was not restricted to supporting mammoth projects: "The bank is prepared to spur on regional development by assisting in the growth of small- and medium-sized businesses."

The EIB, moreover, would be willing to process Irish applications for funding in advance "from the moment the outcome of the referendum is known" so as to ensure that funds would begin flowing into Ireland as soon as possible after Irish accession to the Community on January 1st 1973.

This message was clearly intended for the eyes and ears of undecided voters, but it was also a message to the Irish State, to the semi-states and to the private sector that it was time for them to start getting prepared. Dealing with the bureaucracy in Brussels and representing the country's interests in a competitive arena was going to present a stark challenge for a government service used to operating in a rather laid-back environment.

Ahead of the referendum, the government was involved in extensive nego-tiations with the European Commission. On October 21st 1971 *Business & Finance* reported that "a crunch point had been reached, one that centres around questions of regional policy and incentives for industry". The magazine editorial stressed "the vital importance of protecting the tax holiday [...] the key element for attracting foreign industrialists here".

Dr Paddy Hillery, the man at the heart of the talks as minister for external affairs, stressed the need for an acceleration in industrial development as a means of absorbing those leaving agriculture and narrowing the gap in living standards between Ireland and the original six member states on the European continent. The editorial drew a distinction between what in its eyes were the rule-bound bureaucrats of Brussels, and the political leadership drawn from the member states when it came to assessing their approaches to Ireland's key concerns. "The politically motivated Council of Ministers has been ready to recognise our special difficulties and to grant concessions. The Commission, on the other hand, once again emphasising its role as the guardian of the Treaty of Rome, looked upon the Irish tax holiday scheme with a greater degree of suspicion."

The Commission suggested that it should examine the incentives, hinting that a likely outcome would be a "declaration that the tax holiday contravenes the fair competition provision of the Treaty of Rome". Not surprisingly, the Department of Foreign Affairs reportedly saw this as a "major obstacle in the path of a successful conclusion of the negotiations" and the editorial suggested that "any diminution of what we have to offer – especially with regard to tax incentives – would make the task of the IDA (in attracting foreign investment) well nigh impossible". On a more positive note, it concluded with the suggestion that a solution could exist in the form of a special protocol, "framed in general terms, but sufficiently specific so as to inhibit the Commission from taking action which might slow down our industrial development".

In January 1972, as the date for the vote approached, the author of the magazine's EEC diary, Frank Corr, reported that negotiations on the country's sugar quota were reaching a critical stage and that the "IFA was literally breathing down Dr Hillery's neck". The minister, it seems, faced the prospect of accusations of a 'sell-out' should he accept the EEC's final offer of an annual quota of 140,000 tons. The farmers were pressing him to hold out for 170,000 tons. The shrewd – but sometimes nervy and media shy – Clare doctor-turned-minister could be forgiven for feeling somewhat rattled at this juncture. However, as happened so often in the course of late-night negotiations in Brussels, a deal was pulled together and a serious attempt was made to address Irish concerns.

Later that month Taoiseach Jack Lynch signed the Treaty of Accession. Ireland secured a recognition of its special position as a developing economy. The country was permitted to offer incentives to industry over and above what could be achieved even by a liberal interpretation of the Treaty of Rome.

Critically, at least in the short term, its fishing industry received the comfort blanket of a guarantee to extensively protect its coastal waters. However, over time the value of these guarantees would turn out to be somewhat illusory. Much more soundly based was the guarantee handed out to farmers of a realistic price for their dairy and beef products. As *Business & Finance* put it in its editorial on May 4th 1972, just ahead of the referendum vote: "Our agriculture industry will, at last, be freed from the tyranny of Britain's cheap food policy."

As a result, farmers would be less dependent on direct subsidies from the Irish taxpayer and would be able to draw instead on price supports along with access to a much larger market. Concern was expressed about a likely rise in food prices – one that would impact, in particular, on urban people earning the average industrial wage or below. The business and political establishment, nevertheless, was now free to put up its stalls and begin wooing the populace.

The editor of *Business & Finance* ultimately called for a Yes vote, echoing in the process the views of the vast majority of his readers – by and large men and women of property possessing a degree of financial substance. As the editorial on the eve of the referendum put it, the people were faced with a "choice between a permanent welding with nine other nations in Europe, or cold isolation on the fringe of one of the world's greatest economic unions [...] an isolation warmed by some sort of trading relationship with the EEC, or one of its competitors".

The debate had been marked by great vigour and passion. However, at the end of the day the financial carrots on offer were just too juicy to ignore. Citizens were being offered a ticket to prosperity, or so they were led to believe.

Many proud patriots welcomed the chance to ease the country's dependence on their larger next-door neighbour. Irish farmers had struggled to make headway in a UK market increasingly dominated by rival meat and dairy suppliers from Denmark and New Zealand in spite of the undoubted success of initiatives such as the rollout of the Kerrygold brand.

Paradoxically, the failure of the Anglo-Irish Free Trade Agreement to deliver price increases for Irish farmers actually served to strengthen the arguments put forward by advocates of membership. The EEC was seen as a marketplace in which farmers in Ireland could thrive on the back of a base of price supports. This turned out to be the case, in large part.

CHAPTER 5

Into Europe, into context
By Kyran FitzGerald

MENTALITIES AND IDEOLOGIES HAD TO SHIFT ALONG WITH POLICIES AS IRELAND'S POLITICAL AND BUSINESS ELITE PREPARED FOR EEC ENTRY: CHANGE CAME GRADUALLY, BUT THE TRANSFORMATION WOULD BE TOTAL.

A generation earlier, Irish membership of a large European economic organisation was simply not on the agenda. Indeed, the Irish Republic appeared more isolated than it had ever been amid a climate of hostility in London and Washington as the de Valera government decided to adhere to a policy of neutrality.

For many years after the war, moreover, the country appeared far removed from the continent of Europe despite Irish involvement in efforts to provide aid to war-ravaged populations. The country also benefited from Marshall Aid during the period of the first inter-party government. However, the overall sense is of a country at a considerable remove from a mainland Europe re-establishing itself as an economic force during the 1950s.

Change came gradually. By 1960 the Republic was in the process of becoming a quite different place when it came to its relationships with its neighbours, having adopted the export-oriented pro-investment policies that remain central to its strategy today.

While Taoiseach Éamon de Valera held on to the reins of power, Fianna Fáil was slow to grasp that fundamental change was taking place across the western world with – for example – the Germans rebuilding their economy from the ground up, while Italy embarked on a rapid process of urbanisation and industrialisation. France too, under General de Gaulle from 1958, soon began to prosper while the US, of course, roared ahead economically during the presidency of Eisenhower from 1953 to 1960. Sadly, Ireland remained on the sidelines for much of this period, stagnating while neighbouring economies boomed.

Britain became the main outlet for Ireland's surplus youth, who headed to work on the building sites of southern England and in the huge car factories in the Midlands. Forces for change did emerge, however. The first inter-party government established the Industrial Development Authority while the second, between 1954 and 1957, approved a scheme for export sales relief in the face of fierce opposition from within the Department of Finance.

Fortunately, the once inward-looking Fianna Fáil party also began to alter its outlook. The outstanding figure among the rapidly ageing front ranks of Fianna Fáil was Seán Lemass, the long-time minister of industry and commerce, and during the opposition years the lead contact with the party organisation. Lemass's views on the economy were to undergo a remarkable transformation.

It would be a mistake to assume, however, that Lemass and his close ally TK Whitaker – the head of the Department of Finance from 1956 – were the sole initiators of the transformation in Irish economic policy that became apparent in the late fifties. In fact, Lemass in some respects was a slow learner, although in later years he became a profound enthusiast for the European project.

Much has been written about changes in Irish attitudes towards Europe. However, in 2013 a group of historians under Professor Dermot Keogh produced an excellent book, *Ireland through European Eyes*, which examines the attitudes of key continental west European states towards this country in the period leading up to 1973.

The EEC was established in 1957, having grown out of the Coal and Steel Pact driven in particular by Jean Monnet. According to Mervyn O'Driscoll, senior lecturer in the School of History at UCC, both the UK and Ireland were 'virtual bystanders' when the key early moves towards integration were taking place in the 1950s. Senior civil servants and politicians only belatedly awoke to the significance of the events occurring across the Channel. The Macmillan government in Britain – driven on in large part by the government chief whip Ted Heath, a lifelong enthusiast for the European project – prepared an application for membership and the Irish government followed suit, Lemass having taken over as Taoiseach in 1959.

In July 1961 the application, put together in haste it seems, was forwarded. As O'Driscoll puts it, Irish policymakers "finally appreciated that the EEC [...] offered an alternative to small national state obscurity". At the time, it was a "provincial agricultural economy providing basic foodstuffs for the British urban industrial economy".

What followed was an "arduous battle" to build a case in western Europe for admission. According to Mervyn O'Driscoll, "Ireland, uniquely among the application states, was kept in protracted pre-negotiations from July 1961 to October 1962 in order to ascertain whether it was even worthy of commencing formal entry negotiations".

In contrast, the UK, Denmark and Norway were permitted to enter into full-blown discussions within a few months. Through the 1950s the West German government had, it would appear, serious reservations about Irish foreign policy positioning – ironic this, given the criticism endured by the Irish government over its non-aligned stance during World War Two. Irish neutrality "copperfastened Irish sovereignty as the central political and economic ideology of the nation state".

The Irish government had been quick to recognise the new Federal Republic in 1951, and was also an early supporter of cultural and sporting links with the country emerging from the ashes of war. However, in O'Driscoll's view many officials in Bonn, the German capital, viewed Ireland and its leadership as 'pre-modern' and obsessed with the struggle to end partition.

One can cavil at such apparent hypocrisy, but it is clear that the growing gap between the countries did not serve to boost relations. By 1953 there was a heavy trade imbalance in Germany's favour; the Germans mainly supplying finished goods to Ireland while the Irish exported live cattle, fish and woollen products to Germany. In 1956 the Dublin government was forced to introduce import duties at the height of the economic crisis. The return of Fianna Fáil to government in 1957 opened the way to a change in policy after a period in which the outgoing government suffered from serious internal divisions. Interestingly, the replacement of de Valera as Taoiseach by Seán Lemass, following the elevation of the former to the presidency in 1959, "contributed to a palpable improvement in the bilateral relationship".

At this point, economic ties at ground level were already growing. Between 1955 and 1962, 24 factories with German shareholdings were established in the Republic, most of which arrived after 1959. By the early sixties, German firms were among the top two investors in Ireland, behind the British. Investors were attracted by the low cost of labour – one example being the crane manufacturer Liebherr, which still retains a plant in Killarney.

In December 1960 Lemass told a meeting of the Solicitors' Apprentices' Society that Ireland – while militarily neutral – was not ideologically so. In O'Driscoll's view, what we now had was a "transformation of the tenor of the public debate on EEC membership from 'wait and see' to one of 'how and when'".

Building support

Denis Corboy is an important witness to many of the changes that occurred close to the apex of the Irish elite from the late fifties. He served as honorary director of the Irish Council of the European Movement from the early 1960s and was also the first Irish citizen to work for the European Commission as an adviser, in 1963.

He later headed up the European Commission office in Dublin. As a UCD student from 1954 he was involved in the European Youth Campaign, a European Movement spin-off – this at a time when many young people of his age were more concerned by the IRA Border campaign.

As auditor of the King's Inns Debating Society he chose the Convention on Human Rights as the subject of his inaugural address.

Following the establishment of the Court of Human Rights, a way had been opened for individuals to appeal decisions handed down by courts in a domestic jurisdiction. Corboy recalls his amused astonishment at the wildly contrasting positions adopted by the then Tánaiste Seán MacBride on the European question. At a meeting organised by the European Movement, MacBride emerged as an enthusiastic federalist. But when he later attended a meeting organised by a left-wing group he hit out at the newborn EEC as "the greatest conspiracy".

Denis Corboy certainly enjoyed a degree of access to the corridors of power. He remembers being called to meet with Lemass at his office in the Department of Industry and Commerce to be informed that he was going to propose that Ireland seek membership of the European Community. The future Taoiseach then suggested that Corboy should try to instigate a shake-up at the European Movement, with the aim of involving representatives of industry, agriculture and the trade unions. A new chairman was found in the shape of Garret FitzGerald, then enjoying a growing profile as an economics writer and radio guest. As Lemass put it at the time: "He is a very good choice [...] he has nothing to do with politics."

Corboy believes that Lemass's change of heart on the European question came about because he could see that protectionism was not working. However, he faced opposition – "a closed door" – in the form of traditionally minded colleagues and, in particular, Taoiseach Éamon de Valera.

Denis Corboy recalls the occasion when the head of the College of Europe in Bruges, Henri Brugmans, expressed an interest in meeting de Valera, who was still Taoiseach at the time. Corboy arranged the encounter. The atmosphere between the pair appeared to soften. However, as they parted de Valera said: "You are still a European and I am still a nationalist!"

Another obstacle existed in the form of de Valera's key right-hand man Frank Aiken, then serving as minister of external affairs. When EEC President Walter Hallstein visited Ireland on one occasion, Aiken declined to meet him at the airport – opting to send TK Whitaker, secretary general at the Department of Finance instead. Aiken's thinking permeated the Department of External Affairs at the time. A minimalist approach to European integration was favoured.

Denis Corboy believes that in truth, had the British and Irish applications for membership of the EEC been accepted in 1963 rather than in 1973, this country would have been entirely unprepared. "We had a totally protected industrial structure which was far behind that of any country." However, the groundwork was being laid for the economic reforms that would begin to kick in after 1958 and lead to a fundamental reorientation of the Irish economy and public service. The process would be a gradual one.

Brendan Halligan – the former senator and Dáil deputy, and later the driving force behind the Institute of European Affairs – pointed out in *Europe: The Irish Experience* (edited by Rory O'Donnell in 2000) that as late as 1972, two thirds of our trade was still with the UK, our currency was a derivative of sterling, we shared a common labour market and our agricultural exports almost all ended up in Britain. He recalled: "When I became general secretary of the Labour Party in 1967, it had no links whatsoever with any other social democratic party."

The same attitude, one born of insularity, prevailed in the main political parties: "Europe (with the exception of Lourdes and Rome) was a foreign place." Frank Barry, Professor of International Business and Development at Trinity College Dublin believes, however, that the 1950s is "an underrated decade" when it comes to the history of the country's economic transformation. At a seminar in January 2015, he described some of the key developments in economic policymaking during this period.

He describes as "the most important economic policymaking speech in Irish history" a speech delivered in October 1956 by Taoiseach John A Costello in which he announced the introduction of export profit relief along with a national scheme of industrial grants. Barry believes that there was what amounts to an "unspoken accord" between Costello and his successor but one, Seán Lemass, with respect to this fundamental change in industrial development strategy.

A key aim as far as Costello and his economic advisers were concerned was the attraction of more investment from Britain. This particular goal was not stated in the speech for fear of raising the hackles of key decisionmakers within Fianna Fáil, Frank Barry maintains.

Barry draws an interesting distinction between the focus of the Irish government in the sixties based on trade liberalisation, and that in the fifties which concentrated on boosting export-oriented investment. Lemass had originally opposed the establishment of the Industrial Development Authority, which took place in 1949, as his original preference was for a concentration of power in his long-time fiefdom the Department of Industry and Commerce.

However, in 1953 he made a trip to New York and Ottawa during which he appears to have come around to the idea of acting to open up the Irish economy to US capital investment. From early on the IDA was 'fascinated' by the US – its first US office opened in New York in the late 1950s, being headed up by Count Cyril McCormack, son of the great Irish tenor Count John. On his return to power Lemass pressed ahead with the establishment of the Shannon Development Authority, which soon acted as a magnet for US foreign direct investment.

The run-in to accession

There were few illusions among the commentariat about the challenges facing the country as it prepared for entry to the EEC. *Business & Finance* reporter Bill Ambrose caught the mood when he wrote that "ruthless action is needed" if Irish industry was to avoid a crisis situation. Many who were "slumbering under an imagined tariff blanket" needed to be alerted. "If Irish industry is not aroused, in the next 18 months, it will be too late."

He added: "Outside a narrow range clustered at the top the general quality of home-bred management is very poor." Ambrose quoted an Irish management survey from 1966 that contrasted the strong performance of managers in firms employing more than 500 with the lack of efficiency among those running smaller companies. Certainly, many sectors were in need of rationalisation. For example, in 1972 there were still 38 pork and bacon processing factories operating in the Republic, the same as in 1939. In some cases reorganisation could not be put off.

A reshaping of Bord Bainne as a cooperative-run agency was necessitated due to the EEC prohibition on the use of state-controlled marketing boards. The IFA leader TJ Maher, later an elected MEP, called for an overhaul in the structure of Irish agriculture with the development of a land policy aimed at transferring land into the hands of younger, more vigorous farmers. This goal has yet to be achieved. He also favoured the rationalisation of food processing companies, something that was not happening quickly enough in his view.

In late June the Staines air disaster disrupted preparations for accession in the cruellest way. The disruption to the industrial lobby, and the companies that the 12 business leaders represented, was immediate. The Staines disaster removed many of the businesspeople who had built up close links with officials in Brussels. It meant that the civil service in Dublin took on a greater role in the discussions during the six months or so leading to the accession date.

The loss of such talent was damaging to the national interest, as many of the civil servants of this period tended to be fairly hidebound in their attitudes. That, at least, was a view widely shared by supporters of the European project. But the task that these officials and their political masters faced was a large one indeed.

The challenge was summed up by a young TD, John Bruton, during the November 1972 Dáil debates on the European Communities Bill, the enabling legislation designed to pave the way for the government to pass into law European Community treaties and directives and to adjust existing Irish laws in the process.

As Bruton, a barrister by training, put it: "We are going to bring about a unique situation in the legal history of this country in which we will have two bodies of law in effect at the same time and there will be no certainty where one begins and the other ends."

He suggested that the changes be clarified in specific implementing legislation "so that one can spell out precisely what section of existing law is affected by the proposals". He warned against relying on the courts to carry out this work of interpretation and adaptation as to do so would create "a great opportunity for lawyers to make money debating whether a particular section is affected by a section of Community law".

Charles Haughey – later Taoiseach, but at this point serving on the back benches two and a half years after the Arms Crisis – believed that Ireland was "in the unique position of being a common law country and at the same time having a written constitution [...] because of this we are perhaps more intellectually adapted to the Community system of law than our neighbour [Britain]".

While the civil service machine along with the various business and trade union organisations prepared to meet the challenges of membership, the opponents of the project were laying the groundwork for a period of long drawn-out resistance.

In mid-November came news of the formation of the Irish Sovereignty Movement under the chairmanship of Micheál Ó Loingsigh, former chair of the Common Market Defence Campaign. Its stated objective was the 'defence of Irish democratic rights'. As he put it at the time: "We have every intention of holding the leaders of Fianna Fáil, Fine Gael, the IFA, the Confederation of Irish Industry, the IDA, to the glorious picture they painted of the benefits of EEC membership."

In October it was announced that Patrick Hillery, Minister for External Affairs and TD for Clare, would be leaving Irish politics to assume office as Ireland's first 'Mr Europe', its first European commissioner. Dr Hillery's fortunes had taken a sharp turn for the better since the turbulent period in 1969-70 when he served as the key mouthpiece for the Republic during the rapidly escalating crisis in the North, while simultaneously facing down Republican diehards within the ranks of his party.

Welcoming his appointment, a *Business & Finance* editorial referred to his "dashing visit to the Falls Road" during the crisis in Belfast. It mentioned his 'gauche' speaking style, adding that "no-one doubted his ability for hard bargaining".

Under pressure from various lobby groups, he managed to secure reasonable deals across a wide range of areas from regional development through social affairs to farming and fishing. The editor reminded readers that "as commissioner in Europe, Dr Hillery will have to cut himself away from Irish politics [...] along with the other 13 commissioners, he will act as watchdog over the implementation of the Treaty of Rome".

The hardship of separation from familiar haunts and established relationships was being cushioned by the prospect of an annual salary of £20,000, good money in 1973. For the Taoiseach Jack Lynch, the loss of his key ally – first to Brussels and later, in 1976, to the Phoenix Park – would turn out to be a costly one.

Membership of the EEC proved to be transformative in both a material and a psychological sense. Over time, Irish politicians and officials developed a new set of skills and a broader outlook.

A new generation of lawyers and public representatives led by individuals such as Mary Robinson and David Norris carved out new individual freedoms – making use of the large body of European jurisprudence.

A whole new body of laws began to benefit Irish employees, though benefits for consumers took longer to arrive. It would be well into the 1980s before Peter Sutherland as competition commissioner presided over air transport deregulation. This paved the way for the rise of Ryanair, a company that has contributed greatly to the forging of interpersonal links throughout Europe.

It was at European councils that links between Ireland and Britain were forged. In 1970, Prime Minister Ted Heath declined to take a phonecall from Taoiseach Jack Lynch. This was at the height of the crisis in Derry and Belfast. Yet within 15 years the Hillsborough Agreement had been concluded.

EEC membership transformed provincial Ireland – directly through grants and price supports, and indirectly through the boost to foreign direct investment. In the 1980s industrial Ireland was overhauled dramatically. Early-stage IT investors like Wang replaced labour-intensive operations such as Ferenka. Up until 2000, the story of Ireland and Europe was a positive one indeed. Since then, the picture has been altogether more complicated.

Yet for all that, the progress achieved since 1973 has been little short of miraculous. Ireland reaped the benefits of a generation of European leaders: people like Helmut Schmidt, Hans Dietrich Genscher and Jacques Delors, who remembered the Second World War and sought something better.

We await a new generation of creative European leaders.

CHAPTER 6

Collapse and rebuild: stagnation and inflation in the 1980s
By Kyran Fitzgerald

THE SCALE OF IRELAND'S 1980S ECONOMIC MIRE IS DIFFICULT TO OVERESTIMATE
– AND TURMOIL WAS THE ORDER OF THE DAY IN AN POLITICAL ERA DOMINATED BY
THE FIGURE OF CHARLES HAUGHEY.

Back in 1980, the *Irish Times* journalist Ella Shanahan interviewed a young Sligo politician who had recently entered the cabinet as minister of agriculture.

In those days, Ray MacSharry could come across as edgy and a bit chippy. He was clear about one thing: he was a home-town man. As Shanahan reminded her readers, MacSharry was "the first man to bring a ministerial car to the north-west town". Car or no car, MacSharry would not be moving: "I would rather sign on the dole in Sligo before I would leave."

Less than a decade later he would be on his way to Brussels to serve as agriculture commissioner, following a successful stint as minister for finance. MacSharry would emerge as one of the key players of the 1980s in the Irish political-economic arena. It would be a good decade for smart young politicians with a financial bent – John Bruton, Alan Dukes and Peter Sutherland would all help to shape the decade while still in their thirties. All four men would be forced to operate in the most difficult of circumstances.

The country's education sector would, over this period, be presided over by two formidable female politicians, Gemma Hussey and Mary O'Rourke.

The two were following in the footsteps of Donogh O'Malley and Paddy Hillery as education minister.

O'Malley, minister for education up until his death in 1968, opened a pathway to higher education for a much larger cohort of the population with his scheme for 'free' secondary education. Dr Hillery, his successor, pushed ahead with the development of regional technical colleges that provided a new source of skilled and semi-skilled technician labour for the manufacturing sector.

The education sector would eventually play a major part in the Irish economic recovery after 1993. In 1980, however, the picture was altogether less rosy as officials at the Department of Finance contemplated an emerging fiscal crisis.

This coincided with a period of great political drama and deadlock at the heart of the State. The political battleground would be shaped above all by the rivalry between two old UCD acquaintances, Charles J Haughey and Garret FitzGerald. Three successive general elections between June 1981 and December 1982 almost beggared political parties and politicians at a time when the cost of campaigns had surged as a result of a growing predilection among the parties' planners for US-style electioneering.

Haughey would outlast FitzGerald in high office, but would end the decade sharing the spoils with his bitter former party rival Des O'Malley, who had come to prominence in the wake of the Arms Trial in 1970. Haughey's unexpected accession to the leadership in December 1979 itself plunged the Fianna Fáil party into a series of internal crises that would continue until O'Malley's establishment of a breakaway party, the Progressive Democrats, in late 1985.

The old Fianna Fáil establishment led by former finance minister George Colley could not reconcile itself to Haughey's election. This would result in the authority of the new leader being undermined. The new Taoiseach failed to act on his promise to rapidly rein in the deficit, in large part because he lacked the full backing of his party.

This failure would come to haunt the country as a whole through much of the 1980s. Interestingly, however, Colley's junior at the Department of Finance, Ray MacSharry, backed Haughey in his contest with George

Colley for the posts of party leader and Taoiseach following the resignation of Jack Lynch. Lynch's authority had been undermined largely because of the failure of the plan developed ahead of the 1977 general election aimed at boosting employment and growth. Pressures built up across the system, with large trade union-led marches in protest at high levels of taxation on ordinary PAYE employees, and an outbreak of industrial disputes.

The country's failing economy would be further impacted by the internecine battles within Fianna Fáil. The new Taoiseach lacked the necessary authority to rally his party behind moves to clamp down on government overspending at this crucial stage.

Thousands of jobs were created in the public service in an attempt to massage the figures ahead of a general election that was due by 1982 at the latest. This only served to enhance the sense of dread at the heart of official Ireland. It would be well into 1982 before Ray MacSharry, now minister of finance, would point out to his party leader the unavoidable economic facts of life.

This was the period of GUBU, of events 'grotesque, unbelievable, bizarre and unprecedented', to paraphrase Haughey reacting to the discovery of the bow tie-wearing killer Malcolm MacArthur in the Dalkey apartment of Attorney General Paddy Connolly.

MacSharry's early attempt to rein in spending was soon be aborted by his government's loss of power following the premature deaths of two FF TDs. The new government under Garret FitzGerald would inherit an economy spiralling out of control.

Economic collapse: the background

Auction politics could be said to have arrived early in 1973 when the Fine Gael and Labour parties joined forces with a series of pledges aimed at wooing voters. These included a halving of the level of domestic rates. Fianna Fáil responded with a pledge to abolish domestic rates altogether in an effort to win back middle-class votes.

The 1973 oil crisis produced queues at the petrol pumps and a surge in the oil price level, which helped to derail the national coalition government's economic agenda. By the end of the OPEC oil embargo following the Yom Kippur War, the price of oil had jumped fourfold to around $12 a barrel. This led to a major transfer of wealth to oil-producing nations, and a shift in terms of trade away from oil-importing nations including Ireland.

Central banks cut interest rates in an attempt to stimulate consumption. This only helped to spark further inflation. By the mid-1970s, western nations were caught up in the era of 'stagflation' – economic stagnation coinciding with rates of annual price increases approaching 20%.

At this time the Irish currency was pegged to sterling. In 1976 the UK government was forced to call in the International Monetary Fund. Ireland's major export market was in freefall. It was in this environment that the country faced into a general election in 1977.

The coalition government, and in particular Finance Minister Richie Ryan, had made strenuous attempts to squeeze inflation out of the system and tackle an emerging balance of payments crisis. Ryan was pilloried for initiatives such as a wealth tax, but he had succeeded in turning around the failing economy by 1977. By then the opposition Fianna Fáil party was plotting a return to government, having set up an in-house research think-tank under academic Martin O'Donoghue.

O'Donoghue had left school at the age of 14 to work for the exclusive Dublin restaurant Jammets. He later secured a scholarship to Trinity College and taught in school before becoming an academic, eventually rising to become a professor of economics at TCD. In the 1970s he was viewed within Fianna Fáil as a figure able to challenge Garret FitzGerald in intellectual argument. In his role as adviser to Jack Lynch in government between 1970 and 1973 he was active in the run up to the EEC accession negotiations and was involved in crafting national wage agreements.

But it is for his role as the brains behind the party election manifesto of 1977 that he is arguably best remembered. The manifesto contained a promise that 20,000 new jobs would be created within 12 months. £50m was to be spent on extra posts for gardaí and teachers. Car tax was to be abolished for small- to medium-sized vehicles.

£160m in tax cuts were promised for implementation in late 1977 and in 1978. The *piece de resistance* was the offer of £1,000 as a grant to first-time buyers of new homes. This went down a treat with the voters. The real winner was the building industry. O'Donoghue became one of only five newly elected TDs to enter the cabinet, in his case as the country's first minister of economic planning and development.

Planning in Ireland had been in vogue since the sixties: the economic successes enjoyed by France under General de Gaulle influenced Taoiseach Seán Lemass and his successors. However, this late-1970s mixture of planning and election pledges would prove toxic in an economic environment that turned out to be highly volatile. In the late 1970s the incoming Fianna Fáil government had stuck to a series of manifesto pledges, despite a disastrous shift in the country's terms of trade following the Iranian Revolution.

The second energy crisis prompted a jump in the price of crude oil to almost $40 a barrel within 12 months, creating havoc in the international arena. Other events also conspired to push the Irish economy towards the abyss. The cost of servicing the country's burgeoning national debt was greatly increased as a result of the anti-inflation strategy pursued by the able, but hawkish chairman of the US Federal Reserve, Paul Volcker, from 1979.

Interest rates soared while the value of the US currency also jumped: the result for a country like Ireland with significant levels of dollar-denominated debt was little short of disastrous. Closer to home, Britain's chancellor of the exchequer also pursued an anti-inflation strategy that squeezed demand in the key market for Irish exports.

Unemployment in Britain soared, removing an important outlet for Irish labour. The jobless level would reach three million by 1982. Prime Minister Thatcher found herself against the ropes politically, with even the Conservative Party house journal, *The Daily Telegraph*, calling for her head.

Irish business mans the pumps

The 1970s ended with a famous address to the nation on RTÉ by the new Taoiseach. Haughey certainly talked the talk: "As we stand on the threshold of a new year and start out on a new decade, let us firmly resolve that we are not going to throw away what we have gained or be submerged by the difficulties now facing us," he intoned.

In its editorial, *Business & Finance* revealed itself to be less than impressed. "What a load of waffle! They [the words] sound like a despairing schoolboy's attempt to pad out an essay on citizenship. Charles Haughey's reputation is for toughness and pragmatism and an ability to get things done. He is the sort of leader we need, at present – or so we have assumed."

The BBC extended a warmer welcome to the new Taoiseach, devoting much of an edition of its current affairs programme *Tonight* to a soft-focus piece on Haughey clad in riding jodhpurs at his Abbeville residence near Malahide. The real underlying message was that the running of the State had been handed over to a man who knew a thing or two about how to generate wealth, an Irish Horace Walpole, with more than a dash of old Joe Kennedy thrown in.

The great recession of the 1980s shook Irish business to its foundations. Many established names disappeared. The once-mighty McGrath family lost control of Waterford Glass. Labour-intensive manufacturing firms were hardest hit by a combination of rising input costs, government tax increases and a contracting domestic market.

Losses at State companies such as Irish Steel and fertiliser maker NET soared. By 1984 Irish Shipping was in liquidation, while AIB had to be rescued following its disastrous purchase of the Insurance Corporation of Ireland.

Joe Moore's PMPA proved to be built on quicksand as the liquidators were called in to the largest writer of insurance business in the country. Receiver-liquidators such as John Donnelly, Kevin Kelly, Billy McCann and Tom Grace became household names. The examiner had yet to take his bow in the burgeoning insolvency arena. But many in business adapted – and adapted well, usually through international expansion and innovation. The 1980s was a great decade for Kerry Group, the Smurfit family, Tony Ryan/GPA and Glen Dimplex. The Irish Stock Exchange benefited from large flotations. The IDA began to prepare the way for a foreign direct investment boom. While some semi-state companies ran up huge losses, others embarked on successful diversification.

Ordinary Irish punters were also out in search of great riches. There was great excitement about the possibility of a major oil find off the west and south coastlines. The flames had been fanned by the discovery of a large natural gas field off the Cork coast. A *Business & Finance* editorial warned: 'Exploration – Exercise Caution'.

"In relation to the latest reports, rumours and speculation on the BP consortium oil find off the west coast, it is true that a 5,000 barrels a day flow indicated by the drilling, last year, compared very favourably with the early exploration tests in the now proven North Sea. It is also true that the oil yielded is of good quality and in the jargon of the industry, mobile. But [...] it will take a second exploration well to give any real pointer to the commerciality of such a find," the editorial noted.

"The discovery is in deep waters, some 100 miles off the west coast of Ireland. The technology is complex and costly and while it exists, will require financing of the order of £300m." All of which was "still speculation at this stage, despite the oil share madness which has overtaken the stock exchange – both Irish and in London.

"The omens for the long term are good. There can be little doubt that Irish oil exploration and our currency will benefit from the psychological boost of even a modest field.

"But a sense of proportion is needed. We are, at present, still in danger of jumping the gun." Yet jump the gun they did – in droves. And down they fell, scythed in a mass slaughter of investors. The great Irish oil and gas finds have yet to materialise, though hopes have been raised once more – largely due to deep-sea technology, which has opened up more marginal prospects for development. By the early 1980s, firms such as Aran Energy had withdrawn from exploration off our coast to concentrate on prospecting in the North Sea. The hope of exploration riches had died for a generation.

In December 1980 some glimmers of our technological future could be spotted. *Business & Finance* reported on a 64K microchip holding 64,000 'bits' of information that could fit into an Irish stamp. Most business brochures of the period show executives sitting proudly next to brand new mainframe computers that they had just learned to switch on.

But members of the old guard still walked tall. Joe Moore, chairman of the Private Motorists' Protection Association, was interviewed by *B&F*

reporter Ronnie Hoffman. Moore had started the PMPA following his early retirement from the civil service. Premium income at the company had jumped from £1m in 1970 to £65m in 1980. Total group turnover in 1979 amounted to £86m, a rise of 30% on the preceding year.

As Moore recalled, "motor insurance led to motor cars and garages. Garages led to oil and petrol fuels and even to exploration [...] and to fleets of touring coaches and to tourism". The decision to print a PMPA newssheet led to newspaper production and the acquisition first of a regional – and then a national – newspaper, the *Sunday Journal*.

The PMPA had also moved into banking, acquiring 75% of the equity of Commercial Banking. As the reporter observed: "The PMPA resembles a well-established country store that stocks a little of a great many lines [...] though it may appear messy to the outsider, its proprietor knows every nook and cranny."

Here, the reporter hints at trouble to come: "As its stock in trade grows larger, he begins to know less about the detailed content of each corner." Hoffman noted the chairman's preference for "simple, almost earthy explanation". Said Moore: "Motor insurance has never been profitable for us. It's the investment income that makes the profit."

This self-made man produced what would become a familiar complaint: "We suffer from a terrible handicap in this country. We are Irish." Perhaps these complaints were not unrelated to pressure coming from the Central Bank on the PMPA to reduce its holding in Commercial Banking to 20%. "If the Insurance Corporation (ICI) can own a majority of Credit Finance (Bank), then PMPA can do likewise with Commercial Banking," he said.

The interviewer then referred to an October 1975 analysis of the PMPA's finances that had suggested, on the figures supplied, that the company was technically insolvent. Was it technically insolvent in 1975? Reply: "No, of course not!"

So were the figures wrong? Was the maths wrong? "I never checked the figures. I don't give a damn whether they were right or wrong." He insisted that the method used by the magazine, in its 1975 analysis, was wrong. Moore would later clash with an increasingly concerned Minister of Industry and Commerce Des O'Malley, referring to him as a "tiresome gnat." The concerns aired would be vindicated in dramatic fashion in 1983.

Many larger farmers, too, still seemed to be doing well at the start of the eighties, having successfully ridden the rollercoaster property wave that followed upon Irish entry to the European Community. As *B&F*'s property writer observed, "many Irish farmers who sold their farms at the height of the property boom for an average of £3,500 an acre, bought farms in the UK at around £1,000 an acre and have now sold again to German buyers. Now, they are back in Ireland looking for land, here, prices having slumped to £1,500 per acre, or even less. Despite the drop, no foreigners are rushing to buy Irish land."

The office property market in 1980, meanwhile, was still being propped up by a public service greedy for extra space. Government and semi-state bodies were reported to be taking up more than 50% of the office space coming on the market each year. The national training organisation AnCo, the predecessor of FÁS, was "expanding at a great rate".

Division in the workplace

Employers were not simply fretting about rising wages and inflationary wage claims. It seems that they were wondering whether their staff would turn up at all. The Federated Union of Employers, predecessor of IBEC, had unearthed an absenteeism rate of almost 8%, with a little over one third of these absences being certified by a doctor.

The FUE pointed to a number of major causes: social welfare, working conditions, inadequate personnel problems, social problems such as alcoholism, and the culture of overtime working. Employers were beginning to fight back. The leading Irish cigarette maker, PJ Carroll, announced new control procedures linking bonuses to performance, with better bonuses for those with low rates of absence.

Pfizer, employing 700 at the time, managed to reduce its rate from 11% to below 7%, according to director Joe Cogan. It all harked back to the days when absence rates in rural factories would soar around harvest time.

However, the Irish workplace would undergo significant transformation during the eighties as old-style manufacturing gave way to new high-technology industries and adversarial approaches to industrial relations were upended. Trade unions found themselves on the defensive in sectors that previously appeared impregnable.

In 1983 *Business & Finance* reported that a proposal on the part of the Northern Bank to reduce employment by 350 was "unprecedented in scale on the Irish banking scene". The lion's share of the losses – 280 – were slated to take place in Northern Ireland, then bearing the brunt of the UK economic implosion. The magazine, however, advised readers that there was now a "sharper recognition of the impact of new technology on employment.

"Throughout Europe, for many years, banking and insurance have been at the forefront of job shrinkage. Despite the soothing noises from senior management, financially articulate bank staff can read the balance sheet, too and one of the major obstacles to substantially higher profits is the cost of carrying such huge payrolls."

Business & Finance reported the "startling finding" from research undertaken in the UK that "people actually prefer dealing with machines. They like the cash dispenser. They are perceived as more efficient." While there were no plans in the immediate future (1983) for further large redundancy programmes, the magazine adopted an upbeat approach to the future, suggesting that "talk of staff being released from the drudgery of more boring jobs to more front-of-the-counter dealing with customers was definitely on." It predicted that with the advent of VDUs – visual display machines – able to "conjure up information at the drop of a hat", the need for paper filing would decline and a "new era would arrive".

However, the changes occurring in the early 1980s were not all for the good: *B&F* fretted that "recession and the growing trend of female staff to stay on due to the economic impact of the recession is causing problems, particularly on the promotional ladder. There is a growing bulge in the pipeline at senior banking officer level just below that of assistant branch manager. Something has to be done. This could mean a more generous early retirement scheme for those wishing to go voluntarily."

But elsewhere the winds of change blew with much more rawness, impacting on relationships between workers, management and the middlemen increasingly drawn onto the industrial scene in the wake of financial collapse. In 1983 *B&F*'s unnamed industrial relations commentator reported that "sit-ins by workers resisting the removal of assets from collapsed firms has become the new form of industrial action". At the time, four sit-ins were underway in different parts of the country.

"As hundreds more firms face closure, as premium redundancy terms rapidly become a thing of the past, the spectre of workers filling jails in defiance of court injunctions becomes alarmingly likely." *B&F* predicted that the effects would spill over into the political arena with relationships between the then-governing Fine Gael and Labour parties "reaching their lowest ebb".

Tánaiste Dick Spring, Labour TD for Kerry North, found himself under the cosh in his Tralee heartland following the closure of the Kingdom Tubes plant. The town was then described as Ireland's "worst unemployment black spot". As an unnamed trade union activist told the magazine: "We felt certain that, whatever about factories in other parts of the country, Dick Spring would never allow that one to go."

Politics may well be global but in Ireland it is, above all, local. The one-time poll-topping tánaiste would hold on to his Dáil seat by the skin of his teeth in the subsequent general election in early 1987.

A government under the cosh

The new Fine Gael/Labour coalition, elected in late 1982, would soon find itself navigating stormy waters. Labour, not for the last time, found that participation in government in the heat of an economic crisis was a pretty queasy experience. In February 1983 the young finance minister, Alan Dukes, introduced an austerity budget in an effort to tackle a looming budgetary crisis.

B&F commented that "even before the harshness of this week's budget and the unemployment figures hit home, the Labour Party's honeymoon with the electorate was well and truly over". It saved much of its fire for the lanky Dukes, a 37 year-old economist. On February 17th the editorial accepted that by strongly attacking the balance of payments deficit, the minister had displayed a "seriousness of purpose that should have a soothing effect on foreign investors. That said, the Dukes budget is pretty well without redeeming features. When the minister introduced his taxes on tobacco, drink and petrol in January, we feared that the full budget, when it appeared, would not produce fresh thinking [...] but would rely on the unimaginative nostrums of old.

"The minister has made our nightmare a reality. The assault on expenditure has not materialised. The wretched incubus of the civil service is still in place. The Dukes budget is a civil servant's budget, unimaginative in its exclusive obsession with reducing the deficit. They [the government] are encouraging a black market that would put the Italians to shame. Their pathetic response is to recruit more tax collectors. It is cheaper and more efficient to create a climate in which people are rewarded for effort."

The coalition government introduced a top income tax rate of 65% – though this decision was subsequently reversed. This was an era in which commentators on the business end of the political spectrum were fond of referring to 'white elephants', typically either public projects of dubious worth or cash-gobbling State entities.

A *Business & Finance* article that month carried the headline 'Maintaining the national herd'. The government was complimented in sarcastic terms for its role in the maintenance of the herd through its purchase of the Clondalkin Paper Mills, in west Dublin, in response to its occupation by employees.

It described as "disgraceful" the decision to "capitulate" to the workers in spending £1.75m of taxpayers' money on a "clapped out mill". "The trouble with the plant, in the first place, was that it could not compete with imports from Brazil, France, Germany, thanks to uncompetitive wage demands and government price rises, in areas such as electricity charges."

The Minister of Industry and Commerce, John Bruton, had been forced by political circumstances into a somewhat humiliating u-turn having stated in the Dáil that he did not want "to add another lame duck to the State's long list of nationalised assets".

Trade union leaders such as John Carroll of the Irish Transport and General Workers' Union countered that a big threat to jobs was posed by uncontrolled imports. The editor's finger wagged: 'Dukes must do better'.

Carroll argued that the collapse of flour milling in Dublin and Limerick with the loss of 300 jobs would only be the first of many such collapses. Indeed, in early 1984 Cork would receive a hammer-blow with the closure of the Ford and Dunlop plants, key employers in the city for generations.

Cork, heartland of former Taoiseach Jack Lynch, would be stretched out on the floor economically for years. The loss of the Ford assembly operation alone cost the city 800 jobs directly.

Business and consumers under the cosh

By 1982 it had become apparent to most people in the commercial world that the recession was deep and would be long-lasting. The chief executive of drinks company C&C, Tony O'Brien, was interviewed in 1983 by Aileen O'Toole, then a reporter with *Business & Finance*. C&C was best known for its soft drink brands. However, at the time half its turnover was accounted for by sales of alcoholic beverages.

It had shed 100 employees out of a payroll of 1,500. According to O'Brien – a future president of employers' group IBEC – "we are in a business that is highly vulnerable to government fiscal policies. It makes planning very difficult. Every plan you have made can be destroyed at one stroke of a government minister's pen."

He contended that the recent mini-budget, in early 1983, "took the public by surprise with a number of duty increases including an extra 8p on a glass of spirits. The government may have blown it with those increases. People tend to be very emotive about these rises. The pubs are undoubtedly deserted. We know of some pubs outside Dublin which stay closed until 5.30pm."

This was the fourth year in a row, said O'Brien, that "massive increases" in duties had been introduced. Pleas from an industry employing 38,000 full-time and 15,000 part-time workers "appeared to be falling on deaf ears".

In the year just ended, spirit consumption was down by 17%. By then, the cost of a bottle of scotch whisky was £4 cheaper in Newry than in Dundalk just over the Border. People were making the switch to beer and to "better value drinking". O'Brien touched on a cultural revolution then underway: "Beer drinking is now quite fashionable for females. We had the vodka revolution which was a marvel for 14 years, but now that seems to be over. Now there is a danger that the pubs will turn into beer parlours."

The C&C boss also touched on more long-term changes that were already under way in the world of retailing and distribution. "The power of the multiple supermarkets poses a very serious threat. You have four very powerful ones, who now have around 70% of the Dublin market and taking into account planned developments, they will have 65% of the national market by 1986.

"Their massive buying power could exert great, if not dangerous pressure on manufacturers' margins. Supermarket buyers are big enough to go outside the country for suppliers – for example, a multiple has taken a franchised brand of soft drinks from a German supplier. EEC trade rules prevent any objections being made."

Here, the leading businessman echoed some of the pleas of trade unionist John Carroll. O'Brien noted that "the cost advantages of buying from local suppliers have been eroded because of our ridiculously high energy costs [...] so that they outweigh the cost of freight.

"Imports of soft drinks now account for 10% of the market as against 1%, a few years ago." O'Brien pointed to a curious historical anomaly: water duty, introduced to help pay for the costs of the Boer War at the end of the 19th century. In the 1980s this duty was increased fourfold by the government. C&C was pressing for its abolition.

In an effort to keep down distribution costs – it cost £22,000 to keep a sales rep on the road at the time – the company was looking at the possibility of distributing the products of other companies.

Other high-profile companies were feeling the pinch. Waterford Glass, one of the blue chip stocks on the Irish Stock Exchange, ranked fifth in capitalisation, saw its share price drop by 28% during 1982. Within three years it would be a case of a changing of the guard.

The stake of the long-time owners, the McGrath family, would be acquired by a London investment house and Paddy McGrath, a former senator, would step down as chairman to be replaced by Paddy Hayes, previously head of Ford Ireland. The McGrath family's grip on commercial life had been loosening for some time.

In December 1984 *B&F* would report that the Irish Hospitals' Sweepstake was "fighting for its life". The sweepstake had been a major institution in Irish life since the 1930s, operating out of a sprawling low-rise art deco building in Ballsbridge, south Dublin.

In its heyday 4,000 people – mainly women – operated out of the building. By the end of 1984 just 400 were left working there and soon all would lose their jobs and the building would fall to the developers. McGrath warned of imminent closure if the sweepstake failed to secure the running of the proposed national lottery, a warning that fell on deaf ears. In eighties Ireland there was little room for sentiment.

Elsewhere, the valuation of CRH – Cement Roadstone, Ireland's largest public company – tumbled from £154m at the end of 1981 to £108m a year later. CRH's exposure to the battered construction sector accounted for this share price implosion. According to *B&F*, "opinion is stacked against the group as the recession deepens and cheaper cement imports seep into the country".

Jefferson Smurfit group was Ireland's largest PLC in terms of turnover in 1981, with sales in the year to January 1982 of £491m. During 1982 its share price plunged from 90p to 60p as the paper manufacturer fell prey to a sharp dip in business activity.

In Cork, John Donnelly of accountants Deloitte Haskins Sells was appointed as receiver to the historic Murphy brewery. As an 'insider' told *Business & Finance*, "nobody has invested much in Murphys since 1855". Clearly, this was not a sustainable state of affairs. The Dutch brewing giant Heineken would emerge as a purchaser, but the acquisition was made contingent on the workforce agreeing to new working conditions.

Clothing industry executive Jim O'Leary had no doubt who, in his view, was to blame for the fact that his lingerie company Maylinder was under pressure from imported products. As he told *B&F* in December 1984, "massive wage inflation" was the cause. He was critical of the way wage increases had been negotiated in the clothing trade. As in other low-wage industries, wages were fixed by joint labour committees, the sanctioned increases being legally binding. Interestingly, O'Leary did not believe that the JLCs should be abolished – later, employers would seek their abolition

– but felt that the increases should be open to negotiation. In his view the government was to blame for neglecting labour-intensive industries, saddling them with high rates of PRSI (social security tax) while focusing its attention on what O'Leary termed the "god of high technology".

A different perspective was provided by economist Brendan Dowling, then with stockbrokers J&E Davy. Echoing modern-day concerns about the impact on the economy of a strong euro, Dowling argued for a change in exchange rate policy. In his view, expressed in early 1983, the Irish pound was overvalued and he added that this state of affairs was being "underwritten by massive foreign borrowing".

Back in 1979 the link with sterling had been broken and the Irish pound, or punt, had come into being. Exchange controls had been introduced between Dublin and London. In the past, Irish currency had fallen in value in line with the British pound during periods of prolonged weakness, particularly in the 1960s and 1970s. An important result was a high level of imported inflation, not to mention the importation of UK-style pay demands.

By the mid 1970s inflation in both countries approached 20% and beyond. In March 1979 the European Monetary System, a precursor of the euro, was established with the aim of reducing the degree of fluctuation in European currencies. The currencies were permitted to move up or down within a band of 2.25% either way. National central banks were expected to intervene to prevent the national currency from breaking through either limit.

Brendan Dowling's prescription for dealing with this overvaluation resembled, in some respects, the remedies later put in place at the height of the economic crisis circa 2009-2010. He proposed that incomes be "frozen at current levels" – a sharp decrease in real terms given the prevailing inflation levels – before being allowed to rise at a very modest rate, 2-3% below the weighted average increase across the other EMS partner countries.

His idea was that Ireland would recapture some of the competitiveness it had lost through the implementation of a tight incomes policy. He also proposed reducing foreign borrowing to £575m in 1983, eliminating it

1966: new Taoiseach Jack Lynch and Department of Finance secretary TK Whitaker depart for London to meet UK Prime Minister Harold Wilson.

Dublin's north Docklands, 1959. The area is now a hub of financial services activity, with the IFSC to the left and the Convention Centre Dublin to the right.

Taoiseach Seán Lemass receives his seal of office from President Éamon de Valera, 1959. The changing of the guard was a key moment in economic as well as political history.

Top: Legendary industry figure PV Doyle founded the Doyle Hotel Group in 1964.

Bottom: Trailblazing IDA managing director Michael Killeen was a pivotal figure in remaking the Irish economy.

BUSINESS
and FINANCE

A WEEKLY
SURVEY OF
TRADE/FINANCE
AND THE
PROPERTY MARKET

Vol. 1   No. 1   SEPTEMBER 18, 1964   TWO SHILLINGS

LORD BOYD, MANAGING DIRECTOR OF GUINNESS

GUINNESS TO BREW BEER IN DUBLIN?

Guinness is looking into the possibility of brewing beer at St. James's Gate, Dublin, for the first time in its 205-year history. The beer would be sold through Irish Ale Breweries, which is 66% owned by Guinness.

Full story, page 9

Issue one
of *Business &
Finance*, September
18th 1964. Founded by
editor Nicholas Leonard and
publisher Hugh McLaughlin,
the fledgling title proved
its doubters wrong by
surviving, and then
thriving.

BUSINESS
AND FINANCE

Vol. 3. No. 12.   DECEMBER 2, 1966   **TWO SHILLINGS**
(Including Turnover and Wholesale Tax)

The Ben Dunne phenomenon

Supermarket mogul Ben Dunne Sr **(left)** was a force of nature on the Irish retail scene, his prominence established by the time of this December 1966 front cover. His successor Ben Jr **(below)** plunged the family business into scandal following a Florida drugs bust.

Top: Seán Lemass at the Irish Management Institute Conference in 1966 with Rory Barnes, vice chairman Rigby-Jones, and director Ivor Kenny. **Below:** Pioneering Irish hotelier Paddy Fitzpatrick with film icon Burt Lancaster.

Tony O'Reilly,
1977 and 1994. his
interests extended
from Heinz to Independent
News & Media, Waterford
Wedgwood, Fitzwilton and many
other investments.

Minister for Finance Bertie Ahern with politician and business journalist Shane Ross in 1992. As Taoiseach Ahern presided over the Celtic Tiger boom – which collapsed shortly after he resigned.

Tony Ryan was another colossus of 1980s Irish business, the aviation leasing pioneer overseeing GPA's exponential ascent throughout the decade.

Left: Joe McGough of Bord Bainne (holding trophy), *Business & Finance* Man of the Year 1977, with Minister for Finance Richie Ryan. **Below:** Ford's Marina plant in Cork, founded in 1917, is often considered the starting point in a century-long theme of foreign direct investment in Ireland.

Right: Oonah Keogh, the first woman in the world to join a stock exchange – in Dublin in 1925. New York would first admit a woman in 1967, and London in 1973, though opportunities were otherwise scarce for Irish businesswomen for decades to come.

Right: Tom Roche, founder and driving force of fast-growing building materials firm CRH. **Middle:** The Conference of Free State Chambers of Commerce, Shelbourne Hotel, Dublin, 1st March 1923. **Bottom:** the first meeting of the Federation of Saorstát Industries, October 1932.

Dublin's quays and port have been completely transformed: the building to the right would become the Point Depot, then 3Arena. A Luas terminus, hotel, shopping centre and Holyhead ferry terminals would in time replace many of the factories and warehouses shown.

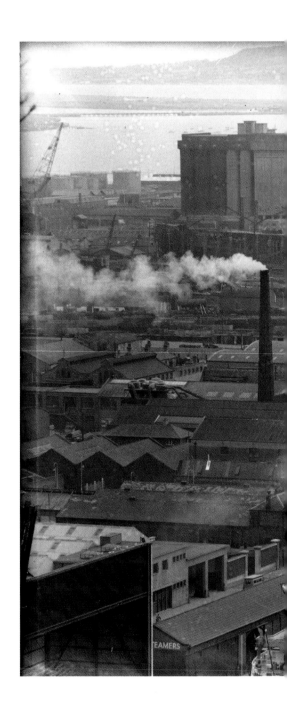

Above: Aer Lingus' acquisition of Boeing 747s was a major milestone in the airline's development. **Below:** Penneys' first retail outlet on Henry Street in Dublin, where the Primark success story began.

3rd APRIL, 1975. 20p (Inc. Tax)

EUROPEAN COMPANY LAW REFORM

Business &Finance

Vol. 11. No. 28.

Left: 1970s themes were repeated in 2016 with the UK's Brexit vote, unbenownst to the designer of this 1975 front cover. On that occasion 67% of voters opted to remain in the nascent EEC.

Right: Likewise, 1960s demands for equal pay for women remain topical. The earnings gap closed incompletely in the intervening years and remains a point of contention. Meanwhile, Patrick Hillery would become president of Ireland – and be succeeded by the country's first woman president, Mary Robinson.

altogether by 1985. The realities of coalition government meant that this proposition was never a runner.

In 1984 the Irish external borrowing requirement reached almost 13% of gross domestic product. Currency fluctuations, however, worked in favour of advocates of depreciation. In August 1979 the punt peaked in value at $2.11 before tumbling down below $1 by January 1985. This represented a boost to the IDA's efforts to secure American investment, but it only increased the headaches being endured by the government given that a high proportion of the national debt was owed in dollars.

The transformation in the position of the dollar in world markets proved to be a double-edged sword indeed.

Hints of recovery

By 1985 the country appeared mired in economic despair. Unemployment had reached the late teens in percentage terms. Confidence was on the floor. Office lettings had fallen from a respectable 750,000 square feet in 1981 to just 245,000 in 1984.

The government was resisting pressure from the public sector unions to implement the award handed down by the public service arbitrator, Hugh Geoghegan SC (later a member of the Supreme Court). By this point ministers were openly engaged in squabbling over the key issue of how to engineer economic revival.

Fine Gael 'young Turks' such as Industry Minister John Bruton and Minister for the Public Service John Boland favoured measures to promote an enterprise culture as well as steps to restructure the public service. Labour under Dick Spring baulked at some of these proposals.

In mid-1984 Boland undertook to release a white paper on public service reform the following autumn. Publication of the white paper fell prey to repeated delay, though the minister did succeed in establishing a new Top-Level Appointments Committee with the aim of ending 'Buggins' turn' and ensuring the promotion of younger talent up the ranks on merit. Under Boland, initiatives such as career breaks for civil servants were also developed.

The government, meanwhile, was busily courting US investors. *Plus ca change...* According to *B&F* reporter John McAleese it was "pulling out all the stops to land chip-making plants". In particular, grants of up to £90m had been sanctioned with the aim of landing US company AMD (Advanced Micro Devices) and Maersk. The two projects promised around 1,500 jobs between them. AMD held out high hopes of opening a £170m plant in Greystones employing up to 800.

Business & Finance reported that the AMD founder, Jerry Sanders, is "not short on colour", explaining that he had nine cars dotted around California and that he sported gem-coloured rings and a sapphire and diamond-studded watch. That year he held a Christmas bash for 8,000 staff in San Francisco. Sanders boasted that he had "never brought a party in under budget, yet!". Greystones never did land this investment, but other plants were in expansionary mode with Nixdorf pledging 200 jobs for its plant in nearby Bray.

In August 1984 the government published a white paper on industrial policy after what was described as an elephantine gestation. A new programme, *Building on Reality*, was launched at Iveagh House that autumn: one of its key proposals was the putting in place of a social employment scheme designed to provide work and a supplementary income for over 100,000 unemployed people.

Inflation gradually began to fall from a peak of almost 30% in 1980 to below 5% in 1987. The first seeds of urban renewal in Dublin were sown with the launch of a regeneration scheme for the Custom House Docks area in 1986.

Elsewhere, the Irish Stock Exchange began to revive, helped in no small part by the upturn in Britain and the so-called 'Big Bang' reform of the stock market. A highpoint was the flotation of Kerry Group in 1986, beginning a process of transformation that would eventually bring considerable wealth to a geographically peripheral part of Ireland while putting the Irish food sector on the global map.

Smurfit Group would also embark on a process of international expansion that would leave it in pole position in the global paper sector. By the time the government collapsed in on itself after more than four years toiling at the recessionary coalface, it was clear that the threat of national bankruptcy or social breakdown had been averted.

However, the electorate was exhausted by the years of austerity and near stagnation. Revenge was enjoyed, if not tasted cold, in the ballot box. A still poisoned – but rather less poisonous – chalice was handed back to Charles Haughey, who soon began to swig with gusto.

CHAPTER 7

Out of the Eighties
By Kyran Fitzgerald

REFORMS AT HOME, EVENTS ABROAD AND DEVELOPMENTS SUCH AS THE IFSC
MEANT THAT THE 1980S ENDED MUCH MORE OPTIMISTICALLY THAN THEY HAD
BEGUN – SETTING THE STAGE FOR THE BRIGHTER NINETIES.

In early 1987 PJ Mara, Fianna Fáil's publicity guru, was getting ready to assume the reins of power on his employer's behalf. It was reported in *Business & Finance* magazine that Mara was reading a biography of Stalin and was a fan of left-wing and right-wing dictators alike. The Fianna Fáil media handler may well have been speaking with his tongue in his cheek. The voters, however, were taking no chances.

Charles Haughey was returned as Taoiseach without an overall majority; the electorate was in no mood to hand over dictatorial powers. Haughey arrived back in Government Buildings undertaking to restore confidence to the country. Ray MacSharry was restored as minister of finance. Fianna Fáil had been vigorous in its condemnation of government cutbacks during the campaign: "Health cuts hurt the old, the sick and the handicapped" was one of its key slogans. MacSharry quickly junked the rhetoric and embarked on an even stiffer round of cuts, with the health service being targeted in particular. The health minister, Rory O'Hanlon, was singled out for particular attention by demonstrators infuriated by the elimination of droves of hospital beds across the system. The finance minister presented a large target for the satirists: *Irish Times* cartoonist Martyn Turner represented him as a Count Dracula figure complete with a mop of dark hair and fangs.

The mood around the time of the handover of power in early 1987 was reflective: there was a real feeling among the country's intellectual movers and shakers that Ireland had largely failed as an economy, and indeed as a society, since independence. This sense of pessimism was conveyed by historians such as Joe Lee, professor of history at UCC.

The broadcaster Gay Byrne had famously informed the readers of *Hot Press* magazine that the country was "banjaxed". Civil service icon TK Whitaker gave an interview to Ivor Kenny, former director of the Irish Management Institute, for his book *In Good Company* late in 1986: in Whitaker's view the public service was in need of deep overhaul. "The civil service has, I fear, suffered deterioration. It is more important to remedy this than to make changes in the structure of parliament, or government.

"I hear with dismay that there has been a considerable politicisation of the senior civil service in the past 25 years or so. This is attributable to a combination of factors: more oppressive ministerial styles, more exacting ministerial requirements." Whitaker called for a restoration of the old position whereby senior officials could speak up and tender advice, without fear, to the minister they served.

He was concerned, in particular, at the fact that secretaries of government departments were now appointed for seven-year terms as opposed to being entitled to serve in the post until they reached retirement age. "I would be afraid that a young man who saw nothing satisfactory ahead following his secretary-ship might be tempted to make a friend of the mammon of iniquity. He might look outside where he could place himself, whom he would be nice to, so that when he goes, they will receive him into their bosom. That could undermine that integrity which is still regarded as the one decent trait of a civil servant."

These remarks would find greater resonance in the years ahead. However, in the late 1980s a very different spirit was abroad.

Financial services revival

Revival of the economy was the top priority and it was expected that business and government should join forces with the achievement of this goal in mind. This was a high watermark for deregulation both at home and abroad.

The mood among business leaders tended to be bullish, and unapologetically so. Following its near-fatal involvement with the Insurance Corporation of Ireland, AIB was very much back in business. As stockbrokers J&E Davy put it at the time, "the bank got out cheap". The cost of the rescue was borne by the banking sector – by customers – as a whole.

In an interview with *Irish Times* journalist Eoin McVey in May 1985, the man who had taken over the bank in the wake of the ICI debacle, Gerry Scanlan, was unapologetic. "I make no apologies to anyone. The most important thing for us to do was to maintain confidence in the bank. We did what was in the best interests of the bank's shareholders, its staff, its depositors, its shareholders and the public at large. What do people want?"

Such bullishness provides an insight into the macho culture of an institution that over the next few decades would land itself in hot water time and time again. By 1990 it would appear that Scanlan's bullishness had reaped rich dividends for his shareholders.

A *Sunday Tribune* profile hailed him as the person "directing one of Ireland's biggest ever success stories". AIB had just announced plans to raise IR£162m in the country's biggest rights issue up to then. The bank had just added Baltimore Bancorp to First Maryland Bancorp in its US portfolio. AIB was also spending £44m on one of the new buildings at the new Custom House Dock complex and had also acquired the stockbroking firm Goodbody James Capel for good measure.

The *Sunday Independent* journalist Martin Fitzpatrick, later – in 2005 – summarised the Lazarus-like recovery of the bank: "On the Ides of March 1985, Scanlan had his worst and his best moment in banking. He had to tell the world his bank needed a £100m loan from the Central Bank and the charity of his fellow banks for a decade to avoid AIB going bust. Without having to forego a single share, he got it." Within a year, the AIB share price had recovered to its pre-March 1985 level, he noted.

AIB had succeeded in persuading the coalition government to push through a rescue plan by pointing to the existential threat to the banking system as a whole should it be allowed to fail. The government could have insisted on taking shares in the institution, but chose not to. The bank, meanwhile, benefited in the full from the huge payback on its investment in First Maryland Bank, which was greatly boosted by the resurgence in the US economy that kicked in around 1984. As Martin Fitzpatrick noted, whereas in 1983 First Maryland Bancorp was valued at around $35m, by 1990 the bank would be worth ten times that.

In January 1987 *Business & Finance* devoted an editorial to changes that were on the way across the European Economic Community. "The EC has embarked on a process to have a free circulation of financial services in place by 1992. This has serious implications for the Irish banking sector." It noted that the emphasis would be "on achieving a relatively rapid freeing of cross-border circulation of financial services".

In November 1987 the editor of *B&F* was moved to welcome the announcement of the complete abolition of exchange controls. One has to have quite a number of body miles clocked up to remember how exchange controls operated at their height in the 1960s when the Irish Republic was part of the sterling zone and when the British currency laboured under the constant threat of devaluations. Tight controls on the movement of capital extended to the amount of currency that holidaymakers could bring with them abroad.

In 1979 exchange controls between the Republic and the UK were introduced following the break of the link with sterling. Now these controls would be removed in line with the drive to free up movements of capital across the European Community.

The Central Bank governor, Tomás Ó Cofaigh, accepted that "on balance, Ireland would benefit from a more liberal international capital regime". The tide of deregulation was also sweeping across the domestic financial services scene. The talk was of privatisation, and of 'demutualisation'. The State-run insurance company Irish Life, the market leader in its sector, was being fattened up for sale by the State by late 1987 when its general manager in the Republic of Ireland, Brian Duncan, asserted that "there is no going back on privatisation".

The new Dublin International Financial Services Centre was being aggressively marketed by the IDA, and a joint public-private working party had been established to advise on what was required in terms of taxation, regulation and physical infrastructure. In May 1987 the government announced that the tax rate for institutions setting up in the IFSC was being reduced from 50% to 10%. Legislation to this effect was enacted the following month and both AIB and Bank of Ireland, wearing the green jersey, announced that they would seek licences to set up shop there.

In October 1987 plans for the development of the site were unveiled: a contract wroth £250m was awarded to a consortium consisting of UK company British Land, the property company Hardwicke, and the Irish building firm McInerney Group. Pádraig O hUiginn, who was heading up the Department of An Taoiseach at the time, predicted that the IFSC "will have a dynamic effect on the economy which has to suffer a profound contractive readjustment in the public sector".

O hUiginn warned that there was no alternative to the castor oil of cutbacks then being forced down the throats of voters. He pointed out that while the economy was on course to increase by around £1bn in size, the country's debt service bill would be £2bn that year and was "growing inexorably". In O hUiginn's view, the IFSC project was a "type of counter-cyclical development measure which will generate construction investment of £250m, employing up to 3,000 people at its peak".

The launch of the IFSC coincided with the events of Black October in 1987. The sharp drop in share prices triggered by the meltdown on Wall Street left the Dublin equity market down 45% from its peak. It also left a huge cloud hanging over the future of the IFSC. However, the pall left by Black October turned out to be relatively short-lived, though the invasion of Kuwait in 1990 was to bring renewed problems, slowing up the physical expansion of the centre in the early 1990s.

By mid-1990 *B&F* journalist Noel Curran (a future director general of RTÉ) was reporting on the "growing optimism in the financial sector due in large measure to the recent success of the IFSC in attracting foreign investment.

"Difficult as it might be for some to accept it looks like the Docklands venture might actually be a success. This is quite a turnaround in fortunes. Only last year, most people had written the venture off [...] people questioned whether we could compete with London, or with smaller centres in Europe such as Luxembourg or Scotland. The big guns like

Chase Manhattan and Dresdner [banks] have arrived. As of now, 70 companies have been approved to trade in the centre and the number of applicants is rising steadily."

Other parts of the financial services industry were also undergoing a shakeup. The Central Bank, by 1989, had been given the power to regulate the country's building societies, which would be given the option to cease being mutuals. According to *Business & Finance*, "some societies were caught off guard by the sweeping powers given to the Central Bank".

Michael Fingleton, managing director of the Irish Nationwide Society, a rising force in the industry, professed to welcome the advent of Central Bank supervision, but he warned that there was a possibility of added bureaucracy which, he suggested, could affect the commerciality of the services provided.

According to Fingleton: "I have no objections so long as the rules are applied to all. But in the case of building society auditors [...] under the new system, they can go over the head of the society to the Central Bank. This is an extraordinary added power for auditors which does not exist anywhere else."

The government was at this stage pursuing a strategy of expansion by means of cutbacks: the idea was that business and consumer confidence could be reignited through a combination of tax-incentivised projects and targeted cutbacks aimed at the public spending bill.

The business community by and large responded positively to the strategy, which was driven from the Departments of Finance and the Taoiseach. In the short term, at least, the baying voices usually emanating from the spending ministries appeared to be stilled.

In January 1989 Ray MacSharry received the accolade of Man of the Year from *Business & Finance*. In some quarters this award was known as the Curse of Belenos (the company that owned the magazine), as the fortunes of recipients usually went into decline shortly thereafter.

MacSharry, however, escaped the curse. He would become a successful agriculture commissioner before returning to Ireland to join a raft of company boards. At the time, the editorial accompanying the award concluded that "there is fresh optimism in the Irish business community, order books are healthy, inflation is at its lowest level in nearly 30 years. People in business are more confident [...] and say it is due to firm management of the economy. One man, in particular, is identified with launching Ireland on the road to recovery."

Such praise may have influenced the decision of the Taoiseach to call an early election the following May following a defeat in the Dáil. In the wake of the poll Haughey was forced to enter into coalition with his long-time political adversary, Des O'Malley. O'Malley's party, the Progressive Democrats, had shed some of its Dáil seats in its second election, the initial excitement around the party's formation having worn off. O'Malley assumed the posts of tánaiste and minister of industry and commerce. The pair made an unlikely couple, but then political life has long thrown up strange bedfellows.

Lazarus starts to rise from the dead

The unlikely alliance benefited from a favourable economic wind. The unemployment rate stood at 18% – however, the economy was growing slowly but steadily. The patient was not yet out and about, but he was sitting up and eating an egg.

Journalist Dan White reported progress in tackling the exchequer deficit, if not the national debt. While the country's debt mountain continued to grow, rising from £23.7bn at the end of 1987 to £24.5bn as at December 31st 1988, equivalent to 133% of GNP, the external borrowing requirement for the year – buoyed by a £250m windfall from a tax amnesty – fell to 3.4%, the lowest in 20 years. White did, however, add words of caution: the figures did not include semi-state debt. Add this to the figures and the total public sector debt rose to £29bn, or 157% of GNP, a hefty debt load by any standard – leaving Ireland with one of the largest public debts relative to national output in the world.

However, Ireland still had a properly functioning banking system and household indebtedness was modest by current standards. The main drag on spending came from high levels of personal taxation that were being reduced under the 'national understanding' agreed with the trade unions and employer groups.

Workers were offered tax reductions as part of a trade-off involving pay restraint. While the IFSC project injected a welcome shot in the arm to the business sector, progress in tackling industrial unrest had the potential to boost competitiveness right across the economy.

Charles Haughey had built close relations with trade union leaders such as Michael Mullen since the 1970s. From the mid-1980s the Fianna Fáil party began to hatch plans for a social partnership that drew much more from the continental European model than from the more adversarial approach then being adopted by the Thatcher government in Britain.

The Thatcher administration opted to abandon the old cosy relationship with the trade unions pursued by its predecessor under the Labour prime ministers Wilson and Callaghan. The practice of offering beer and sandwiches at No 10 Downing Street to trade union leaders such as Jack Jones of the TGWU was seen as having been discredited by events during the 'Winter of Discontent' in late 1978 and early 1979.

The union leaders were seen as having failed to control the militants in their ranks. Images of rubbish bags mounting up in central London served to boost the Tory cause in the run in to the May 1979 general election.

The Tories opted for draconian legislation. However, Fianna Fáil believed that a German-style model could be made to operate, albeit with much more of a top-down, national focus to the social partnership model. The Fine Gael-Labour administration had become embroiled in conflict with the teachers' unions and in particular with the ASTI, led since 1980 by Kieran Mulvey, later to head up the new Labour Relations Commission.

In a feature in 1989, *Business & Finance* welcomed the advent of what it termed the 'New Realism' in industrial relations. It noted, in particular, that the number of work days lost through strikes had fallen dramatically from the peak levels of the late 1970s. In 1979 the figure peaked at 1.427 million days lost. Between 1980 and 1986 the number of days lost fluctuated between a high of 437,000 (1982) and a low of 311,000 (1983). In 1987 270,000 days were lost to disputes, but the equivalent figure for 1988 was just 130,000.

Business & Finance's unnamed correspondent (usually Pat Sweeney, the RTÉ industrial relations correspondent) suggested that years of recession "could be said to have created a climate of realism of their own accord". Many organisations had shed labour, accelerating the introduction of new technology and new work practices.

Workers had been "frightened off militancy by the possible loss of their jobs". The correspondent also noted that "the management of people problems has attained a status reserved years ago for production, finance, or marketing". A more emollient attitude towards human resource management was reflected in the stance adopted by John Dunne, the reflective head of the Federated Union of Employers, which handled IR issues on behalf of firms in both the public and private sectors.

According to Dunne, as quoted in the article, "the economic position and the precarious position of the national finances led the FUE to believe that the way out of the crisis lay in the development of a consensus". But the FUE leader also believed that some resort to legislation would also be required as part of an effort aimed at curbing strike activity.

According to Dunne: "We have the most antiquated industrial relations system in Europe. Industrial action must be made something of a last resort." The *B&F* special correspondent also warned against too much complacency, pointing out that "it has often been said that industrial militancy in Ireland waxes and wanes with growth and contraction in the national economy".

What was clear, however, is that key trade union leaders including Bill Attley, Phil Flynn and Peter Cassells had signed up to a consensual approach to national-level wage determination, one that was underpinned in the initial stages by a policy of tax cuts aimed at boosting workers' real take-home pay. It finally dawned on many union members and not just their leadership that large pay claims were simply unrealistic in a world of sharp disinflation and increasing international competitiveness.

A wind from the east

Political events in eastern Europe began to speed up dramatically from June 1989 following the accession to power of a non-communist Polish government under Prime Minister Tadeusz Mazowiecki. In the late summer the Hungarian government opened its border with the west, sparking a flood of exits westward by 'holidaymakers' from the east. This outflow, in turn, undermined the regime in East Germany. Crowds of protesters began to gather *en masse* in cities such as Leipzig. By the end of November the East German regime had fallen, followed by the Berlin Wall.

Further east, China under its paramount leader Deng Xiaoping, one of the key transformative leaders of the 20th century, was presiding over an opening up of its economy following the long hiatus under Chairman Mao. The impact would be felt before long by more traditional Irish manufacturers, many of whom had lost competitiveness as a result of soaring wage levels.

By 1970 Waterford Crystal, an Irish manufacturing icon, employed 3,000 people at what was then the world's largest crystal glassmaking facility. It had been a PLC since 1966 and was controlled by the McGrath family.

In 1986 3,430 were employed at Kilbarry on the western outskirts of the city, engaged in the traditional mouth-blowing and hand-cutting of glass. The original glass factory in the port city had been established just after the Second World War by two Czech émigrés, Charles Bacik (father of Senator Ivana Bacik) and designer Miroslav Havel.

Havel, as his son Brian later recounted, persuaded his employees to "manipulate molten glass from the furnace to produce a blown piece of crystal that was relatively thin at the top, but thickened towards the base". Crystal chandeliers from Waterford began to feature extensively in US consumer publications from the late 1950s. Marketeer Con Dooley came up with a host of design names, such as Lismore, that appealed to the US consumer. Eventually US sales accounted for three quarters of group crystal turnover.

However, by the late 1980s Waterford Crystal was already facing a struggle for survival. Its sales in the US were hit badly by a drop in the value of the dollar, from parity with the Irish pound in late 1984 to $1.60 by the end of 1987. Pre-tax losses of £11m for 1987 were recorded and plans were in place to shed 1,000 jobs by mid-1988.

The fall of the Wall meant that lower-cost producers in regions such as Bohemia, the birthplace of crystal-making, would be coming onstream.

Trade unions at the plant had driven what in retrospect appears like a very hard bargain with management. The perks on offer to employees included downpayments towards the houses being built in nearby suburbs by house builders McInerney.

Waterford Glass staff parties were the stuff of legend. Eventually, however, the really rich payouts would go to the firms of consultants who would descend on the plant at regular intervals. As *Business & Finance* observed at the time, average cost per employee in Waterford stood at $36,200, whereas cost per employee at Baccarat and at Lenox, their main competitors in the US, amounted to $24,300 and $22,000 respectively.

Now a new factor had entered the equation: competition from the east. Waterford was facing into a battle for its very existence. Following major restructuring and an investment by a consortium under businessman Tony O'Reilly, the crystal plant would enjoy renewed success in the late 1990s. The Kilbarry plant eventually closed in 2009.

Competition from the east brought changes to many other long-established industries. Packard Electric employed around 1,100 people supplying harnesses to car plants. By the late eighties, European car manufacturer customers were coming under increased pressure from the Japanese. This in turn put downward pressure on the price of the harnesses produced at the plant in Tallaght. The Packard plant was affected by a succession of disputes. In an effort to keep the plant open, management moved the plant to just-in-time manufacturing.

A new head of HR, Niall Saul, was brought in to negotiate a 15-point plan including a no-strike agreement and binding arbitration, as he recalled in a 1999 interview with *Industrial Relations News*. The plan included a guarantee of no compulsory redundancies and measures to address employee grievances. Saul was accused of strikebreaking, but the peace proposals were narrowly accepted in a ballot. The revamp worked for several years, but the plant eventually closed in 1996. In truth, the restructuring bought time – but such added time for a manufacturing plant in an era of high unemployment was not to be sniffed at.

The new buildings springing up at the IFSC were only part of a wider investment upsurge that began to take place from the late 1980s. In 1989 the chip maker Intel decided to build its first European manufacturing operation in Leixlip. It was a major coup for the Industrial Development Authority and a signal that Ireland was back in business.

New homegrown international entities were emerging. One of the most interesting movers was Glen Dimplex, which by the late 1980s was the largest manufacturer of central heaters and small appliances in these islands. In 1986 it expanded into the US, acquiring a company called Hamilton Beach for $120m.

As CEO Martin Naughton recalled, in January 1987 goodwill towards his company among US institutions was high as he and his team went from coast to coast selling bonds. The Glen Dimplex bond issue was nearly undone by the scandal surrounding junk bond king Ivan Boesky. However, Glen Dimplex still managed to raise $65m. At the time Naughton commented that "it is a quantum leap for us which makes us as big in North America as we are in Europe".

Glen Dimplex had come a long way since Naughton had established Glen Electric in Newry with £60,000 in loans from the Northern Ireland Finance Corporation. The company started manufacturing electric heaters at the start of the oil crisis in late 1973.

By 1987 its total workforce exceeded 4,000, of whom more than 1,200 were employed in Ireland. Glen Dimplex was proof that traditional manufacturing activity could be profitably carried on in Ireland given sound day-to-day management and a sensible acquisition strategy.

By 1992 its annual turnover would exceed £200m sterling, though Naughton by then had second thoughts about his US acquisition. As he put it to reporter Daire O'Brien, "acquisitions are a great buzz, but you can become a junkie".

The glitterati

The newspapers abounded with profiles – generally favourable; on occasions fawning – of the great and good of Irish business. Few received a more positive press than Michael Smurfit, chairman/CEO of Jefferson Smurfit Group. The group was expanding rapidly at this time. During the 1980s it established itself as a major supplier of print and packaging in the US, entering into a joint venture with the Morgan Stanley Leveraged Equity Fund to acquire paper board and packaging producer Container Corporation of America in 1986. The acquisition cost $1.2bn.

Smurfit was a major investor in *Business & Finance* magazine. It continued to invest in media publications into the 1990s and in 1989 it launched the US publication *The Irish Voice*. By 1988 the USA accounted for 65% of its profits, while it controlled 20% of the paperboard market in Venezuela and Colombia. In 1989 the group restructured its US operation using junk bonds and generating $1.2bn in fresh resources. Michael Smurfit's reputation in Ireland had reached its pinnacle: he was seen as having generated huge value for shareholders. His AGMs were highly organised affairs. Shareholders purred happily over their coffee and biscuits.

If Smurfit was the inventive strategist then Howard Kilroy was his sensible right-hand man, playing a restraining role where necessary. As chairman of Telecom Éireann Smurfit played a public role, overseeing a major programme of investment and job-shedding. Eventually, by the late 1980s, large inroads had been made into the lengthy waiting lists for telephones that had been such a feature of the service.

An *Irish Press* profile in September 1990 concluded that "apart from Tony O'Reilly, he [Smurfit] would have few, if any peers, in Irish industry. Apart from his own IR£1bn Smurfit Group, he has numerous other interests and holds directorships of leading companies such as AIB and has served as chairman of the Irish Racing Board," *Irish Press* business editor John Lattimore observed.

The writer also highlighted the scale of the transformation achieved at Telecom Éireann under the aegis of Smurfit. "At the time it [the company] was vested in 1984, it was losing more than £100m a year. Standards of service and efficiency were generally held to be abysmal."

The restructuring came at a cost in scarce State resources, and in jobs. Between 1985 and 1989 1,500 jobs were shed, with a further 700 going by the end of 1990. John Lattimore also noted that the chairman "continually advocated the privatisation of Telecom Éireann and his opinion seems to be shared by the government". However, this happy event would not come to pass until 1999.

Smurfit was garlanded with honours and almost weighed down with personal wealth. Writing in the *Sunday Independent*, journalist Sam Smyth drew comparisons between Smurfit and another high-flying figure, GPA founder Tony Ryan. Smyth pointed out that Smurfit had represented Ireland diplomatically as consul in Monaco, fiefdom of the late Princess Grace and Prince Rainier, since August 1988 "for an annual honorarium of £250 – barely the price of a brace of bottles of his favourite wine (Chateau Petrus)".

He pointed out that Tony Ryan "has collected a glittering gallery of former politicians and diplomats on the board of his fabulously successful GPA" (including former Taoiseach Garret FitzGerald, former UK chancellor of the exchequer Nigel Lawson, and former ICI chief executive and TV presenter Sir John Harvey-Jones).

Ryan had himself, in 1990, just been appointed honorary consul of Mexico in Ireland. In 1990 GPA (or Guinness Peat Aviation) had emerged as a highly successful aviation finance business trading out of the Shannon Free Zone. Its executives circled the globe hunting for leasing deals and following a punishing schedule for which they earned rewards beyond the wildest dreams of most people in the Ireland of the time.

GPA was not quoted on the stock exchange but as *Irish Independent* business editor Brendan Keenan noted, the placement of GPA shares with Air Canada at $630 each had valued the company at almost $4bn (or IR£2.6bn). Ryan's stake was valued at £208m, and the stake held by Aer Lingus, his former employer, stood at around £250m – "this might be as much as the net worth of the rest of the airline put together", Keenan suggested. In an allusion to the Honorary Consul of novelist Graham Greene, Sam Smyth added: "It is difficult to imagine Doctors Smurfit and Ryan, bleary eyed and reeking of gin, early in the morning, shuffling through a cluttered desk for a temporary passport."

The US publication *Forbes* estimated that Smurfit's salary package in 1989 was worth $9.3m – "Dr Smurfit will not reveal the true figure, but says that it was a big number." *The European* magazine pointed out that the paper and packaging boss lived beside Europe's greatest casino in Monte Carlo, and owned another apartment in Trump Towers, Manhattan.

It reported that he dined from time to time with the latter's developer, property mogul (and later US president) Donald Trump.

"Other buddies include Larry Goodman, Tony O'Reilly and Albert Reynolds [Ireland's finance minister in 1990]. He occasionally meets corporate raider Sir James Goldsmith." In another piece, the *Irish Independent* social columnist Angela Phelan pointed to some of the Telecom chairman's "very best friends" or VBFs, including 'beef baron' Larry Goodman, "a partner in several property deals".

Smurfit's former wife Norma had recalled to Whelan their life in the sixties, when the Smurfit family enjoyed Heinz beans and Cross and Blackwell spaghetti in their suburban home in Stillorgan, and when the young couple would chill out on Saturday nights with trips to the fashionable Martello Roof on the top of the Intercontinental Hotel (later Jurys) in Ballsbridge.

The food sector reawakens

Away from the glitterati, significant developments were occurring close to the heartland of the rural economy. By the end of the decade the development of an international food business based out of Ireland was underway.

Kerry Group was leading the charge, but umbrella group ICOS was meeting resistance to its efforts to facilitate amalgamations among Irish co-ops. By the time Kerry Group founder Denis Brosnan stood down as CEO in 2002 the company had annual sales of €3.7bn and after-tax profits of more than €200m, with operations in almost 20 countries around the globe.

Two key early turning points can be identified: the company's flotation on the stock exchange in 1986, and its 1988 acquisition of US company Beatreme Food Ingredients for $130m – the equivalent of its market capitalisation at the time. The group transformed itself in stages into a fully fledged international business focused on food ingredients. Revenues grew from IR£300m in 1987 to £755m in 1991. By 2003 the combined farmer shareholding was worth close to €1bn.

Kerry Group was one of the first major Irish companies to become a global player rather than simply run a large exporting business out of Ireland, as was the case with Waterford Crystal. Elsewhere, the food business sought to face up to the challenges posed by its overreliance on commodity exports.

The goal being pursued by reformers was the building of new Irish food brands. No-one was more keen on this message than the man behind the enduringly successful Irish butter brand Kerrygold, Tony O'Reilly. The task was not a straightforward one.

In December 1989 Dr Noel Cawley – the managing director of Bord Bainne, the company charged with promoting sales of Irish dairy produce – gave an interview to *Business & Finance*. At the time, people were calling on the agency to put its energies into creating another international Irish food brand besides Kerrygold as part of the effort to reduce the country's reliance on the export of bulk commodities.

Cawley's response was blunt: "Bord Bainne has no interest in developing another brand, which costs a huge amount of money [...] very few new brands are being launched by dairy companies. Instead, the Kerrygold label will be extended to many more products in the next few years. I foresee a Kerrygold smoked salmon and even a Kerrygold spring water.

"We won't be jumping into new products without guaranteeing that the mistakes of the past are not repeated." He instanced the association of Kerrygold with pigmeat producers. The pigmeat was not of high enough standard and the Kerrygold image was put at risk.

One man seemingly determined to reshape the food industry was 'beef baron' Larry Goodman. His stock market vehicle Food Industries PLC proposed a plan to three north east co-ops for an amalgamation of their business with Food Industries, a company valued in January 1990 at around IR£130m.

Food Industries had already acquired Bailieboro Co-op following a hard-fought battle in 1988. Goodman was also stake-building in two large UK companies, Unigate and Berisford. The shakeup on the processing side was not unrelated to the growing influence of the large supermarket multiples and their supermarket buying teams. Dunnes Stores and Quinnsworth, the latter then owned by British Group ABF, exerted an increasingly tight grip on the domestic supermarket business, forcing many Irish food groups on the defensive. The success of Goodman's meat-boning operations was built on a combination of knowledge of the Common Agricultural Policy (CAP) and its complex mechanisms, and the ability of Goodman and his team to meet the needs of UK multiples.

Holding the line

In 1989 Ray MacSharry took over as EC commissioner for agriculture after just under two years at the Department of Finance. 'Mac The Knife' had made his name by cutting government borrowing by more than 2.5% of GDP in just nine months. His task now was to oversee major reforms to the CAP while ensuring that the interests of Irish farmers and other food producers was upheld.

In 1992 the *Financial Times* journalist David Gardiner reviewed the record of MacSharry in Brussels: "As commissioner, he faced the unanimous opposition of farm ministers to his plans for the most radical overhaul of the CAP in its 30-year history. He glowered through a year of abuse yet by May [1991], the reform had been almost bludgeoned through."

At one point the farming commissioner found himself confronting the powerful head of the Commission, Jacques Delors, a former French finance minister and the man who had spearheaded the European Commission's revival. As Gardner observed at the time, "no-one had publicly taken on probably the most powerful chief the Commission has had".

But then, "brought up in one of the toughest schools of politics, the Fianna Fáil party [...] MacSharry is no stranger to the black arts of political street fighting". MacSharry, while pressing for reform at home, stood accused by a US government pressing for heavy cuts in agricultural supports of jeopardising a four-year effort to liberalise world trade.

In 1993 MacSharry's predecessor as EU commissioner, Peter Sutherland, would take charge of the global trade liberalisation effort as director general of GATT, the General Agreement on Tariffs and Trade (later the World Trade Organisation).

MacSharry responded by accusing the Americans of a campaign of intimidation. He insisted that he was offering them cuts in EU supports amounting to 30%. His position was further complicated by the collapse, in August 1990, of the Goodman Group hot on the heels of the Iraqi invasion of Kuwait. Ironically, the commissioner had himself been employed in an abattoir as a teenager.

In 1990 Kieran Cook and Tim Dickson of the *Financial Times* penned another profile of the commissioner. "Loyalty is central to MacSharry, but he has few close political friends. He is not known as a particularly social animal – he wears a Pioneer pin [...] an Irish sign of a lifetime's abstinence from alcohol.

"MacSharry's at times abrasive style has served him well in the rough and tumble of routine EC farm price talks, where till recently he appeared to have succeeded in keeping the EC's once-again burgeoning farm spending under control." The writers contrasted him with his Irish predecessor, Peter Sutherland, who "quickly learned the finer arts of Brussels, carefully cultivating contacts and alliances with his fellow commissioners".

Society columnist Angela Phelan was more impressed with MacSharry's emerging image as a man about Brussels. Writing about him in December 1992, shortly before his return home, she painted a picture of the commissioner "in his snappy double-breasted suit, crisp white shirt, discreet silk tie [...] you could see yourself on the shine of his shoes [...] he is every inch the totally assured, sartorially elegant Eurocrat".

"It is indeed a long way from life as a cattle drover [...] driving his uncles' live cattle on the boats to Scotland."

The country's top businesspeople must have clinked their champagne glasses with some confidence as the troubled 1980s gave way to a new decade. The new year promised much in the way of prosperity for this elite, at least. The reforms in competition initiated by Peter Sutherland had begun to transform air travel, removing a major competitive barrier for Irish exporters.

From America, the talk was of 'the end of history', but that old donkey would soon show that he was not done for yet. Saddam Hussein would dispatch his tanks into Kuwait in August, barely six months after the world had celebrated the fall of the Berlin Wall. Two of Ireland's business icons, Larry Goodman and Tony Ryan, would be heavily impacted by this event. Emergency legislation would be forced through the Dáil in an effort to rescue Goodman Group that August.

Scandals and tragedy would soon overtake Greencore and Irish Life, and by autumn 1991 the reputations of some of Ireland's best-known businessmen would be called into question.

The era of the tribunal was about to dawn.

CHAPTER 8

Living dangerously: 1989-1991
By Brian O'Connor

THE TURN OF THE DECADE SAW SOLUTIONS TO SOME OLD PROBLEMS – AND PERHAPS SIGNS OF SUCCESSES AND FAILURES TO COME, IN A PARTICULARLY EXCITING TIME TO BE EDITOR OF BUSINESS & FINANCE.

Living Dangerously was the theme of *Business and Finance*'s annual review and outlook in December 1990. But the perils differed from those that overwhelmed the economy nearly two decades later.

By the end of 1990, mid-way through my two-year stint editing *B&F*, the dangers were mostly coming from outside. International recession, particularly severe in the UK where the boom of the late Thatcher years had imploded, threatened to slow Irish economic growth to a crawl. The global climate was stormy. The historic breakup of the Soviet Union and its empire of satellite states in eastern Europe was gathering momentum, with President Mikhail Gorbachev fighting for survival.

In the Middle East, Iraqi dictator Saddam Hussein had sent his bombers to attack Kuwait in August, following with a full-scale invasion that was to trigger the first Gulf War. Stock markets slumped: Irish shares fell by about 32% over the year. Currencies came under pressure – though it was not until September 16th 1992 that UK Chancellor Norman Lamont finally announced sterling's departure from the European Monetary System. The Irish pound was hovering at about 90p sterling, and floating upwards as sterling fell.

In the event, some subdued Irish economic growth was achieved in 1991, which turned out better than initially feared. But shocks from abroad rocked the economy and led to one spectacular corporate collapse. On the political front, Charles Haughey was Taoiseach, Albert Reynolds minister for finance, and Des O'Malley ran Industry and Commerce. Speculation about Haughey's future, after 12 years leading Fianna Fáil, was growing: Ray MacSharry, agriculture commissioner in Brussels, was one of those tipped to succeed him.

Dick Spring led Labour, and John Bruton was elected unopposed as leader of Fine Gael when Alan Dukes resigned after the party trailed in third place in the presidential election. This poll had blown winds of change through the Phoenix Park with the election of Mary Robinson, the first woman to become Ireland's head of State.

The Industrial Development Authority also had the wind behind it as its drive to attract foreign investment reached warp speed. Under Kieran McGowan, who had succeeded Padraic White, the IDA was cock-a-hoop after landing major projects from Dell, Motorola, Seagate Technology and Intel (the last for a controversially large IR£87m package). Dell and Intel would play a significant part in the later boom years. In Dublin's derelict Docklands, the fledgling International Financial Services Centre was beginning to attract some serious tenants.

Looking back at the Irish corporate scene in 1990, it seems like another age in many ways. In the supermarket aisles Dunnes Stores and Quinnsworth were fighting it out for supremacy; Tesco would not arrive for another seven years. On the Irish Stock Exchange the list of quoted companies included Waterford Wedgwood, Irish Distillers, PJ Carroll (taken over during 1990), Clondalkin Paper Mills, Arnotts, New Ireland Assurance and Woodchester. Some of these businesses have survived, but their ownership has changed drastically. Only a handful of the leading quoted companies of that day – Cement Roadstone Holdings, United Drug, Bank of Ireland – are still independent.

The public sector and the semi-state companies loomed large in business life. In 1991 the government launched its first privatisation, the Irish Sugar Company, which was then run by Chris Comerford. Irish Life, under David Kingston and boasting a dominant share of the life assurance market, was set to follow.

The food industry was undergoing major changes. The traditional co-op structures were being challenged: Mitchelstown and Ballyclough co-ops had merged to form Dairygold; Avonmore and Waterford Foods embarked on difficult merger talks. Larry Goodman, the 'Beef Baron', laid siege to Lough Egish and Killeshandra co-ops.

Soon Goodman's Anglo-Irish Beef group had more than co-ops to worry about. By mid-1990 his exposure to Iraq and international expansion, including stakes in UK-quoted Berisford and Unigate, accompanied by a rising tide of debt, had brought his private empire to the brink. In September 1990 a *Business & Finance* scoop revealed that Goodman's empire owed £442m to 33 local and international banks. Not only was much of the funding unsecured, but it emerged that many of the lenders did not realise how much debt the empire was carrying.

Goodman complained that the government had not provided enough credit cover for his exports to Iraq, but he had also lost heavily on his investment in trading group Berisford in particular. His group was put in the hands of examiner Peter Fitzpatrick and chunks of it were put up for sale. It was a chastening blow for the driven and widely admired Goodman, and a hammer blow for the food industry. It could be called the first Anglo-Irish crisis – though its scale pales into insignificance beside the €34bn that the other Anglo was to cost.

Over the years that followed, the resourceful Goodman eventually rebuilt much of his business. But his travails were evidence of how difficult it was to find the truth about personal wealth and the true standing of private ventures. At that time many of the country's largest companies were private and the information they were legally required to disclose was minimal, which did not make the work of reporting and analysing any easier.

In trying to report on Irish business in those days, I often reflected on the many very substantial companies where we obtained only an occasional glimpse of what they were doing: hidden 'big beasts', whether family-owned or subsidiaries of multinationals. Their size often dwarfed the stock market-quoted companies about which we wrote copiously, simply because information was accessible. Sometimes the coverage of these private empires was unduly deferential because it was the only way to report on them at all. Disclosure requirements are greater now, but I think there are still many large ventures whose scale is only glimpsed in the rankings of the top 500 companies. In a world further complicated by tax planning and transfer pricing issues, this is a barrier to an informed analysis of what is happening.

On August 2nd 1990 *Business & Finance* looked at the value of quoted shareholdings of leading Irish business families, acknowledging that these might be only part of the picture of their overall wealth. Tipperary's Tony Ryan topped the list, though not on the strength of Ryanair. Ryan owned 5% of the Bank of Ireland, but his main asset was his holding in Guinness Peat Aviation, the leasing group he founded and built into a global leader, which was then valued at more than £2bn.

The spectacular fall of GPA, and the remarkable rise of Ryanair, were still some way off. Ryanair, then run by PJ McGoldrick, had begun moving its London flights from Luton Airport to the newly built Stansted. Entrenched opponents were contesting its right to landing 'slots' at Irish airports.

Guinness was still an independent company and the family holding was valued at £302m. Property investor Robin Power, the Gallagher family at Abbey and the Murtaghs at Kingspan – still a small company – also featured in the top ten.

The main private shareholders were largely male. Only two women ranked in the top 50: Agnes McArdle Murphy of Clondalkin and Elizabeth Nelson of Jurys Hotels. Yet women were on the march. One of the highlights of my spell at *Business & Finance* was when President Mary Robinson presented our Businessman of the Year award to Neil McCann of Fyffes, who had built his company from a small fruit shop in Dundalk to IR£700m a year in sales. We announced that the award would in future be called Business Person of the Year (though sadly this did not last).

Fyffes was one of the rare success stories in the food industry. For most of the sector, 1990 was an *annus horribilis*. This began with the collapse into receivership of Ballybay Meats when the year was just five days old. The collapse was remarkable because it came just nine months after Ballybay's modern pig processing plant in Co Monaghan had been opened by Minister for Health Rory O'Hanlon (father of comedian Ardal). The plant had been grant-aided both by the IDA, which had handed over £813,000 to the company, and the EU, while Ballybay owed the State rescue agency Fóir Teoranta £600,000 from previous State support.

One of the issues that emerged was the purchase and re-sale of Hungarian pork, which was much cheaper than pork from Ireland or the market leader, Denmark. Ballybay's managers complained that the company had been victim of a "campaign of vilification". All this was not exactly helpful to the Irish meat industry's export drive. In an ironic twist, Ballybay ended up being owned by Goodman.

It was not only cheap meat from eastern Europe that was affecting the EU food market. Irish dairy exports fell sharply in 1990 and Bord Bainne reported that weak markets had been further hit by intense competition from the east. More than half of Irish butter production and nearly half of skimmed milk output for the year had to be sold into the EU's intervention system.

In the financial markets the level of interest rates was very different from the present day. One-month money on the interbank market cost more than 10%. In August 1990 Irish Permanent cut mortgage rates by 0.45% to 11.65%. In December, Ulster Bank was advertising its Reserve 90 ninety-day deposit account, paying between 8.75% and 9.75% interest.

Three companies floated on the Irish Stock Exchange during 1990 (down from seven in 1989). The three were food group Golden Vale, chemists' distributor Cahill May Roberts and print group Dakota.

The only major share to show any notable gain over the year was Printech. At the other end of the scale, video retailer Xtra-vision slumped 94% before being taken over, McInerney Properties fell 93%, Seafield 83%, CLF Yeoman 74%, IWP (Irish Wire Products) 73%, Food Industries 61%, IAWS 58% and Norish 57%; while Heiton, Waterford Wedgwood and John Teeling's CountyGlen each fell 56%. There was one promising newcomer, however: pharmaceutical group Elan Corporation made its debut on the Unlisted Securities Market and its shares soared 53% in 11 months.

Irish entrepreneurs continued to innovate and grow their businesses. Cooley Distillery, which John Teeling had founded in 1987 to challenge the dominance of Irish Distillers, was laying down its first whiskey. Ryan Hotels, owner of the Gresham, was the second-largest hotel group after PV Doyle's Doyle Group. Ryan's chairman Conor McCarthy also chaired Irish Life and the Irish Export Board, Córas Tráchtála. Ray McLoughlin's James Crean Group expanded to the continent with its first Dutch acquisition.

Oil and mining exploration companies were active. In Mozambique, explorer Kenmare Resources persevered through two years of negotiations to reach a significant agreement to develop mineral sands. In some other hopefuls, much of the activity was on the stock market.

In the media, RTÉ was feeling the draught of competition from new radio challengers such as 98FM, Century and Capital. With the internet only a dotcom on the horizon, newspapers were still seen as investments that could make money. Tony O'Reilly's Independent Newspapers was strengthening its grip on its home market. The Irish Press (where I had worked from 1975 to 1986) was battling on, having ceded a 50% stake in its papers to Ingersoll Group of the US. Vincent Browne ruled at *The Sunday Tribune*, which was seeking new investors: Independent Newspapers had acquired 29.9%. *The Sunday Business Post* was launched in 1989, a challenge to *Business & Finance*'s role as the leading business weekly.

In paper and packaging, Jefferson Smurfit Group was Ireland's biggest company in 1991 and the fifth-largest papermaker in the world, with 32,000 employees. Smurfit had pulled off a brilliantly timed part-exit from the US when recession was looming, effectively selling half the US business and releasing £675m cash.

One of the changes working its way through Irish business was the growth of a class of battle-hardened managers from the best home-grown companies such as Smurfit and CRH. With the experience they gained at home and abroad, many of these managers went on to set up their own businesses.

The professions were changing. Accountancy firms were consolidating: Deloitte Haskins and Sells Haughey Boland announced plans to merge with Touche Ross. The legal profession was booming. In two decades from 1970, the number of solicitors in Ireland quadrupled to 3,500 – one for every 824 of the population. The top five firms, ranked by registered solicitors and based on the 1990 *Law Directory*, were A&L Goodbody (67), McCann FitzGerald (63), Arthur Cox (49), Wm Fry (36) and Matheson Ormsby Prentice (32). *Business & Finance* estimated their annual fee income at £11m for Goodbody and McCann FitzGerald, £9m for Cox, £7.5m for Fry and £5m for Matheson.

Another theme from *Business & Finance*'s cover story on 'The Law Boom' was the rise of women, who in 1970 had accounted for 25% of new solicitors. By 1990 that had risen to 55%. Although two of the top four firms still had no female partners, the trend was unmistakable. This report, on August 15th 1991, marked the end of my stint at *Business & Finance*. It seems fitting that it ended much as it had begun, with women – led by President Robinson – making their way to the top.

The years when the economy went into overdrive and credit growth ballooned to 30% a year were still distant. Nonetheless, every economic commentator with any sensitivity needs to ask: should I have seen trouble coming? In 1990 the meltdown was far away – but were there clues to be seen?

Economists at Davy Stockbrokers forecast that the 1991 public sector pay bill, before providing for any pay round, would rise by 8.5%. The cumulative effect of such pay increases was inflating the cost of the public sector and storing up trouble for the exchequer – ultimately leading to the bizarre situation whereby Irish politicians and public servants were paid far more than their counterparts in much larger countries in Europe.

Issues of accountability in the public sector were also evident, an issue that was aired in *Business & Finance*. A few years later, in 1995, Cathal Guiomard wrote in his book *The Irish Disease and How to Cure It: Common Sense Economics for a Competitive World*: "In the public sector, it is unheard of for senior managers of public companies, no matter how loss-making, to be called to account."

Anglo Irish Bank was still a minnow, with market value of about £30m. It did target the UK for expansion – in time for the early 1990s property crash. Its losses were contained at £7m to £8m, and it survived easily, but perhaps this was an early warning.

Looking back now, the good things that stand out about the early 1990s include the progress made by the best Irish companies, such as CRH and Smurfit, in building themselves into global businesses, and the remarkable success of the IDA in devising a strategy of going after world-leading growth sectors in technology and pharmaceuticals, and in following through by delivering major investments from the likes of Intel and Dell.

This was the solid part of the foundation on which the turbocharged economic growth of the Tiger years was built. The collapsible parts of the edifice – easy credit, euphoric excess and the loss of the plot – were added later.

IRELAND IN 1990

President:	Mary Robinson
Taoiseach:	Charles J Haughey
Minister for Finance:	Albert Reynolds
Currency:	Irish pound (=92p sterling)
Stock Exchange:	ISEQ index 1,205
Three-month interbank rate:	10.75%
European Union:	12 member states, 12 currencies
Property:	Large house, Blackrock, Dublin £390,000
	Three-bedroom house, Harold's Cross £60,000
	Three-bed house, Ballincollig, Cork £40,000
Business & Finance cover price:	£1.50

At December 14th 1990

TOP TEN SHAREHOLDING FAMILIES

At July 20th 1990
Value of holdings (IR£m)

Guinness:	302
Tony Ryan:	231
Smurfit:	154
Tony O'Reilly:	126
Larry Goodman:	61
McCanns (Fyffes):	42
Robin Power:	25
Gleesons (Smurfit):	17
Murtaghs (Kingspan):	16
Gallaghers (Abbey):	12

Business & Finance, August 2nd 1990

CHAPTER 9

Setting the scene: Ireland on the eve of the Tiger
By Kyran Fitzgerald

SOCIAL PARTNERSHIP, FOREIGN DIRECT INVESTMENT, CURRENCY CRISES, EUROPEAN REFORM AND TRIBUNALS WERE AMONG THE TALKING POINTS IN THE YEARS JUST BEFORE THE CELTIC TIGER REARED ITS HEAD.

Charles Haughey, towards the end of his period in office, famously joked that he would – like the leaders of China – go on for a very long time. His former minister of justice, Seán Doherty, had other ideas. Revenge would be served up cold by him, following years of political neglect, on a popular RTÉ late night show, *Nighthawks*. The former minister would make his bombshell disclosures concerning the Taoiseach's knowledge of dubious practices carried out at his department.

The Roscommon politician was no longer prepared to bear full responsibility for practices sanctioned from on high. The departure of Haughey would not be long delayed. His parting line, "I have done the State some service", was delivered with style to a packed Dáil Éireann.

His replacement, Albert Reynolds, had thrown down the gauntlet before departing government just months before, mounting an unsuccessful challenge to his leader prior to his resignation as minister for finance.

The Longford-Westmeath TD and owner of leading midlands-based petfood manufacturer C&D Foods seized hold of the Taoiseach's crown. He assumed power at a time when the economy was beginning to enter a recovery phase, but during a period when scandals were starting to engulf many at the heart of the political class.

This was a period of rapid political change. Reynolds led a right-of-centre coalition with the Progressive Democrats until November 1992, when an early general election was precipitated. The 'Spring tide' boosted the Dáil representation of Labour under Dick Spring to more than 30 TDs.

The Labour leader – to the chagrin of many of his supporters – decided to lead his party into coalition with Fianna Fáil. This in turn prompted many commentators to assume that a FF/Labour centre-left coalition could remain in power for a generation.

The new administration was socially liberal. The new minister for justice, Máire Geoghegan-Quinn, shepherded through legislation overhauling the laws on homosexuality. Ireland's first minister for equality and law reform, Mervyn Taylor, entered the cabinet. Geoghegan-Quinn also passed extensive legislation dealing with money laundering. As Taoiseach, Reynolds continued his predecessor's commitment to the social partnership model under which the trade unions agreed to wage restraint in return for tax cuts and a range of social policy initiatives. Funding for labour market intervention through the State jobs agency FÁS was boosted.

Reynolds was pragmatic, but ultimately his stubbornness – and in particular an attempt to spin the findings of the Beef Tribunal following its publication in summer 1994 – proved fatal to his relationship with Dick Spring. The tribunal of inquiry had been established in May 1991 to examine, in particular, relations between the Goodman Group and the government. This, in turn, set the stage for the fall of the government when the Brendan Smyth scandal erupted in autumn 1994.

Bertie Ahern had continued under Albert Reynolds as finance minister, having made his reputation in the Department of Labour as a dealmaker and negotiator. As finance minister he was at the heart of controversy when the government sought to defend the punt within the EC's Exchange Rate Mechanism against attacks from within the financial markets from September 1992 to February 1993. Interest rates soared during this period, pushing many businesses close to the edge and causing great pain for householders with significant borrowings.

Ahern "has little room for manoeuvre", Dan McLoughlin of Riada Stockbrokers warned, in a report presented as the new finance minister got ready to present his first budget early in 1993. "Public spending looks set to rise at least twice the rate of GNP. The EBR (external borrowing requirement) looks set to come in at around IR£1.1bn. Fuelling the increases [...] the seemingly inexorable rise in unemployment. Despite underlying inflation of just 1.3%, total public spending and pay will rise by around 10% this year."

And he added that including the public pay bill – up by 50% over the preceding six years – and debt servicing costs, "of the £11bn Ahern will spend, this year, £7bn is already spoken for before he utters a word".

The early 1990s has, in retrospect, an eerily familiar look to it in other respects. In September 1991 leading Irish businessmen Dermot Desmond and Michael Smurfit were caught up in speculation surrounding property deals in the run up to State telephone company Telecom Éireann's acquisition of the former Johnston Mooney and O'Brien bakery for its planned head-quarters on a large site in Ballsbridge, Dublin 4.

Smurfit soon stepped aside as chairman of the company at the request of the Taoiseach, Haughey. As Smurfit disclosed in his autobiography, relations between the two men never recovered following the request. Dermot Desmond stood down as chairman of Aer Rianta in October 1991. An inquiry under John Glackin, an inspector appointed by the Department of Industry and Commerce, was established and it would be faced with several legal challenges before its report was finally issued.

A major force behind the launch of the IFSC and a series of business ventures, particularly in the technology and communications sector, Desmond remains a prominent figure in Irish business with a net worth well in excess of €1bn. His stockbroking firm NCB rose during the 1980s to become Ireland's largest independent stockbroker, challenging the established firms.

In the early 1990s he sold NCB to Ulster Bank for close to €50m. Desmond went on to invest in a number of software startups before estab-lishing his investment vehicle IIU in 1995. During this period he acquired London City Airport for £23m, later making a huge profit on its sale. Other profitable investments at the time included Baltimore Technologies, which rose to become a darling of the London Stock Exchange at the height of the dotcom boom around the turn of the millennium.

The Glackin Report in 1993 came as the Beef Tribunal approached its end point. It was around this time that the whole idea of a 'golden circle' of connected Irish business parties operating at the intersection between business and politics began to exert a grip on the public consciousness. However, few could have conjured up in their imaginations the sheer scale of the disclosures that would emerge over the following two decades – disclosures that would eventually undermine the faith of so many in their public representatives.

If the Glackin Report was the appetiser, and a juicy one at that, then the Beef Tribunal certainly served up a succulent main course to those interested in examining the relationships between big business and the political class.

Politicians from the smaller parties in Dáil Éireann made the running, with the Labour Party leader Dick Spring to the forefront. The establishment of the tribunal was precipitated by the Granada TV programme *World in Action*, presented by business journalist Susan O'Keeffe, containing bombshell revelations from Goodman insiders.

However, Larry Goodman's back was already to the wall. The Gulf War had exposed the flaws in his strategy, involving reliance on the supply of beef to Saddam Hussein's Iraq. Goodman Group was left heavily exposed following the Iraqi invasion of Kuwait early in August 1990.

In an effort to prop up the group, the government rushed through legislation providing for protection for group management from its creditors through a new procedure known as examinership, modelled on US Chapter 11 proceedings.

On August 23rd 1990 *Business & Finance* editor Brian O'Connor and reporter Dan White warned that Larry Goodman was facing an uphill survival struggle. In their view, "the lifeboat sent out by the government is smaller and carrying less fuel than Goodman hoped". In the Dáil it was alleged that Larry Goodman was seeking guarantees from the State of up to £300m.

The collapse of Goodman Group was viewed as a seismic event. Goodman was the dominant figure in the Irish meat-processing sector, an individual with close links to the government, someone whose companies had received large dollops of grant aid from the IDA.

The taxpayer was now left on the hook for hundreds of millions of Irish pounds in the form of export credit guarantees. According to *B&F*, Larry Goodman was "said to be bitterly disappointed that the Companies (Amendment) legislation offers only four months to put together a rescue plan. He had hoped for 12 months." The minister of industry and commerce, Des O'Malley, told the Dáil that Goodman International and its subsidiaries owed the banks £460m and that most of the debts were short-term. A further £200m was owed in the form of bank guarantees.

Labour Party leader Dick Spring concluded that "the Goodman enterprise is finished" and that it was time to "put a more honest entity in its place". According to Dan White, the weakness of the beef trade was "brutally exposed" – "were it not for the panoply of EC support measures, there would be very few customers for Irish beef". The industry had "failed to move on from subsidised commodity trading", he added, pointing to the failure of Agra Trading's marketing plan, the "one serious effort to rebrand Irish beef". He concluded that the industry "is likely to endure many more painful shocks, in the next few years".

Shocks did emerge, but from an unexpected direction. In 1990, concerns about the threat to human safety from beef products began to escalate in the UK where the agriculture minister, John Gummer, attracted much unfavourable publicity after he was pictured plying his little daughter with a burger as part of an ill-judged effort to show that the industry had his full confidence.

The spread of BSE and its human equivalent CJD cost hundreds of lives, many hundreds of millions of pounds and led to the closing off of key markets to beef exporters in these islands. Countless livelihoods would be undermined as a result of an ill-thought-out decision by the UK government to cut back on inspections of key facilities. Many families counted the cost of a lack of scruple in the implementation of safety measures along the food production chain.

A strong whiff of manure

In eighties Ireland many considered that only the naïve paid their taxes. Very high marginal rates of tax appeared to provide many tax evaders with a free pass in terms of social acceptance. The task of efficient tax administration appeared to be beyond the capacity of the Irish Revenue as then constituted. It was the norm among many self-employed to demand payment in cash for services delivered, or about to be rendered. But many in full-time PAYE posts were equally lacking in scruple.

During the 1990s a quiet revolution in tax collection and in attitudes towards tax evasion took place. The revolution was driven in part by a steady drop in tax rates, a drop that was part of the negotiated industrial settlement reached between the government and the social partners. A major overhaul in the Revenue Commissioners, at the same time, provided officials with ammunition in the fight against tax evaders.

This revolution was instigated in part by a series of tax amnesties that attracted much controversy at the time, but resulted in many income-earners being attracted out of the black economy. Between 1988 and 1993 five separate tax amnesties were introduced. The first amnesty in 1988 was expected to net the exchequer less than £100m. In fact, it attracted £500m into the national coffers.

Many, however, baulked at initiatives that in effect rewarded those who had engaged in criminal behaviour. In July 1993 the Irish correspondent of the London *Independent*, Alan Murdoch, wrote a piece about that year's controversial amnesty that attracted press headlines such as 'Crime Does Pay'.

Murdoch explained the motivation behind the initiative: "Faced with the alternative of a £500m deficit in next January's budget, the prime minister [Taoiseach] committed to wooing a generation of large-scale cash fiddlers. Without their cash he has little chance of reducing draconian tax rates, lifted to 57% on incomes over IR£10,500."

The reaction to the 1993 amnesty was especially fierce. Tax officials argued that the amnesty was unnecessary as they were already preparing intensive crackdowns on high-evader sections of society. The 1988 income tax amnesty exempted debtor taxpayers from accumulated interest and late payment penalties, whereas the 1993 amnesty went further in actually wiping some of the tax owed.

The State would only take a 15% levy on the hot money declared – it was expected to bring in £300m nevertheless. Such pragmatism was to be a feature of Irish governments in the 1990s and beyond; this essentially amoral approach would eventually culminate in the self-destructive behaviour that marked the peak of the boom in Ireland, one that was evident across all levels of society from government politicians and officials to bankers and professional advisers.

Ironically, some of the country's elite chose to ignore the amnesties despite having salted away large sums in accounts held offshore by Ansbacher Bank in the Cayman Islands. In 2002 the existence of these accounts would be exposed in a report prepared and published by the then director of corporate enforcement, Paul Appleby.

Many of the country's top business figures and professionals would face acute embarrassment, not to mention financial penalties, as a result of the disclosures. The wave of scandal swept over the country's semi-state sector, and across much of local government – in the greater Dublin area in particular.

In September 1991, following the privatisation of the Irish Sugar Company (today known as Greencore), top management at the company found themselves under investigation. The minister of industry and commerce, Des O'Malley, appointed leading lawyer Maurice Curran to examine payments made to its chief executive, Chris Comerford.

The Greencore affair surfaced in the *Sunday Independent*, where journalist Sam Smyth reported on allegations that Comerford was the beneficial owner of a Jersey-registered company, Talmino, which in turn had a 24% interest in Gladebrook, which owned 49% of Sugar Distributors Ltd, a business that was acquired by the Irish Sugar Company.

Comerford had a strong reputation as a CEO, but Curran concluded that he had breached company law through a failure to make disclosures of payments. The chief executive resigned quickly, retreating into private life. Two High Court inspectors, Aidan Barry and Ciaran Foley – a prominent accountant and barrister, respectively – were appointed. The inspectors considered the allegations in their 1992 report, but did not reach a definitive conclusion.

Speaking in a Dáil debate following the report's release on March 13th, Fine Gael finance spokesman Michael Noonan posed a number of questions:

"did a small group of public servants conspire to sell their holding in the Irish Sugar Company at an inflated price?" He questioned why, in that event, they were not stopped by the Department of Finance, by the minister (Bertie Ahern) or by the minister of agriculture.

He noted that the inspectors were silent on the question as to whether the transactions were improper or illegal. "I know it is a widely held view among professional people in this country that dog does not eat dog. I believe, however, that the taxpayer who paid £1.1m for this report was at least entitled to one bite." A file was sent to the Director of Public Prosecutions but no prosecutions resulted.

As the academic and author Elaine Byrne has noted in her book *Political Corruption in Ireland, 1922-2010: A Cracked Harp?* it was at this time that the expression 'Golden Circle' became part of the lexicon. Many scandals occurred or originated in this period. The origins of the Flood/Mahon Tribunal can be traced back to this time, when large swathes of land were rezoned by councillors under the influence of developers, and rumours swirled around the then Dublin county manager George Redmond.

According to Byrne, "this period was distinct from previous scandals because it marked the gravest form of corruption, that of State capture within political decision making".

The EU and the shift towards affluence

If Ireland was being rocked by scandals, this was also a time of economic regeneration – a recovery that is attributable in large part to developments at the heart of the European Union project.

Anyone who visited the capital of Europe, Brussels, in the early 1980s would have been struck by a sense of drift about the place. Many EU officials appeared to be underworked, their bosses caught up by issues of protocol. The president of the Commission, Gaston Thorn, was a politician lacking in clout.

The real action occurred down the road from the Commission's Berlaymont building HQ – at the Council of Ministers, where lengthy late-night haggling occurred between ministers from the member states. When the heads of government met they did so in the knowledge that they would face a handbagging from Britain's increasingly eurosceptical prime minister, who scored points at home via regular requests for concessions on the budget.

In the first half of the eighties, most of the EC was caught up in recession and much of the activity was out on the streets where the continent's farmers staged energetic protests. The Commission seemed engrossed in the challenge of absorbing Spain and Portugal, the latest countries to join the European Community.

The advent of the presidency of Jacques Delors, in January 1985, was a transformative event. Delors was a senior member of the French Socialist Party who had just served under President Francois Mitterand from 1981 as the country's finance minister. Delors had previously reached across the political frontier to serve an earlier Gaullist prime minister, Jacques Chaban-Delmas, as an adviser in 1969.

Delors' arrival in Brussels sparked a period of intense activity with the launch of the internal market project, a deadline of 1992 being set for completion. From 1985 to 1988, a key ally and occasional adversary was the former Irish attorney general Peter Sutherland, first appointed to office by Garret FitzGerald in June 1981 at the age of just 35. FitzGerald's subsequent decision to select the lawyer as Ireland's nominee to the European Commission in succession to Dick Burke was to prove of great significance.

Sutherland, in turn, was able to draw greatly on the fund of goodwill across Europe built up by FitzGerald during his tenure as minister of foreign affairs between 1973 and 1977. FitzGerald was unusual in that he sought not merely to represent the Irish national interest in negotiations, but sought to build personal relationships with senior European politicians such as the German foreign minister Hans-Dietrich Genscher.

In April 1985 the *Irish Times* correspondent John Cooney reported that Europe's youngest-ever commissioner was "making his mark where it counts". Sutherland was said to be playing an important role in "clearing the decks for a serious push forward in the area of institutional development". According to Cooney, "last year, when I visited Brussels, there was a mood of weary cynicism [...] This began to change with the meeting in France of the new Commission."

Sutherland initially served as social affairs minister but his real impact came as competition commissioner, where he played a key role in the liberalisation of the aviation market across Europe. Delors and Sutherland could be said to have acted as the midwives of the low-cost transport revolution that propelled Ryanair, in particular, into pole position in the market.

An elderly British Tory peer, Lord Cockfield – Thatcher's nominee – also played a key role in the development of the internal market project, which set out to tackle the multiplicity of barriers that were placed in the way of trade across the Community. The UK PM did not approve of Lord Cockfield's zeal – he served only one term in Brussels before being replaced by former home secretary Leon Brittan.

Cockfield, a former chancellor of the Duchy of Lancaster, had been expected to follow a eurosceptic line. Instead he produced a huge white paper listing around 300 barriers to trade, and containing a timetable for their abolition.

The opening of markets in Europe to exports provided a massive boost for an export- and foreign investment-dependent country like Ireland, helping in no small part to explain why US investor interest in the country grew so significantly by the end of the 1980s. Across Ireland in the late eighties seminars were held to assist businesspeople and professionals to prepare for the changes due under the '1992 project' of EC internal market reforms.

While tariff and quota restrictions between member states had gone by the 1980s, many non-tariff barriers had remained – France being a particular offender in this regard. Air fares, meanwhile, were kept artificially high by the IATA air cartel. The reforms engineered under the successive Delors presidencies played a transformative role. As *Business & Finance* reported in December 1989, the European Community was "entering the 1990s on a wave of self confidence".

In a 1988 interview with *The Sunday Tribune*, *The Guardian*'s European Affairs editor John Palmer summed up Delors as follows: "Delors has brought to the European presidency greater vision and intellectual rigour than any incumbent since the early 'heroic' days after the EC's foundation. A temperamental, not to say volatile character, given to extremes of euphoria and depression, he clearly stands heads and shoulders above his fellow commissioners." Palmer, however, added that Delors was an admirer of Peter Sutherland, "in spite of the occasional blazing rows".

In 1991 *The Irish Times* interviewed Sutherland who, by now, was serving as chairman of AIB. The former competition commissioner was well ensconced as a member of the great and the good, also serving as chairman of Shannon Aerospace, and as a director of James Crean and CRH, both PLCs.

"As AIB chairman, Sutherland has taken up the cudgels against criticism of excessive bank charges," the newspaper reported. Sutherland accepted that the bank, however, needed to raise its game. Agreeing that the bank's opening hours are "inconvenient", he added: "We need to be cost efficient and to introduce new technology [...] queues must be reduced."

He had no doubt that '1992', the completion of the internal market, would bring more competition from the foreign banking sector, something he welcomed. He also promised that he would not remain on as AIB chairman for more than six years: "the role requires new blood, every so often."

As for the future: "I don't agree that we have seen the halcyon days [...] the theme of the day is globalisation. It is totally changing the environment for investment banks."

In July 1993 Sutherland would assume office as director general of the World Trade Organisation, stepping down from his position at AIB and later resigning from its board. He would bring to fruition the 'Uruguay Round' by the end of 1993, putting in place what is described as 'the biggest trade agreement in history'. He would also join the board of investment bank Goldman Sachs, benefiting from the financial largesse that accrued to leading players in global finance as the world economy rebounded during what became known as the Goldilocks Era. Sutherland became chairman of Goldman Sachs International in 1995, also becoming a partner at the firm soon after. In 1998 Goldman Sachs was floated on the stock exchange and partners such as Sutherland cashed in.

An early Euro-crisis

The benefits of globalisation would spread to the furthest corners of the globe, with China a particular beneficiary. However, by the early 1990s there were already signs of blowback from communities and countries that felt threatened by the wave of competition from the east, and by threats, real or imagined, to their nation state.

In May 1992 the Danes rejected the Maastricht Treaty put before it by the European Community by a margin of 50,000 votes. The treaty, which created the European Union and laid the groundwork for the establishment of the euro, was stalled. The following September, French voters accepted the treaty by a wafer-thin 51% majority. The resulting uncertainty helped spark the currency crisis and the UK's exit from the Exchange Rate Mechanism (ERM), followed by a period of acute uncertainty in Ireland and Portugal, with both countries forced eventually to accept devaluations.

The treaty was eventually ratified after the Danes were offered certain opt-outs and persuaded in consequence to ratify the treaty, which passed into law later in 1993. Under its terms, convergence criteria were put in place. A member country's debt was to be limited to 60% of GDP, with a cap of 3% on the annual deficit also being introduced.

Common EU justice and foreign policy 'pillars' were put in place. The Irish government used its position of leverage to extract increased funding from Brussels, at the Edinburgh Summit, for investment projects and labour market interventions. Ireland arguably had earned its spurs by then.

The country endured a traumatic period in later 1992 and early 1993. In September 1992, the economist Austin Hughes reported for *B&F* on the events surrounding Britain's enforced exit from the ERM, an exit – at the hands of financial speculators – that destroyed the Tories' reputation for sound economic management and paved the way for the Labour landslide of 1997. As Hughes wrote: "Since [...] Danish voters rejected the Maastricht Treaty, sentiment on the financial markets has become increasingly gloomy. The astonishing events of the past week suggest that these fears were completely justified [...]

"It is especially disturbing that the recent chaos and shakeup in the exchange rate mechanism of the ERM has not served to unwind the pressures that brought it about. [...] There can be little doubt that the seeds of the UK's misfortunes lay in the weakness of the UK economy. The Treasury engaged in a dangerous game of bluff with the markets [...] in the end, their avowed determination to take whatever measures were needed to defend sterling rang hollow."

Hughes pointed a finger, however, at the Germans and at their central bank in particular. In his view, the clear inference from the statements of the bank's president, Helmut Schlesinger, that sterling was overvalued "set in motion the trail of events that led to sterling's collapse". Britain's enforced exit from the European Monetary System helped to boost the forces of euro-scepticism across the Irish Sea. The reverberations are still being felt today.

The Irish currency found itself under attack and the economy under siege from September 1992 through until the following February, when devaluation of the punt freed the economy from its shackles.

In the early 1990s, boom-times appeared to be far away. *Business & Finance* reported on a 'white collar jobs squeeze'. The number of executive jobs advertised had fallen from 6,530 in 1990 to 4,187 in 1991 and 3,920 in 1992.

According to the magazine's reporter Carmel Joyce, writing in December 1992, the St Vincent de Paul was also "feeling the pinch". The organisation had spent almost £12m fighting poverty in the year ended March 1992. According to its finance chairman, Frank Casey, "the situation has got materially worse since [lending] rates went up [...] if the pressure on rates continues, it will get very much worse".

The body was calling on the government to "give due recognition to the poor in any future partnership structure such as the PESP", the Programme for Economic and Social Progress. This indeed happened, with the social and voluntary pillar forming a part of subsequent social partnership negotiations.

Foreign investment troubles

In February 1993 a *B&F* editorial sternly admonished the government over its decision to send the minister of enterprise and employment, Ruairi Quinn, to the US "cap in hand, begging Digital Corporation to save its Galway plant". In the editor's view, "the whole Digital saga illustrates, once again, the flawed nature of Irish industrial policy [...]

"Digital illustrates the mobility of the vast majority of overseas companies located in Ireland. Their loyalty is purely a function of tax rates, grant aids and the fortunes of the individual company [...] a sceptic might argue that the development agencies are part of the problem rather than part of the solution [...] it is far easier to attract a small number of large multinationals than to nurture a large number of small indigenous companies."

Some time earlier the businessman Jim Culliton had proposed, in a major report, that the IDA be broken into two parts: domestic and overseas. Culliton's proposal was eventually put into effect in 1998 when Enterprise Ireland assumed the domestic industry functions of the IDA. The Digital plant in Galway closed in 1993, but before long the number of jobs created by spinoffs from the closure more than made up for the jobs lost.

A similar tale could be told in relation to GPA, the aircraft leasing company that was arguably the great home-grown Irish entrepreneurial success story of the 1980s. The collapse of GPA following its aborted flotation in 1992 was a huge disappointment. A great Irish success story appeared to turn to ashes.

Tony Ryan, GPA's founder, was a victim of a mix of personal hubris, bad luck in the form of global events (the Gulf War) and poor advice. GPA was taken over by GE and became a shadow of its former self, but out of the ashes of GPA emerged a host of companies run by former employees, and Ireland today is a major centre of the international leasing sector.

Tony Ryan bounced back via the extraordinary success of Ryanair. Indeed, the 1990s brought its share of individual recovery stories alongside a rebounding economy. Goodman lenders, with certain exceptions, decided that they needed Larry Goodman's skills after all, and the Louth man eventually regained control of his beef empire.

Meanwhile, Ryan's young protégés Denis O'Brien and Michael O'Leary played their part in the relaunch of the Irish economy in the 1990s. In 1991 O'Brien founded Esat Telecom and immediately applied to the minister for communications, Séamus Brennan, for a telecommunications licence. Few doubted that the State telephone monopoly could not be allowed to persist indefinitely. The government, however, resisted attempts to permit such competition in the fixed-line market, ignoring a 1990 EU Services Directive providing for such competition.

When the government finally gave way, it did so only in a partial sense: new entrants would be allowed to connect up business customers to their networks on lines rented from Telecom Éireann. O'Brien and his colleagues insisted that TÉ was engaging in systematic obstruction as they set out to expand their share of the market.

His canny response was to appoint Pádraig O hUiginn, the retired government official who had been at Charles Haughey's right-hand side, to the Esat board. Esat's first CEO, Doug Goldschmidt, had worked as head of regulatory affairs at a leading US satellite company and had in-depth knowledge of the EU regulatory environment. He knew that the European Commission was prepared to force the State to issue a second mobile licence.

The Department of Communications first raised this possibility in 1993. The mobile licence was finally issued to Esat following a competition in 1996; the handling of the competition was later investigated in detail by the Moriarty Tribunal. In a submission to the tribunal, Esat Digifone pointed out that in eventually securing a share of the market in excess of 40% it would become "the most successful second entrant ever in a European Union mobile market". In 1993 Esat Telecom was also granted a licence to operate a long-distance service, and in 1994, through the introduction of autodialling, Esat managed to dramatically reduce the backlogs on its fixed-line service.

In January 1994 Michael O'Leary – another figure with whom we have become familiar – took over as chief executive at the cash-strapped airline Ryanair, having served since 1991 as deputy to PJ McGoldrick, the man brought in to steady the Ryanair ship following the departure of Eugene O'Neill, the eighties face of the company.

There were few signs then that O'Leary, along with Tony Ryan and later David Bonderman, was about to reshape European aviation, helping in the process to rebuild the Ryan family's wealth.

Ireland's social partnership model

In February 1993 *B&F* published figures collated by Dr Bill Roche, director of research at the Michael Smurfit Graduate School of Business, outlining the scale of the decline in trade union membership since the onset of the 1980s slump. Between 1980 and 1987, union membership had fallen by 70,000 and the gains achieved during the 1970s were "almost totally wiped out".

Roche reported a "growing belief that trade unions face marginalisation". This perceived weakness helps in no small part to explain the positive reaction on the part of seasoned union leaders to an informal approach on behalf of the leader of the opposition, Charles Haughey, ahead of the 1987 election.

The details of this courtship, and its end result – the unveiling of social partnership – are set out in *Saving The Future – How Social Partnership Shaped Ireland's Economic Success* by industrial relations journalists Tim Hastings, Brian Sheehan and Pádraig Yeates (Hastings, as it happens, succeeded Pat Sweeney as *B&F*'s unnamed industrial affairs columnist).

The book details how Haughey was "particularly impressed by the German chancellor and SPD leader Helmut Schmidt". The German social partnership model appeared to be particularly attractive in the light of the Irish experience of wage-driven inflation and industrial unrest in the 1970s and early 1980s.

The 'tough cop' Ray MacSharry met with the Public Services Committee of ICTU, the Congress of Trade Unions, to warn them that "the place is bust". As the authors concluded, "the trade unions were under pressure. Declining membership, falling living standards, rising taxation and fears about privatisation and possible tough labour legislation persuaded many of the leading trade union thinkers that a return to national agreements would also be the best option to protect their institutional interests and the interests of their membership."

In 1987 the unemployment rate had reached 18%, up from 7% in 1979, and by 1987 the debt/GNP ratio stood at 130% (roughly equivalent to the level in 2014). The employers' body, the FUE (Federated Union of Employers) was "persuaded to enter into an agreement on pay in the PNR [Programme for National Recovery] and thereafter remained a strong advocate of the centralised bargaining approach". It helped that FUE leader John Dunne was "one of those people with the capacity to take the big picture view".

Putting together a national deal under which the unions accepted pay moderation in return for agreement on tax cuts was not necessarily a straightforward exercise. As senior SIPTU official Patricia King told the authors:

"The easiest thing is to stay running with the members. The hardest thing is to lead them into the big picture."

However, the reassurance that came in the wake of a successful national pay agreement was of considerable assistance when it came to the campaign to attract foreign direct investment. Kieran McGowan, IDA chief executive in the 1990s, has concluded that the social partnership agreements were a "huge help when selling Ireland to companies against the UK". This is ironic given that US investors – the key to Ireland's industrial recovery in the 1990s – did not believe in dealing directly with trade unions.

Through the 1990s tensions would persist. The unions would press unsuccessfully for union recognition. The country would experience the 'Blue Flu' Garda and nurses' disputes. However, the successive national agreements would hold at least until the great crash of 2008.

Irish workers would find themselves operating in a rapidly changing environment as the 1990s unfolded. Employees in manufacturing and the country's farming community would find themselves in the crosshairs of an emerging global economy.

Back in 1993, *B&F* contributor Clifford Coonan reported from Guangdong in southern China on the rapid development already under way in the three special economic zones that had been created under the leadership of Deng Xiaoping. Thousands of firms were spreading out along the new 'superhighways' as China appeared to put the trauma of the events in Tiananmen Square, just five years previously, behind them.

Asia's road to prosperity would not be straightforward. In 1997/98, a financial implosion in countries including South Korea, Thailand, Indonesia – and also Russia – would cause a jolt to the world financial system, reminding people that the world of global finance could be a dangerous, unpredictable place.

A dream dies - at least for now

By the early 1990s the Irish economy struggled with huge legacy issues, but real signs of recovery were in place. However, for the punters who had staked heavily on the fortunes of Irish oil exploration companies the picture was altogether different. In an article headed 'Dry Hole – The Exploration

Crisis', *B&F* reporter James Kirby pointed out that 18,000 shareholders in Atlantic Resources, exploration vehicle of the businessman Tony O'Reilly, had accepted 2.7p a share for a stock that had been worth £2 each back in 1983.

Wrote Kirby: "In 1989, the sector had a market capitalisation of £439m. Today, the market value of the 20 companies making up Ireland's quoted securities market is just £147m – less than half the value of Kerry Group [...] funding is now a critical issue for almost every company in the sector [...] there are fears that future rights issues and cash calls will be ignored by investors," he said, noting the 70% fall in the value of resources shares over the preceding three years.

Aidan Heavey of Tullow Oil, subsequently a major Irish exploration success story, said this at the time: "People are sick to death of companies continually asking their shareholders for money." Sean Finlay of Celtic Gold observed: "The crux of the funding crisis in this industry is that investors now have other places to put their money in." On a more positive note, while exploration off Ireland's shores was becalmed, the prospects for the country's zinc mines onshore looked fairly good. The Finnish company Outokumpu had acquired the former Tara Mines complex, while Ivernia was actively developing the zinc mines at Lisheen.

Dramatic change

Ireland changed dramatically between the late 1970s and early 1990s. The early period was defined by the charged relationship between the middle-class moderniser Garret FitzGerald and the more earthy nationalistic Charles Haughey – who ironically would emerge as a driving force for reform in the late 1980s following a period of relative stasis when FitzGerald and Dick Spring sought to hold the line against the forces leading to social and financial breakdown, unleashed in large part by previous Fianna Fáil administrations.

Deregulation transformed the building society movement and the banking sector, producing negative as well as positive impacts. The new focus on selling in banking would prove disastrous after 2000, when global financial forces unleashed a boom that grew out of control.

Europe, in those days, was accepted more uncritically, and with good reason, as a force for reform. The flaws in the Euro project – neither federal fish, nor confederal fowl – had yet to become apparent.

The Irish courts played an important but perhaps disruptive role in tax reform through the decision of the Supreme Court in the Murphy case. Married couples benefited from the ruling, but single earners suffered in consequence. The tax system came under fierce challenge in the 1980s, but the seeds were laid down for a reform that led to greater public acceptance of taxation from the 1990s on. The era of 'cash up front' ended, at least as far as many professionals were concerned.

However, new forms of greed would emerge as the economic boom matured. By 2000, Ireland had become a major IT and pharma hub. Ten years earlier, foreign pharmaceutical firms were already well established, but the development of serious IT and finance clusters had yet to happen.

Many of the issues of today were voiced with equal vigour in the *Business & Finance* editions of yesteryear. Along the way, cartoonist Bob Fannin kept readers smiling. In late 1992 he produced an image of a man with tousled hair (resembling finance minister Bertie Ahern) chanting: "We will not devalue... we will not devalue". A large key is shown attached to the man's back. That summer the British minister of culture, David Mellor, was forced to resign in the wake of a sex scandal. Fannin's cartoon linked this event with the Barcelona Olympic games. His caption, accompanying a drawing of Mellor on the floor: "And next up for the horizontal floor gymnastics section, we have David Mellor for GB."

On September 3rd 1992, Bob informed readers that the Beef Tribunal was "resuming next week". Four cows were cartooned sitting on a front row, with men in suits ranked behind them.

CHAPTER 10

Enterprising women leave their mark
By Aileen O'Toole

AILEEN O'TOOLE, FORMER BUSINESS & FINANCE EDITOR AND CO-FOUNDER OF THE SUNDAY BUSINESS POST, HAS CLOSELY FOLLOWED THE WOMEN-IN-BUSINESS NARRATIVE THROUGHOUT HER CAREER AS A JOURNALIST AND AN ENTREPRENEUR.

Selecting a theme for my contribution to this book took all of ten seconds, if even that. A book that records and reflects on the history of Irish business should acknowledge the achievements of Irish female entrepreneurs. It should chronicle the risks taken by Irish entrepreneurial women, as well as the obstacles they encountered and usually overcame. It should not be a dry academic treatise on Irish industrial policy and gender equality. Instead, it should offer insights and anecdotes about Irish female entrepreneurs, some well-known and others less well-known.

With greater participation by women in corporate life, the chapter should also question why half the population is still under-represented in leadership roles – on company boards, among senior management teams, and as owner-managers of businesses. With many of the barriers removed, why is there still such a gender imbalance in corporate Ireland?

That's a big, big theme, and one that could easily justify a book, not a chapter. So with due regard for the editor's word count, I embark on this chapter knowing that it will not be comprehensive and that much of it will be drawn on personal experience, observations and reflections.

My career has spanned a period in Ireland's history that saw a transformation in our economic fortunes, due in no small measure to foreign direct investment (FDI) and the emergence of an entrepreneurial culture. It covers a period in which there has been greater participation by Irish women in the workforce and many barriers to advancement had been removed. Up to a few years before I left school in the mid-1970s women were forced to leave the public service upon marriage, a rule that was also in place in many businesses. It was illegal for companies to take on female apprentices until the mid-1970s.

Women could not secure credit from a bank without their husbands, fathers, brothers or other male relatives in tow to sign the papers. And there were many similar practices in place that might appear to my daughter's generation to belong to the pages of the history books – yet they were rampant scarcely four decades ago.

Leaving school when I did provided me with career options denied to my counterparts in previous decades, but they were still way short of the opportunities that are available today. Commerce was not a subject option in many girls' schools and the numbers opting for business-related third-level courses were low. However, through opportunities or circumstances, women began to break through in Irish business, albeit in modest numbers, from the late 1970s onwards.

It was during that period that I joined *Business & Finance*. Nine years later and still in my 20s I became the magazine's editor, the first female business editor in Ireland. The fact that I presided over a then-weekly magazine in the late 1980s carrying a prominent 'Man of the Week' slot was probably the most discussed feature of my editorship. The reasons for this merit an explanation, as does my dalliance with entrepreneurship in competition with *Business & Finance*, both of which I will return to later.

My career – first in media and then in business – has given me access to Irish business leaders, politicians, policymakers, economists and entrepreneurs. I've probably interviewed, known or met dozens of Irish female entrepreneurs. However, it is only since I left journalism in 2000 that I feel I have got to really know many female entrepreneurs, and indeed other women who command senior roles in Irish life. That's because many such women are not always comfortable talking to journalists and prefer to keep a lower profile than their male counterparts.

That is one of very many differences between how men and women approach their careers. Women are disinclined to apply for promotional opportunities if they feel they cannot fulfil all of the role's requirements. Men don't have similar inhibitions. In establishing and developing businesses, the main driver for a female entrepreneur is often about validating a business idea rather than financial reward. Not so with male entrepreneurs.

When it comes to performance, women tend to exceed the expectations they set for themselves and by their superiors or their investors. Niche VC funds have been established to only back female entrepreneurs and do so, they argue, because they'll deliver higher returns.

Among female-led early-stage entrepreneurs in Ireland, there continues to be the inclination to set low financial targets and not apply for the full supports available from State agencies. Their male counterparts have no such inhibitions: set high targets and seek all the grants they can get. The females tend to exceed their targets but the men don't; somehow the numbers meet around the middle.

The research that tracks this leads to a simple fact: women are wired differently. Recognising those differences puts a context on this reflection on women in entrepreneurial, leadership and corporate roles over the course of *Business & Finance*'s 50-year lifetime.

A different path

Many of the first group of female entrepreneurs I met, and in some cases interviewed, did not follow the classic entrepreneurial path. Instead, family tragedies and other circumstances left them holding the reins of modest businesses. Carol Moffett of Moffett Engineering and Mairéad Sorensen of Chez Nous (now Butlers Irish Chocolates) were both in their early 20s and at college when their fathers died and they took charge of their family businesses.

In Carol's case, that was a two-person engineering business based in Clontibret, Co Monaghan. In 1972, when she was studying languages at Trinity College Dublin, her world was "turned upside down" following the sudden death of her father. She told her tutor she needed to take a year off to "sort out domestic problems" but didn't return to Trinity. She got some initial sympathy from customers who "were surprised at a young lass coming into them [...] to sell friction saws and moulds", as she told Ivor Kenny in *Out on their Own: Conversations with Irish Entrepreneurs*. From that period to the mid-1990s she transformed Moffett Engineering into an international business, with customers in over 40 countries and a headcount of 250.

Mairéad and her brother took her late father's chocolate company from a modest operation on Dublin's Lad Lane to a premier coffee and chocolate brand. Such is the strength of the Butlers brand that there was outrage among coffee addicts that there was no Butlers outlet when Terminal Two opened in Dublin Airport in 2010. While her training as a nurse might not have prepared her for the world of business in the 1970s, Mairéad has argued that she was always a trader. At the age of seven she cut up Christmas cards and sold them as holy pictures to make enough money to buy a bunny, much to her mother's annoyance.

A Limerick woman, Mirette Corboy, took charge of a construction business on the death of her husband and in the 1980s became not only the first female president of the Construction Industry Federation, but the first female leader of a construction body anywhere in the world. It was the sudden death of her former boss that led Clare woman Angela Collins O'Mahony to a steeplejack business, scaling church spires even when she was pregnant. Angela was a journalist's dream interviewee, full of anecdotes and good humour.

Another woman who inherited a family business was Mary Guiney, who assumed the management of the iconic Clerys department store on Dublin's O'Connell Street on the death of her husband in 1967. She shunned the limelight, refused all media interviews and was admired for her business acumen and her commitment to customer service. She remained active in the business well beyond what some consider normal retirement age and retained the title of chairwoman until her death in 2004 at the age of 103.

Other women inherited family businesses and developed new strategies. In some cases that path was not smooth. Freda Hayes took charge of her family business, Blarney Woollen Mills, which had been started by her father Christy. Freda was the one who took Blarney national, built a national and international brand, and acquired Kilkenny Design. A family dispute led to a schism with her siblings and the decision to leave and establish another business, Meadows and Byrne. Eight years on, the dispute was resolved and Freda re-joined the Blarney fold along with the Meadows and Byrne homeware stores.

Margaret Heffernan of Dunnes Stores assumed control of the family business in trying circumstances – the arrest of her brother Ben Dunne following a drugs bust in Florida in the early 1990s. That incident had enormous political and business repercussions and led to a dispute played out in the media, which the Dunne family had eschewed. Margaret kept her counsel, presiding over Ireland's largest retailer and overcoming what was perhaps the greatest reputational crisis ever faced by any Irish company.

For other women, the route to establishing a business began with a deep passion, be it for food, dance or fashion. Myrtle Allen's interest in artisan foods was the foundation not only for the Ballymaloe brand but for the creation of a new quality Irish tourism product in the 1960s. Myrtle's daughter-in-law Darina and then her daughter-in-law Rachel ensured that not only were the Ballymaloe values preserved, but the brand was extended into a cookery school, new products, TV shows and books.

Another woman of a similar generation to Myrtle Allen, Anna May McHugh, took her inspiration from rural Ireland. Her involvement in the Irish Countrywomen's Association led her to a career in event management, although such a label was probably not put on her career back then or maybe even now. The National Ploughing Championships is the largest of its kind in the world. Now in her 70s, Anna May continues to be its driving force, evidenced by the numbers – 280,000 spectators and commercial revenues from some 1,700 stands.

Moya Doherty, an old schoolfriend, was working as a TV producer. She wanted to showcase Irish music and dance in the Eurovision, which she was producing for RTÉ in 1994. The spine-tingling interval act stole the show and led Moya to risk everything she had to turn it into a new and ambitious show. The global phenomenon that is *Riverdance* has been seen by over 25 million people, making Moya Ireland's leading entrepreneur in the arts sector. It would have been far easier and less risky for Moya to rest on her laurels after *Riverdance* was established. Instead she pursued new ventures, creating new formats to celebrate dance and art. Moya and husband John Colgan invested heavily in those projects. Some didn't work out; some did.

In the fickle business of fashion, Ireland has produced some world-renowned talent. The late Sybil Connolly was probably the first Irish fashion entrepreneur to develop a global brand, designing for Tiffanys in the 1950s and for loyal customers like Elizabeth Taylor, Jackie Kennedy and Julie Andrews.

She operated from Georgian Dublin for a long period, in a house and mews on Merrion Square where she happily hosted international clients and from where she proved a strong supporter of Ireland's tweed and linen industries. Sybil's trademark pleated linen adorned the room of the house. She patiently explained the complex manufacturing process to journalists like me, about how it was necessary to closely pleat up to nine yards of linen handkerchiefs to produce only one yard of fabric. A dress made from this pleated linen could be packed away in a suitcase and emerge "unscathed", making it popular with her couture customers.

Today, also on Merrion Square is the home and showrooms of probably Ireland's most successful fashion designer, Louise Kennedy – who numbers presidents, princesses and other personalities among her client base. Mary Robinson wore an electric blue Louise Kennedy number when she was inaugurated as Ireland's first female president, while in 2014 Sabina Higgins, wife of President Michael D Higgins, chose off-the-peg Louise Kennedy numbers for the first ever State visit to the UK, and won praise for her style and elegance.

Other Irish women set up businesses, most likely in services, because it gave them more flexibility in reconciling work with family life. Eileen O'Mara Walsh established a tourism business called O'Mara Travel, and was Club Med's Irish representative – but probably had her highest profile as the chair of the State-owned Great Southern Hotels. She established her business after the company she worked for ran into problems and Eileen saw opportunities in continuing to provide inbound travel services. As a single mother she also felt that working for herself would afford her more freedom than working for someone else.

While women were noticeably absent in other sectors, the same could not be said for Irish travel and tourism, which has produced its fair share of women leaders. On marketing trips to the US, Eileen recalls that "many powerful Irish women took centre stage". Mary Britton, who ran the Sandhouse Hotel in Rosnowlagh in Co Donegal, Eithne Fitzpatrick of the Fitzpatrick Hotel Group, Irene Quinn of the Ballymascanlon Hotel in Dundalk, and Nancy FitzGerald and Dilly Griffith – who set up an organisation to market farmhouse holidays – were among those who attended giant US travel conventions and hosted tour operators to secure a slot on their itineraries. They were all effectively promoting their family businesses – so too did women like Mary Bowe of Marlfield House in Gorey and Myrtle Allen in Ballymaloe.

Several outward travel businesses were also led by women, the best-known of whom was Gillian Bowler of Budget Travel. In fact, Gillian epitomised female entrepreneurship: no feature or news story in the 1980s about women in business was complete without quotes and pictures of Gillian, who died in late 2016. She provided access to journalists and insights on running a business that were difficult to secure from other sources.

Starting out in a one-room basement, and grateful that the rent was paid in arrears, Gillian and her partner created one of the country's best-known travel companies. "I think I am a dogged person. If I don't achieve my goal instantly, that doesn't mean that I will give up. I will always have it in the back of my mind and work patiently towards it," she told Ivor Kenny.

Rarities on the scene

That rollcall – by no means complete – may give the impression that there were many Irish female entrepreneurs or even female senior executives on the Irish business scene. The opposite was the case. For a business journalist, identifying a female entrepreneur or executive was a rarity and finding those who would be interviewed was rarer still. In my 11-year career at *Business & Finance* I can only remember a handful of women who graced the magazine's cover or were profiled or interviewed at length.

Gillian was probably the first I encountered who saw the value of PR in the development of her business. With her trademark sunglasses holding back her long hair, Gillian graced the pages of newspapers and magazines. The strategy worked: the way Gillian packaged and marketed affordable sun holidays created a leading travel brand and led to the takeover of Budget by Granada.

Angela Collins O'Mahony had a fascinating story to tell about her steeplejack business – revitalising the business, climbing church steeples and ultimately helping the IDA to secure a US company to locate in her native west Clare. She landed big PR hits that transformed her business. Her first appearance on *The Late Late Show* was transformational for her business. Unlike many female executives, she wasn't afraid to tell a few fibs to market her business.

In an interview she gave me for my book *The Pace Setters* in 1987, she told me about her first appearance on *The Late Late Show*: "I think I said that I had 22 men, which seemed to be a nice number and I said that we had all sorts of contracts. I think the reality is that we had three men, we had one contract a week and we were all sharing the same ladder. But it was my big chance… everything exploded after the *Late Late*."

Mary Finan was one of Ireland's top PR consultants, with top clients like Michael Smurfit and Tony Ryan, and was famously described in a magazine profile as a "Roscommon ball of fire". She attracted media attention in her own right – and deservedly so, given her role in growing a significant communications business and fulfilling a myriad of board positions. She has chaired RTÉ, is a former president of the Dublin Chamber of Commerce and has sat on a variety of cultural and commercial boards, including the Gate Theatre and Canada Life.

Margaret Downes, a partner with Ernst and Young, became the first woman to chair the Institute of Chartered Accountants and was keen to raise the institute's profile. Some women were beginning to break through in professional services firms, in banking, and in stockbroking. Vivienne Jupp rose through the ranks of Arthur Andersen, now Accenture, to become its first female partner in Europe and later to become global managing director. Among the accountancy firms, women like Marie O'Connor

(PwC) and Niamh Marshall (KPMG) blazed a trail by becoming the first female partners in their respective firms.

Statistics speak for themselves

There has been much analysis about the slow emergence of women into leadership roles and starting their own businesses in Ireland. Despite a supposedly more level playing pitch between the genders, a number of anomalies remain. Girls outperform boys in the Leaving Certificate, yet males outnumber females in securing college places for science, technology, engineering and maths (STEM) and in securing jobs in science and technology.

Women continue to not put themselves forward for promotion, and often question headhunters on why they would be considered suitable for senior roles. And when it comes to creating businesses their inclination is to play it safe; to think small.

In the corporate world, it has been argued that there was a 'pipeline' problem: typically, senior roles are filled from the ranks of middle managers, who are filled from the ranks of junior positions. With low participation by women in business disciplines at third level, with disincentives such as the marriage bar in place in commercial entities as well as in the public sector, and with many women opting to leave the workforce to rear their children, the argument goes that the number of women in that 'pipeline' is low.

But is it really as simple as that? I am unconvinced. If it is a pipeline problem it would have long been resolved, given that there has been a healthy intake of women into third level and into business since the early 1980s. There are a number of other forces at play, a fact evident in many research studies and which would correlate with my experience and that of other women I know.

Many women are not prepared to play the corporate game, like the networking on the golf course, in the same way as men. They are not always front of mind when it comes to senior roles, or indeed for board roles. They are also inclined to undersell their achievements and not put themselves forward for new roles. Facebook's Sheryl Sandberg drills into such issues through an evidence-based analysis in her ground-breaking book *Lean In*. While the book caused debate, I for one found that I could relate to much of what she highlighted.

There's also the D word – discrimination. It was rampant in Irish corporate life in the 1970s and 1980s and became less prevalent from the 1990s on. The best candidates who happened to be women were often overlooked for promotion on the grounds of gender. Employers routinely asked women about marriage and their family commitments at job interviews, questions that were never asked of men. These days such questioning is illegal but there is anecdotal evidence that some employers continue to pass over female candidates, fearing that maternity leave or family commitments would cause undue disruption. Some females I know or know of take off their wedding and engagement rings before job interviews.

Rather than whinge about sexist comments or discrimination, some female leaders just got on with the job. In an interview with Ivor Kenny, Carol Moffett explained her transition from languages student to international businesswoman, and one who subsequently sold the family business in the late nineties for a reported £30 million: "I am clear about my goals and the pursuit of them. When I arrive in somebody's office and he is surprised I feel I have his full and undivided attention for about 60 seconds. I have a major advantage over a man coming to do the same job.

"If people try to treat me frivolously, I nip it very quickly in the bud. It is usually a very junior person who would try that on. Though on occasion it can happen with a senior person. I was at a dinner for 32 people and was the only woman present. The man beside me asked 'Mrs Moffett are you in your husband's business?' 'No. I don't have a husband.' He said: 'I am very sorry'."

Freda Hayes of Blarney had been running her own business and failed in her early attempts to get a mortgage in the 1980s when she was a single parent. "The building society turned me down first time until my husband would sign. I said 'I'm separated, I don't have a relationship with my husband, I can't get in touch with him'. We nearly came to blows." She eventually got a mortgage.

The late Nuala Fennell certainly believes that the D word was in evidence, so much so that as minister for women's affairs she set up the Women in Business programme "as a counter-balance to traditional thinking and ingrained discrimination". The under-representation of women among start-up businesses in the mid 1980s was "appalling", she said. Among the main IDA scheme for small businesses, female-led businesses accounted for just 3%.

She established the Women in Business programme to address this and it ran awareness campaigns and provided services to women interested in setting up their own companies. In Dundalk a phenomenal 250 attended a seminar, one of many that attracted similar large numbers throughout the country. Academic Joyce O'Connor was commissioned by the IDA to conduct the first detailed study on female entrepreneurship. She likens the Women in Business programme to being like a "movement".

The then-head of the IDA, Padraic White, needed little convincing that women were an untapped source for new enterprises. In the US, businesses led by women were the fastest-growing sector among small businesses. His wife, Mary White, was a highly successful entrepreneur, a co-founder of the luxury chocolate company Lir.

Delving into the reasons why more women did not seek state supports, Joyce O'Connor's study found that females who ran businesses, some without state aid, had different skills than men – secretarial, teaching or craft roles – whereas men had more business experience.

Recalling that period, she feels that there was a "mindset" about enterprise around that time – state supports were focused on manufacturing, which was in decline, and there was little focus on services, which was not seen as having as much economic value. Women were more likely to establish service rather than manufacturing businesses. Women like Anne Heraty, who became a founder of the publicly listed CPL recruitment business, would not have been seen to be a candidate for support because her business was in services.

Nuala Fennell's programme succeeded in doing more than packing out hotel rooms for seminars, but delivered leads for the development agencies – there was a 200% spike in the number of feasibility grant applications from females, albeit from a low base. But the Women in Business programme came to a thumping halt, killed off by new Minister for Industry Albert Reynolds.

The manner in which it was abandoned annoyed not only his political opponents, but also many women who had been encouraged by the initiative. In her memoir the late Nuala Fennell allowed the words in an *Irish Times* editorial convey the mood: "If the Women in Business enterprise agency was 'patronising', as the minister for industry believes, then there are a lot of women willing to be patronised."

Editorial battles

As for me, I feel privileged to have received so many opportunities and to have only experienced discrimination on a few occasions. Having studied journalism at college and worked briefly for a trade publication, I joined *Business & Finance* magazine as a reporter in 1978. I knew little about business and rarely read business stories. The then editor, the late Jim Dunne, mentored me and gave me career opportunities denied to many of my journalistic peers.

As a rookie business journalist I was initially a curiosity. Company AGMs, press conferences and events and corporate gatherings that business journalists covered were usually all-male affairs. My arrival on the circuit changed that. "Gentlemen and lady" was how many a chairman started his address to an AGM or networking event I attended.

The Cork Chamber of Commerce dinner was one of the biggest gatherings in the country. I was invited to the annual dinner in the early 1980s. There were possibly 800 in the room – the black tie dress code made it easy to identify other female attendees, half a dozen at best. Between courses, I went to powder my nose – which caused ripples among the waiting staff. The ladies' toilets doubled that night as the store for the bar, such was the need for space at a sell-out event, and such was the scarcity of female attendees.

I visited many factories and other workplaces where the absence of women in senior roles was evidenced by the lack of female toilets. It was not uncommon to conduct an interview or attend an event in the CEO's office or in a boardroom but then be ushered by a (female) secretary to the female facilities on the factory floor if nature called. While the practice of not putting such facilities in place died out, I had a weird déjà vu moment in the late 1990s. I was one of two female guests at a lunch in the boardroom of a newly refurbished executive wing at the head office of large company. I asked to use the facilities and was again escorted away from the plush surroundings where the all-male executive team worked into a noisy and dreary factory floor and towards the only ladies' facilities in the building.

Back to *Business & Finance*: by the age of 27 I had become the magazine's deputy editor. While I had been subjected to occasional sexist comments, my approach was to shrug them off and just get on with the job. When Jim Dunne gave his notice following an approach from *The Irish Times* in 1987, I was immediately eliminated as a contender. "The Irish business community is not ready to accept a female editor of *Business & Finance* magazine," I was told.

I was devastated. However, attempts to find an editor from other media outlets failed and by default I became editor of *Business & Finance* at the age of 29. The appointment put me, and indeed the magazine, under the spotlight.

The most frequent question I was asked was about my intentions for the Man of the Week slot. I fudged it while I tried, and ultimately failed, to convince the magazine's management that it should be renamed to a more neutral Person of the Week. The absence of any women on the cover of the magazine, or indeed as contenders for that slot, was given as the main argument against the change.

Those two years of my editorship were the most challenging of my career. My mentor had moved on but continued to guide and support me. I fought and lost not only the battle to rename the Man of the Week slot but to implement other changes to the magazine's editorial mix. In mid-1989 I had a clash with management about an issue of editorial independence. It confirmed what I had long suspected: I did not have the editorial freedom that an editor should enjoy.

On a Friday evening I decided to hand in my notice. I committed to working a three-month notice period to give the magazine a chance to find a replacement. I didn't even serve a day. On Monday morning I arrived in the office to find all my personal belongings in a black refuse bag on my desk. I was told that I wouldn't be serving my notice and was given a cheque. I left that day with the refuse bag but without the opportunity to say goodbye to my colleagues.

The story of my abrupt departure travelled rapidly through media circles but I kept to the mantra that I had left for 'personal reasons'. I decided I'd take the summer off to think about what I'd do next. That never happened. Within a matter of days, former colleague Frank Fitzgibbon called and suggested that we have a chat about a business idea. A classic entrepreneur, Frank had floated many such ideas by me and usually they evaporated within weeks. This one didn't.

In early June of 1989, Frank and a few other colleagues met in my home to discuss his idea of launching a new Sunday business newspaper. By the following November the first edition of *The Sunday Business Post* was launched, and with it the most exciting and often head-wrecking phase of my career.

I regard the experience as a founding shareholder and executive director of *The Sunday Business Post* to be the MBA I never did. My experience as a business journalist and an editor did not equip me for the reality of being a part-owner of a high-risk publishing venture. While we correctly spotted the market opportunity, attracted talented journalists (like Matt Cooper and Susan O'Keeffe from *Business & Finance*), we were an imbalanced team. We lacked the commercial and managerial skills and experience to turn an editorial product into a viable business.

We lurched from crisis to crisis, made substantial losses and were on the point of extinction on several occasions in the early 1990s. The founding team of four had shrunk to two – editor Damien Kiberd and I – within the newspaper's first couple of years.

It took a woman, Barbara Nugent, with commercial experience and dynamism to put us on a path to survival, and ultimately to realising some value from a hard slog and personal risk – the sale of the newspaper to a PLC in 1997.

Three years later, another 11-year phase in my career ended. I decided to leave the newspaper, primarily because the working hours required in producing a Sunday newspaper were difficult to reconcile with my role as a mother to three young children. While my husband was a full-time parent, I felt I was missing out on much of my children's early years.

I had no immediate career plans. Leaving a business that I co-founded was akin to walking out on members of a family. I felt that wrench for years and often regretted my decision. But I also had an inkling that I wanted to take my career in another direction, away from media. This I did through founding a strategy consultancy business specialising in digital marketing and communications, and in advocacy endeavours. The most high-profile one was the Ideas Campaign, a citizens' initiative designed to generate ideas for Irish economic recovery and renewal in 2009.

Identifying the reasons

My own entrepreneurial endeavours have left me with a fascination with female entrepreneurship and a curiosity about why more women weren't establishing their own businesses. And among those who were, the businesses were not as bold or ambitious as those started by men.

Women "represent a large pool of entrepreneurial potential in Europe", according to the EU Commission's 2020 Entrepreneurship Plan. Ireland shares common challenges with other countries, not only in the EU, in harnessing that potential. The statistics speak volumes. Females are under-represented among those engaged in entrepreneurial activity, from aspiring entrepreneurs to those who own and manage their own businesses.

The Global Entrepreneurship Monitor (GEM) is a large-scale global study carried out annually in 69 countries, including Ireland. It shows that only 4% of the female adult population start businesses, compared with the OECD average of 5.8% and the EU average of 5.2%. That's quite a gap. The ratio of men to women among early-stage entrepreneurs is 2.5:1, while among established owner-managers it is 2.2:1.

There had been a narrowing of the gap in early-stage entrepreneurship between 2012 and the previous year – yet it was not caused by more women starting businesses, but by a decline in men creating businesses. The GEM shows that there are differences in the types of businesses that Irish women start, with consumer services being the top category for new female-led businesses.

Paula Fitzsimons, the co-author of the GEM studies, is well-placed to analyse the data, identify the trends and offer insights on why women have been disinclined to establish their own businesses. Not only is she a leading expert in entrepreneurship and gender diversity, but she is the instigator of a ground-breaking programme designed to address the imbalance. She is gaining a growing international reputation for how this and other programmes she launched can stimulate entrepreneurship.

The seeds for Paula's interest in entrepreneurship were sown when she worked in IDA Ireland and where, as the agency's press officer, I got to know her. Through GEM and her consultancy work, Paula has identified the factors that prevent Irishwomen from starting their own businesses. Women tend to lack confidence in their own skills and their abilities. They have a fear of failure. They do not have the networks or know of role models to whom they can aspire. They have concerns about childcare and work-life balance.

And for those who do start businesses, many do not have growth aspirations. That led Paula to establish Going for Growth, a programme that provides peer support to women in developing growth strategies for their businesses. To date, over 300 female entrepreneurs have participated in the programme whereby leading female entrepreneurs probe and guide the participants on a range of growth-related topics.

The programme, supported by Enterprise Ireland and other State sources, has helped these female entrepreneurs to be more ambitious and to deliver revenue and employment growth. It is described by the OECD as an "inspiring" example of inclusive entrepreneurial policy: Paula is now in demand to advise other countries on stimulating female entrepreneurship and in 2014 Finland became the first outside Ireland to pilot the project.

While many women are not always comfortable with the concept of "female-only" programmes or incentives, there is no escaping the reality: they work. For several years, Enterprise Ireland had experienced few women among the founding teams of what it terms "scaling businesses" – those that were on a potential growth trajectory. Just seven of the 90 High Potential Start Up (HPSU) programme companies were female-led or had a female on the founding team in 2012.

Furthermore, at an earlier stage in the life-cycle of an enterprising business, women tended to under-promise and over-deliver. Research confirmed some of the traits identified in the GEM and other work exploring female entrepreneurship – issues around confidence, risk aversion, technical knowledge and access to capital.

Enterprise Ireland decided to launch its female-only Competitive Start Fund, which provides capital of up to €50,000 in equity finance plus access to other supports for businesses with potential. The first funding call for this female-only programme attracted 87 applications, compared to just 16 from female applicants in rounds that were open to both men and women. At the time of writing, close on 30 businesses have been approved under that female programme, while Enterprise Ireland is also supporting a range of other awareness and training programmes as part of its focus on female entrepreneurship.

Promoting female entrepreneurship is very much back on the policy agenda. Not since Nuala Fennell's programme in the mid-1980s has there been such a focus on encouraging more Irish women to go out on their own. There are a number of differences this time. There is now a recognition of the economic value of services businesses, which female entrepreneurs tend to focus on. The supports available are more extensive and go beyond grants to help resolve underlying issues of confidence and access to role models.

The promoters of many of those programmes aim that they will eventually become redundant; that women will overcome the barriers – perceived or real – to starting their own businesses.

Media portrayals

Knowing how important role models and the portrayal of female business leaders are to furthering entrepreneurship, these days I find myself reviewing and analysing how the Irish media portray female entrepreneurs and other business leaders.

Women are featured more frequently in the business media than during my time; unsurprising given that more women are in senior roles than in the 1970s and 1980s. Two PLCs are run by women: Siobhán Talbot of

Glanbia and Anne Heraty of CPL. Professional services firms have more women in senior roles – and at one point recently, at least four Irish legal firms had female managing partners.

The 2014 *Irish Times* Top 100 Companies said that 25% of all C-suite roles were held by women. That dominated the headlines. Analysing the data, the women were dominant in HR and marketing, commanding 60% and 55% of the roles respectively – but among CEOs they held just 11% of the roles.

Among start-ups and early-stage entrepreneurial businesses, more women are featured in the media. Business editors and reporters appear to make conscious decisions to achieve a greater gender balance. They are sometimes hampered by the fact that many women do not want to put themselves forward for media interviews. Initiatives such as Women On Air have sought to ensure that there are more female voices on broadcast media, and that there is a greater pool of women from all types of sectors prepared to be interviewed.

For me, the issue is not how frequently business or professional women are portrayed in the media, but often how. The treatment of Facebook's Sheryl Sandberg in *The Irish Times* is a case in point. In early 2014 the outlet carried a photograph and a short paragraph about the National Union of Journalists (NUJ) honouring Mary Maher, one of the newspaper's crusading female journalists who changed how women were portrayed in the 1970s.

Her peers included Geraldine Kennedy, the former *Irish Times* editor; Nell McCafferty, the firebrand columnist; and the late Caroline Walsh, a gifted literary editor. The short piece about the NUJ honouring Mary Maher noted how she was the first woman retained by *The Irish Times* following marriage. It was news to me that in common with many gifted public servants who were forced to leave on marriage, the same practice had applied to the newspaper until the late 1960s.

A few weeks after that piece appeared, *The Irish Times* carried a feature on Sheryl Sandberg on its lifestyle page. Promoted on page one above the newspaper's masthead as "Sandberg's style: profiling the face of Facebook", the feature took up three quarters of a page and included three photographs, one of which was a full head-to-toe shot. The article described her as a "no-nonsense dresser", a "43-year-old billionaire" (twice), a mother of two with a "fit body, which is toned in her home gym" and who shows off her body in "fitted dresses".

What did Sheryl Sandberg do to deserve such treatment in Ireland's leading quality newspaper? The rationale was that her book, *Lean In*, did "not have a sentence [...] about presenting oneself for the office" and that her preference for not discussing her own style in "an office full of young men in hoodies" justified this piece.

The *Irish Times* piece riled me, as it did many other professional women I know. The irony that the newspaper was recording the achievements of Mary Maher, one of a band of journalists who broke the mould about how women were portrayed in the media, and then sought to ridicule a highly successful businesswoman over her dress code was breathtaking. The fact that Sheryl Sandberg never set out to write a style manual seemed irrelevant.

Successful businesswomen are subject to a different treatment in the media than men. When, if ever, would the same newspaper carry such a lengthy piece about male business leaders accompanied by similar photographs of their different "looks"? Would Google's Larry Page be described as a 41 year-old father of two who favoured bright T-shirts? Are businessmen routinely described by reference to their age, marital/ partnership status, the numbers of offspring and their efforts to achieve work/life balance?

This different approach, and the often-intrusive nature of the media's coverage of women, contributes to the belief among many female entrepreneurs and businesswomen that they are better off avoiding the media. The much-held belief that the media is generally hostile to business success, and particularly to successful women, leads to many adopting a low media profile. And that in turn feeds into the perception that there is an absence of role models in business.

The counter-arguments that I often try to put – that media exposure is good for business, and more female business role models are needed in the media – are often difficult to carry. Many women interested in encouraging other women in business choose to do so in other ways: as official and unofficial mentors, as advisers to fledgling businesses, as speakers at events, and increasingly as supporters for initiatives designed to support female-led businesses to grow. They tend to be generous with their time despite a range of other commitments, do not seek remuneration or recognition, and studiously avoid media attention.

A promising future

It would be wrong to end on a negative note. Some businesses are prioritising the retention and motivation of female talent and have programmes in place to support women's career progression. A new generation of female business leaders is emerging. Many I don't know, but from afar I am impressed.

After she had her first child in 2013, Sonia Flynn, regional director at Facebook Ireland, didn't race back to the office or feel she needed to be in daily contact with it. Instead, she took eight months off and was in touch with the office intermittently. "It sent a positive message (to her colleagues) that you can have your family and then come back to work," she told *The Irish Times*. It also sent a signal that she had total faith in the team she had assembled.

On corporate boards there is a growing recognition that good governance and gender diversity are complementary. There have been a series of recent appointments of women to PLC and State boards, and a growing recognition that there is no shortage of talented female contenders for board roles – only an awareness gap. The Board Diversity Initiative, conceived by Vivienne Jupp and Anne-Marie Taylor, aims to increase the visibility of potential female board candidates.

There is also the potential that quotas may be introduced by the EU for listed companies. I'm probably not the only one to have mixed views on quotas, particularly regarding the negative messages they could send that appointments are not necessarily being made on merit. A better approach would be for boards and other senior figures to recognise the value of gender diversity and the skills and experience that those female candidates can offer.

With that purpose, it would be a breakthrough if more male leaders would mentor females with potential. I feel I am the beneficiary of such mentorship.

And for that I am eternally grateful to the late Jim Dunne.

CHAPTER 11

Semi-states: from public to private
By Fearghal O'Connor

COMMERCIAL STATE-OWNED COMPANIES PLAYED A CRUCIAL ROLE IN FIELDS SUCH AS ENERGY AND TELECOMMUNICATIONS THROUGHOUT POST-INDEPENDENCE IRELAND.

In a nondescript office block behind a Starbucks and a gym on Dublin's Shelbourne Road lies perhaps the most important room in Ireland. It also stands – in all its high-tech glory – as a symbol of the positive achievements and technical abilities of a group of oft-maligned companies: Ireland's commercial semi-state organisations.

One could argue that the cabinet room in Government Buildings or the Dáil chamber in Leinster House, or even the boardrooms of the country's biggest banks and businesses, are more influential spaces. But Eirgrid's National Control Centre on Shelbourne Road is where Ireland's electricity network is controlled. In this quiet, tech-laden space the country's lights are kept on and the flows of energy that are the very lifeblood of the economy are regulated and managed every moment of every day.

So important is this room to the smooth running of the electricity system that an exact replica stands in a permanent state of readiness at an undisclosed location five miles away. A failure by the engineers in this room to constantly match electricity supply to demand would lead to unthinkable blackouts. Colour-coded lines on a huge digital screen that dominates the room display the state of all the key lines on the network. Rows of red digits deliver real-time information about electricity demand and supply.

For the uninitiated it all looks very impressive, but for those who understand the significance of the information on display it is even more impressive again. There is good reason why US energy secretary Steven Chu, congresswoman Nancy Pelosi and a number of British ministers have been among the visitors to the National Control Centre: it is the beating heart of an Irish energy revolution that is being watched closely from abroad and driven in no small part by cooperation between high-tech energy companies in the private sector and commercial semi-state companies such as Eirgrid and ESB.

For what the red digits on the wall show – and what the engineers in the room facilitate – is that Ireland's energy needs are being satisfied by huge amounts of renewable wind power on a daily basis. With climate change and energy security ever-increasing concerns for almost every country on the planet, Eirgrid's National Control Centre, and the developing smart electricity grid it controls, are seen as a testbed for groundbreaking technology that could revolutionise the energy systems of the future.

What is most remarkable is that it is only a few short years since Ireland faced a huge energy crisis. Government-owned electricity provider ESB completely dominated an electricity market that had been forced to turn on diesel generators just to keep the lights on.

This growing energy crisis was followed swiftly by an even bigger problem: the collapse of the entire economy as the property bubble came spectacularly undone. Suddenly semi-state companies such as ESB, Bord Gáis and Bord na Móna were being lined up on the auction block. Through often barren economic decades right back to the 1920s, these companies in their different guises had sometimes proved to be among the few sustainable sources of good employment and economic growth.

Much debate raged around the advantages and disadvantages of privatisation and increased competition in the crucial sectors that these companies controlled long before the International Monetary Fund came to town in 2010. For so long an engine of growth, the big network-controlling semi-state monopolies were often seen as part of the problem that had driven up the price of doing business and made it even harder for Irish business to react when the floor fell out of the Celtic Tiger.

Something had to change, and given that the semi-states had always played such a crucial role they were a prime target. Nevertheless, the 1999 sell-off of semi-state telecoms giant Eircom had long provided a salutary lesson in how not to handle a crucial national network, and dimmed the appetite of many to see another crucial industry thrown open to the vagaries of the market.

But with the country in a €46 billion hole, the time seemed right to cash in what many saw as the last remaining jewels in Ireland's tarnished crown.

From the beginning

The genesis of the peculiar institution that is the Irish semi-state goes all the way back to the difficult post-revolutionary days of the 1920s. Ireland had been mostly bypassed by the Industrial Revolution that had allowed other European economies, most notably Britain, to develop great cities and modern infrastructure. Belfast was the industrial heart of the island, reaching its pinnacle in 1912 as the *Titanic* set sail from the Harland and Wolff shipyard. Its subsequent sinking was not just a harbinger of the death and destruction of the looming Great War, but also of the decline of Belfast as a great industrial centre. Either way, partition would ensure that the North's industrial base would play no part in the economy of the newly born Irish Free State in 1922.

Further south, Dublin was a slum-riven city saturated with poverty. Ten years of upheaval that had seen Dublin become the stage for bitter and violent strikes, a destructive and bloody uprising, the subsequent War of Independence and a divisive civil war left the city in no shape to be the economic driver of the fledgling Free State. Ireland was a country just a few short decades out of famine and the electrification revolution that was sweeping developed countries was slow to arrive. A few select locations around the country did have access to this incredible new power source. Dublin Corporation's Electricity Department built the famous Pigeon House power station in 1903, but widespread power would have to wait.

Nevertheless, as early as 1901 the potential of Ireland's rivers to generate electricity had been recognised but no projects got off the ground. This lack of development meant that by the time the Free State was born it contained just 36,000 electricity users and, according to Diarmaid Ferriter's *The Transformation of Ireland 1900-2000*, just one of its 300 creameries used the new power source.

But then in 1925 came a transformative move by the new government when it approved the harnessing of the River Shannon for the generation of electrical power at Ardnacrusha, Co Clare. According to Ferriter, the decision was not only a far-sighted and innovative one but also "the government's most significant gesture in the direction of industrialisation".

"It deservedly received huge media coverage, and became an important symbol of the potential for constructive use of Irish natural resources," he wrote: government-commissioned paintings depicted Ireland's revolutionary gunmen being replaced by bureaucrats intent on modernity.

The major contract was given to Germany's Siemens, marking the beginning of the company's long relationship with Ireland. It also marked the first time that an independent Irish government had the vision and bravery to look so far from home to bring in foreign expertise to help develop the local economy. It would be at least 40 more years before a government would realise the huge potential of attracting the outside world to do business in Ireland.

When Ardnacrusha opened in 1929 it instantly met all of Ireland's energy needs and was put under the management of the newly formed Electricity Supply Board. Today the dam still supplies approximately 2% of national peak demand for power.

By 1937, Ardnacrusha's ability to meet energy demand had fallen to 87% and ESB set about planning a series of other hydroelectric plants at Poulaphouca, Golden Falls, Leixlip, Clady, Cliff, Cathleen's Falls, Carrigadrohid and Inniscarra. This accounted for 75% of the country's inland water power potential, and the ESB had completed all of the projects by 1949.

Nevertheless, despite these huge developments the new power source was a distant rumour to many. By 1945 just 2% of rural homes had an electricity supply, compared to 85% and 98% in rural Denmark and Holland respectively. That sparked what is perhaps the ESB's greatest legacy to the country: the Rural Electrification Scheme.

Between 1946 and 1979 the company connected in excess of 420,000 customers in rural Ireland, making possible the 1960s' economic boom that heralded a new age of modernity after decades of emigration, stagnation and literal darkness. Indeed, such was the success of the company's rollout that by 1962, 96% of 800 areas designated had an electricity supply. Until the end of World War II just 2,000 miles of electrical lines ran across the country. Some 30 years later, 75,000 miles of new line had been built – putting protests around current-day expansion into perspective.

The period also saw the ESB move away from renewable but limited hydro power, starting with the building of the North Wall power station in Dublin. Later decades saw the company build huge stations such as Poolbeg in Dublin, Aghada in Cork and Moneypoint in Co Clare, not to mention its transformation of Turlough Hill, a mountain in Wicklow, into a huge pumped storage facility that opened in 1974.

Peak peat

History has not always been kind to the foresight of the first Free State governments in terms of economic development. Schoolchildren may have learned for generations that Ireland was a country with no natural resources, as if to explain the lack of opportunity that awaited them beyond the classroom. But apart from its rivers, there was one other quintessentially Irish raw material that was exploited: peat.

The beginnings of the peat industry in Ireland had its roots in the private sector. As at Ardnacrusha, German ingenuity was once again brought in to supply huge excavators to extract peat from Turraun bog in Co Offaly, where a peat-fired power station was built to power the equipment. This led to the establishment of a turf distribution network in Dublin.

But great events were soon to shape the industry and ensure that it too became a ward of the State. After a decade in the wilderness, Éamon de Valera secured victory in the 1932 general election for his new Fianna Fáil party. He quickly abolished the hated oath of allegiance to the king and withheld land annuities owed to Britain as part of the 1921 Anglo-Irish Treaty. A damaging trade war kicked off between the two countries, with levies and sanctions imposed on goods travelling both ways across the Irish Sea.

With British coal now a more expensive commodity to acquire, the bog that lay in a blanket across the Irish midlands suddenly became a more potent natural resource and the government established the Turf Development Board, the precursor to Bord na Móna. It was led by Fianna Fáil industry and commerce minister Todd Andrews, who was to have a huge influence on the development of a number of semi-state companies, not least Bord na Móna.

Andrews set about establishing schemes to stimulate private turf production, set standards for density and moisture content, fix prices and organise distribution, as well as setting up cooperative societies for the marketing of turf. A government delegation had visited German and Russian bogs in 1935 on fact-finding missions but the arrival of World War II saw such international cooperation become an impossibility. As the horrors of war began to unfold across Europe, Ireland slipped into the lonely isolation of the Emergency and the turf industry became a matter of economic life or death.

By 1941 coal imports for domestic use had fallen drastically and Hugo Flinn was appointed turf controller. He marshalled the country's turf cutters "like an army general", according to Diarmaid Ferriter. Under his direction four major projects were established, the largest of which – the Kildare Scheme – involved the drainage of 24,000 acres of bog and the building of 14 residential camps to house the workers. The scheme produced some 600,000 tonnes of turf in the period to its closure in 1947.

Such was the scale of the effort that the country managed to fuel itself through the war. Prior to 1939 the country's annual fuel consumption was 2.5m tons of imported coal and 3.5m tons of turf, according to Ferriter. Flinn's efforts pushed turf production to more than 4.5m per annum during the war years, and by 1942 over 26,000 people were employed on more than 800 bogs.

"These endeavours also laid the foundations for a modern turf industry in the post-war period," wrote Ferriter. "If this was as close as most Irish people got to digging in the trenches it is also the case that, like soldiering, it invoked a sense of camaraderie and a spirit of cooperation; a severe test had been successfully met."

When the war ended, the Turf Development Board was transformed into Bord na Móna and an ambitious development plan was enacted to provide two ESB turf-fired power stations. The new State company was to develop 24 bogs to produce over a million tonnes of sod-peat per annum. A further development programme in the 1950s obliged the ESB to build four more turf-fired power stations and the industry got a further boost from the oil crisis in the 1970s.

All of these stations have since been shut, but the link between the country's electricity supply and its bogs has been maintained with three new, more efficient stations built over the last decade. Increasingly, however, Bord na Móna has sought to diversify away from producing peat from Ireland's dwindling bogs, themselves important natural habitats. Instead, the company has attempted to create a more sustainable future through the increased use of biomass and major plans for wind energy development on the vast tracts of land it controls across some of the most isolated parts of the country.

Public opinion and the political climate have not been kind to these plans and in April 2014 the company was forced to abandon its €1bn Clean Energy Hub project to export renewable energy to the UK due to the lack of an intergovernmental deal.

The plan for the largest onshore wind farm development in Europe, along with competing plans by private companies, became a huge political issue for the Fine Gael/Labour government as local communities organised themselves against proposals that would have seen Bord na Móna erect up to 600 huge turbines on cutaway bog sites in Offaly and Kildare. For now, the project looks to be dead, leaving the company at a crossroads.

Floating or sinking?

The morning of July 8th 1999 was a hot one in New York City. As Minister for Public Enterprise Mary O'Rourke arrived in Wall Street she was greeted by an Irish street carnival worthy of the early days of the Celtic Tiger. After months of government-led hype, Eircom was about to float on the stock exchange and the Irish public were to share in the bonanza, or so the theory went.

But the tale of how Eircom, an offshoot of the Government department responsible for the development of Ireland's telecommunications systems, ultimately ended up in the largest examinership in Irish corporate history is one filled with regret and debt, and is a cautionary tale of how not to develop crucial network infrastructure.

When Telecom Éireann, later to be rebranded Eircom, was hived off from the Department of Post and Telegraphs in 1984 to begin life as a semi-state organisation, the changes that lay ahead in the industry – mobile phones, the worldwide web and broadband – were almost impossible to predict. Nevertheless, the new State company made a promising start. It invested huge amounts into turning Ireland's previously backward analogue phone system into one of the most advanced digital networks in Europe.

With the European Union insisting on more competition in the Irish telecommunications market, the government also saw a chance to raise money for itself and to encourage voters to cash in on the expected windfall. 500,000 took the bait, paying €3.90 per share.

Initially it seemed like a great success. The government raised €6 billion overnight and the shares rose as high as €4.77 as the optimism of the IPO on Wall Street carried on through the summer. But what slowly unfolded was a sharp lesson for a government and its people that markets can fall as well as rise.

In September, Europe's telecommunications industry took a hit on the markets. While other, bigger players recovered through the autumn, Eircom dropped below its IPO price and stayed there.

In 1996, in preparation for the full privatisation, the government had sold off 20% of the company to two strategic investors, the Dutch KPN and Swedish Telia. Their stake would later grow to 35% and a further 15% was handed over to workers through a share ownership trust known as ESOT. As newly floated Eircom struggled to maintain its IPO price, KPN and Telia dropped a bombshell: they were selling their stake.

Thousands of first-time share-owning Irish people watched in horror as the investment that had been sold to them as a sure thing came undone. Most ended up losing a third of their money, apart from the smart few who had taken profits quickly in July.

The sale of the KPN and Telia stake kicked off a huge takeover battle between consortia led by Denis O'Brien and Tony O'Reilly. O'Reilly's Valentia group won out after striking a deal with the ESOT to double its stake. The company that had been worth more than €10bn in July 1999 was snapped up for just €3.2bn. Worse still, Valentia funded the purchase with €2.7bn of debt, which it loaded on to the now-private company's balance sheet. A second flotation of the company in 2004 saw Valentia make almost €1bn from its brief ownership.

What followed was a period of Eircom being passed from one set of owners to the next, with new debt landing on its balance sheet at every stage. By 2010, Singapore-based STT was able to pick up the company for just €39m and its debts had risen to €3.8bn. That ultimately led to the company's lenders taking control of it and putting it through the biggest examinership in Irish corporate history, the first time in more than a decade that debt was removed from Eircom's balance sheet rather than piled on to it.

While all of that was going on, the telecommunications world was undergoing a revolution. The Irish government had offloaded not just its business interest in the industry but also its effective control of how it would develop, because it no longer had any interest beyond regulation over the Eircom network, which was still a monopoly. With Eircom's private owners generally more interested in flipping the company for profit than developing any long-term strategy for it to partake in the communications revolution, that meant that Ireland's network began to rapidly fall behind competitors in technological terms.

By 2012 Irish people were paying the second-highest cost per megabit of data in the EU, according to pressure group Ireland Offline. Its regular report that year into the state of broadband services, until recently utterly dependent on Eircom investment, made clear the scale of the gulf that had developed for an economy that was dependent on a high-skilled, computer-literate workforce.

"We are stagnant in terms of upload and download speeds; however, the likes of Bulgaria, Moldova, Belarus, Romania, Zimbabwe and Nigeria are still ahead of us for download speeds and we are battling to stay ahead of Laos in terms of upload speeds. We are 74th in the world for upload speeds, with Libya, a country with no government, catching us up fast," it said. It was hardly surprising that even as the economy fell asunder in 2008, the privatisation of other State assets, particularly the valuable semi-states, was viewed darkly through the prism of the Eircom experience.

Lessons learned

The lessons of the Eircom debacle were hard-learned. No government would consider such a total selloff of a crucial network business again. As energy prices rose, for example, and the electricity market cried out for more competition, a far more cautious approach was taken towards a mooted privatisation of the ESB. Much of this caution was down to the powerful unions in the company, but the idea of handing over another crucial national infrastructure network would have been politically impossible given the situation with the country's broadband network.

Assets such as generating stations were sold to try and remove the monopoly situation in the market, but responsibility for the network – with the crucial National Control Centre at its heart – was passed to a new commercial State entity, Eirgrid. It has since been able to concentrate on innovation and expansion of the electricity network to meet the challenges of greatly increased renewable energy, free of any overhanging threat of privatisation.

Bord Gáis was another State company to enjoy a more strategic approach from government in recent times, doubtless learned from the Eircom experience. Ironically, its history is firmly rooted in the success of private-sector speculation. Even to this day, private-sector oil and gas exploration companies look to the seas around Ireland as a possible new and lucrative hydrocarbon province.

The first big breakthrough came in 1971 and there have been very few since. Marathon Petroleum had struck natural gas off the Old Head of Kinsale in Co Cork. By 1976 the gas was ready to come ashore and the government established Bord Gáis Éireann as the State's gas development agency. Much of the gas was destined for two ESB power stations but the new company set about bringing the new cheap, clean and efficient energy source to homes and businesses around Ireland.

Central to that work was the building of a 240km pipeline between Cork and Dublin. The spread of the new energy source throughout the capital coincided with a ban on smoky fuels and the city's increasingly bad smog problem was wiped out almost overnight.

In 1993 a new sub-sea gas interconnector pipeline linked Loughshinny in north Co Dublin and Moffat in Scotland. With the promise of huge amounts of new gas discoveries failing to materialise since Marathon's original discovery, the new pipeline gave customers and industry the reassurance that the supply would not run dry when Kinsale was exhausted. This link to the wider European network meant that Bord Gáis could continue to rapidly expand its network almost nationwide. The discovery of a new field at Corrib – the subject of a torturous planning battle – meant that the new interconnector might even be used for export rather than import.

By 2006, all of this expansion meant that Bord Gáis's turnover had jumped by a third in just one year to surge past the €1bn mark. With profits of almost €100m it was perhaps the shiniest jewel in the semi-state crown. Little wonder then that when the IMF and European Union examined a list of State assets that Ireland could sell to help itself out of financial armageddon, Bord Gáis was top of the pile.

Nevertheless, this sale was very different to the Eircom debacle. Bord Gáis's vital network was retained by the State. A trio of companies – Centrica, Brookfield Renewable Energy Partners and Icon Infrastructure – paid €1.12bn for the company's gas and electricity supply, as well as 17 windfarms.

Given the strength of the overall business established by Bord Gáis, critics have argued that the price paid for its retail business, its wind farms and a modern gas-powered electricity generating station was way too low. To many, the government had its back against the wall when it agreed what some believe amounted to little more than a fire sale to keep the EU/IMF Troika at bay.

But as so often before, the semi-state sector was there to provide a way out for a nation in need. Just how appropriate such strong State involvement in energy, telecommunications and the network industries of the future will be remains to be seen in the challenging decades ahead.

CHAPTER 12

Aer Lingus and Ryanair: an intertwined history
By Fearghal O'Connor and Ruraidh Conlon O'Reilly

TWO OF IRELAND'S MOST RECOGNISABLE GLOBAL BRANDS – ITS TWO AIRLINES – HAVE BOTH UNDERGONE HUGE TRANSFORMATIONS IN THE MIDST OF THEIR FIERCE RIVALRY.

It is March 2013, and a large group of European aviation journalists have gathered in a conference room at the EU Commission in Brussels. They are there to discuss the problems, challenges and opportunities facing European aviation. The topics are wide-ranging: the proposed new European Open Skies system, the long-overdue transformation of Europe's air traffic control system, Russia's belligerent approach to European airlines and a host of other aviation matters.

But one persistent topic excites more passion than any other: the unstoppable expansion of Ryanair across Europe. German journalists express horror at how the Irish upstart treats its passengers. Estonians demand it be encouraged to deliver more passengers further east. French reporters grow passionate about taxation matters. Scandinavians demand action on labour laws. British journalists barely contain their disdain for its chief executive Michael O'Leary but privately tell their favourite Ryanair stag weekend tales, while Irish journalists ask endless questions about Ryanair's attempts to take over Aer Lingus.

One Commission official sighs at the workload the airline creates. Correspondence from Ryanair, much of it berating EU policy, greatly exceeds the amount that the Commission receives from any other airline in Europe, he whispers. There are wry smiles when EU transport commissioner Siim Kallas tells the group that O'Leary is not "enemy number one" of the European Union.

O'Leary has long revelled in making a nuisance of himself with officialdom. The airline's infamous cartoon of public enterprise minister Mary O'Rourke in the bath, its branding of a British prime minister as 'Greedy Gordon', its relentless abuse of Bertie Ahern as a ditherer and its cartoon of Silvio Berlusconi holding the infamous Ryanair calendar were just some of the more conspicuous examples.

Such stunts have long characterised the airline's uniquely aggressive approach to public relations. But one year on from the Brussels gathering, all that has seemingly changed. Europe's aviation journalists are once again gathered in a room discussing the Irish airline, but this time everybody is smiling. Uncharacteristically, Ryanair is paying the bill: there is a free bar in the corner and no-one is going hungry or thirsty. The overarching theme of the no-expenses-spared gathering on the banks of the Thames overlooking London's iconic Tower Bridge is designed to suggest just one basic message. Ryanair has changed.

Behind the change of attitude is the airline's ambition to grow its passenger numbers from just over 80 million passengers per annum to 110m in five years, helping to fill the 175 new planes it has on order. Michael O'Leary's bullishness has long symbolised a less-than-customer-friendly approach that is seen by many as a major impediment to that growth. Is that the reason behind the new nice guy image, he is asked? "It's not an image. It's real. I've always been a nice guy, just misunderstood," he shoots back, while a string quartet plays in the background and a scrum of reporters pushes closer to catch every O'Leary utterance on all aviation-related topics imaginable, and more besides.

The flag carrier

After years of fending off unwanted – and, to many, mischievous – takeover attempts by Ryanair, there is likely to be few at Aer Lingus headquarters who would describe O'Leary simply as "a nice guy". The history of the two airlines was intimately entwined long before the original takeover attempt in 2006. To understand the 'challenger' mantle that Ryanair still cherishes, it is important to first understand the special role that Aer Lingus found itself playing as national airline in a country attempting to forge a newly independent identity.

The first Aer Lingus flight flew from Baldonnel Aerodrome in Dublin to Bristol on May 27th 1936. The aircraft was a five-seater De Havilland Dragon biplane and the first year of operation saw the new airline carry 800 passengers and 3.5 tonnes of freight on routes to Bristol, Liverpool and the Isle of Man. By 1940 the airline had acquired the first of its much larger DC-3 aircraft and moved its base of operations north of the city to Collinstown, where Dublin Airport would grow. That year it carried 5,000 passengers but growth came to an abrupt halt due to the war raging in Europe. As the 1950s kicked off, Aer Lingus was growing again with regular services to Britain as well as Amsterdam and Paris. The fact that it used its new fleet of Vickers Viscounts to establish the first scheduled service by any airline to Lourdes was perhaps a reflection of Irish priorities abroad at the time.

By 1958 Aer Lingus began flying from Shannon to New York and Boston, and with the arrival of a fleet of three Boeing 707s in 1966 this transatlantic service was extended to Chicago and Montreal. This move into the jet age was the beginning of the modern Aer Lingus. By the 1980s Aer Lingus was carrying over two million passengers per annum as well as 66,000 tons of cargo, employed over 6,000 people, had total revenues of £100m and, courtesy of a friendly understanding with British Airways, utterly dominated air traffic in and out of Ireland.

Perhaps the biggest milestone for the airline during this period of expansion came in 1971, when it bought two 397-seater Boeing 747 jets. It turned out, initially at least, to be a bad buy – but it was also a sign that the airline was ready to compete with the biggest and the best. Aer Lingus now provided a confident expression of a modern Ireland at some of the world's major airports. In reality, the country itself struggled to keep pace with the symbolism.

What nobody knew at the time was that the 747 deal would also open an unprecedented career path for one Aer Lingus employee who would go on to create the world's biggest aircraft leasing company and, perhaps more importantly, a revolutionary airline of his own that would turn everything Aer Lingus thought it understood about the aviation business on its head.

Enter Tony Ryan

Back in the sixties and early seventies Tony Ryan was very much a company man. Having worked his way up through the ranks at Shannon Airport without particularly shining, he had finally found a role with a degree of independence. As Aer Lingus station manager at New York's JFK he began to show the tough, ruthless streak that would later win him great riches. Glamorous, Ray-Ban wearing Aer Lingus pilots of the era used to "drive him nuts" and his conflicts with them became legendary, according to *Tony Ryan: Ireland's Aviator*, the biography of him written by Richard Aldous.

His tough stance with the pilots had put Ryan on the radar of the airline's management back in Dublin. So with his family tiring of life in the US, Ryan took a less than glamorous-sounding role heading up the Aer Lingus leasing department. It was a fateful move. The oil crisis had struck and Aer Lingus was stuck with two brand-new Boeing 747 Jumbo Jets. The jets may have been the pride of early seventies Ireland but they were also half-empty all winter and a massive financial drag on the airline. The difficult task fell to Ryan to find some other airline to lease them for half the year.

After travelling the world seeking a deal, Ryan hit the jackpot in Thailand with Air Siam, reportedly nicknamed 'Air Heroin' in the industry. The high-risk nature of the deal meant that Aer Lingus had to establish a 'snatch squad' for the 747 and its staff in case Air Siam ran into trouble and the precious jet became impounded. Ryan was sent to Thailand to take care of the jet and the Aer Lingus crew that would operate it.

It was during his adventures in Bangkok that the slow metamorphosis from company man to global aviation entrepreneur, described brilliantly by Aldous, truly became apparent. He was certainly mixing in the right circles at this stage of his career. Politicians such as Jack Lynch and Des O'Malley learned to call upon Ryan when help was needed travelling in what was then a difficult part of the world. The relationship with the latter would prove significant when, decades later, the future PD leader would prove a key supporter and driver of the aviation deregulation that would make the Ryanair revolution possible.

But long before Ryan established Ryanair he had convinced Aer Lingus to invest in a new leasing business called Guinness Peat Aviation (GPA). Ryan had spotted a huge opportunity and left Aer Lingus to establish the new company. Its rise was phenomenal. Ryan convinced airlines to lease rather than buy aircraft and, from its base in Shannon, it became the world's largest commercial aircraft leasing company, valued at $4 billion. But then disaster struck. In the wake of the Gulf War in 1992 the company's IPO flopped.

Others might have crumbled under the intense pressure, but not Tony Ryan. The failure of the IPO allowed Ryan to concentrate on another struggling project, the fledgling Ryanair. Since its establishment in 1984, Ryanair has grown from a small airline flying the short journey from Waterford to Gatwick with a 15-seat Embraer Bandeirante turboprop aircraft. This was followed by a second route, to Luton, and in its first year the airline carried 82,000 passengers.

Nevertheless, Ryanair looked set for failure. Competition had brought about a doubling of passenger numbers between Ireland and the UK since 1986. Yet despite this competition Aer Lingus still held the upper hand. In the wake of the first Gulf War, the State airline had received IR£175m in a rescue package from the government under the Cahill Plan, named after then-chairman Bernie Cahill. Ryanair appeared to be on its knees, and in 1993 Aer Lingus offered to buy Ryanair for IR£20m. That was not to be, and both airlines went their separate ways.

The Cahill Plan spurred Aer Lingus on to a restructuring that eventually saw it fare much better than most of the western world's legacy carriers at the time. But in a difficult, volatile and rapidly changing business, financial problems were never far away and handouts from government were less acceptable as an answer. Aer Lingus was seen by many as an obvious candidate for privatisation but powerful unions, political jitters, the furore over the botched privatisation of Eircom and the terrorist attacks of September 2001 all ensured that the process became a long-drawn-out saga.

The airline shaped up for privatisation under new young chief executive Willie Walsh, a former pilot with the airline and later chief executive of IAG, the parent company of British Airways and Iberia. An impressive plan for transatlantic expansion hung on the need for an outside injection of cash for new long-haul aircraft. All the while, Aer Lingus began to look and feel more and more like the increasingly aggressive Ryanair it was struggling to compete with – low fares, outsourcing, brash adverts and an increasingly intelligent use of the internet as the key sales channel. Aer Lingus boomed, yet the management team became increasingly frustrated waiting for the government to set privatisation in motion. By 2004 they could wait no longer and Walsh and his colleagues announced an ill-fated management buyout proposal. This was given a swift rebuke by the politicians and Walsh soon departed. Along with him went arguably the best possible moment for the privatisation of Aer Lingus. Spiralling oil prices, the continuing threat of global terrorism, pension difficulties and a feeling that the moment had passed all conspired to ensure that when it was eventually floated in September 2006, a distinct lack of ambition in the share price was key to ensuring success.

Protracted battles

The €2.20 flotation price for Aer Lingus had Michael O'Leary rubbing his hands with glee. If Aer Lingus had boomed under Walsh, it was nothing compared to the stratospheric Europe-conquering performance of Ryanair under O'Leary. With a second business disaster staring Tony Ryan in the face, he had tasked his right-hand man O'Leary with turning around the airline in 1991. O'Leary had visited the US and witnessed first-hand how an intense focus on costs had helped Southwest Airlines revolutionise the short-haul model there. As the EU deregulated the European aviation market, O'Leary set about implementing the ideas he had picked up at Southwest with ruthless efficiency – first as deputy chief executive, but by 1994 as chief executive.

O'Leary's no-nonsense approach did not always chime with Tony Ryan's view of where the airline should pitch itself. Indeed, when Michael O'Leary stood up at Ryanair's AGM in September 2013 and promised to stop annoying customers and to end the airline's macho culture, Ryan must have been looking down from above and smiling wryly.

Ryan had spent the tumultuous early days of Ryanair attempting to tame the more extreme cost-cutting desires of O'Leary, then his personal assistant. Ryan, who had a taste for luxury, was always somewhat conflicted about the direction of Ryanair from the beginning. Cheap and cheerful "does not have to mean shite", he once said in defence of his vision for the airline.

Tensions mounted as O'Leary insisted to Ryan in a letter, quoted by Aldous, that Ryanair was not a quality product and that it would "get no return for style or elegance". "We are the Woolworths of the industry," said O'Leary. When Ryan finally appointed O'Leary chief executive, his former underling dropped the "cheerful" part of Ryan's vision for the carrier and concentrated solely on "cheap". It led to huge tensions between the two, with Ryan ultimately pushed aside, although not before he had made a second fortune from the airline.

By 1995 the O'Leary model was on its way to becoming a Europe-wide phenomenon. Ryanair celebrated its tenth birthday by carrying 2.25m passengers. The real game-changer came in 1998 when, after floating on the Dublin and New York stock exchanges the year previously, the airline placed a $2bn order for 45 new Boeing 737-800 series aircraft.

Three years later – in 2001, in the wake of the 9/11 attacks – Ryanair followed up with a new order for 155 more 737-800 aircraft at what was believed to be a substantial discount, with a further order of 100 aircraft coming two years later. The drip-feed of these highly efficient new aircraft into new bases and routes throughout Europe over the next eight years, combined with even greater focus on cutting costs and boosting ancillary revenues, meant that Ryanair's growth was unstoppable. By 2003 the airline was carrying more than 21m annually. Three years later, with EU expansion helping to further its reach, passenger numbers had doubled to over 42m.

The key ingredient remained the cost-cutting that allowed it to greatly undercut the fare prices offered by all of its competitors in every country in Europe. A simple analysis carried out by *Business & Finance* in July 2007 of two corresponding Ryanair and Aer Lingus 737 flights explained in detail how this worked for the two equivalent flights by the two airlines carrying 189 passengers out of Dublin. For starters, the fuel efficiency of Ryanair's brand new fleet was way ahead of Aer Lingus and most others, even down to the use of specially modified wingtips that increased fuel efficiency.

On the ground, Ryanair would check in its flight using just one person at one desk; Aer Lingus used two. Aer Lingus had at least one separate staff member boarding the flight. Ryanair had none – rather, this was done by flight attendants who would also have done light cleaning onboard the aircraft. Aer Lingus had five flight attendants, Ryanair had four. Aer Lingus had a pension, a sick pay scheme and paid the Dublin Airport Authority for staff parking; Ryanair provided none of those things. Ryanair staff were likely to be employed not by Ryanair but by a recruitment agency and, unlike in Aer Lingus, were entitled to no extra shift allowances for weekends, night shifts or early starts. Ryanair's ground operations workers were even expected to pay €288 for their own uniform.

So when Aer Lingus floated at €2.20 in 2006, no-one saw it coming – but O'Leary was in prime position to snap up what he saw as a bargain and the chance to create an Irish super-carrier. Sadly for O'Leary, that is not how European, Irish and British regulators viewed his audacious buyout plan and it was turned down on three occasions.

In 2012, as Ryanair launched yet another attempted takeover, the *Financial Times* branded its five-year pursuit of Aer Lingus as "a waste of time and effort" for both companies. The new bid was likely to mean months of legal fees and management distraction for both carriers, it said. "That might be indulged in boom times. In an age of austerity, it is an extravagance that needs to end," the column said. The EU Commission agreed.

But just why did the chief executive of Ryanair so badly want the much smaller Aer Lingus? Many analysts suggest it was just another step in Ryanair's pursuit of growth and total domination. It already had about 12% of the entire European aviation market. O'Leary had long and loudly targeted 100m passengers per annum for the airline. But he may have seen Aer Lingus, and its nine million passengers, as a shortcut to achieving that goal as well as adding new possibilities to what has been a very rigid business model.

Some analysts believed that Aer Lingus could provide him with a secondary brand in his stable that was closer in feel to EasyJet, which had made gains on Ryanair with its slightly more upmarket feel and routes into Europe's major airports. The fact that Ryanair itself has since directly targeted this more business-oriented market lends credence to the theory. Another theory is that O'Leary might have used Aer Lingus and its long-established transatlantic service as a testing ground for his long-rumoured expansion to the US. Buying Aer Lingus would give O'Leary US slots, infrastructure and invaluable transat-lantic expertise as well as an initial fleet of seven long-haul Airbus A330s. The cost of buying such a fleet – with new Airbus A330s likely to cost anywhere from €100m upwards – could be worth the purchase price of Aer Lingus alone.

20th May 1982. 80p (Incl. Tax)

BUSINESS AND FINANCE

TECHNOLOGY AND THE TOWN HALL

O'MALLEY— IN DEFENCE OF PRIVATE ENTERPRISE

- Apartment market still has sparkle
- Irish clothes for trendy Germans
- At the Irish Press a.g.m.

Left: Soon-to-be Haughey nemesis and Progressive Democrats founder Des O'Malley, 1982. His break with Fianna Fáil was a defining moment of the '80s, and the PDs pursued free markets and deregulation in several coalitions before being wiped out as the Celtic Tiger drew to a close.

Below: The tumultuous 1980s. Fine Gael's Garret FitzGerald dissolves the Dáil, 1982. There would be three elections in 18 months.

Pictured: packaging magnate Michael Smurfit on his feet in 1991, as Dermot Desmond watches on from the top table. Both had risen to amass money and influence in the previous decade.

Visionary ESB chairman and CEO Paddy Moriarty.

Jeremiah (Jerry) Dempsey, first general manager of Aer Lingus, the State airline founded in 1936.

David Kennedy was chief executive of Aer Lingus between 1974 and 1988, going on to become a prominent figure in national and international boardrooms.

Top: Current Smurfit Kappa CEO Tony Smurfit, his father Michael Smurfit and *Business & Finance* publisher Ian Hyland in 2017. **Left:** Michael Fingleton, pictured circa 1993, was one of the highest-profile bankers in the country via his Irish Nationwide Building Society.

Right: Express Dairies, Irish Sugar and Aer Lingus veteran Bernie Cahill. **Below:** Charles Haughey shares a cup of tea with prominent retailer Fergal Quinn and EEC Commissioner Peter Sutherland.

Dermot Desmond became a billionnaire via his National City Brokers stockbroking firm, his International Investment & Underwriting vehicle, and a wide gamut of investments – as well as driving the International Financial Services Centre in Dublin.

Top: Prominent car dealer – and later bestselling author – Bill Cullen. **Bottom:** Construction industry veteran George Sisk, a key figure in the growth of the 1859-founded Sisk Group.

Peter Sutherland in the mid-1990s, as World Trade Organisation director-general. Associated with Fine Gael, much of his work focused on trade liberalisation in the European and global economies.

Pictured: Soon-to-depart Taoiseach Albert Reynolds and Tony O'Reilly with much to discuss as they open the O'Reilly Hall at UCD in late 1994.

Pictured: Seán Quinn, 1988. The quarrying magnate became Ireland's richest man but his downfall would be ignominious as the Celtic Tiger collapsed.

Privatisation permutations

Ryanair is not the only airline that has wanted a piece of Aer Lingus. In May 2012, Middle Eastern giant Etihad bought a 3% stake in the airline, raising it to more than 4% as part of a strategy of buying stakes in airlines that can help feed traffic to its huge Abu Dhabi base. By now the Aer Lingus privatisation was already one of the longest-running sagas in Irish business, and its resolution would not be possible without the return of a key Aer Lingus figure: Willie Walsh.

After the failed management buyout in 2005 Walsh had swiftly found himself CEO of British Airways via Virgin Atlantic, rising to head up BA parent group International Airlines Group, or IAG. He had navigated significant challenges with characteristic resolve at BA: strikes, a hugely competitive and changing industry, a monumental crisis with the botched opening of Heathrow Terminal 5 in 2008, and the volcanic ash shutdown in 2010.

Walsh was one of three key figures piloting the merger with Spanish carrier Iberia in 2011, a £5bn deal to create a London- and Madrid-listed global giant that, at the time of writing, is the sixth largest in the world. Among the key advantages for both airlines was that BA would now gain access to Iberia's South American business, with North America similarly unlocked for the Spanish carrier.

In December 2014 Walsh made his second move for Aer Lingus, in €1.23bn and then €1.28bn bids rejected by the Irish airline. Early in the new year the Aer Lingus board finally agreed at €1.36bn, or €2.55 per share.

It had already been an eventful period for the airline, with the prominent Christoph Mueller's tenure as CEO being combined with roles at Tourism Ireland and An Post. By the time the IAG bid arrived Muller absented himself from the decision as he stood to gain from the sale – and was on his way to Malaysian Airlines, widely regarded as one of the toughest jobs in world aviation after the loss of two planes in separate disasters.

His replacement was Dubliner Stephen Kavanagh, who had joined the airline in 1988. Together with chairman Colm Barrington, intense months of activity followed as the complexities of the carrier's role were untangled: its valuable Heathrow slots, its jobs and pension scheme, concerns from government and tourism over access to the island, the opposition of Virgin Atlantic founder

Richard Branson, competition hurdles, and Ryanair's sore-thumb 29.8% shareholding. In May the government sold its 25% holding, followed by Ryanair's agreement in July – and by August 18th the matter was settled. "We'd like to welcome Aer Lingus into IAG," said Walsh, whose career had now come full-circle. "It will remain an iconic Irish brand with its base and management team in Ireland but will now grow as part of a strong, profitable airline group. This means new routes and more jobs benefiting customers, employees and the Irish economy and tourism."

A change of culture?

Ryanair also reached a crossroads. In March 2013 its share price jumped to its highest level in nearly six years after it announced a massive deal to buy 175 so-called Next Generation 737 aircraft from Boeing for $15.6bn. It was the US firm's largest ever order from a European airline and the largest ever order of anything by any Irish company. The plan was to boost Ryanair's fleet to 400 aircraft and allow it to grow traffic by about 5% a year, it said at the time. Aviation analysts were gushing in their praise. "Carlsberg doesn't do airlines, but if it did..." began Goodbody's morning briefing note the following day. "No debt, surging free cash-flow, a 10% dividend in sight, buybacks, and an amazing management. Thank you Ireland!" wrote Seeking Alpha.

But the positive sentiment did not last long. That August the UK Competition Commission confirmed its decision that Ryanair must cut its 29.8% stake in Aer Lingus to no more than 5%. The competition regulator said that Ryanair's minority shareholding had led or may be expected to lead to a substantial lessening of competition between airlines on routes between Britain and Ireland.

Aer Lingus had to bear the brunt of the investor reaction to the news and its share price fell nearly 4%. Worse was to follow for Ryanair. In September the airline was forced to issue a warning to the markets about its traffic target for the year, blaming increased price competition and the continuing effect of austerity across Europe. Investors long accustomed to nothing but bullish announcements from Ryanair reacted badly and its share price plunged despite the carrier's announcement that it was going to focus more on customer satisfaction.

November brought even worse news. Ryanair's share price tumbled the most in five years, down more than 12%, after it cut its forecast for full-year profits. Most other airlines could only dream of the sort of profit forecast that Ryanair had announced: it was predicting not a loss but full-year profits of around €510m. This was down from a previous forecast of between €570m and €600m.

Ryanair's culture had always been rigorously questioned by those who hated the notion that air travel had become little more than a bus service with passengers herded onboard tightly packed 737s and forced to grab whatever seat they could get – like it or lump it. Michael O'Leary revelled in churning out controversial ideas such as selling tickets for standing-room flights and charging to use the toilets.

But suddenly the figures seemed to be suggesting that this approach had reached its natural limit and that Ryanair needed to try something different. The airline was characteristically quick to react and made changes to or abandoned some of the things most despised by customers such as the lack of allocated seating, extra bag fees and exorbitant excess baggage fees.

O'Leary, who in the past had publicly given short shrift to individual customer complaints, also took to Twitter to answer questions from unhappy fliers. While it was hard to tell where a genuine desire to change ended and shameless spin began, it was a big step for a man who just a year earlier answered a customer complaint about boarding card fees by telling a newspaper the person was "stupid".

Ryanair may not have managed to take over Aer Lingus, but it was certainly starting to speak a bit like the former national airline once did with television adverts, hints at a business class product and a friendlier approach to travel agents. It all added up to an apparent major change of culture. Nevertheless, it is also something of an about-turn from some of the key cost-cutting and revenue-raising measures that analysts say made Ryanair the behemoth of the low-cost aviation sector that it is today.

Having pushed Ryanair beyond the 120m passengers per annum mark on which the airline had set its targets, it is likely to go down as one of the great corporate transformations of our times.

CHAPTER 13

Banking: boom, bubble and bust
By John Walsh

THE IRISH BANKING COLLAPSE WAS CAUSED BY A "MASSIVE INTELLECTUAL FAILURE",
IN THE WORDS OF ONE INSIDER – WITH SOCIETY LEFT TO PICK UP THE PIECES IN
A TASK THAT LINGERS ON AND ON.

AIB's 2001 annual general meeting was a pivotal moment in the formation
of the Irish financial and property bubble. The AIB management team, led
by chief executive Michael Buckley, faced a barrage of criticism from angry
shareholders. However, the widespread disaffection was not because of a
slump in profits, but rather the pedestrian pace of AIB's revenue growth
compared to Anglo Irish Bank.

Anglo was the *arriviste* of the Irish banking world. From very modest
beginnings in the late 1980s, by the early 2000s it had become a player
on the booming Irish property market. In January of 2005, when Seanie
Fitzpatrick stood down as CEO of Anglo Irish Bank and moved into the
position of chairman, profit before tax stood at €504 million, lending had
reached €24bn and lending for 2004 alone came in at €6.3bn, which was up
35% on the previous year.

The results had been nothing short of spectacular. Over a decade, the
bank went from gross assets of just £3.14bn (€4bn) in 1997 to €95bn by the
end of 2007. In 1997 it was worth just €250m. In 2007 it was worth €12.4bn,
ranking fourth on the stock exchange league table after AIB, CRH and Bank
of Ireland. For investors who were lucky enough to buy into Anglo early on
it was the stock exchange equivalent of winning the lottery, according to one
Dublin-based analyst. In 1997 it was possible to buy Anglo shares for just

81p (€1.03). In February 2007 they had climbed to €16.10 (€32.20 when the 2005 share split is taken into account). So anyone who bought 1,000 Anglo shares for €1,030 in 1997 would have shares worth €32,220 a decade later.

AIB shareholders wanted a piece of the action and soon they got it. Following the 2001 AGM, AIB would embrace property lending with abandon – a move that would have disastrous and costly consequences for the Irish taxpayer.

The Irish stock market breached the 10,000 barrier for the first time in its history in February 2007, fuelled in no small part by Irish financials. There were six domestic banks: AIB, Bank of Ireland, Anglo Irish Bank, Irish Nationwide, EBS and Irish Life and Permanent. There were also a number of foreign-owned banks, including Ulster Bank, Danske Bank, ACC/Rabobank and Bank of Scotland.

By 2015, Anglo Irish Bank and Irish Nationwide had been liquidated. EBS had been folded into AIB, which was 99.8% owned by the government following a €20.8bn bailout in 2011. Irish Life has been sold to the Canadian Great West LifeCo. Permanent TSB, which was 99.2% owned by the State, has been part-privatised.

Danske has closed down the bulk of its Irish operations. Bank of Scotland has pulled out of the Irish market, as has ACC. Despite questionmarks over the future of Ulster Bank for much of 2013 and 2014, Royal Bank of Scotland decided to keep it as part of its core operations following a review.

Responsibility for the collapse of the Irish banking system can be attributed to domestic and international factors alike. In the late 1990s, the chairman of the US Federal Reserve, Alan Greenspan, lowered interest rates to historic lows on fears that the Y2K 'millennium bug' would wreak havoc with the technology infrastructure.

Greenspan maintained a low interest rate policy in the early 2000s to counter the effects of the collapse of the internet bubble. Globalisation of financial services meant that cheap credit was sloshing through the arteries of the international banking system. The advent of the single currency accelerated capital flows through the eurozone. Much of this cheap credit was finding its way into the property market, not just in Ireland but in much of the EU and the US. Financial engineering was coming up with increasingly complex products such as asset-backed securities (ABS) and collateralised debt obligations (CDO). These products sliced and diced bank loans, particularly to the property sector, and repackaged them for investors, often with triple-A credit ratings regardless of the underlying quality of the assets. The aim was to spread risk throughout the market.

However, when the US property market started to falter in early 2008, the opaqueness of these complex financial products wreaked havoc across financial markets. Instead of spreading risk, it was impossible to discern which banks were carrying junk assets. There was a scramble to unwind positions. The interbank lending market dried up as banks became increasingly suspicious of each other's solvency.

Property overheats

Irish banks had, for the most part, shied away from the ABS and CDO markets. But they had become massively exposed to an overheating domestic property market. Moreover, during the 2000s Irish banks had become heavily reliant on the wholesale money markets to fund lending activities. When this funding line stopped suddenly following the collapse of Lehman Brothers on September 14th 2008, Irish banks were left in a perilous state.

The government introduced the State guarantee of the banking system on September 28th that year, providing unlimited cover for all depositors, senior bondholders and subordinated bondholders in Irish banks. In other words, the Irish government was now on the hook for roughly €400bn, which was three times the size of the country's GDP.

The rationale for the move was that Irish banks were finding it extremely hard to secure day-to-day funding. A radical and unprecedented move such as the State guarantee was needed to shore up confidence in the banking system and ensure that liquidity would come back into the sector.

Taoiseach Brian Cowen and Minister for Finance Brian Lenihan both said that they made that fateful decision because they accepted as bone fides the word of the chairmen and chief executives of the six Irish banks that they were facing a problem of liquidity, not solvency. As it has now transpired, the Irish banks were insolvent, and in the case of Anglo hopelessly insolvent.

In 2009 Lenihan, as finance minister, would set up the National Asset Management Agency (Nama). Ireland's bad bank would eventually pay just over €32bn for €74bn in property loans from the domestic banks. Combined losses at Anglo and Nationwide reached €35bn. Both banks were amalgamated and became the Irish Bank Resolution Corporation. In February 2013, IBRC was liquidated as part of a deal by the Irish government to refinance €27bn of promissory notes, which carried a €3.1bn repayment each year for ten years, with long-dated bonds that had an average maturity of 37.5 years.

Fallout

The State has taken legal action against a number of former banking executives. Anglo arranged a temporary €7.5bn loan from Irish Life and Permanent in September 2008 to make its own deposit base look much healthier than it was when the 2008 financial accounts were being prepared. Three banking executives, Willie McAteer, John Bowe and Denis Casey, were jailed for periods up to two years and nine months for their role in these transactions.

The businessman Seán Quinn had amassed a potentially explosive 25% stake in Anglo Irish Bank through a high-risk and high-leveraged investment instrument known as contracts for difference (CFD) in the years leading up to 2008. The unwinding of this CFD position threatened the future of the bank. Anglo arranged €451m in non-recourse loans for ten of the bank's biggest clients in the summer of 2008 to buy the bank's shares and thus enable Quinn to reduce his shareholding in the bank in an orderly manner.

Seán Fitzpatrick, CEO of Anglo Irish Bank from its inception in 1986 until 2005, was acquitted by the High Court in a case relating to the 'Maple Ten' in 2014, although Anglo executives Pat Whelan and Willie McAteer were found guilty.

There have been a number of reports into the banking crisis. The Nyberg Report, Regling and Watson Report, and the Honohan Report all preceded the Oireachtas Banking Inquiry. The three reports came to the same broad conclusions: a lax regulatory framework and an ineffective regulator, a concentration of risk in the property sector, poor risk management and corporate governance standards in the banks, groupthink in the media, and inappropriate fiscal policies that stoked a massive credit-fuelled bubble.

Between 2008 and 2011 there was a complete overhaul of the management teams across the domestic banking system. Eugene Sheehy stood down as chief executive of AIB in 2009. He appeared before the Banking Inquiry, along with former chairman Dermot Gleeson, in June of 2015. He apologised for his role in the economic crisis.

"I'm very sorry for what happened and my role in these events. I know a lot of people were let down and feel very angry – deservedly so [...] I take personal responsibility for my actions and omissions," said Sheehy.

"I agree with a description offered by a colleague who, reflecting on the crisis, described our approach as a massive intellectual failure. This failure led to the triumph of models, consensus and market pressure over experience and common sense."

Sheehy was replaced by Colm Doherty, who was chief executive of AIB from 2009 for one year. He was forced to resign amid political pressure. Doherty had been with the bank for a number of years prior to its nationalisation. He was replaced by David Duffy, who stayed with the bank between 2011 and 2015 when he left to take up a position as chief executive of Clydesdale Bank in the UK.

Richie Boucher took over at the helm of Bank of Ireland in 2009 following the resignation of Brian Goggin, with Francesca McDonagh in turn replacing Boucher in 2017. The bank had avoided majority State-ownership through private investment from Wilbur Ross and Fairfax, and the government retains a 14% stake.

At the time of writing there are a number of cases pending against Michael Fingleton, the former chief executive of Irish Nationwide, as well as a number of other directors with the bank: in legal as well as economic terms, the bailout saga lingers on.

CHAPTER 14

Turf wars: the Irish horse racing industry
By Ian Parker

ITS LEGENDARY JOCKEYS, OWNERS AND TRAINERS HAVE MADE IRELAND A PRIMARY PLAYER IN HORSE RACING – WHERE SPORT AND BUSINESS GO HAND IN HAND, AND EXTREME PERSONALITIES ARE TO BE FOUND.

The many-faceted entity that is Irish horse racing today is worth an estimated €1bn to the economy annually and employs approximately 16,000 people in its various sectors. The sport of horse racing exists in tandem with, and is heavily dependent upon, an enormously successful bloodstock industry that would simply not exist in its present form without the input of some of the key people whose exploits we will come to shortly.

But first, what exactly is horse racing? The immediate answer is that it is best understood as two sports, or at least two codes: National Hunt racing over jumps, where horses are bred principally for stamina and endurance; and racing on the flat, where the breeding emphasis is on speed. In crude terms, flat racing is where the money is, an international sport which, at the highest level, can deliver hugely lucrative returns to the owners of champion racehorses once these star performers are retired to the breeding shed.

Jumps racing, for its part, is a comparatively parochial affair with a strong following in Britain and Ireland – but very much the poor relation to the flat game in the other main racing jurisdictions apart from, perhaps, France. It is not unknown for those who train racehorses to compete in both codes, of course, and any history of modern Irish racing could only begin by discussing the man who achieved unprecedented success first as

National Hunt trainer and then as the flat trainer to whom all others must yield, the late Vincent O'Brien. Born in 1917 in Churchtown, Co Cork, O'Brien trained his first winner at Limerick Junction racecourse in 1943. His achievements in NH racing in the 15 or so years thereafter are the stuff of jumps racing legend and were only brought to a halt by his own decision to concentrate on the flat from the end of the 1950s onward.

Cottage Rake won the Gold Cup at Cheltenham on three successive occasions from 1948, Hatton's Grace won the Champion Hurdle at the same venue three times in a row (1949-51), while Knock Hard also lifted the Gold Cup in 1953.

Of all the many facts that can be cited as evidence of O'Brien's mastery of the art of training jumps horses, however, his extraordinary feat of winning the Aintree Grand National three years in a row with three different horses (Early Mist, 1953; Royal Tan, 1954; and Quare Times in 1955) is perhaps the most striking. A quick look at the list of winners of the world's most famous steeplechase in the first half of the 20th century reveals the names of just four horses trained in Ireland. So in the course of serially snatching the biggest and most prestigious prizes that NH racing had to offer in Britain from the late forties onwards, O'Brien was not merely announcing his own incipient pre-eminence among trainers but striking a blow for Irish racing in general, and setting a precedent for much that was to follow throughout the next half-century and beyond.

The defining difference between horses that run at the highest level on the flat and those over jumps is that the overwhelming majority of the latter are geldings, or castrated male horses. This fact alone accounts for the huge difference in financial implication of owning a Classic-winning colt on the flat versus even an all-time great jumps horse. Thus Anne, Duchess of Westminster was in no position to capitalise on the genes of her beloved Arkle once the finest steeplechaser of them all retired through injury in 1967, as the great gelding lacked the physical wherewithal to pass his qualities on to succeeding generations as a stallion.

For Vincent O'Brien, as the 1950s drew to a close, widening the scope of his ambition to include an assault on the upper echelons of flat racing necessarily meant attracting investment from wealthy owners outside

Ireland. Having already won the Irish Derby in 1953 with Chamier, O'Brien acquired five yearlings for American owner John McShain, one of which, Ballymoss, became his first true flat racing champion, numbering the Irish Derby and English St Leger in 1957, and the Prix de L'Arc de Triomphe at Longchamp in 1958 among an impressive haul of Group One wins.

O'Brien saddled his first of six Epsom Derby winners with Larkspur in 1962 for Raymond R Guest, US ambassador to Ireland from 1965 to 1968, but it was the win of Sir Ivor for the same owner in '68 that held the greater portent of things to come. Sir Ivor was American-bred, sent to Ireland to be trained by O'Brien, and the horse rewarded his connections' faith by also winning the 2,000 Guineas and Champion Stakes at Newmarket before rounding off his racing career with victory in the Washington DC International in the country of his birth.

Sir Ivor went on to become a highly successful and influential stallion in his own right but it was the 1968 purchase, on O'Brien's advice, of a Canadian-bred yearling by American businessman Charles Engelhard that proved instrumental in changing the course of racing and breeding history. Nijinsky was a son of Northern Dancer, champion North American racehorse of 1964 but as yet unproven as a stallion. Nijinsky's deeds on the racetrack in England and Ireland, from his two-year-old season in 1969 through his all-conquering campaign of 1970, singlehandedly secured Northern Dancer's reputation as a sire of champions while adding confirmation, if such were needed by this point, of his trainer's genius for the identification and handling of equine talent.

Nijinsky's capture of the elusive Triple Crown of British flat racing (2,000 Guineas over one mile, Epsom Derby over a mile and a half, and St Leger over a mile and three quarters) in 1970 was the first such since 1935 and has yet to be emulated almost half a century later. Nijinsky too proved an outstanding stallion, siring three subsequent Derby winners including Golden Fleece, which gave O'Brien the last of his six winners in the Epsom classic in 1982.

His racing achievements further emboldened O'Brien, along with his son-in-law and now business partner John Magnier, to mine the rich seam of American thoroughbred bloodstock through the acquisition of yearlings at the Keeneland Sales in Kentucky, most of them sired by Northern Dancer. Such an undertaking required capital, of course, and much of this was provided by Robert Sangster, the colourful Vernons Pools heir whose teaming up with O'Brien and Magnier laid the foundation for what later became Coolmore Stud.

For the racing public, however, O'Brien's most visible ally from the late sixties to the early 1980s was Lester Piggott. Arguably the finest of all flat jockeys, Piggott recorded four of his record-breaking nine victories in the Epsom Derby aboard horses trained at Ballydoyle. The taciturn Englishman followed his wins on Sir Ivor and Nijinsky with an unforgettable drive aboard Roberto in 1972 before steering The Minstrel to victory in Sangster's colours in 1977. While sporting the famous green and blue silks, Piggott also won the Prix de L'Arc at Longchamp in successive years (1977-78) aboard the remarkable O'Brien-trained Alleged. But from the late seventies onwards Sangster and Co's most furious battles were being fought not only on the racetrack but, increasingly, at the sales.

Bidding wars commence

The entry of oil-derived Arab money into the world of international bloodstock, largely from Dubai's Maktoum family as well as the Saudi Prince Khalid Abdullah, had a hugely inflationary effect on yearling prices. Through 1975-84 the original Coolmore Syndicate was at the very height of its powers on the track, with Sangster finishing as leading owner in the UK on five occasions. But the ever-escalating bidding wars with Sheikh Mohammed al Maktoum in particular were becoming strictly unwinnable. Sangster and his partners may have trumped the Sheikh's world-record purchase of the Northern Dancer yearling Snaafi Dancer for $10.2 million in 1982 with their own acquisition of Seattle Dancer for $13.1 million in 1984, but the campaign was becoming unsustainable.

The details of a couple of unofficial 'summit' meetings that Sheikh Mohammed held with Sangster, Magnier and O'Brien as well as the Niarchos family and others in 1985 have never been disclosed, but the result was a decline in prices at yearling sales in succeeding years. As the 1980s drew to a close the now-septuagenarian O'Brien's stable entered a period of gradual but perceptible decline as the decisive influence of Middle Eastern investment began to be reflected in the dominance of Sheikh Mohammed-backed trainers like Henry Cecil and Michael Stoute of the flat racing scene, particularly in the UK.

In 1987 Leopardstown racecourse inaugurated the Vincent O'Brien Gold Cup, a three-mile Grade One steeplechase run in February and conceived as an important stepping stone for horses thought good enough to contest the Gold Cup at Cheltenham a month later. Now firmly established on the Irish racing calendar as the Hennessy Gold Cup after that company took over the sponsorship in 1991, the race's original title was a fitting tribute to the man who achieved so much in the NH sphere, the branch of the sport perhaps closer to the hearts of the majority of this country's racing fans.

The winter game is undoubtedly attritional and dangerous, but in spite of this (and partly because of it) jumps racing's star horses and jockeys excite the interest of the Irish sporting public to an extent that their flat counterparts, with rare exceptions, struggle to match. The other element that gives the NH code's top performers the edge with the general public is familiarity.

While in flat racing a top Classic-winning colt will as likely as not be bundled off to stud at the end of his three-year-old season, many jumps-bred horses will not even see a racecourse until they are four or five years old. Thereafter, however, a horse with the talent to reach the top over hurdles or fences can, if also blessed with durability and the good fortune to remain relatively injury-free, race at a high level until its age becomes numbered in double digits and perhaps a year or two beyond.

In the affections and esteem of jump racing devotees there has always been an informal hierarchy that tends to place the best staying steeplechasers at the very top. Horses that truly excel in open company over hurdles such as the recent multiple Grade One-winning Champion Hurdler Hurricane Fly (trained by Willie Mullins) are usually kept over the smaller obstacles for the duration of their careers, particularly if they are adjudged physically unsuitable to tackling fences, but in general the preferred trajectory for a promising young jumper would see him start off over hurdles before progressing to the sterner jumping test as he reaches maturity. This historical bias betrays the rural, cross-country roots of

National Hunt, and for many jumps aficionados steeplechasing remains literally the name of the game.

Exceptions to the general norm regarding the differing career paths taken by flat- and NH-bred stock abound, of course, particularly in recent times as the National Hunt herd is increasingly infiltrated by stallions and broodmares with flat pedigrees. The history of NH racing is anyway littered with the names of top jumps horses bred to be useful – or even top-class – performers on the flat. Easily the best horse answering to the latter description is the mighty Istabraq, masterfully trained by Aidan O'Brien to win three Champion Hurdles (1998-2000) at Cheltenham having won the two-and-a-half mile novice race there in '97.

Acquired under ultimately poignant circumstances by JP McManus on the recommendation of the late John Durkan, Istabraq is a three-parts brother to the 1984 Epsom Derby winner Secreto. Although regally bred, the colt had been a little weak and immature while running as a three-year-old on the flat for John Gosden. Gelded and given time to grow into his frame, the horse developed into the classiest Champion Hurdler of the modern era, and only the intervention of a foot-and-mouth outbreak in 2001, which saw the cancellation of the Cheltenham Festival that year, denied Istabraq a likely historic fourth victory in the two-mile championship.

In the 1970s a much more extreme case, from a breeding standpoint, was the legendary three-time Aintree Grand National winner Red Rum. Bred to race over a mile, the Ginger McCain-trained bay famously gained his last win at Liverpool in 1977 at the age of 12 over the gruelling four-and-a-half mile trip. Rather less well-known is the fact that he won on his debut at the same racecourse ten years earlier over five furlongs. Although probably the most popular English-trained chaser of the 20th century, Red Rum was bred in Co Kilkenny, a reminder that the threads of racing and breeding in Britain and Ireland are so intertwined as to be inextricable.

With 26 racecourses between North and South (racing is administered on an all-Ireland basis) this country has more courses per capita than anywhere in the world. The Curragh in Co Kildare is the established home of Irish flat racing, with all Classics being decided there each year. Leopardstown is a globally recognised Group One track on the flat, with the Irish Champion

Stakes in early September one of the glittering prizes on the late-season itinerary of international flat racing. It is also a Grade One jumps track, with the four-day Christmas meeting at the Foxrock venue arguably the most prestigious jumps fixture of the year.

The other meeting contending for that status is the season-ending festival at Punchestown in late April/early May, an event whose steady growth in recent times has seen it blossom into a genuine celebration of jumps racing. Fairyhouse hosts the Irish Grand National on Easter Monday each year and hosts numerous Grade One races during the winter, while Navan and Naas provide high-class jumping fare throughout the core NH season. With all that said, however, a notional quest to locate the soul of Irish National Hunt racing would terminate not in Kildare, south Dublin or Co Meath but in a large field in deepest Gloucestershire.

The Cheltenham Festival in March now dominates the landscape of jumps racing on both sides of the Irish Sea to such an extent that for some it has a distorting effect on the rest of the National Hunt season. Be that as it may, the allure of the great meeting from an Irish point of view has been building for over seven decades, since the Cheltenham Gold Cup itself began to outgrow its original status as a Grand National trial in the post-war era.

Tom Dreaper will forever be synonymous with Cheltenham for his association with the horse who is still rated, by common consent, the greatest chaser in the history of National Hunt racing. Arkle's career in the middle years of the 1960s set an impossibly high benchmark for every staying chaser that has run in Britain or Ireland since. His record Timeform rating of 212 has never been seriously threatened although, remarkably, his stablemate and contemporary Flying Bolt holds the nearest rating of 210. Whether this is a reflection of the vagaries of the rating system, which is at all times more subjective than one is led to believe, is a matter for debate.

What is not in doubt is that Arkle's victories under his regular jockey Pat Taaffe – not just in Grade One events like the Cheltenham Gold Cup, which he won three times in a row from 1964, but in handicaps while conceding huge amounts of weight to top-class chasers in races like the Hennessy Gold Cup (1964 and '65) and Irish Grand National (1964) – give him an unanswerable claim to his spot at the very summit. His triumph in the Irish National in '64 was the fourth in an amazing sequence of seven consecutive wins in the race for his trainer. Dreaper won the race ten times in all, also winning the Gold Cup at Cheltenham with Prince Regent in 1946 and Fort Leney in '68. He achieved a total of 26 wins at the Cheltenham Festival in a stellar career before illness enforced a handover of responsibilities to his son Jim in 1972.

Great bloodlines

A feature of racing in Ireland is the prominence of a number of bloodlines, both human and equine: dynasties of overachievers who exert a disproportionate influence on the sport through succeeding generations. Dreaper's rivals among Irish National Hunt trainers throughout the prime of his career in the 1950s and sixties included Dan Moore, who saddled the great L'Escargot to win the Cheltenham Gold Cup in 1970 and Aintree Grand National in '75 before handing over training duties to his son Arthur that same year.

But it was another of Dreaper's colleagues from the training ranks whose surname resonates most loudly through to the present day. The late Paddy Mullins trained his first winner in 1953 and trained winners every year thereafter until his retirement in 2005. Although best known as a trainer of jumpers, two of his biggest wins came on the level, with Hurry Harriet claiming the English Champion Stakes at Newmarket in 1973 and, in an extraordinary late climax to the Kilkenny man's career, Vintage Tipple claimed the Irish St Leger at the Curragh under Frankie Dettori in 2003.

Mullins is best remembered, however, for his handling of the great mare Dawn Run, who won the Champion Hurdle at Cheltenham in 1984 and returned, under jockey Jonjo O'Neill, to win perhaps the most celebrated running of the Cheltenham Gold Cup in the race's history in 1986. In fighting back up the famous hill to get her head in front to prevail in a heartstopping finish against Wayward Lad and Forgive 'N' Forget, Dawn Run became the first and to date the only horse to win both the Champion Hurdle and Gold Cup. Her premature death in a race in France later that season was a blow to jumps racing in Ireland, and the country would go on to endure a thin time of it at the Cheltenham Festival for the next five or six years before a revival in fortunes in the early 1990s.

Mullins' son Tom took over the Doninga stables at Goresbridge upon Paddy's 2005 retirement but it is Tom's brother Willie who had already begun to match, and would in time threaten to surpass, their father's achievements as a trainer. Having taken out a licence to train in 1988, the strength of the former top amateur jockey's stable had been building steadily from the early nineties onwards when Florida Pearl became the stable's first superstar, following on from his win in the Cheltenham Bumper in 1997 to become arguably the best chaser not to win the Gold Cup in recent decades – winning a host of Grade One and other graded races both at home and in the UK in a lengthy career that culminated in a emotional fourth victory in the Irish Hennessy at Leopardstown on his final start in 2004.

Many a good NH trainer would count himself lucky to put one horse of Florida Pearl's quality through his hands, but the likeable chestnut's many victories were but a foretaste of what was to follow at Mullins' Closutton stable in Co Carlow. Hedgehunter claimed the Aintree Grand National in 2005 for owner Trevor Hemmings under Ruby Walsh, the best NH jockey of modern times, whose partnership with Mullins has been an incalculably important factor in the stable's ongoing success.

In 2009 Mikael D'Haguenet became Mullins' first Cheltenham Festival winner for owner Rich Ricci, the American financier whose decision to place virtually all of his horses, many very expensively acquired, at Closutton has yielded spectacular results in the years since. 2009 was also the year that mare Quevega claimed the first of her six consecutive wins in the David Nicholson Mares' hurdle at Cheltenham. That Mullins had the luxury of running a mare patently capable of contesting Grade Ones in open company mainly in races restricted to her own sex is an indication of the strength in depth at her trainer's disposal. Also, the management of the mare's career over such an extended period, and the longevity of the now-retired Hurricane Fly's tenure at the top of the hurdling division, are testament to Mullins' uncommonly sure touch with top-class horses.

In 2011 Mullins became the sole beneficiary of wealthy English owner Graham Wylie's dispersal of his powerful string upon the enforced ending of his association with the disgraced trainer Howard Johnson. So along with substantial support from Gigginstown Stud, owned by Ryanair boss Michael O'Leary – though they would part ways in 2016 – Mullins has for some time been in an unbeatably strong position to dominate Irish jumps racing, and his dozens of winners at the Cheltenham Festival tell their own story.

In flat racing, Aidan O'Brien has mirrored Mullins' recent success levels over jumps since the late 1990s. Crowned champion jumps trainer with the assistance of his now-wife Anne-Marie Crowley from her father Joe's Piltown base in the early-to-mid nineties, in 1996 O'Brien assumed the role once occupied by his illustrious namesake Vincent (no relation) as effectively private trainer to the Coolmore organisation at Ballydoyle in Co Tipperary. His record since Desert King won the Irish 2,000 Guineas in 1997 simply defies belief. Still in his 40s, O'Brien has trained over 250 Group One winners around the world.

The only basis for a grudging response to such an astonishing level of achievement is to point out that O'Brien has had more ammunition than anyone else to fire at the best races throughout his time in the job. While this is a harsh view, there is maybe some justice in it as the modern incarnation of Coolmore Stud, under the direction of John Magnier, makes even the original Sangster-backed syndicate from Vincent O'Brien's halcyon days as a trainer look underpowered by comparison. The strategy employed by Sangster, Magnier and O'Brien in the 1970s of selling champion colts on to syndicates to stand at stud proved enormously profitable for a time. However, it was Magnier's decision to have Coolmore standing its own stallions at its base in Fethard that laid the groundwork for what was to follow.

Fittingly, it was a son of Northern Dancer that helped propel Coolmore to its current position as a globally dominant bloodstock company. Sadler's Wells was a tough and classy Group One-winning performer on the track, winning the Group One Eclipse Stakes for Vincent O'Brien in 1984, but will be remembered chiefly for his exploits as a stallion. A very selective list of champions sired by Sadler's Wells could include 2002 Epsom Derby winner High Chaparral, French Derby and Prix de L'Arc winner Montjeu (trained by John Hammond), and the great stayer Yeats whose four consecutive wins in the Gold Cup at Royal Ascot from 2006 did so much to restore the prestige of that venerable race, but the most significant name of all is Galileo, the 2001 Epsom Derby winner who has taken on his late progenitor's mantle as the most successful stallion in the world.

Montjeu apart, all of the above were trained by Aidan O'Brien – but flat racing in Ireland is far from a one-man show, despite Ballydoyle's undoubted dominance. Dermot Weld, best known domestically for his annual assault on the marvellous Galway Races at Ballybrit, where he is perennially crowned top trainer, is perhaps the finest dual-purpose in the country at present. He is also the best modern inheritor of Vincent O'Brien's pioneering willingness to chase the biggest racing prizes overseas, sending Vintage Crop to Australia to become the first Northern hemisphere-trained horse to win the Melbourne Cup, in 1993, and repeating the trick with Media Puzzle in 2002.

In 2009 a half-brother to Galileo, Sea the Stars, ran up a sequence of six wins beginning with the 2,000 Guineas at Newmarket and finishing with victory at Longchamp in the Prix de L'Arc de Triomphe. Along the way the Epsom Derby and Irish Champion Stakes fell the way of the incomparable son of Cape Cross, whose campaign was guided with typically understated mastery by his trainer John Oxx.

Aidan O'Brien's one-time mentor, the veteran Wexford trainer Jim Bolger, meanwhile, has enjoyed enormous vindication in the last decade or so of his decision to invest early and often in the progeny of Galileo – chiefly with New Approach, who won the Epsom Derby in 2008, and with that horse's son Dawn Approach, who landed the 2013 2,000 Guineas at Newmarket in the Godolphin blue of Sheikh Mohammed.

Racing in Ireland today faces many challenges, not the least of which is the continuing struggle to receive a fair financial return from the off-course betting industry. Attendances at the less-glamorous midweek meetings have long been a matter of concern, as has the continuing decline in the on-course betting ring as so many punters' business has migrated online. The big festival meetings are still extremely successful, however, reflecting a similar pattern in the UK, and the sport can look to the future with relative confidence.

CHAPTER 15

The media: stability or turbulence?
By Ian Maleney

IN PRINT, ON THE AIRWAVES AND NOW ONLINE, THE IRISH MEDIA LANDSCAPE HAS CHANGED ENORMOUSLY IN THE PAST SIX DECADES OR SO – WITH THE PACE OF THAT CHANGE ONLY ACCELERATING IN RECENT YEARS.

Depending on how you look at it, the story of the media in Ireland since the end of the Second World War can be one of calm stability or constant and dramatic turbulence. Most of the major institutions that had been established by the middle of the last century are still around today, in one form or another. Of the four largest newspaper businesses in the country in 1950, three can still claim that status. The other has disintegrated entirely.

RTÉ continues to be the predominant force in Irish television and radio, as it has always been, despite the significant challenges it has faced in the last quarter of a century. Many new ventures have been established across a multitude of media markets, particularly since the 1980s, and almost as many have disappeared again. The arrival of the internet has led to previously unimaginable shifts in the habits of news and entertainment audiences, but many of the old guard have adapted reasonably well – if not without some painful readjustments – to this new paradigm.

Perhaps more than any other industry, the media reflects and informs the social and moral consciousness of its time. For that reason, the story of the media in Ireland is not simply one of business. Yes, there are many interesting and illuminating aspects to the financial side of this resource-hungry, semi-abstract business, but underneath the circulation numbers, underneath the never-ending search for capital and the vicissitudes of an ultra-competitive marketplace, lies something deeper and more telling.

National and local newspapers have for a century and a half provided the most detailed record we have of what the country thinks, what the country does and how the country feels. Radio brought music, drama and a sense of possibility to a people in dire need of it.

Television, from day one, has been seen, as John Bowman puts it, as "a window and a mirror" – allowing us to see out into the world, and at the same time to see ourselves reflected. What face we want to see in that mirror has been a question at the heart of the Irish media since its beginning. It has so often been through the media, from the front page of a paper to *The Late Late Show* to the headline on a website, that Ireland has discovered itself in the modern world, learned of its faults and its indiscretions, its corruptions, its successes, its glories. The media, underneath it all, is what gets us talking.

In 1931 Éamon de Valera founded *The Irish Press*, a newspaper with staunch republican leanings – a contrast to what he saw as the pro-British, pro-estab-lishment bias of the existing press. "The establishment of *The Irish Press* was as seismic an event, in its own way, as the birth of 2RN," noted the media historian, author and former senator John Horgan, referring to the first radio station in the State. "It was – and remained – unique in 20th century Ireland as the only national newspaper to have been established which had an overt relationship with a national political party."

However, it was De Valera himself, rather than the Fianna Fáil party, who was the controlling director of the company. Though the paper had no formal link to Fianna Fáil, de Valera could step in at any time with the power to assume any function associated with the management and control of the newspaper. "This was a sophisticated formula," writes Horgan. "Setting the paper at arm's length from the party in this way had two distinct advantages: it created at least a veneer of political independence, however transparent this might be in practice, and it protected the paper and its journalists from the type of constant interference by party committee which would have probably guaranteed its commercial ruin."

From the outset, *The Irish Press* competed strongly with the Independent Newspapers group, founded by William Martin Murphy in 1904 and operated for most of the century by his descendants. *The Irish Press* was based in Burgh Quay in Dublin, with its rivals just across the river on Middle Abbey Street. Between them they managed to reach a vast swathe of the Irish population, with the *Irish Independent* focused on a growing Catholic middle class and the *Press* generally seen more as a working class or farmers' paper. Though it was not particularly severe, this divide largely mirrored the split between Fine Gael and Fianna Fáil.

The period immediately after World War II was an important one for the Irish media. The newspapers had been heavily censored during the war, but with some semblance of economic and social normality returning in the years after 1945 paper circulation and journalistic activity improved. This time was, according to Horgan, the highpoint of conservatism in the *Irish Independent*, which was known as a particularly religious paper – the rosary was often said in the head office, with everyone kneeling before a rotating wooden statue of the Virgin Mary.

By the early fifties a new generation of younger journalists was emerging under editorial and management structures that had largely been in place since the early 1930s. Their youthful energy matched the frustrations of younger politicians who were beginning to grumble at the continued presence of their own moribund elders. Cabinet leaks, once an impropriety in a world of very cosy political journalism, were beginning to become more common, most notably in the 'Backbencher' column of *The Irish Times*' short-lived *Evening Mail* venture.

The appointment in 1951 of Benedict Kiely, a novelist, as literary editor of *The Irish Press* turned that paper into a haven for younger, more radical Irish writers including John Banville, Brendan Behan and Patrick Kavanagh. By 1953, the *Irish Independent* and *The Irish Press* were both selling around 200,000 copies a day, five or six times that of their nearest rivals. The biggest market was Sunday papers, with the *Sunday Independent* selling 395,507 copies a week and *The Sunday Press* 378,454. The *Evening Press* would launch in 1954, and would compete directly with the Independent group's *Evening Herald* in a frantic, news-hungry, sometimes bitter battle for the evening scoops.

The tug-of-war between the Independent group and the Press group was a long and turbulent one, a fight that did not end until the latter finally folded in 1995. As late as 1993, the then editor of *The Irish Press*, Hugh Lambert, could say that the *Independent* was "a successful expression of the callowness of modern Ireland – it's all about acquisition". The Press's attachment to its founding values – "to celebrate plain decent Irish living, [to be] a paper of the plain people, of the farm- or factory-worker", as Lambert said – would ultimately leave it struggling to survive in a rapidly changing Ireland.

Independent Newspapers would suffer no such problems. The group was run by the Murphy and Chance families for almost three-quarters of a century, but when change came it came quickly. Though the ultimate change of ownership came in 1973, with businessman Tony O'Reilly acquiring control of the group from chairman TV Murphy, some lesser-known figures also played an important part in modernising an ageing, albeit successful, business.

The first was Bartle Pitcher, who joined the company in 1958, when its business practices were described as 'Edwardian', and rose to become general manager ten years later. He oversaw the first acquisition of a new title by the group in 1967-68, acquiring the *Drogheda Independent* for £40,000. There was Vinnie Doyle, who started at *The Irish Press* in 1958 before eventually becoming editor of the *Irish Independent* in 1981. Doyle headed the title for 24 years, taking it from what he recalled as a paper "steeped in tradition and staffed by righteous men, many of whom were slaves to what had been politically correct in the fifties", through to the internet age. The final part of the puzzle was Joe Hayes, a former brand manager from the cigarette industry, who joined Independent Newspapers in 1978 and immediately set about modernising its marketing strategies with such success that no competitor could ignore it. As Michael Brophy, former editor of *The Star* would recall, "Joe has had an impact on the newspaper industry greater than any other single person".

Tony O'Reilly was a young Irish businessman and former rugby star who had launched the Kerrygold brand and climbed the corporate ladder with Heinz, the American food giant. Under O'Reilly's stewardship Independent Newspapers would gradually expand its operations outwards from Middle Abbey Street, first taking control of regional papers all along the eastern seaboard, as well as the well-respected *Kerryman*. By the 1980s the organisation had begun to spread abroad, acquiring large and profitable media businesses in Australia, New Zealand, India and the UK. By 2008 it was active in 22 countries on four continents, owning over 200 print titles, more than 130 radio stations and over 100 commercial websites. It holds a 50% stake in the *Irish Daily Star*, and ran *The Sunday Tribune* for 18 years before its closure in 2011.

Over the years its interests have expanded into outdoor advertising space and digital communication networks, highlighting the globalised diversification of the company in search of new markets. The company was extremely profitable during the time of O'Reilly's expansion, paying out an average dividend of €14 million a year in the decade leading up to 2006, and a record €30m in 2007. O'Reilly and his sons reduced their stake in the company in recent years, and have been succeeded as a controlling interest by Denis O'Brien.

Independent News and Media's transition from the 'Edwardian' practices of the 1950s and 1960s into one of the largest media companies in the world has not been achieved without strife. In 2004 the company moved its headquarters in Dublin from Middle Abbey Street to Talbot Street, and shed over 200 jobs in the process. Of the 360 jobs that remained in 2012 half were journalists; many of the former clerical and production staff were let go and their duties either shared among the remaining staff or outsourced entirely.

While the other major newspapers in Ireland have seen some changes, none have experienced the kind of expansion that INM has pursued. *The Irish Times'* restructuring as a trust in 1974 has allowed it to weather many financial storms by re-investing the paper's (sometimes rare) profits back into the business, though its expensive investments in property websites – seen as a way of offsetting the loss of traditional real estate classifieds – have not been so successful. The 2013 receivership of Thomas Crosbie Holdings, which had run the *Examiner* in Cork for 170 years, led to the foundation of a new Crosbie family company, Landmark Media Investments, which took control of the paper and many of its other media interests.

The Irish Press group remained in the hands of the de Valera family right up until its closure in 1995, though it survived until then thanks only to the investment of £5m by the American newspaper magnate Ralph Ingersoll in 1989. The group had fallen desperately behind in the decade leading up to this investment, needing new presses (a huge investment) and a modern approach to marketing that it didn't possess. An attempt to transition from broadsheet to tabloid in 1988 was a disaster, and many of the group's auxiliary papers and freesheets had to be closed down. The circulation of *The Irish Press* fell from a high of 104,000 in 1981 – a year characterised by much intrigue and excitement around the leadership of Fianna Fáil – to just under 66,000 in 1989.

The increasingly powerful position held by INM (which controlled 51% of the market in 1990), as well as the injection of so much fresh blood and fresh capital into the Irish market in the 1980s – particularly through the brash and hugely successful new voice of the *Sunday World*, also owned by the Independent group – left the Press out of touch and struggling to connect with its former readership. In a situation described as "one of the most competitive newspaper markets in the world" by former Press employee and subsequent founder-editor of *The Sunday Business Post* Damien Kiberd, *The Irish Press* was falling between stools. "If you don't deliver the ABC1 reader at an effective cost per thousand to the advertiser, you can't create the argument that enables you to sell ads," said Kiberd in 1993. "That's where *The Irish Press* and the *Evening Press* and *The Sunday Press* have fallen down in their battle with Independent Newspapers." By the end of 1994 things had got so bad that INM were considering taking over the Press, but a combination of the Competition Authority and a breakdown in worker relations at the under-pressure group eventually scuppered all hopes of any deals, and the paper closed in 1995.

The small screen

The first broadcast on Teilifís Éireann on New Year's Eve 1961 must go down as one of the most important events in the history of Irish media. A decade of behind-the-scenes negotiations between governments and civil servants had gone into the establishment of the public service broadcaster, and as many as 15 proposals to establish a private broadcaster were eventually rebuffed. As with 2RN, the country's first national radio station, the new broadcaster was expected to need as little financial support from the State as possible, and was set up – unlike the BBC – to sell advertising and pursue commercial opportunities from the beginning.

The context provided by the BBC is important in this story. For many years before the introduction of Teilifís Éireann, a significant portion of the population had been able to tune in to BBC and ITV programmes coming from the UK. This exposure, mostly for people on the east coast and near the

Border, had the effect of heightening expectations for the nascent indigenous service. As one viewer informed the journalist Norris Davidson while waiting for the new channel's first pictures to emerge, Teilifís Éireann's test card was not as good as the BBC's.

"In other countries a newly launched television service was expected to offer a two- or three-hour schedule each night," writes John Bowman in his history of RTÉ, *Window And Mirror*. "But the Irish case was different: much of the country was in the multi-channel area with competition from arguably the best television anywhere." If the new channel was to succeed, it would have to operate "beyond its resources" right from the start. Those resources were stretched significantly by the live televised visit of John F Kennedy in 1963, which stands as one of the station's first major achievements – RTÉ footage was viewed the world over.

The station's early days were marked by a strange mix of penny-pinching experimentalism. As well as securing various American and BBC programmes, which were cheaper to broadcast than native productions, the station was soon producing weekly teleplays, with respected English theatre producer Hilton Edwards somewhat reluctantly at the head of that department. The station in general was run by Edward J Roth, a young and inexperienced American who had successfully applied to be the first director general of the combined radio and television service.

In fact, despite the regular worries of the political and religious establishments about the decadent and immoral influence of foreign television, many of the station's key early figures came from abroad. Michael Barry, a hugely experienced producer and former head of drama at the BBC, was the first head of programmes. His successor was Gunnar Rugheimer, a Swedish man with a colourful past described by John Bowman as "not only combative, but also innovative, energetic, experimental and highly successful". He head-hunted Gay Byrne to present *The Late Late Show*, and his current affairs programme *Division* was the first to feature political party spokespeople. Rugheimer would later bring the hit show *Dallas* to the BBC.

One of the most important facets of RTÉ's formation was its structure of governance. The broadcaster was conceived as being entirely separate from any government department, overseen instead by an elected authority. This independence marked a significant shift from the earlier policy with 2RN, and allowed the broadcaster a certain degree of resistance against the pressures of church and state. The public broadcast was, for the first time, outside of direct state control.

Some problems did inevitably arise, not least on the *Late Late*, which regularly courted controversy by pushing the envelope of what was up for discussion. More than any other programme, *The Late Late Show* in its early years caught and expanded the mood of the nation. As Tom Inglis wrote in his book *Moral Monopoly*, television had introduced "a constant advocacy for an individualist, consumerist, sexualised, urban lifestyle that broke the unquestioning 'respect for the cloth', and has forced the church into giving a public account of itself". At a time when as many as one in eight boys sitting the Leaving Cert were entering the priesthood and the power of the Catholic church was near-total, the *Late Late*'s regular delving into religion, sex and politics, combined with the unwavering moral centre of its immensely popular presenter, made for an unmissable weekly event.

Other incidents were more difficult to contain. The publication of *Sit Down and Be Counted*, an excoriating account of the station's faults by three recently resigned producers, exposed the inner workings of RTÉ for the first time and turned its balance between home-grown and foreign-bought productions into a political football. Ambitious but aborted attempts by RTÉ journalists to enter north Vietnam and the breakaway state of Biafra in the late 1960s drew attention to the broadcaster's investigative journalism, or lack thereof. Both attempts collapsed under government pressure. An investigation by the *7 Days* programme into moneylending in Dublin proved highly embarrassing for the government and An Garda Siochána, with a 51-day tribunal being established not to examine the moneylending, but rather the making of the documentary. Even though the journalists were largely vindicated, the episode had a chilling effect on future investigations.

Perhaps the most politically important incident of all occurred in Derry in 1968, when a peaceful civil rights march was set upon by baton-wielding RUC officers. "Inspired by Martin Luther King's tactics in the United States, the movement had held earlier marches that summer without making much impact," writes Bowman of the incident. "It was the police response on this occasion and the fact that it had been captured by television which made the difference. Most especially it was the news film taken by Gay O'Brien of RTÉ which proved most dramatic, 'capturing the chaos and the fury of the baton charge close up'. It was the circulation and worldwide impact of this film footage which dramatised for millions of television viewers across the world 'that something was very wrong in Northern Ireland'."

This event was a starting gun for what would later be known as the Troubles, a conflict that would have far-reaching consequences for the media in Ireland. In October 1971 Gerry Collins, Minister for Posts and Telegraphs, issued a directive under Section 31 ordering RTÉ to "refrain from broadcasting any matter that could be calculated to promote the aims and activities of any organisation which engages in, promotes, encourages or advocates the attainment of any particular objective by violent means". The RTÉ Authority complained that the order was too vague but the minister refused to clarify his wording, claiming that it spoke for itself. Following repeated attempts by journalists to test this order, including the verbatim reading of an interview with an IRA member on television, the authority was sacked by Jack Lynch's government in November 1972. Section 31 remained in force until 1994, depriving RTÉ – and, by extension, the public record – of much important information from a pivotal time in the history of the State.

Meanwhile, RTÉ, despite being a public broadcaster, has never been free from the pressure of commercial activity. While it has been somewhat insulated from the priority to operate at a profit, it has always been dependent on advertising revenue to survive. Never was this clearer than during Ray Burke's time as minister for communications. Burke was a key figure in attempting to open up the broadcasting space to private initiative, typically at the financial expense of RTÉ. Even without domestic competition RTÉ had, like all other Irish media, a significant competitor in the form of British television, which has been widely available in Ireland for many years. The impact of this competition, somewhat hidden and unofficial, has been, in John Horgan's words, "intense".

Fianna Fáil, of which Burke was a member, had promised commercial radio to its supporters as far back as 1981, and RTÉ spent much of the 1980s anticipating its arrival. This preparation took the form of a thorough analysis of its financial standing, which eventually led to major management changes as well as the shedding of 320 jobs. This strategy worked. By 1987 the station had doubled its profits. In 1988, having lost over 200 staff, RTÉ's share of multi-channel viewers had increased by 14%. Television had been turned around, but lacking the finance to pursue capital investment, and lacking any solid backing from the ever-changing government, radio was proving a more difficult beast. At the time of Burke becoming minister in 1987, RTÉ had another problem: pirate radio.

By the end of the 1980s pirate radio was big business. The biggest stations, Sunshine and Q102, had audiences outnumbering RTÉ's own Radio 2. In the Border counties, pirates were claiming huge numbers of Northern Irish listeners and advertisers. To deal with their increased presence, and acknowledging that they were not likely to disappear any time soon, Burke set out a plan to enable the establishment of commercial radio for the first time. As Horgan notes, there were 13 applications for the two available Dublin licences and 72 for the 24 provincial ones. Dublin-based Capital Radio, which was later renamed FM104, was the first to go on-air, in July 1989.

A little later a franchise for a national commercial station was awarded to Century Radio, the first station to be licensed as a direct competitor for RTÉ on a national basis. This, according to Horgan, appeared to be a personal initiative by the minister for communications, and was not originally part of the plan at all. The launch of Century was more difficult than envisaged as it struggled to raise its profile without well-known presenters, and so struggled to attract the necessary advertising revenue.

Horgan recounts that it was at this point that the minister intervened most dramatically, with a proposal that RTÉ's second radio service "should become a cultural and educational service (thus leaving the popular music field completely at the disposal of the commercial sector), that up to a quarter of the licence fee should be diverted from RTÉ to support the public service obligations of the commercial channels, and that RTÉ advertising should be capped, thus diverting revenue from that source into the commercial sector". Needless to say, these proposals caused no end of controversy.

After a strike by radio workers the first two proposals were forgotten, but the third was enacted in 1990. The amount of advertising time on RTÉ was reduced by a quarter, and the revenue generated from advertising was capped at the amount generated by the licence fee. Given that the government controlled the cost of the licence fee, and showed little or no inclination to increase it, this meant that RTÉ's commercial capabilities were severely reduced.

Century eventually closed in 1991, unable to sustain itself on the 6% of the national audience it had captured, and in 2000 a tribunal found that Burke had received a £30,000 donation from Oliver Barry, one of Century's directors, during the establishment of the station. The tribunal also found that the minister had intervened repeatedly on the side of Century in disputes between it and the State broadcaster. The cap on RTÉ's advertising revenue was removed in 1993 after the election of a new Fianna Fáil-Labour government.

Denis O'Brien, these days the largest holder of Independent News and Media shares, was also involved in the early days of commercial radio, turning his local Dublin radio station 98FM into a major media empire. 98FM was one of very few of the initial radio licences to be successful, with O'Brien claiming in 1992 that only two of the new stations were actually making a profit. Now operating under the name Communicorp, O'Brien's stable includes all of Ireland's independent national stations – most notably Today FM and Newstalk – as well as some smaller regional stations. Communicorp is also active outside of Ireland, operating a variety of stations in the UK and Bulgaria. One of the last remaining major pirates, the alternative music station Phantom FM, went legal in 2003 and eventually became TXFM, which was part-owned by Communicorp before folding in 2016.

The story of commercial television in Ireland is perhaps less complex, but just as fraught with failure. The eventual establishment of TV3 came about after a decade of struggle, and several changes of ownership and direction. Since its establishment by Canadian company Canwest and a consortium made up of Windmill Lane Productions and Paul McGuinness, it has changed hands several times. At the time of writing it is owned by Liberty Global, the world's largest international cable company, and operated through Virgin Media.

In recent years it has launched a second channel, called 3E, to expand its entertainment coverage and has made more significant moves into sports broadcasting, challenging RTÉ for the rights to international tournaments like the Six Nations, the Rugby World Cup and the UEFA European Championships.

UTV Ireland was established in January 2015 and its schedule included some high-profile presenters like Pat Kenny and Chris Donoghue, alongside popular soaps like *Coronation Street* and. The station was purchased by ITV, and then Virgin Media before being rebranded as "female-focused" be3.

Going digital

Irish newspapers have now spent over two decades online, with *The Irish Times* the first major paper to establish a digital presence, in 1994. Despite this time online, it's still difficult to say what effect the transition, or part-transition at least, to digital has had on Irish media. All of the major papers operate busy websites, and most have dedicated mobile applications. The most significant shift has perhaps been the emergence of new digital-native players in the media scene, with outlets like Distilled Media group, headed up by TheJournal.ie, and former *Magill* editor John Ryan's Broadsheet.ie, "a satirical news and pop-culture source", cornering large parts of a more casual, socially-networked market.

The internet has also forced a change in how news is distributed. Gradually the power of the long-established physical distribution networks has been eroded, and social networks and aggregator sites like Reddit have largely taken its place. This has greatly changed the pace and style of how a media organisation operates. Back in 1993 Conor Brady, then editor of *The Irish Times*, suggested that "the future of serious newspapers like ourselves lies in analysis and in offering the readers a deeper comprehension of the events that swirl around them. The future is in investigation and in good descriptive writing rather than presenting people with a huge amalgam of nuggets of news."

Almost a quarter of a century later, Brady has largely been proven right – though the reality is perhaps less positive than he would have hoped. While the expensive work of reporting news is still important, particularly for legacy media like the major newspapers, such news is rarely, if ever, profitable. It doesn't matter as much now if you publish a story first; what matters is where a story is first seen – a value shift from the production of news to its distribution.

This has combined with an ever-greater focus on analysis and opinion, with the value of comment-generating columnists higher than ever.

The downward pressure put on digital revenues over recent years as advertising models have shifted to extract more value for advertisers' money, as well as the loss to print revenues of almost all small-scale advertising, has had a deeply deleterious effect on most Irish media. Many now sell third-party advertising on their websites and apps, as well as engaging in "advertorial" – sponsored content that looks like journalism – in order to pay the bills. The previously intense pressures exerted by larger media organisations like the BBC have multiplied many times over; it is just as quick and easy to read the news on *The Guardian* or *New York Times* as it is to find it on a domestic source. *The Irish Times* has begun to operate a paywall, charging for access to more than ten articles a week. The *Irish Independent* has not yet gone down this route, hoping to achieve a critical mass of traffic to drive advertising. It is as yet unclear which of these strategies will be successful, or to what extent either will be.

RTÉ's online broadcasting output is centred mostly on the RTÉ Player, where its programmes are made available for viewing at any time on any device. Bowman writes that in 2010 Geraldine O'Leary, commercial director of RTÉ television, argued that RTÉ had to see its role changing from being a broadcaster to a content provider. Individuals could now choose where and when to watch content: "it might be mobile or the internet with the RTÉ Player – it's about making sure it's available. Rather than say technology is working against television, it's the reverse, it's actually working for us."

RTÉ now broadcasts many sports events and several TV shows live online, as well as making all its live radio available worldwide, and has made a portion of its archives available for free through the RTÉ Player. Much like the BBC and ITV, RTÉ has had to work around the fact that people using the online service may not possess a television, or a TV licence. Unlike the BBC, it has had to negotiate the placement of advertisements through its online channels: as with so many elements of the Irish media landscape as it moves from the traditional to the digital, that process is still ongoing.

CHAPTER 16

A farm and food future
By Ian Maleney

AS LOCAL CO-OPERATIVES TURNED INTO CORPORATE GIANTS AND FARMING TECHNIQUES WERE REVOLUTIONISED, THE IRISH COUNTRYSIDE MOVED A LONG WAY AWAY FROM ITS PASTORAL DE VALERA PAST.

The latter half of the 20th century was a time of dramatic change in Irish agriculture. A sector that had seen very little development in the previous three centuries underwent fundamental shifts in technology, organisation and orientation. In particular, the 20-year period between 1966 and 1986 utterly revolutionised Irish farming – and through it, Irish society more generally. The image of Ireland as a sleepy backwater full of unproductive farmers was completely discredited, as was the more kindly dream of the traditional farmstead as a locus of authentic Irish culture.

Farming became, during this pivotal period, a real business. Modern ideas around productivity, analysis, technology and finance have all become a central part of the average farmer's daily life, even as the struggle to make a living from farming has driven so many off the land entirely. For many farmers the stakes were higher, but so too were the potential returns.

The Anglo-Irish Free Trade Area came into effect on January 1st 1966 and saw the end of many trade obstacles with Britain, then – as now – Ireland's most important trading partner. This was followed by Ireland joining the EEC in 1973, which brought money and expertise into the country at a previously unknown level. It is fair to say that no other single event in modern times has had a greater impact on the Irish farmer than accession to the EU.

The availability of a giant common market opened Ireland up to trade in a way not previously seen. Since joining the EU, the Irish farmer has more and more displayed an internationalist outlook, seeking opportunities on every continent of a globalised marketplace. The development of the traditional, farmer-owned dairy co-operatives into diversified agribusiness behemoths is just the most visible result of this change in attitude. That change echoes down to the most basic levels of how Irish farmers manage their land, their animals and their crops.

Today, the face of farming is very different than it was half a century ago, with higher levels of education and ever-increasing farm sizes becoming the norm. With a decreasing amount of people working the land, farming is more concentrated and far more tightly organised. Environmental awareness and stewardship are now important facets of the farmer's responsibilities. The image of the landscape as a rich, biodiverse and beautiful place is now very much a part of the branding and marketing for Irish produce, and an important one in charging a premium for that produce.

Thus, the contrast with the post-Emergency period is stark. During the war, food supply had been the primary concern and many farmers were encouraged to take up tillage in place of their more usual dairy and dry-stock enterprises. Farming at this time consisted mostly of gradually moving animals across the country, with cattle raised in the west and south finished in the "ranches" of the east midlands before being exported, on the hoof, from Dublin. It was a low-margin, low-tech business model that required little investment and offered few significant rewards for most farmers. Dairy farmers had it slightly better, as the drive for co-operative organisation that began in earnest around the beginning of the 20th century had proliferated widely. Dairy farmers were more organised, and they had more control over the processing and exporting of their product than livestock farmers.

The roots of the big changes in Irish agriculture in the 1960s were laid first by the co-operative movement. This farmer-led movement was joined by important organisations like Macra Na Feirme in 1944, the Irish Creamery Milk Suppliers' Association in 1950 and the National (later Irish) Farmers' Association in 1955. These, along with IAOS (now the Irish Co-Operative Organisation Society), were some of the most influential farming organisations in Ireland, and remain so today. John Feehan, one of Ireland's leading agricultural academics, has noted that important innovations in the period immediately after the Second World War included the introduction of artificial insemination in 1964, co-operative livestock auction marts in 1955 (replacing the traditional town square cattle fair, in spite of fierce opposition from cattle dealers) and co-operative pig fattening units in 1959.

Another important organisation was Bord Bainne, founded in 1960 and led by the young Tony O'Reilly, who would go on to become Ireland's first billionaire and one of the most successful businessmen of his generation. Bord Bainne operated as a central marketing organisation for Irish dairy products being offered for export, and flourished in the years directly after the Anglo-Irish Free Trade Agreement. "Although only 26 when he took the reins of Bord Bainne, O'Reilly quickly shaped it into a professionally managed, outward-looking, entrepreneurial organisation," writes James Kennelly in his book *The Kerry Way*. "With the advent of the Anglo-Irish Free Trade Agreement in 1965, the quota for Irish butter to the United Kingdom was increased dramatically, and Bord Bainne took advantage of this opening by marketing the first branded Irish butter to be exported, Kerrygold, which was to meet with considerable success."

The political background to these developments cannot be underestimated. The publication of the First Programme For Economic Expansion in 1958 was a watershed moment in Irish business, signalling a more open, more active, more dynamic approach from the government in how it wanted the Irish economy to function. One element of this programme was to encourage the rationalisation of Irish agriculture, particularly the creamery co-operatives, which were numerous (there were 606 separate creamery premises in Ireland in 1962) and often inefficient. IOAS announced its plans to pursue rationalisation between co-operatives, with a programme of amalgamations being put in place from 1966.

This strategy resulted in the formation of the so-called 'Big Five' co-operatives: Golden Vale, Avonmore, Waterford, Ballyclough and Mitchelstown. The federalised North Kerry Co-Operatives soon made this a Big Six by joining with the rest of the county and becoming Kerry Co-operative Creameries in 1974. The Kerry Co-op is a vital organisation in the history of Irish agriculture, with its rapid change and development over the last 45 years providing a telling example of the wider changes within Irish agriculture and agribusiness.

In 1971 North Kerry Co-Operatives had founded North Kerry Milk Products, a company part-owned by the co-operative alongside the Dairy Disposal Company (the State-owned dairy company) and Erie Casein Ltd, an American company that specialised in casein, a protein found in milk and used as a food ingredient. Together they opened a milk processing factory in Listowel, itself the culmination of over a decade of work by the head of the North Kerry Co-Op, Eddie Hayes. A young executive from Golden Vale, Denis Brosnan, was brought in to oversee the building of the factory and to run the company. Aged just 27, he began his work in a caravan on the building site with no phone and no staff, and began factory production only six months later, in June 1972.

Brosnan would lead the company's executive team through the tuber-culosis crises of the late 1970s, the 'Milk Wars' with Golden Vale in the early 1980s, and the rapid expansion of the company from the mid-1980s through to his retirement from the group in 2002. Kerry, in all its various formations from NKMP to today's Kerry Group, has been first through the gate at so many key junctures. It was the first to undergo the more rigorous testing for tuberculosis that formed part of the Bovine Disease Eradication Scheme, TB having decimated dairy herds in 1979 and cost Kerry 20% of its milk supply. It was the first co-op to diversify its core business after the destructive price wars with Golden Vale impacted on its balance sheet from 1982, the same time that the EU introduced milk quotas and called a halt to the unrestricted growth of the previous decade.

Kerry was also the first co-op to become a publicly listed company, listing on the stock market in 1986 as it sought more capital to further its expansion in the US and the UK in particular. The acquisition of

American food ingredient business Beatreme in 1988 for $130m – a sum greater than Kerry's own market capitalisation at the time – was the first significant fruit of this decision, and it marked a fundamental shift in terms of ambition and reach for an Irish agribusiness. In 15 years, a group of Kerry farmers had travelled from a caravan in a muddy car park outside Listowel to seal massive acquisitions in the World Trade Centre. The Kerry Group tested the limits of the Irish market sooner than any other company, and it was the first to fully grasp the opportunities available on the global stage.

The other big co-operatives were soon to follow in Kerry's footsteps. Golden Vale battled hard with Kerry for control of the south-west before going public in 1990, but its growth stagnated throughout the following decade and Kerry acquired the company in 2001. At that time, Kerry's share price was 21 times higher than its first listing, while Golden Vale's hadn't changed at all. Mitchelstown and Ballyclough merged to form Dairygold, which is still one of Ireland's biggest farmer-led co-operatives. Avonmore and Waterford also merged in 1997 after a long and sometimes fractious negotiation, and rebranded as Glanbia in 1999.

Both companies had seen impressive growth after their listings on the stock exchange in 1988. Between 1987 and 1993, employment at Avonmore rose from 1,381 to 6,219 and turnover grew from £263m to £1.129bn, with a far greater share of that income sourced from outside Ireland. A series of acquisitions in Irish meat and dairy, as well as growing operations in the UK and US, were paying off. The acquisition of a number of small cheese plants in the USA formed the basis of what is now Glanbia's market-leading US Cheese business. In 2016 Glanbia posted its seventh consecutive year of double-digit growth and it claims 12-13% share in the global sports nutrition market, which is estimated to be worth €10bn.

Perhaps the most important aspect of the Kerry Group's public floatation was the nature of its management structure, and the relationship between the original farmer-shareholders from the co-operative and the new investors. From the beginning of Kerry Co-Op in 1972 there had been a fruitful distance between the management and the shareholders. There was no doubt in anyone's mind that the co-op was to be run as a business. When the time came to list the Kerry Group, the initial share offering was for 20% of the new company, with the farmer-shareholders retaining 80% and, significantly, control of the company through their elected board. This was much the same as it had always been, but with one key difference: the transferral of shares in the co-op (which offer no return on capital) to shares in the group (which do) made many Kerry farmers millionaires overnight. It would be ten years before a need for increased capital investment would drive the farmers' share of the company below 51%. Today the co-op retains a 13.7% stake in the group, worth over €1.8bn.

Kennelly, in his book on the Kerry Group, highlights some of the questions that have dogged this transition from co-op to PLC — not just for the Kerry Group, but for Irish agriculture as a whole. "Not only were there economic business issues at stake, but serious and deep philosophical issues as well," he writes. "What was the prime obligation of a co-operative organisation? What were the uses of competition, and should co-operative organisations compete just as other business organisations do? Should co-operatives be limited to certain geographic territories, and to certain businesses? Kerry's actions had thrown these questions into very sharp relief, and the debate would rage on for years."

The cheque in the post

It's important to remember the key political milestones underpinning the rapid and radical development of Irish agriculture after 1960. The political drive towards EEC membership led by the Lemass and Lynch governments was a cornerstone of that decade's rationalisation and increased competitiveness. When EEC membership was attained, the Common Agricultural Policy gave Irish farmers access to an essentially unlimited market. A fundamental aspect of the CAP was guaranteed high prices for unlimited production, something that allowed agricultural productivity to increase without affecting the price in the way one would normally expect.

"Aid money poured into the country, with 81% of all funding received from Europe going to agriculture," says Ethel Crowley in her book *Land*

Matters. "The seventies was the most prosperous decade in the history of Irish agriculture, with real farm incomes doubling in 1978 compared to 1970."

According to Crowley, the CAP greatly influenced what farmers "produced, how they produced it, how much they produced and how much they earned for that produce. Peasant farming was to be discouraged and farmers were encouraged to be 'progressive' in their thinking. The rewards for those who were in a position to make this mental shift were enormous."

Crowley outlines the five main aims of the CAP as such: 1) To increase agricultural productivity by promoting technical progress and the best use of labour; 2) To ensure a fair standard of living for the farming community; 3) To stabilise markets; 4) To guarantee regular food supplies; 5) To ensure reasonable prices for consumers.

According to John Feehan, these aims combined with a greater scientific understanding of the processes underlying plant and animal husbandry in Ireland, increased mechanisation, and the increased use of fertilisers, pesticides and herbicides to drive Irish agriculture into a modern age. "The EEC's Common Agricultural Policy proved enormously successful in increasing the volumes of food and drink produced within Europe," writes Feehan in *Farming In Ireland*, "but was accompanied by unforeseen environmental, social and economic costs that have forced the dismantling and restructuring of the CAP to a more sustainable policy".

By 1987, Irish wheat farmers were getting a 51% higher price for their produce than the world average, while butter prices were 80% higher and beef prices 90% higher. Sugar-beet farmers were paid five times the going world rate for their sugar. This had a serious impact on food markets outside the EU, most notably in Africa and Asia, and was not sustainable from an economic point of view – it is a basic tenet of markets that prices and supply cannot continue to rise together forever. Also, a growing public awareness of the situation, which essentially amounted to massive subsidies for farmers at the cost of the taxpayer (and, in a less politically toxic way, the environment) was putting an increasing amount of pressure on politicians.

The first reform of the CAP in 1984 saw the introduction of quotas to restrict surpluses, which were becoming a serious problem particularly in dairy. The second reform of CAP in 1992 was more wide-reaching in that it attempted to tackle the impact of the EU's productivist approach to agriculture on the natural environment without affecting farm incomes or trade prices. These reforms, most visible in the long-running REPS scheme, attempted to offset the environmental impact of resource-intensive farming with a programme of grants to aid in the development of extensive, nature-aware farming. Land would be left empty for periods of the year, hedges would be re-sowed and maintained and certain areas would benefit from being 'specially protected areas', which meant that farmers would get grants for maintaining the land in a way beneficial to particular wildlife.

While REPS certainly helped to maintain farm incomes, it also furthered the split between intensive and extensive farming, with certain areas now more reliant than ever on what was essentially a form of farmer welfare. GLAS, the scheme that replaced REPS in 2015, has many of the same goals, being focused on grants for low-input, low-carbon farming that promotes biodiversity and environmental sustainability. Those productive farmers with enough land and significant margins could ignore REPS/GLAS entirely, and carry on much as they had been doing. Smaller farmers, particularly those in peripheral areas, have been assigned the role of stewards rather than farmers, and their numbers continue to decline dramatically.

"Between 1994 and 2001, farm numbers declined by almost 40,000, from 159,000 to 120,300," reports Crowley. "The number of farms of over 50ha remained static and those of under 20ha showed substantial decline." According to recent figures there are around 140,000 farmers in receipt of some form of payment from the Department of Agriculture today (with a little over 30,000 involved in the first rollout of GLAS), but it is estimated that some 60% of them are part-time. Among the part-time farmers, some 80% have a farm income below €20,000. Incomes are particularly low along the west coast, where farms are typically much smaller. Income disparity is likely to be further entrenched since the removal of milk quotas in 2015, which has allowed larger farmers – often through taking on a significant amount of debt – to rapidly expand their dairy production. What effect the removal of dairy quotas will have on the CAP's environmental aims remains to be seen.

Farming meets tourism

The success of Kerrygold cannot be forgotten: it was the first branded Irish butter sold to the export market, and its huge popularity at home and abroad is something that others have continually tried to recreate. A key part of the brand's success was its marketing as an Irish product, using the rolling green fields and pastoral lifestyle often associated with rural Ireland as a tool to attract customers. This strategy, and its attendant imagery, have been used time and time again in the decades since.

Bord Bia, the Irish State agency tasked with promoting sales of Irish food and horticulture both abroad and in Ireland itself, was created in 1994 as an amalgamation of Córas Beostoic agus Feola (the Irish Meat and Livestock Board) and the food promotion activities of the Irish Trade Board. It has attempted to build the image of Irish food as a premium product using the Bord Bia Quality Assurance Mark and marketing campaigns focused on Ireland's natural grasslands and coastlines. Bord Bia's success in this can be measured the fact that a RepTrak survey declared it to be "Ireland's most reputable organisation".

Though Bord Bia and Fáilte Ireland (the Irish Tourism Board) are in no way integrated, they share a common strategy of advertising Ireland to potential visitors and customers as a natural, wholesome and sometimes wild place. There is a great degree of sympathy between large-scale tourist initiatives, such as the construction of the Wild Atlantic Way tourist trail, and the marketing of Irish food products over the last ten years. Both seek to put a premium on the experience of Ireland and its food as a distinct tradition, with its roots literally in the soil and the sea.

This is particularly important for Irish food in a world with an ever-increasing focus on health, wellbeing and environmental sustainability, as well as growing concerns about obesity and lifestyle-related diseases. As Bord Bia's latest strategy document outlines, "the perception of Ireland in a marketplace that is placing a growing emphasis on how and where our food is produced remains strongly positive. Our grass-based production systems, our island status and our ocean wealth are key strengths that highlight our green credentials."

Despite this focus on green, sustainable food production, the take-up of organic farming in Ireland has been slow. Only 1.3% of farmers in Ireland are certified as organic, though the government has set a target of raising that to 5% by 2020 in its *Food Harvest 2020* document. There are perhaps two primary reasons for this slow take-up of organics: firstly, a lack of knowledge and advice available for those who wish to make the change, and secondly a lack of resources. Making the switch to organic production, even though it promises higher margins of return, has never been cheap. A 2002 study found the average investment required to be €357/ha for drystock farms, €949/ha on dairy farms and €253/ha on tillage farms, and incomes would naturally decrease during the conversion process. For smaller or part-time farmers, who might theoretically benefit most from such a change, it is a large risk to take.

The numbers are increasing though. As at February 2013 there were 1,639 organic operators in Ireland with over 52,000ha of land under organic production methods, which equates to just under 1.2% of our utilisable agricultural area. There were 981 organic dry-stock farms and 41,381 organic non-dairy cattle in Ireland, an increase of 19% in cattle farms and a 38% increase in cattle numbers since 2007. While Ireland is largely self-sufficient for organic meat, there are significant opportunities for export growth, particularly in central Europe. The development of organic dairy and tillage is at the heart of the State's current Organic Farming Action Plan.

It remains to be seen whether the intended growth of organic farming, which builds on the long-standing aims of Irish food producers to create value-added premium products, can be achieved in a marketplace that has typically rewarded intensive production techniques. The image of the small-scale organic producer is at odds with the efficient, mechanised farmer on a large-scale consolidated farm. As Bord Bia has pointed out, an awareness of where food originates and the methods of its production are becoming central components of consumer sentiment across Europe and elsewhere. If this continues, and if it is met with the same kinds of support that intensive farming has received, then we may see a significant growth in organic farming in this country over the coming years.

CHAPTER 17

The Evolution of Chambers of Commerce
By Susan McDermott, Chambers Ireland

FROM THEIR ROOTS IN THE 18TH CENTURY, CHAMBERS OF COMMERCE HAVE EVOLVED IN THEIR FOCUS, THEIR OFFERING AND THEIR OVERSEAS LINKS TO BUILD INFLUENCE NATIONALLY, LOCALLY AND IN EUROPE.

Chambers of Commerce in Ireland pre-date independence, with some individual chambers dating back as far as the 1780s and early 1800s: Dublin Chamber was founded in 1783, Waterford Chamber 1787, Limerick Chamber 1807 and Cork Chamber 1819. Chambers in major cities and towns generally have a rich, extensive individual history. The evolution of the network of chambers around the country since the 1950s can be traced through the prism of the national coordination body, Chambers Ireland.

The Association of Chambers of Commerce of the Irish Free State was founded in 1923 following Irish independence. Chambers in Ireland had previously been aligned to the UK and in the aftermath of independence the need for a national organisation for Irish chambers became clear. The legal entity continues today under the trading name of Chambers Ireland, which was introduced in 2005.

The organisation originally shared an office space with the Dublin Chamber of Commerce at Commercial Buildings on Dame Street in Dublin, a three-storey building that was demolished and replaced by the Central Bank of Ireland building in 1980, and then later at 7 Clare Street until moving to its own office premises on Merrion Square in the early 1990s. The original remit of the association was to "communicate the opinions of the chambers of commerce, separately or unitedly, to the government or to the various departments", "to petition the Oireachtas on any matter affecting trade, commerce, manufacture or shipping" and "to attain those advantages by united action which each chamber would have more difficulty in accomplishing in its separate capacity".

By the 1950s the remit of the organisation had not changed dramatically. The primary focus was to represent the interests of business across Ireland and communicate the opinions and concerns of the network to government. In 1952 the Chamber of Commerce *Journal* was launched to increase communication to chamber members on the work of the organisation. According to his research on chambers of commerce in the UK and Ireland, University of Cambridge Professor Robert Bennett notes that prior to the launch of the *Journal* the organisation had focused chiefly as a vehicle to organise meetings and exchange views.

From the 1950s and sixties onwards there was a new focus on the needs of each chamber and strengthening the network of chambers affiliated to the Association of Chambers. At the 1965 AGM much attention was paid to the image of the organisation and it was held that the "real strength of the association is measured by the yardstick as to how active the member chambers are in their own field". Attention was placed on whether inactive chambers should be allowed to remain part of the association: "If a local chamber is not prepared to take action in its own name for the redress of any commercial difficulties existing in its own sphere of influence then it is not entitled to call itself a chamber of commerce nor to be affiliated to this association."

An ongoing analysis of the strength of the chamber network was a constant discussion point for the organisation. For many reasons, the size and success of local chambers through history has fluctuated whether due to economic factors or the availability of volunteerism. Conversations and analysis of the activity of individual chambers, and those that had affiliated or disaffiliated, frequently took place at association AGMs as an assessment of the strength of the network. The accreditation system for chamber membership modernised with the organisation and from the mid-1990s a more stringent system was put in place so that local chambers had to achieve an accreditation stamp through meeting the relevant standards across various areas such as strategy to drive local economic development, capacity to research and represent concerns of local business to key decisionmakers, and commitment to developing strong links between business and education. The 1998 annual report references the accredited chamber network as "effectively a new business organisation in Ireland, founded on the strong tradition and voluntary commitment of business people to chambers of commerce". Increasingly Chambers Ireland took on a role of assisting capacity-building within the network and brand management as well as its traditional national lobbying role.

The organisation and the chamber network rebranded in 2005 and became known by its current trading name, Chambers Ireland. This re-launch included a uniform branding and logo for affiliated chambers. Rules for affiliation were updated to reflect the needs of the modern chamber network. Current rules for affiliation with Chambers Ireland include minimum membership requirements, appropriate organisation and governance structures, and ability to lobby, represent and communicate on behalf of members. Increasingly, individual chambers are also working collectively as regions, particularly to profile regional infrastructure needs.

Policy development and lobbying

The capacity of the organisation to develop policy and to engage in lobbying has grown dramatically since the 1950s. In its early years the Association of Chambers in Ireland focused its lobbying activities on a major submission to government on the annual budget. From the 1960s the development of policy positions and lobbying activity began to gather pace and since then the association has expanded the many ways in which it represents business at a national level.

The ability of the organisation to communicate its lobbying and policy work has also improved since the Chamber *Journal* was originally launched in 1952. It was re-launched in the early 1990s to improve the communications of the organisation at a national level and the magazine became known as *Inside Business* from the early 1990s. It became the most widely distributed business magazine in Ireland. The current Chambers Ireland magazine, *InBusiness*, is published quarterly and available to read in hard copy and digital versions. It is a combination of policy content from Chambers Ireland and the chamber network, and commercial features of interest to Irish business.

To improve network communications further and to showcase the annual work and achievements of the organisation, the first *Association Yearbook* was published in 1993 and has been published each year since. It is now known as the *InBusiness Yearbook* and is distributed across the chamber network and among corporate partners and patrons.

Certain key national policy issues have reoccurred frequently for the local chambers throughout recent decades – for example, increasing business costs, commercial rates, regional development, investment in infrastructure and local economic development are key policy issues that reflect the ongoing need for business to see progress and improvement in such areas.

The organisation also moved increasingly towards a focus on local government, and from the 1980s was developing policy positions on local government issues. Local authority structures and finances, the collection of commercial rates and how to improve local economic development have been ongoing and important issues for chamber members and an important policy area for the national organisation. Along with this, the need for government to invest in the infrastructure necessary for the local, regional and national economy to grow has been a continuous focus of policy development. A region cannot attract investment and businesses struggle to grow without the development of essential infrastructure such as transport links or facilitating the enablement of modern technology.

The evolution of the economy can be illustrated by comparison. For example, in 1982 some of the key policy issues being raised by the organisation were the cost to business of tax collection, aid to small industries by the IDA, the development of Sunday trading, as well as ongoing policy engagement with the European chambers and the International Chamber of Commerce (ICC). This developed, and by 1993 there was a greater focus on the need for a broader taxation base for local government as businesses were suffering due to increased commercial rates that were having a direct adverse economic impact on businesses' cost structures and hindering prospects for growth and employment.

While many policy issues reoccur as priorities, it is noteworthy that the economic and policy concerns of the organisation in 1998 do not differ significantly from those of the present, reflecting in part the cyclical nature of the economy. In 1998 the economy was in Celtic Tiger mode and growing rapidly; the economy today may not be booming at such a level but is growing steadily following a period of economic turmoil.

The Chambers of Commerce of Ireland's advice then was that the government consider the 'Celtic Squirrel' approach in planning for Ireland's future development: there should be investment in infrastructure – not just transport, but also IT and environmental protection works – "whilst simultaneously husbanding our resources, resisting inflationary pressures and restraining current expenditure".

In 2016 Chambers Ireland repeatedly called for investment in infrastructure, transport, housing, broadband and water, and also mirrored the call from 1998 that the competitiveness of Irish business must be protected. Then the challenge to competitiveness came from entering monetary union, whereas today the potential implications from Brexit and weak global demand pose a threat. The organisation continues to represent the concerns of business across the chamber network and as politics and the economy can be cyclical, so too are the issues that concern Irish business.

The physical presence of the chamber network ensures that policy development will reflect all regions of the country. The organisation has significantly increased its level of external representation in recent decades. Businesses rely on chambers to represent their policy needs at local, regional, national and international levels and to improve the environment in which business can operate in Ireland. In the 1970s and eighties the organisation represented the chamber network on several important national councils and committees – for example, the Irish Shippers Council or the Irish Trade Facilitation Committee (IREPO).

The increased policy output of the organisation reflects the increasing challenges for business in a globalised world. As trade has become more globalised and the modern Irish economy became a very open market operating within the eurozone and trading across the world, the policy remit of the organisation now reflects the reality of Irish business within a global context. As such, the organisation not only represents the chamber network on important national councils and committees where it inputs into domestic policy; it also represents the Irish chamber network at European and global levels.

International engagement

The association's engagement with Northern Irish chambers prior to the 1950s largely mirrored the level of political engagement as there was limited cross-Border dialogue in the early decades of partition. 1965 was the first time that an Irish Taoiseach met with the Prime Minister of Northern Ireland, when Seán Lemass travelled to Belfast to meet Terence O'Neill. Coinciding with political developments, the chambers in Ireland also identified opportunities to be gained from increased cooperation with Northern Ireland.

In 1964-65 the Dundalk Chamber arranged cross-Border trade talks between chambers of commerce in Belfast, Dublin, Dundalk and Newry. The objective was to explore "ways and means as to where cooperation can best be extended with the maximum beneficial results to both areas". The Association of Chambers was fully supportive of such work and acknowledged the "very pleasant climate being created which must hold out great potentialities for cooperation in the field of business, tourism, power and light, and industrial research in the years that lie ahead".

Since the 1960s the Irish chamber network continued to explore opportunities to develop such links. In 1967 the London Chamber of Commerce's Irish office visited members of Dublin and Limerick chambers to discuss mutual concerns.

At the same time the Association of Chambers of Commerce of Ireland wanted to strengthen ties with the Association of Chambers of Commerce in Britain and the Northern Ireland Chamber of Commerce to discuss a range of common concerns, particularly to discuss the approaching change to decimal coinage.

During the Troubles the business community was ahead of the political world in that trade continued across the Border and business owners were more willing to pursue practical areas for north-south cooperation throughout the late 1980s and early 1990s. The 1992 annual report highlights the increased cooperation between the business communities North and South, noting that "Chambers of Commerce Ireland and the Northern Ireland Chamber of Commerce and Industry received approval from government for activities under the Interreg Programme for a project to support the development of cross-Border linkages". This project became known as Chamberlink, a European Economic Interest Group (EIIG) established by the Chambers of Commerce of Ireland and by the Northern Ireland Chamber of Commerce in 1994. It received funding under Interreg 1 and both unionist-dominated and nationalist-dominated areas were included.

In 1998 the Chamber of Commerce Ireland and the Northern Ireland Chamber of Commerce and Industry worked closely under the umbrella of Chamberlink to unlock the potential that lies within the Belfast Agreement and "to encourage the very practical (and profitable) development of new structures and institutions which will facilitate trade on the island and for the island to grow".

This North-South relationship continued to evolve and develop in the post-agreement context, with many working relationships and joint initiatives between individual chambers along the Border. In January 2016 Chambers Ireland and the Northern Ireland Chamber of Commerce and Industry formally affiliated for the first time. In light of the Brexit vote in the UK, this affiliation between the two organisations has gained a new importance.

In 1958 the Permanent Conference of Chambers of Commerce and Industry of the EEC (CPCCI) was set up in Strasbourg, leading to a whole new range of direct contacts between the chambers of various countries across Europe. The Association of Chambers of Ireland joined the CPCCI in 1961 and continues to be an active member of the organisation now known as Eurochambres. The remit of the CPCCI was to tackle all questions raised by the expansion and construction of the EEC and to "try to arrive at a common position on various matters which are then submitted to the relevant department of the Commission of the European Communities".

The composition of chambers in continental Europe is very different to the Irish and British chamber organisations. European chambers are mostly institutions subject to public law, were set up by act of the public authorities, and there is a body of law specifically to govern them. By contrast, chambers in Ireland and the UK are private companies without direct government support.

Ireland joined the EEC in 1973 and at that year's association AGM voted to update the memorandum of association mandating it "to establish relations and to cooperate, federate, maintain communications with or become affiliated to business organisations or other bodies existing for similar objects whether in Ireland or elsewhere". This reflected the new European and global focus of the organisation.

The Association of Chambers formally joined the International Chamber of Commerce (ICC) in 1979. The need for greater links to chambers globally was becoming more important in a rapidly changing world: as far back as 1964 there were discussions about the steps necessary to establish a national committee of the ICC in Ireland and the importance of expanding the new relationship with a global body.

Chambers Ireland, through its membership of the ICC, provides the Irish chamber network with valuable information on areas of international policy such as trade finance, customs, intellectual property and cross-border dispute resolution. It also provides members with access to global communities specialising in the core elements of international trade.

With a long history of representing business interests in Ireland, chambers of commerce have made a significant contribution to the history of Irish business. The chamber network is currently Ireland's largest business network, with members affiliated from all across Ireland and with an on-the-ground presence in every major town and city.

The progress made throughout the 20th century by the organisation at national level and by chambers at local level has ensured that the term 'chamber of commerce' is well known in Ireland as offering strong representation on behalf of members and as an important networking opportunity for businesses to share ideas, exchange contacts and improve the business environment in which they operate.

CHAPTER 18

Boom-bust-boom: the Irish tech revolution
By Ed Micheau

THE TECH BUBBLE BURST MERCILESSLY JUST AFTER THE TURN OF THE MILLENNIUM, WRITES A FORMER BUSINESS & FINANCE MARKETS EDITOR – BUT TECH IN IRELAND WOULD HAVE ITS DAY.

March 10th, 2000. For many, the date is etched in the memory like a birthday or that anniversary reminder that you dare not forget. It was the date on which the Nasdaq Composite index reached the seemingly magical milestone of 5,408.62. The date that marked the peak of the spectacular dotcom boom and the beginning of the equally breathtaking dotcom crash. The date that personal fortunes, either real or imaginary on paper, began to evaporate.

Conventional wisdom has it that when the tipping point came there was no huge surprise; the real surprise was that it had taken so long. Between Q4 1998 and Q1 2000, the Nasdaq tripled in value and at peak, tech stocks – once the poor relation on Wall Street – accounted for more than one third of the value of all stocks in the US.

Not that everyone was partial to conventional wisdom. Spare a thought for the strategist from Warburg Dillion Read, who on the very day that Nasdaq was scaling what would prove to be its all-time peak, proclaimed to *The New York Times*: "I don't see the end in sight."

Blinded by the light of the so-called New Paradigm, the failure to see beyond the obvious had many historical parallels. A century and a half previously, Scottish writer Charles Mackay had written extensively on the history of popular follies in his book *Extraordinary Popular Delusions and the Madness of Crowds*. Perhaps we can be accused of hindsightism now, but as extraordinary popular delusions go, the dotcom crowd and advocates of the late 1990s suffered from a particularly virulent form of madness.

Out of a total of 450 initial public offerings (IPOs) in the US in 1999, the vast majority of which were internet- or technology-related, no fewer than 117 of the companies saw the valuation of their stock more than double on the first day of trading. The three highest IPO day-one gains of all time in the US were recorded within a year: Va Linux, soaring no less than 697% in value on day one, Globe.com up 606%, and Foundry Networks rising by 525% on its debut.

At the end of its first day of trading, Va Linux had risen from $30 to $239.25, in the process giving it a value of $4 billion, or approximately half the market capitalisation of Apple Computer, prompting the memorable headline in *The New York Times*: 'A tiny company with dim prospects goes public with a bang'.

Intoxicated on bubble inflation in the months prior, a series of books were published whose prognostications for the future direction of the Dow Jones index, fuelled by the technology new paradigm, were pitched at near biblical levels: *Dow 36,000*, *Dow 40,000*, and – not to be outdone – *Dow 100,000*.

Some years later James Glassman, author of *Dow 36,000* and subsequently an undersecretary of state for public diplomacy at the grace and favour of President George W Bush, remained unrepentant about his central thesis, stating that the Dow would dutifully pass the 36,000 threshold one day. A stopped clock, and all of that.

The above introduction is made by way of context: an international context. As a small open island economy emerging from the dark shadow of prolonged recessions, near financial insolvency and mass emigration throughout the 1980s, the following decade had seen stabilisation in the Irish economy and then, mid-way through the 1990s, a return of that illusive creature – economic growth.

In the period 1993-2000, gross domestic product per capita in the Republic of Ireland all but doubled to $28,921. As the original Celtic Tiger roared away, the economy rang out the old millennium with 8.4% GDP growth in 1999 and rang in the new one with a whopping 9.9% growth figure in 2000.

Given the openness of the economy – with a focus on exports and interaction with the wider world through trade and improved travel and telecommunications – it was hardly surprising that there would be a newfound receptiveness to fresh external ideas and trends. As one century ended, it seemed apt that new technologies and the potential therein would be embraced by a new generation of young entrepreneurs. Ireland would not remain immune from the dotcom mania. And with the economy roaring away, such a mindset was imbued with a new confidence and an increased appetite for risk.

That sense of the possible had more than percolated down to the environs of *Business & Finance* magazine, located as it was back then in No 50 Fitzwilliam Square. Amid the faded but beautiful Georgian grandeur of the square, Dublin 2 became something of a hotbed for a new popular concept: the 'tech start-up', as twentysomething and thirtysomething professionals discarded their ties and their suits and their safe and pensionable jobs and headed off to dotcom land.

Entrepreneurs and venture capitalists assembled at the Red Box for monthly sessions of First Tuesday, where an experienced guest speaker would give a pep talk that was then followed by a number of aspiring start-up principals who were each given three minutes to make a pitch for funding and support.

There was something very appropriate about the venue, a disused train station at the top of Harcourt Street: where once trains had helped drive the industrial revolution, everyone would now be transported to the brave new world of the 21st century via the information superhighway. Old was giving way to new as the business lexicon changed and adapted to the coming age of technology. Companies soon were categorised as New Economy or Old Economy.

Those companies in the New Economy space quickly found themselves being lovebombed by private equity and venture capital. It is probably fair to say now, again with hindsight, that some projects attracted seed investment even without a good business plan. Business plans based on a seemingly brilliant concept, but written down on the back on envelopes, were not entirely apocryphal.

A new wave of frontier Irish tech companies began to populate the business pages of *Business & Finance* and the financial press in the late 1990s – Aldiscon, Apion, Baltimore, CBT, Euristix, Iona, Riverdeep and Trintech to name but a few. An examination of *Business & Finance* backissues proves fascinating, chronicling the rise of technology as represented by increased coverage in the magazine.

The issue of November 11th 1999 typified the period. Fran Rooney, CEO of Baltimore Technologies, was the recipient of the Business Person of the Month award after Baltimore had successfully floated on Nasdaq in October, raised stg£106m and traded at $36 per share, or some 50% higher than its IPO launch price.

Elsewhere in the same issue it was noted that Cross Atlantic Capital Partners had invested £2m for a 20% stake in UCD campus company Nanomat, while ICC Venture Capital was injecting £2.1m into Limerick technology firm Aisling Microsystems. Meanwhile, the Nasdaq, which was expanding with the launch of a new pan-European market, broke the 3,000 mark in the US just 12 months after breaching the 2,000 level, and was sporting an eye-bulging price-earnings multiple of 50 plus.

The story of the rise and fall of Baltimore Technologies is well documented but worth touching on. Baltimore was expanding rapidly in 1999 and early 2000 through a combination of organic growth and a number of acquisitions as it expanded its core e-security solutions offering called Public Key Infra-structure (PKI).

It was Fran Rooney, perhaps, who captured the zeitgeist of the time most memorably when asked what his business philosophy was: "GBF: Get Big Fast," said Rooney. True to his philosophy, and funded by the stock market's runaway appetite for growth stocks, Baltimore made a couple of massive acquisitions including the stg£703.5m purchase of the UK-based Content Technologies Holdings in September 2000 in a deal that gave the Irish company access to 6,000 customers and 6m users around the world.

In the short term, the Get Big Fast philosophy appeared to be working. Such was the pace of development that by February 2000, the encryption software newcomer to the stock market had eclipsed the market capitalisation of Bank of Ireland, which had been in existence since 1783. There are few better examples of the New Economy v Old Economy split in Ireland than this moment.

In that same month, and although not officially disclosed, it was reported that Paine Webber had made a $20 million investment for 5% of the Dublin-based financial services company Enba, valuing it at $400m. A supplier of internet banking infrastructure, including a contract with the UK's first internet bank, First E, Enba by this stage had raised $55m in funding from the likes of CGU, Intel and Morgan Stanley, and was employing 240 people in Dublin.

New creatures, old dinosaurs

The technology revolution was producing new forms and new creatures, snapping away at the heels of the old dinosaurs. At press conferences, banks and media companies were peppered with questions such as "do you have an internet strategy, and if so what is it?" Those who had not appended an internet dimension were vulnerable to investors and media alike shying away from their story.

Old Economy stocks began to go out of fashion with the markets. When Philip Lynch, then CEO of IAWS, was announced on October 15th 1998 as the magazine's Business Person of the Month, the foods company had announced pre-tax profits of £26.2m on turnover of £675.3m for the year to July 31st 1998. Despite the solid performance, and the *B&F* accolade, the share price of IAWS had nevertheless almost halved in value to £1.60 per share since the beginning of the year as the trend to New Economy stocks began to take hold.

Others were more easily swayed and decided that if you can't beat them, you may as well join them. Eircom was a good example of this trend. Floated in July 1999, the old Telecom Éireann became Eircom, an old-fashioned telephone company in need of a good internet story. Over the period, Eircom would take a 51% stake in Ebeon, a technology company that developed commercial applications of digital technology for clients offering services or products over the internet and mobile phones. In 1999 it went a step further and established its own internal internet business named Rondomondo, an online publishing house. But just as the new empires were being assembled the music stopped. And in the immediate era post-March 10th 2000, the kites that flew highest fell the hardest to the ground.

Baltimore by this time had become large enough in value to enter the FTSE 100 index in London, and at peak scaled to a stratospheric market capitalisation in excess of $13 billion. Within months, over 90% of this valuation was wiped out.

The above is not designed to single out Rooney or Baltimore or any other of the local dotcoms and techs that were ultimately doomed to failure. Their reference here is rather to provide practical Irish examples of companies that were very much products of their time and place.

Indeed, Baltimore was emblematic of a wider global malaise: Ireland had become caught up in a global contagion of boom and bust. And in the crash there were no sacred cows. The example provided by Microsoft is instructive of the spectacular nature of those boom and bust days – and of the salient fact that even the giants of the industry were levelled. As the biggest beast in the jungle back in 1999, its stock climbed and soared to an all-time high of $118.75 on December 22nd 1999, or the equivalent today of $42.65 allowing for dividends and stock splits in the intervening period. Just under a year later, on December 20th 2000, Microsoft too had succumbed to the dotcom crash, plummeting to $15.06 in today's money – a fall of 64% in less than 12 months and a telling indication of the magnitude of the tech implosion.

Va Linux, the IPO record-breaker on prior-year earnings of a mere $84,000 and on revenues of $5.5m, would a year later be valued at $8.49 per share, down from over $200 per share. The aggregate impact was equally staggering. Between March 2000 and October 2002, US companies saw in excess of $5 trillion wiped off their valuations. Of the Irish technology companies referenced above – Aldiscon, Apion, Baltimore, CBT, Euristix, Iona, Riverdeep and Trintech – none survived as independent entities, either being sold or succumbing to the crash.

Enba would not engineer a revolution in the banking industry. In January 2001 Ebeon would have the dubious distinction of becoming the first large Dublin-based e-commerce business to collapse, with the loss of 170 jobs. Eircom's wider internet portfolio would unravel over the following months.

Not everyone was taken in by the hype of the era, it should be said. In November 1999, *Business & Finance*'s 'London Letter' sagely opined: "One day the tech bubble will overheat and crash, but for now it is running away." It is also worth noting that not all was lost. Some Irish entrepreneurs and shareholders were fortunate enough or smart enough to sell their companies before the crash.

The best example was the Belfast-based tech entrepreneur Gilbert Little and a close network of investors, who in the summer of 1999 – and two years after selling another company, Aldiscon, for £57m to Logica – sold Apion to Phone.com for $239m. Apion had been at the forefront of internet technology with its Wireless Application Protocol (WAP), which enabled mobile phones to access the internet and email. Enterprise Ireland, with an 8.5% stake in Apion, earned an estimated $20m from the deal.

In a separate twist of fate, Jim Mountjoy, one of the original co-founders of Baltimore Technologies, sold his Dún Laoghaire-based business Euristix to Fore Systems for £59m in February 1999 – the largest acquisition ever of an Irish tech company at that time. Mountjoy and co-founder Bryan Alton each netted $14.5m in the deal.

Trintech, which at one point in 2000 was valued at $4.5 billion after it had floated on the Nasdaq and the German Neuer Markt, was eventually sold for $93m in 2010. In one respect Trintech was both a victim and survivor of the dotcom crash, changing its business model in the post-crash period to develop new products in the area of financial governance and risk management, and yielding founder Cyril McGuire $27m on disposal.

Throughout the tech boom years, and in their aftermath, many of the down and out in the Old Economy simply continued getting on with the day-to-day job of building a business.

There are few better examples of the era than sales, marketing and support services conglomerate DCC, which as part of its 20th birthday celebrations released a presentation on its performance in this period. From April 1st 1994 to March 31st 2014 DCC grew revenues from stg£0.2 billion to £11.2 billion, operating profits from £18m to £208m, and produced free cashflow in the period of £2 billion. It is an extraordinary performance by any measure.

A subsequent historical irony was the position of the Irish banks, which although upstaged by the tech upstarts at the time, would themselves succumb to a different bubble and one of entirely different proportions at a domestic level.

Few remained untouched. Closer to home, and in keeping with the spirit of the times, *Business & Finance* also dabbled in the space with its iCommerce venture, which did not ultimately get off the ground. On a personal level, I packed my bags to go and work for internet company Digiserve, an online portal venture that did not fly due to a combination of factors – not least a prolonged hiatus in the rollout of high-speed broadband.

A decade and a half on from the peak and crash, there has been much conversation about whether the tech industry is once again back in or approaching bubble levels. John Kennedy, technology editor of *Business & Finance* from 1998 to 2002, and now editor of *Silicon Republic*, is better placed than most to provide contextualisation. "While many parallels can be drawn between the wild optimism pre-2000 and today, it is worth noting that established technology players like Apple, Microsoft, IBM, Oracle and SAP marched on almost oblivious to the carnage of the dotcom bubble bursting. It was business as usual.

"It is also worth noting that many countries didn't start receiving broadband until 2002 and you could argue that had the technology been around earlier some of the dotcoms might have survived. YouTube for example, which was founded in 2005 and bought a year later by Google for $1.6bn, wouldn't have stood a chance in a world of 56k dial-up modems."

On a broader level, the technology sector has the appearance of an accelerated form of corporate Darwinism. As one tech firm or concept goes bust, something superior or more adaptive quickly takes its place. The world goes on.

From an Ireland Inc perspective, the irony of the tale in recent years has been the remarkable resilience and development of the technology industry in Ireland *vis a vis* the overall economy. Despite what was arguably the worst financial and economic crash in the history of the State from late 2008 onwards, the tech industry here in Ireland not only held its own but has expanded significantly.

So although Ireland Inc was falling off a cliff in early 2009, the tech industry here was on the cusp of significant inward investment that is being sustained until the present day. The success of Ireland Inc and IDA Ireland in helping to attract this investment is borne out in figures supplied by the latter.

According to the IDA, 164 new international technology companies set up operations in the Republic in the period from January 1st 2009 until December 31st 2013. Included in this list are some of the best-known tech companies on the planet: Dropbox, LinkedIn, PayPal (Dundalk) and Twitter. In addition to new companies being established, 90 existing international technology companies expanded their operations here in the same period including Facebook, Google Ireland, IBM, Microsoft, Salesforce and SAP. In March 2014, Intel announced that it had invested $5 billion at its Leixlip operations over the previous three years, the single largest private investment in the history of the State.

That these levels of inward investment and expansion have occurred during a period when the global economy was badly hit by a financial crisis points to the enduring strength, continued development and growing importance of technology in a globalised world. That these levels of inward investment and expansion have occurred during a period when Ireland was close to bankruptcy points to the attractiveness of the State as an emerging technology hub with critical mass.

'The Silicon Valley of Europe' is how Brian Halligan, senior lecturer at Massachusetts Institute of Technology, describes Ireland. For Halligan it is not just an academic description, having put his money where his mouth is and located the company he co-founded, Hubspot, in the so-called Silicon Docks of the Grand Canal Dock area in Dublin. By the time of a 2014 study, 36,000 people in Ireland were employed by companies whose headquarters are on the west coast of the US.

While it must be acknowledged that tax is an important factor in the location of these businesses here in Ireland, there are other factors too including the benefits of critical mass, labour availability and so on. The

European Commission took a high-profile interest in Apple's Irish tax breaks, and it is an issue that needs to be clarified and sorted out, but the general subject of tax is really a subject for another day, in another chapter, in another book.

No less than other industries, the multinational composition of the technology industry in Ireland means it is exposed to international trends and mobility. But this is the same of all industries, no more and no less in the case of tech.

Intel, which employs around 4,500 people here, has been in Ireland since 1989. The roots are deep, and while its Irish operations must remain competitive, the ability of the Leixlip plant to outperform others in the Intel family has been a key factor in the ongoing levels of investment by the US multinational here. The multinational composition of the industry here throws down a challenge to indigenous players to produce the technology equivalent of world-class Irish multinational companies such as Glanbia, Kerry Group or Kingspan Group.

Statistical data is also supportive of the notion that technology is becoming increasingly embedded throughout the local economy. A report commissioned by cable operator UPC and carried out by research firm Amárach estimated the value of the Irish internet economy in 2014 to be in the order of €8.4 billion, or a not inconsiderable 5% of GDP. By 2016 that figure was 6%, with UPC having become Virgin Media in a high-profile transformation in the meantime.

The rise in the digital economy that we are currently witnessing is reflected by improvements in high-speed broadband penetration. With our corporation tax regime likely to come under continued scrutiny in the years ahead, gaining competitive advantages against our EU competitors is imperative. Unlike the dotcom era, the infrastructure of high-speed broadband is now almost in place to enable the digital economy to take off. In historical terms, it is not surprising that many of the revolutionaries of the late 1990s were subsumed by the revolution and that a new paradigm in economics did not hold sway.

But that isn't really the point. Bubbles are often more about the inherent goldrush mentality of the herd. They say more about the nature of greed than the industries they inflate. In many ways it is no longer an Us versus Them game; Old Economy v New Economy. To varying degrees, everyone in the economy is now tied up or in some way exposed to technology. The logic of the technology ideology of the late 1990s is still with us and is in many ways inescapable. And with the emergence of big data, the next-generation technological revolution has already begun. That such a seachange is already upon us is evidenced by Microsoft's change of direction from a 'products and services' company to one focusing on being 'cloud first, mobile first'.

This relentless march of innovation provides large-scale opportunities for Ireland Inc. Who better to sum this up than Colm Grealy, who as co-founder with Barry Flanagain of Ireland On-line in 1993, effectively pioneered the introduction of the internet into Ireland on a commercial basis?

"Today we are witnessing a more cautious but equally ambitious approach to tech investments. The growth of mobile internet usage combined with cloud-based services is driving a high volume of new internet start-ups. Health and financial services are now changing fundamentally, driven by new innovative companies delivering fresh services via mobile and tablet devices.

"It is hard not to feel that we are just going through another early phase of innovation in what may prove to be a continuous evolution driven by innovation in networks and technology for decades to come," said Grealy.

A recent personal family gathering provided a revealing snapshot of the times we live in. There together were grandad and his five year-old grand-daughter swiping freely and successfully on an iPad. It was a scene that is replicated in many households in Ireland today, technology straddling the generations. Regardless of the dotcom crash of 2000 and regardless of the lofty valuations of some tech companies today on Wall Street, technology is here to stay. It is all around us. It hasn't gone away, you know.

CHAPTER 19

Retail: the eternal price war
By Stephen Wynne-Jones

IRISH RETAIL'S 20TH CENTURY GROWTH WAS BASED ON INNOVATIONS SUCH AS SHOPPING CENTRES, OWN-BRANDS AND SELLING PRODUCTS FROM AISLES – BUT THE ARRIVAL OF GERMAN DISCOUNTERS MADE THE SECTOR FOCUS ON PRICE.

When, in June of 2015, news of a proposed high-profile revamp of Stillorgan Shopping Centre hit the headlines, it marked a new chapter in the evolution of Ireland's oldest shopping mall. According to the centre's owners, real estate firm Kennedy Wilson, a "full glass canopy" would now be placed atop the famously open-air mall for the first time, with extra care taken to ensure that it retained "the local community atmosphere that differentiates it from other centres".

That "community atmosphere" dates all the way back to 1966, when locals gathered to witness singer Dickie Rock officially open the centre during what was a period of upheaval in the Irish retail sector. Stillorgan was a development that "set the style in Ireland for the shopping of the future", as a *Woman's Way* editorial put it the following March.

"Here you park your car in comfort... then park your young children in the free nursery provided... stroll leisurely about your business on traffic free malls... and wind up, if you like, with something to eat in our fabulous new restaurant and coffee shop." It would become, the authors explained, "an integral part of modern life".

The vision for Stillorgan was the brainchild of the polo neck-wearing entrepreneur Pat Quinn, just one of a handful of retail pioneers that emerged during the Seán Lemass/Jack Lynch era. Just down the road, in Cornelscourt, Ben Dunne Senior was fashioning a destination outlet that would remain a flagship for his nascent Dunnes Stores operation for decades to come. On the Northside, the ebullient Feargal Quinn was establishing what would become one of Ireland's best-loved (and arguably most-missed) supermarket brands: Superquinn. In Cork, Jack Musgrave was overseeing the transition of the country's leading wholesaler into a retail powerhouse, alongside his nephew Hugh Mackeown. And in textiles, a young Arthur Ryan was about to turn the world of ladieswear on its head with the launch of a new 'fast fashion' chain, Penneys.

Fast-forward half a century and it is somewhat of an understatement to suggest that the grocery vista has changed a great deal since retail sophistication first came to suburbia. Today, when consumers are asked for their retail preferences they may look to Aldi, Lidl or Tesco; foreign-owned chains that now account for some 40% of the Irish market. They may think of SuperValu, battling for market leadership following its absorption of the Superquinn brand, or perhaps Dunnes Stores, balancing its long-standing price credentials with internal family struggles. But the more things change the more they stay the same, as the old adage goes, and retailer concerns over the buying power of the multiples, below-cost selling, product provenance and – most of all – the need to offer good value are just as prevalent today as they were five decades ago.

The opportunist

In November 1960 a young Feargal Quinn opened his first store on a 210 square-metre site on Dundalk's Clanbrassil Street with a workforce of eight. The store offered the brand new concept of 'self-service shopping', as experienced by the young Quinn on a year's break in France – in those days all products in an Irish store were located behind the counter. It was so new that many bemused shoppers walked home with the wire baskets they picked up at the front door beside a sign that encouraged them to 'Please Take One'.

Quinn and his team weren't prepared to stop there, visiting stores in Europe, the US and even Australia to 'borrow' successful concepts and bring them back to Ireland. The in-house bakery, which would go on to adorn the entrance to so many Superquinn stores, was introduced following a trip to a Carrefour outlet in Caerphilly in Wales; while its SuperClub loyalty programme, Ireland's first, was launched around the same time as a similar scheme in Belgium. New fresh departments were rolled out all the time: Pizza Kitchen, Pasta Kitchen… although a short-lived Soup Kitchen at its Blanchardstown outlet didn't hit the mark with the locals for obvious reasons.

Describing the opening of Superquinn Finglas in 1970, the *Irish Independent* described the dapper Quinn as "the type of competent young Irish executive who instills more confidence in our ability to succeed in Common Market conditions than a hundred platitudinous speeches". A born entrepreneur, the future senator's eye for detail remained keener than most, right up to the sale of Superquinn to property firm Select Retail Holdings in 2004.

Indeed, when the announcement came that Musgrave Group – which took over the Superquinn portfolio in 2011 – was going to 'retire' the brand, it was the fate of another Quinn-introduced concept, the famous sausages (which followed a fact-finding mission to Nuremberg) that garnered the most reaction from customers. During what was described as Musgrave's busiest ever day on Twitter, the announcement was made that the Superquinn sausages would remain, and still do to this day.

A new era

It was Feargal too, along with Quinnsworth under Canadian Galen Weston (who bought the chain from Pat Quinn in 1971) who introduced the concept of private label, in-house brands that were initially known as 'generics'. Quinn's effort, Thrift, with stark white packaging and bold exclamation – 'That's Thrift!' – was followed swiftly by Weston's Yellow Pack, ushering in a new competitive element to the grocery space.

Such outside-the-box thinking inevitably led to a number of missteps: Quinn's decision to place all Thrift items into a single lane at Superquinn led to the concept being dubbed the 'social welfare' aisle, while Quinnsworth drew the ire of the Irish Goods Council, creators of the Guaranteed Irish brand, who accused the retailer of using Yellow Pack as cover for delisting Irish products from its shelves. However, the foundations were laid for countless others to follow: Dunnes soon rolled out its St Bernard brand, while Homestead, arguably Ireland's most famous store brand range, followed in 1983, introduced by the National Grocers' Wholesale Alliance (NGWA).

Today, private label accounts for more than one fifth of all products purchased in supermarkets, and has become a sophisticated business with multiple tiers evident in most major product categories (such as Tesco's Value/House Brand/Finest matrix). In addition, retailers increasingly use private labels to promote their 'Irish' credentials – particularly at Aldi and Lidl, where the in-store range is composed almost entirely of generic items.

On the back of the generics boom, the dawn of computerisation was another of the biggest quantum leaps for the grocery industry, ushering in a new era of efficiency for the sector.

Musgrave operational director John Smith summed up the potential of the computer age back in 1983 when he told *Checkout* magazine that "computerisation will be essential in the future, to control modern retailing, but the medium-sized retailer who lets his enthusiasm for computer technology run away with him is asking for real trouble. Computerisation pays, but only when the volume is big – and I mean real big." What the late Smith might have made of today's high-tech retail world, where stock levels and pricing can be manipulated at the click of a mouse, is anyone's guess.

Here too, however, there were teething problems, such as those that accompanied the introduction of barcode scanning in the 1980s. While barcodes had been around for the best part of a decade, the first store to offer the service in Ireland was an L&N outlet in Ballincollig, Co Cork, where the technology was introduced with a view to improving customer service. However, "as with all unique systems, it has some unique problems, too", *Checkout* reported at the time. "For example, in the dairy section, Yoplait twin tub yoghurt packs have bar coding on one tub only. Customers invariably prefer to buy just one tub and tend to break the pack. Should they take the barcoded one up to the checkout, they will be charged for two, and if they choose the one without coding, they can get it for nothing. The store has now remedied this by price-labelling each tub."

But while the modern retail environment owes much to various chains' technological breakthroughs, the bargain-hunting mentality so prevalent in today's marketplace can arguably be traced to one company. When Co Down-born Ben Dunne used his savings to open the first Dunnes Stores on Patrick St in Cork in 1944, he emblazoned the words 'Better Value' in metre-high black paint above the door, thus commencing one of the most intriguing (and sometimes scandalous) chronicles in Irish business history.

Better Value Beats Them All

The Dunne family has been likened in the past to the Ewings in *Dallas*, except with the soap opera taking place almost exclusively behind closed doors. In a rare interview in the early seventies, Dunne affirmed the importance of family control, saying that "public companies are like the government. The government has the privilege of spending money foolishly, and public companies are no better."

But family ownership made Dunnes an agile business, able to move quicker than many of his rivals. When groceries were first introduced to Dunnes in 1960, the retailer positioned its (then costly to source) fruit and veg significantly cheaper than its rivals. Around the same time that Feargal Quinn was encouraging consumers to browse the aisles in Dundalk, Dunnes was doing likewise on Dublin's South Great George's St, where its head office still resides.

As *The Irish Press* wrote in 1971, "Dunnes Stores – just mention the name anywhere throughout the length and breadth of Ireland, and it stands for something big, something great and unique, something that gets right down to the basic needs of the Irish people. You cannot think of Dunnes Stores without thinking of Better Value."

Yet as Dunnes Stores expanded nationwide in the sixties and seventies, it was rare for any journalist to succeed in peeling back the layers of the Dunne family structure: if a hack managed to succeed in getting Ben on the phone, he or she was often met with a brusque response: "Dunnes Stores: better value beats them all" – and the sound of the receiver being slammed down.

If Ben Senior, who passed away in 1983, was rightly considered a pioneer, it was under the guidance of the next generation that the retailer would go on to become an industry powerhouse boasting a quarter of the market, a position it has retained for the best part of two decades. However, as the business grew so did the allure. Bar the Guinness heirs, few Irish business families have graced the front pages as much as the Dunnes – not always for the right reasons.

This was perhaps best encapsulated in the life and times of Ben Dunne Jr, a man whose retail career both began and ended with a bang. Having survived a traumatic kidnapping by the IRA in 1981, Dunne went on to lead Dunnes through some of its most successful years of growth, only to see his reputation soured by an unfortunate episode in a Florida hotel room 11 years later. That dalliance was a misstep too many for the publicity-shy family, and in 1993 he was ousted from the firm by his sister, Margaret Heffernan, the eldest of Ben Senior's six children – and a businesswoman with a reputation for taking short shrift with those not allied to her cause.

Ben Junior, to his credit, has since proven himself to be unsinkable, shaking off the revelations uncovered by the McCracken and Moriarty Tribunals in the late nineties to reinvent himself as an astute fitness centre operator. Speaking to *The Sunday Times* in 2012, he said that he would "hate" to still be in the supermarket business, adding that his siblings still involved in the business "seem to be fighting a lot of people". He also noted that Dunnes' current policy of not talking to the media has made it "faceless".

Born leader

'Faceless' she may be – public appearances are rare as hen's teeth – but Margaret Heffernan certainly doesn't lack backbone. She was just two when her father opened his first store, in 1944, and by the age of 14 was employed on the shop floor of the family's Cork outlet. In 1964 she was appointed a director of Dunnes Stores, and set about building a legacy of philanthropy: she founded the People in Need Trust in 1988, and was awarded the Dublin Lord Mayor's Millennium Award for her charity work.

But as the doyenne of the Irish grocery trade, Heffernan cuts a formidable figure. Back in 1992, she is reported to have told solicitor Noel Smyth: "I'm sorry the little bastard didn't go to jail", referring to her brother's American misadventure. In the mid-nineties she stood up to the unions' demand for fairer workplace conditions, which led to the closure of stores for more than three weeks (Mandate trade union has since referred to Dunnes as the "most difficult" retailer it has ever dealt with). More recently, she was reported as telling former

Dunnes finance chief Larry Howard that she "either wanted fucking men or mice", prior to a High Court case over the latter's expulsion from operations.

Working alongside her brother Frank (as well as a litany of loyal lieutenants over the years including Dick Reeves, Tommy Carmody, Dan Barrett and John McNiffe), Heffernan's position as the kingmaker behind the Dunnes empire makes her one of Irish grocery's most enigmatic characters. Conferring an honorary doctorate from the National University of Ireland on Heffernan in 2007, Dr Michael Murphy of UCC said that "in other countries with formal state honours schemes, Margaret Heffernan would have been knighted or admitted to the Legion d'Honneur".

At Dunnes, sources close to the retailer say it's "her way or the highway", and as a leader Heffernan has proven herself to be steadfast in her determination to give customers what they want: Better Value. At the time of writing, Dunnes holds about 21% of the Irish grocery market according to market share figures from Kantar Worldpanel, despite practically no new store openings – its rivals continue to open stores at a rapid rate. When Mandate called a one-day picket outside its stores in 2015, Dunnes responded with a 24-hour promotion offering 20% off all online orders. The retailer also recently put it up to discounters Aldi and Lidl by engaging in a massive vouchering campaign, which has seen it enjoy higher growth than any of its mainstream competitors over the last few quarters.

Under Heffernan's watchful eye, Dunnes will continue to do things its way – and as long as the retailer remains synonymous with its founder's Better Value promise, change is unlikely to be forthcoming at South Great George's St.

The Ryan line

If Ben Dunne Senior instilled a shrewd business acumen in his daughter Margaret, the same can be said for one of his protégés, Arthur Ryan. Ryan, the son of a Cork-born insurance clerk, had built a reputation for himself in London at swanky department stores such as Swan and Edgar at Piccadilly Circus, and soon became a member of Dunne's 'dream team' at his Cornelscourt flagship in the mid sixties.

But it was at Associated British Foods, under the control of Galen Weston, that Ryan would become a household name. Having convinced his boss that value fashion was an area with huge potential, Ryan was put in charge of the newly-acquired Todd Burns and Co department store on Mary St in Dublin, which upon reopening in 1969 was rebranded Penneys.

The store was soon followed by a sister outlet in Cork in 1971, and an expansion into the mainland UK in 1973 under the Primark banner (American fashion chain JC Penney was eyeing an entry to the British market at the time, and the two names were deemed too similar).

Under Ryan's leadership the business flourished, yet the "creator, driving force, and inspiration" behind its growth (as George Weston, ABF chief executive dubbed Ryan) remained notoriously private, shunning interviews and photoshoots, and conducting incognito store visits flanked by a security detail. On his retirement from the business in 2009 after 40 years of service, a brief statement from Ryan indicated that he was "extremely proud" of all that Primark achieved under his tenure; an understated end to an astonishingly successful career.

Today, Primark is an empire stretching right across Europe, boasting stores in Spain, Germany, the Netherlands, Belgium, Austria, and recently France, the land of haute couture. According to Associated British Foods' 2016 report, its retail division brought in revenues just shy of £6bn, and adjusted operating profit was at £689m: there were now 315 stores in 11 countries, including five in the USA. The world, it seems, is Primark's cut-price oyster.

While his name no longer appears on the company balance sheet, the modus operandi created under Ryan's leadership continues to be the cornerstone of Primark's success, as if its founder was cheering each new venture on from the sidelines. In private, of course.

Groupthink

While the likes of Primark, Superquinn, Quinnsworth and Dunnes are domestic success stories, a raft of international suitors have also thrown their hat in the ring, with Tesco arguably the most prominent. However, while the Cheshunt-based retailer vies for grocery market leadership here, its initial foray across the Irish Sea proved less triumphant.

Tesco's entry into Ireland owes a lot to a Welshman, Albert Gubay, who established the 3 Guys chain in the late 1970s, offering a new type of shopping experience built around an EDLP ('every day low price' model) – limited assortment coupled with keen pricing. Gubay's aggressive business style earned him both friends and enemies in the trade: Ben Dunne Senior, so the story goes, expressed particular distaste for the entrepreneur, dubbing him 'Gubby'. Having shaken up the trade with a new style of retailing, Gubay would make his most significant transaction in 1979, selling his 49% stake in 3 Guys to Tesco, paving the way for the UK retail giant's first overseas investment.

Announcing a £10 million investment in its fledgling Irish operation – quite a sum in those days – Tesco's promise, as espoused by then managing director Ian MacLaurin, was to create a wholly new shopping experience, tailored to the whims of the Irish consumer. "We have no intention of trying to impose an alien character on our Irish operation," he told *Checkout* magazine in March 1979. "Our objective is to adapt our thinking to the Irish experience, rather than the other way round. To do otherwise would be commercial madness, and while we are many things, mad we are not."

While initial sales proved positive, customer feedback was mixed: a survey carried out by Lansdowne Market Research in 1983 found that while 57% of shoppers believed Tesco to have a 'very good' or 'fairly good' range of products, just 40% felt that it was 'very/fairly good' at stocking Irish produce, well behind its competitors Dunnes (64%), Quinnsworth (63%) and Superquinn (90%). As Tesco upped its capital expenditure, most notably with the opening of a flash new flagship store in Nutgrove, Co Dublin, in November 1984, its marketing strategy remained unmistakably British, with massive shelf space afforded to the likes of Marmite and Cadbury's Smash, brands with limited appeal in this country. Irish consumers weren't convinced, and in March 1986 Tesco announced its ignominious departure, selling its Irish operation to the H Williams chain.

One more time

Some 11 years later, however, the retailer was back – under the guidance of the bullish Terry Leahy, just weeks into what would turn out to be a defining period in Tesco's history. While its purchase of Power's Supermarkets, which operated Quinnsworth, for £630 million in 1997 was met with some resistance from business groups, Tesco set about redefining its image as a supporter of all things 'Irish'. "I think people [...] were suspicious of Tesco, because we'd been there before, hadn't done a great job," Leahy told *The Irish Times* back in 2008. "It was clear that we were going to have to earn our reputation in Ireland."

Tesco (at a group level) became the biggest purchaser of Irish food and drink in the world, with an Indecon report finding that the retailer purchases €1.57bn worth of Irish products every year. Tesco Ireland accounts for around €600m of that.

But the bigger you are, the more are ready to cut you down, and Tesco's leadership position saw it come under fire from farming groups, supplier organisations and independent retailers. In addition, the recent financial scandal at its UK parent, coupled with the fact that as in the old MacLaurin days Tesco Ireland does not reveal its profits, means that many shoppers still retain an aura of suspicion about the retail giant.

Tesco isn't the only international retailer to have staked a claim for a piece of Ireland's retail landscape, of course. The purchase of Powers sparked a flurry of takeover rumours in the late nineties and early 2000s, with Asda, Sainsbury's and others reportedly declaring 'expressions of interest' in the Irish market. In 1997 Safeway announced the proposed opening of 20 stores in the Republic, in conjunction with Sir Anthony O'Reilly's Fitzwilton Group, a development that never materialised. A year later, Sainsbury's was 'strongly linked' with a move for Roches Stores' nine Irish outlets; in 2000, a deal to sell Dunnes Stores to the then-Walmart owned Asda chain was reportedly at an 'advanced stage' (rumours that recirculated in 2008). In 2014 it emerged that Feargal Quinn was on the verge of selling Superquinn to Sainsbury's in 2004, only for the newly appointed chief executive at the UK retailer, Justin King, to back out at the last minute.

The period did, however, see the arrival of Aldi and Lidl, two low-key German discount chains built around a philosophy not dissimilar to that of Gubay's limited assortment model. In the early part of the last decade, the 'stack em high, sell em cheap' mindset espoused by both was very much out of kilter with the tendencies of the Celtic Tiger generation. Commenting on the opening of Aldi's first two stores, on Parnell St in Dublin and Ballincollig in Co Cork, the *Irish Independent* wrote in 1999 that "many people at first could be turned off by the German discount group's stores. Products are sold from the cardboard boxes in which they were delivered, and sit on pallets dropped on the store floor by forklifts. All costs are stripped down to the bare minimum."

Few could have predicted the impact these young upstarts would have on the Irish retail landscape in the years to come.

Looking ahead

That Aldi and Lidl now hold around a fifth of the market between them is testament to both retailers' aggressive focus on pricing, as well as a rapid expansion drive with store numbers for each growing well into three figures. While recent years have seen both embrace local suppliers, and develop an 'Irish' message, it is their value credentials, cultivated in their native Germany, that keep customers coming back. Having seen double-digit sales growth almost consistently since 2011, Aldi and Lidl have every right to be optimistic about their growth prospects, with Aldi announcing the opening of a second Irish headquarters in Mitchelstown to support the discounter's growth in the south west.

In May 2012 Tesco Ireland's then-chief executive Tony Keohane told a Deloitte seminar in Dublin that consumers are now entering "a new order. We're not going to go back to where we were in 2008. This is where we're at now." His words now seem all the more prescient. Aldi and Lidl have become synonymous with the post-downturn generation, who still retain a hunger for recession-era value yet seek quality and provenance as standard.

While Dunnes, Tesco and SuperValu, their key competitors, hold around two thirds of the market between them, all three are conscious of the German juggernaut roaring just over their shoulders. The key differentials that defined Irish retail over the decades have been redefined around price, and all understand the risk involved in thinking otherwise. While the wider macroeconomic environment shows real signs of recovery, the supermarket trade is a still a place where value is king, special offers are expected rather than wished for, and measurable growth remains stunted.

At Stillorgan Shopping Centre, planners are hopeful that a new glass canopy will be enough to draw shoppers back to 'where it all began' in suburban grocery. Retailers, especially those caught in a prolonged discount cycle, will be hoping that it doesn't turn out to be a glass ceiling.

CHAPTER 20

Case Study: Primark

FOUNDED IN 1969 BY ARTHUR RYAN, PRIMARK HAS BECOME A GLOBAL RETAIL GIANT WITH OVER 340 STORES IN 11 COUNTRIES. THE COMPANY IS NOW GUIDED BY PAUL MARCHANT AND HIS TEAM AT THE COMPANY'S MARY STREET HQ.

Primark is an international retailer that offers high-quality fashion at value-for-money prices: put simply, "amazing fashion, amazing prices". The company prides itself on offering something for everyone and has a wide selection of products available across womenswear, menswear, childrenswear, homeware, beauty, activewear and gifts, including licensed ranges such as Disney and Warner Bros, which continue to provide some of its most popular pieces.

At September 2017, Primark has over 340 stores, with over 13.5 million square feet of selling space in 11 countries: the Republic of Ireland, UK, Spain, Germany, Portugal, Netherlands, Belgium, Austria, France, Italy and the north-east of the USA. It employs over 70,000 people. The company has number one volume market share in the UK, Republic of Ireland, Spain and Portugal. For the year ending September 2016 its net sales were £5,949m, with a net operating profit of £689m.

Primark is a subsidiary of Associated British Foods PLC, a diversified international food, ingredients and retail group with global sales of £13.4bn, over 130,000 employees and operations in 50 countries.

Primark began in Ireland as Penneys, with its first store on Dublin's Mary Street, in the heart of the north inner city, in 1969. The economic landscape at that time was particularly challenging – however, Penneys founder Arthur Ryan saw the opportunity in 'value fashion'.

Ryan had always viewed the business as one that would thrive beyond the shores of Ireland. The company's move into the UK market in 1974 followed just five years after opening the first Dublin store. The name Primark was conceived when the company expanded to the UK and another retailer had the rights to use the Penneys name there: Primark still operates under the Penneys name in Ireland, where it has 37 stores, and the company is known as Primark in the other ten countries where it trades.

The next decades were spent building and consolidating its presence in Ireland and the UK before taking on its next challenges. Between 1995 and 2000, Primark acquired a number of stores in the UK from BHS, Co-Op and C&A. In 2005, the acquisition of Littlewoods by ABF PLC comprising an estate of 120 premises was completed, of which 41 stores were transferred to Primark (many of the other sites were in cities and towns where Primark already had a presence).

By 2006 Primark was a company with 143 stores, 18,000 employees and £1,309m in sales. It was then that Primark began its European expansion: it saw opportunities to bring the Primark brand to the rest of Europe, and to shake up the competitive landscape. Primark opened its first store in Spain in May 2006, its first store in the Netherlands in 2008, in Portugal, Germany and Belgium in 2009, in Austria in 2012, in France in 2014, the USA in 2015 and Italy in 2016.

In 2009 Paul Marchant was appointed chief executive of Primark, while Arthur Ryan remained chairman, a position he still holds today. Before joining Primark, Marchant was chief operating officer of New Look. He also held senior positions at Debenhams, Topman and River Island.

In recent years Primark looked outside Europe, and in September 2015 opened its first US store, Downtown Crossing, in Boston's landmark Burnham building. Since then the company has opened a further seven stores in the north-east of the USA, and will open its ninth US store in Brooklyn in 2018. As a country with close ties to Ireland and Europe, the US offers a clear opportunity for Primark to take a unique position in the market. Primark is a compelling proposition for American customers and the States' fluid property market offers potential to build scale and strong price position versus US competition.

In October 2015 Primark opened a flagship store in Gran Via, Madrid. It is Primark's largest store in Spain, with a retail area of 133,000 square foot covering five floors. Located in the historic building of Almacenes Madrid-Paris, the store combines history with cutting-edge design.

In April 2016 Primark entered its 11th market with the opening of its first Italian store in the Il Centro shopping centre, about 12km from fashion capital Milan. At the time of writing, the company operates four stores in Italy.

Primark's international headquarters are above its first ever store, Mary Street in Dublin. The office space was extensively redeveloped in 2015 and renamed Arthur Ryan House in honour of the founder and chairman. The expansive open-plan office space features over 40 meeting rooms, a fashion press room, a photo studio, a café and a coffee bar, as well as a wellbeing exercise studio for employees. The award-winning space showcases Primark's dynamic brand and heritage and is designed to provide employees with a closer connection to the company's retail stores. Primark also has regional offices in Reading, Essen, Paris, Madrid and Boston.

The company has also focused on upgrading the back-of-house area in its stores to create a more motivating work environment for employees. First trialled with the opening of its Leeds Trinity store in 2013, this concept has been rolled out in all of its new stores and a number of existing stores have been upgraded as part of its planned refurbishment. They are designed with a completely open-plan, fresh, modern look and feel, and feedback from employees has been very positive across all markets.

The core of Primark's innovation is in its business model. It is no surprise that some people are astonished at how Primark combine fashion and affordability. But there's no secret. In fact, it's quite simple. From the clothing it sources to the way it organises its stores, Primark's business is based on doing some simple things differently from other retailers, which is how it can keep prices low.

Primark sells a lot of items, which means it is able to make savings from buying in bulk for all its stores. It also tries to be as efficient as possible when transporting products from factories to stores. This includes things like asking suppliers to pack t-shirts so that they are ready for the salesfloor. Primark designs clothes that offer the latest trends, but does not use expensive hangers, tags or labels. The company has a global supply chain sourcing products from 39 countries and its business directly contributes to the employment of more than 700,000 workers. 98% of Primark's factories are shared with other high street brands.

Primark is committed to the highest ethical standards. It requires suppliers and factories that commit to making its products to do so in factories with good working conditions so that people are treated decently and paid a fair wage. Primark does not own factories and is very selective about who it works with. It places orders with factories and suppliers that manufacture products on its behalf.

To make it onto Primark's approved factory list, each factory is vetted to internationally-recognised standards set out in the Primark Code of Conduct. The code covers areas such as pay, employment policies and health and safety. Once approved, it is the job of Primark's Ethical Trade and Environmental Sustainability Team, a group of more than 90 experts based in key sourcing countries, to monitor compliance. They audit every factory at least once a year, and sometimes more, to check whether international standards are being met.

The team carries out over 3,000 audits in the factories making Primark's products. The company also works with suppliers, factories and local partners to deliver training and programmes that help factories address locally relevant issues and needs.

Store environment plays an important part in inspiring customers and engaging them in the fun and fashion of Primark. Over the last few years, significant advances have been made in window presentation, visual merchandising, digital communication and the look and feel of each department.

Primark's latest store design offers an enhanced customer experience including access to free wi-fi, trend rooms, recharge areas, customer seating areas and showrooms where groups of friends can try on clothes together. Primark has also opened coffee shops with third parties in a number of stores in the UK and Republic of Ireland, and has plans to roll these out to more stores in all markets.

The retailer has a strong digital presence and a high level of customer engagement, with over 10 million followers across its social media channels. From the latest beauty tutorial videos, to live streaming of its press events and store openings, its fans can get inspired 24/7 and keep up with Primark's new lines. Its website Primark.com is a hub of content where customers can create wish lists, get the latest styling advice and upload their looks to Primania.

Primark is expanding its store footprint in existing markets and continues to invest in infrastructure including depots, technology, people, and an on-going refurbishment programme for its older stores. The company's new flagship store in Birmingham Pavilions is scheduled for completion in December 2018: it will showcase four floors of fashion over 160,000 square feet of retail space, which will make it the largest Primark store to date.

CHAPTER 21

The management revolution
By the Irish Management Institute

THE DEVELOPMENT OF THE IRISH MANAGEMENT INSTITUTE IS A STORY OF HOW RESEARCH AND EDUCATION INJECTED GLOBAL IDEAS AND NEW ENERGY INTO IRISH BUSINESS.

In the 1950s, as TK Whitaker described it, the country was "enveloped in a palpable air of despondency", with miniscule exports and a stagnant industrial base reliant on protectionist government policies to avoid foreign competition. Ireland was an agricultural country, and the original industrial base was a legacy of British business, followed by the formation by a Seán Lemass-inspired Irish government of relatively large state enterprises such as the ESB, Bord na Móna and Irish Sugar to create both employment and an industrial infrastructure.

By the fifties the era of protectionism was coming to an end. The seeds of the European Economic Community had been sown by the creation of the Coal and Steel Community in Europe. Meanwhile, in Ireland the educational base was low. Most people left school with barely a primary education: university, and management roles, were seen as the preserve of the elite classes.

Courage, leadership and fresh ideas were needed. Michael Dargan, by now Aer Lingus services manager in New York, was one of those to show the way. He was introduced to the American Association of Managers, pioneers in management training. Dargan was determined to bring this management expertise home to Ireland, and recruited a cohort of like-minded volunteers, an interesting mix of Irish and foreign executives: Tommy Hogan (Plessey), Colm Barnes, Dillon Digby (Pye), Peter Owens (Domas), Liam Boyd (TWA), Michael Fitzpatrick, Dermot O'Flynn (JJ O'Hara and Co) and TC Wade (Esso).

They met in the Domas office upstairs in 76 Grafton Street, initially to form a study group based on the AMA and papers, but then raised their ambition: "to promote the science of management in all its aspects, provide guidance and educational facilities for management personnel: collect and disseminate knowledge of management problems among its members to improving management practice". A collegiate framework was created for managers to meet and exchange experience through conferences and study groups, drawing ideas from private and public sectors, including dialogue with senior civil servants, unusual for that era.

Their belief was that there was an outstanding need in Ireland to promote "the science of industrial management" and apply management methods to a moribund industrial base – and so the Irish Management Institute was founded, with the first formal meeting in the Shelbourne Hotel on May 1st 1952. A landmark inaugural meeting in the Gresham Hotel on Dec 9th 1952 was addressed by Lemass, Lord Mayor Andrew Clarkin, Dargan and Sir Charles Harvey of Guinness, among others.

Around this time Lemass, as minister of industry and commerce, together with the redoubtable department secretary John Leydon, were considering a similar initiative prompted by the Organisation for European Economic Cooperation's proposal for a European Institute of Management.

On April 23rd 1952, in Lemass's enforced absence through illness, Minister for External Affairs Frank Aiken, assisted by officials JA Cassidy and JJ McElligott, met with leading semi-state executives JP Beddy (head of the pioneering IDA), Todd Andrews (Bord na Móna, and for many years a leading figure in Irish politics), RF Browne (ESB), TC Courtney (CIE) and Jeremiah Dempsey (Aer Lingus), together with private-sector bosses, most notably Sir Charles Harvey, assistant MD of Guinness, a staunch champion of management development –

presumably encouraged by Sir Hugh Beaver, head of Guinness in London and chairman of the five-year-old British Institute of Management. Charles Harvey is honoured to this day by an eponymous award.

Minister Frank Aiken pointed out that the constraint was not a shortage of labour or even capital, but weaknesses "in the technique of business management", especially in a small newly independent country with an agrarian economy. The superiority of the US in management education was clear, with 600 colleges offering degrees in business management – in contrast to none in Ireland except the fledgling B. Comm in UCD, which had an accountancy focus.

Professor George O'Brien of UCD was the sole representative of academia, a sign of the central dilemma in management education: academia in general held management education in disdain, regarding it as a mercantile subject not amenable to research and teaching. While industry needed – and wanted – management training, it could sponsor such an initiative. Academics lacked the necessary experience to credibly impart knowledge in an area where most 'theory' comes from practitioners. Sir Hugh Beaver at the British Institute of Management remarked that English universities did not accept that business management contained a sufficiently high intellectual content to justify a faculty at a university or the conferring of a degree.

Programmes and participants

Beaver distinguished between pre-career learning and the study by practising managers of management techniques: this distinction remained central to IMI's ethos throughout the following decades, informing such ground-breaking programmes (never 'courses') as the MPP – Management Practice Programme for CEOs, now running over 40 years, and the Business Development Programme for owner-managers.

This subtle – but crucial – distinction formed the hallmark of IMI's teaching philosophy. Management, with its nuances and variability, cannot seriously be taught through conventional means such as lectures but can really only be learned through experience, guided by educated practitioners. Such 'action learning' is the IMI's core tenet. Often mistakenly perceived as the simple addition of a project to a 'course', it requires the participant (never 'student') to take responsibility for his or her own learning – and requires the programme to adapt to the emerging needs of the developing learner, flexing the curriculum to suit (an administrative complexity as well as a pedagogical quandary, one that invariably defeats bureaucratic educational establishments).

Action learning of this sort involves not just action, but mindful reflection by the participant to extract the learnings – often about their own personality, beliefs and assumptions. A programme, to be successful, changes the inner man or woman rather than merely filling the brain with buckets of knowledge. To paraphrase Churchill: people always want to learn but don't always want to be taught!

This mantra was reinforced by successive IMI leaders, notably Ivor Kenny, who brought the IMI from a semi-detached house in Leeson Park and an annual budget of €30k through Orwell Road (now the Russian Embassy) to the 12-acre National Management Centre in Sandyford. Kenny echoed Pascale's 1662 premise that "people are generally better persuaded by the reasons they themselves have discovered than those which have come into the minds of others".

This extensive campus, on the Myerscough estate, five miles from Grafton Street, opened by Labour Minister Michael O'Leary on September 25th 1974, was selected because it was convenient to both UCD in the new Belfield grounds as well as Trinity College. Indeed, IMI's subsequent degrees, up to MSc level, were awarded by Trinity College.

From the outset, it was envisaged that IMI would draw from universities and industry, but retain separation to maintain the focus on the practice of management. There was a cross-flow of such luminaries as Brefni Tomlin (who joined IMI in 1962 as a researcher) and Jerry Liston who was IMI chairman 1995-1997 and later headed the Smurfit School of Business in UCD at Carysfort. Liston had the further distinction of making IMI financially self-reliant by 1997 and of bringing the IMI National Forum Conference to Belfast to promote cross-Border cooperation.

This new National Management Centre was seen as a symbol of Ireland's emergence from the gloom of the impoverished fifties. Self-confidence was now evident. Lemass's industrialisation policy was paying off in spades, aided by an energetic IDA that brought Digital to Galway in 1970 – paving a path for IBM, Apple, Wang, Nixdorf and peripheral manufacturers throughout Ireland.

The IMI pioneered collaboration with state and private bodies, trying – and often failing – to form alliances with such bodies as the Nationwide Business Organisation, the Confederation of Irish Industry, the Federated Union of Employers and the Federation of Irish Industry. Informal cooperation remained high, especially with the senior echelons of the civil service and with Taoisigh from Lemass onwards who promoted the idea, right through Lynch, Haughey, Reynolds and Enda Kenny. It was this ease of access that provided the opportunity to have the crucial conversations between major stakeholders across private and public sectors. Garret FitzGerald, a visionary Taoiseach, was an IMI lecturer as far back as the early sixties.

Conference calls

The crucible for these conversations was the National Management Conference, which came of age in 1963 with a keynote address from Seán Lemass on the need for modernisation: "There is a signpost to the future that our industrial leaders must read very clearly. Obsolete procedures or equipment, defects of management or operatives' training, or restrictive practices bolstering up costs will no longer be made possible by protective tariffs... It is one of the difficulties of the situation that the firms who are represented at conferences like this are those least in need of exhortations to efficiency, and those who need the advice are hardest to contact."

The conference had been almost exclusively male: now the role of women was being embraced, and their proper inclusion was regarded by Ivor Kenny as being the point at which the conference turned from a male bastion into a community with a social dimension that broadened those "crucial conversations". In the prescient 1969 conference, by now traditionally held in Killarney, the theme was leadership and the need for change: Ivor Kenny declared that "change will not merely be an academic subject... It will be something that will be happening at an increasing pace to all of us. It will require change – sometimes painful change – within ourselves: change in our attitudes and in our behaviour. It will involve a process of continuing learning, not just for managers, but for every level in the organisation. It will require leadership that is flexible and adaptive... More than this, it will also require the unchanging qualities of enterprise, realism, courage and determination. Enterprise that can see beyond what it might be, that sees the opportunities and not merely the difficulties, enterprise that does not suffer from the Irish disease – resolving problems by talking about them."

This conference also signalled the need for corporations to show social responsibility, with JG Bavinck of Philips NL, Cardinal Conway and, perhaps surprisingly, David Rockefeller of Chase Manhattan Bank flagging the emerging issues of rising expectation, social complexity and limited natural resources: "We must continue to be profit-oriented, for it is upon profit that our enterprises – and, in my view, our free societies – ultimately depends. At the same time, though, we must keep in touch with men who are not essentially profit-oriented – that troublesome but creative minority of academics and intellectuals who can help us identify emerging social problems before they reach crisis proportions."

Jack Lynch opened the 1970 conference – and a few days later fired Charles Haughey and Neil Blaney, prominent ministers, for their involvement in conspiring to import arms illegally.

The IMI's commitment to attracting leading speakers was absolute – even bringing speakers, when necessary, by private jet from Paris to Killarney. The National Management Conference remains an annual fixture, with the 2016 conference entitled Managing Disruption, Seizing Opportunity. The effects of globalisation were central, with much discussion on the impact of Brexit and the opportunities and threats that emanate from the more recent economic powerhouse, China.

IMI's success in pioneering management development created a plethora of competitors, from independent consultants to colleges nationwide now creating their own business degrees. The universities were not idle during this period, bringing many increasingly specific degrees into being: Trinity had introduced the MSA (master of science in administration) as a one-year full-time course as far back as 1964, rivalling UCD's two-year part-time formula. Both were welcomed by the IMI, especially by Guinness's Charles Harvey, as helping IMI fulfil its mission of management development: the IMI awarded a medal in Harvey's name to outstanding candidates from either programme, the first winner being Patrick J Murphy, later chairman of the Arts Council.

Nonetheless, there remained reticence about becoming 'the handmaids of industry' in some universities. Similarly, IMI was averse to what it saw as 'credentialism' in universities and questioned universities' enclosed environment.

New techniques

Coinciding with the rise of MBAs, there was an explosion in new management techniques fuelled by such successes as Harold Geneen's (ITT) management by objectives, Shell's rational planning, GE's divisionalisation, BCG's portfolio management, and Greiner's pattern of organisation evolution.

In parallel, the human relations and behaviouralist schools were prominent, allied to the progressive staff policies of the fledgling computer makers on the US East Coast, and software and IC companies in Silicon Valley. Work itself had become more complex, much less manual: knowledge was the new currency. New techniques were hailed as silver bullets, often only to become denigrated as fads. In practice, many of these 'fads' had value but were undermined by poor application in practice.

The rise of Japan and the east brought whole new perspectives, and radically new management techniques, but with some difficulties in crossing over to new work cultures. The Toyota techniques are ubiquitous and have been transferred, in new form, into software and venture creation fields.

In this IMI was ambitious, bringing a catalogue of visionary figures to Ireland. Peter Drucker came in 1969: 600 people crammed in to hear him speak on The Effective Executive. Henry Mintzberg came in 1977 to debunk the myths of management. Michael Porter came, at great cost, to talk about his five forces in analysing industries. Tom Peters came In Search of Excellence.

Sumantra Ghoshal, Dave Beckhard, Chris Argyris, Doug McClelland, John Kotter, Gary Hamel, Rita McGrath, Costas Markides, Jeffrey Pfeffer, Charles O'Reilly, Charles Handy, Michael Beer, Edward de Bono, Dave Ulrich, Richard Pascale, Don Sull, Gareth Jones, Robert Kaplan, Nancy Kline, Doug Silsbee, David Clutterbuck, Daniel Pink, David Goleman, Jack Welsh, Rosabeth Moss Kanter, Lynda Gratton, Mauborgne and Kim plus a host of other literati all came to Ireland, courtesy of IMI.

Intriguingly, that pioneering wave has largely passed through, and there are now fewer iconic gurus. Perhaps this is because of indigestion with the flux of earlier experts and perceived fads, or because the new frontier is in the mind as the west seeks innovations that will free it from the need to compete with ultra-low cost economies. The new gurus, aided by the ability to probe the impulses of the brain through scans such as MRI, are advising us on creativity, innovation, group intuition and impulse control with a continuing focus on coaching, mentoring, transformational leadership and mass collaboration as organisations become more elaborate.

The next generation will depend for their prosperity on developing managerial techniques that will resolve the above problems. Since the fifties, the IMI has played its part in advancing management and industry. The art and science of management has always defied exact definition; the inner world of the mind is the next frontier – almost impenetrable, but surely a superbly rewarding prize. As Ivor Kenny (sadly departed in 2016) said, the future is not a fixed singular entity but is there to be invented.

In the final analysis, it is ideas that rule the world, and IMI is well placed to stimulate the crucial conversations that could bring those ideas to fruition in the new world of work.

This short history is based on the comprehensive works of Ivor Kenny, Tom Cox and many former IMI staff to whom a debt of gratitude is owed: the reader is urged to consult their original works.

CHAPTER 22

Directing investment: FDI and the IDA

FOREIGN DIRECT INVESTMENT HAS BEEN A KEYSTONE OF IRISH ECONOMIC POLICY – WITH THE EVER-EVOLVING INDUSTRIAL DEVELOPMENT AUTHORITY AT THE CENTRE OF THINGS SINCE THE 1950S.

The Industrial Development Authority was founded in 1949 by the Fine Gael-led inter-party government of the day. Its mission, then as now, was to promote the growth and development of industry in Ireland. The distinct strategies the authority has implemented in pursuit of this goal were often radical, typically forceful and, by its own standards, usually successful. The IDA's connections to successive Irish governments and the globalised business world make it a fine mirror in which to trace the political and economic (and even, to a lesser degree, cultural) trends of the last 70 years.

The IDA originated in an era when state-led protectionism was established in Ireland as economic common sense. The lean years of the Emergency did not provoke an immediate shift from the economic strategies of the 1930s: high tariffs on imported goods, strategic focus on indigenous industry for indigenous consumption, and limited export trade with any market other than the UK. While Ireland of the 1940s and early 1950s is often seen as a small, inefficient and closed economy, this isn't entirely true. It wasn't so much closed as open only in a particular direction: the Irish State was incredibly reliant on, even shaped by the needs of, the British economy.

By the late 1940s, however, the strategy of protectionism was facing some significant challenges. Irish academic Paul F Donnelly lists "inefficiency, the saturated domestic market, migration from the land, increasing unemployment and emigration, and a deteriorating balance of payments" as a formidable set of stormclouds gathering over the State's economic policy at this time. "In general the scope for protectionist measures to expand industrial employment had reached its limits by the Second World War and industrial employment actually contracted between 1946 and 1951," write Andy Bielenberg and Raymond Ryan in their book *An Economic History of Ireland Since Independence*. "Protected industries were unable to take advantage of the gradual re-opening of export markets in the aftermath of the Second World War."

The IDA was formed in 1949 as part of the Department of Industry and Commerce, and was initially briefed to "stimulate, support and develop export-led business and enterprise in Ireland". Its sister organisation, Foras Tionscal, was charged with approving grants and aids to business. While the authority initially favoured the overall strategy of protectionism, according to Donnelly, "the IDA's view gradually changed to seeing export-led industrialisation as the only way to develop the Irish economy and foreign investment as a source for such industrialisation".

Foreign capital

The authority soon made several recommendations to lighten the burden of that task, including that the restrictions on foreign capital in Ireland be eased. These restrictions were enshrined in law by virtue of the Control of Manufactures Act of 1932. The Act was ostensibly designed to ensure that industries established in the Irish Free State would be Irish-controlled, though an amendment in 1934 made significant concessions to British industry.

Over the course of the 1950s, the protectionist ideology set out in the Control of Manufactures Act would gradually be swept away as government strategy changed to maximise foreign direct investment. The first major shift came in 1956, with the Finance Act's Export Profits Tax Relief introducing preferential corporation taxation for exporting companies. After that year, companies setting up in Ireland were guaranteed 15 years of tax-free profits on exports, with gradual introduction of tax for the five years after that. The Control of Manufactures Act itself was partially repealed in 1958, and fully abolished a little while later. This meant that the profits made by foreign companies, which exported practically all products manufactured in Ireland, could then be fully repatriated, essentially tax-free, for the next two decades. Padraic White, later managing director of the IDA, described this combination of policies as "the IDA's most distinctive investment incentive, and over time its most powerful single weapon in the international industrial promotion battle".

The growing official focus on foreign direct investment did not have an immediate impact on the wider economy. "The performance of the industrial sector overall between 1949 and 1958 remained relatively dismal," write Bielenberg and Ryan, "with the volume of industrial output expanding by a mere 23% in these years, compared with a figure of 73% achieved by all OEEC countries". 1958 was, however, a pivotal year. The announcement of the First Programme for Economic Expansion by Taoiseach Seán Lemass and TK Whitaker heralded a new sense of cohesion and purpose in government strategy, which benefited the IDA greatly.

According to Donnelly, the programme positioned the IDA as "the focal organisation for attracting FDI, effectively turning it into an investment promotion agency". In the years after 1958 the IDA increased investment in marketing campaigns and opened offices in the USA and Europe in the hope of attracting new businesses to the country. Compared to the 1950s, progress was certainly made: 450 foreign companies negotiated new projects or major expansions with the IDA in the 1960s, employing 34,000 people by 1972. At the same time the IDA was increasingly frustrated at the limitations of its organisational structure. It remained under the control of the Department of Industry and Commerce, and was staffed by civil servants. Internally it was felt that official restrictions on hiring and the need for budgetary approval for every expense were hampering the authority's effectiveness.

The IDA and Foras Tionscal enlisted the American consultancy Arthur D Little to assist in "a major reappraisal" of Ireland's industrial development apparatus. The review concluded that "achieving full employment rested on encouraging foreign firms to establish operations in the country". It also recommended that the IDA be given far greater powers to support its efforts in this regard. Padraic White has since written that the Americans were essentially given the script the IDA wanted to hear. Armed with the apparently independent recommendations, the authority approached the government, which duly obliged with the relevant legislation.

The Industrial Development Act 1969 "streamlined agencies dealing with industrial development and concentrated the expertise within an expanded IDA having full control over its own international operations", writes Donnelly. The outgoing chairman of the 'old' IDA, John Walsh, was replaced by Michael Killeen, director designate of the 'new' IDA, in November of 1969. The appointment of a young director (Killeen was only 42 at the time) precipitated perhaps the most dynamic and tumultuous decade of the authority's history.

Killeen's appointment and the structural re-organisation quickly led to rapid growth for the IDA. "Inside eight months, the IDA, which retained its six overseas offices, had assembled 230 staff," writes White, who was himself hired during this time. "Just over half came from the civil service, with years of experience in promoting industrial investment from within a government department. The remaining hundred or so had come straight from the marketplace."

Building on the energy, expertise and ambition of the new staff, along with the increased financial freedom, the 1970s saw the IDA take a far more proactive approach to securing industrial development in Ireland. The strategy began with "cold callers" – IDA employees who specialised in securing, without prior encouragement, meetings with the executives of companies who could potentially be persuaded to invest in Ireland. This was followed by a greatly increased amount of presentations tailored to specific target companies. In 1971 the IDA made presentations to 105 different companies; by 1973 that number was 2,600. This was combined with a greater presence on the ground in foreign cities as the number of foreign offices tripled to 18 by 1979.

To challenge the still-dominant image (particularly in the US) of Ireland as a backward, rural, romantic place, the IDA created advertising campaigns focused on a modern, business-friendly Ireland, filled with tax incentives and highly-skilled labour. The students of Trinity College and UCD featured heavily, with one caption declaring: "Hire them before they hire you!" When Ireland's membership of the EEC was secured in 1973, the benefits of access to the common market were made a cornerstone of the IDA's message. Package trips were organised for business journalists, with 60 journalists arriving for a tour of the State's business and industrial showpieces in 1974. This directly resulted in over 500 articles on the Irish business landscape being printed around the world.

The IDA was also becoming more selective in terms of the types of companies and industries it aimed to attract. In the mid-1970s the authority began to specifically target pharmaceutical and electronics manufacturers. In the year 2000 White would call these industries the keys to the IDA's success. The first wave of electronics-based manufacturing in Ireland was based in large, foreign-owned plants that produced components for electronic devices but, according to Bielenberg and Ryan, "did not locate research and development facilities in Ireland and had few linkages with local suppliers". Generating these "linkages" became a key part of the IDA's strategy, though it would be quite some time before it was even marginally achieved.

"Prior to the selective strategy that emerged in the early 1970s," writes Donnelly, "Ireland had no electronics industry to speak of, but by 1982, some 130 of the world's leading electronics companies were manufacturing in Ireland". The IDA focused on chemicals and electronics because both industries were seen as having "significant growth potential in global terms". Those companies were attracted to Ireland because of low labour costs, low taxation, access to the common market and the lobbying efforts of the IDA.

At this time the IDA was in a unique position, described by Donnelly as a "Janus-faced" coordinating mechanism. On one side, the IDA could liaise directly and autonomously with foreign industry. On the other, it could interface and negotiate, on behalf of foreign industry, with the Irish government.

During the 1970s it was the sole arbiter of all relationships between foreign capital and the Irish State, giving it a huge influence on State policy and the location of industry within Ireland. Against the recommendations of the Buchanan Report (1969), which suggested that Irish industrial development should be concentrated in particular strategic urban "growth centres", the IDA instead "brought jobs to the people" (White) by locating industries in small towns scattered across the country. Bielenberg and Ryan write that this was in line with the short-term political needs of the politicians too, who were keen to ensure their own constituencies were not passed over.

Though not operated by the IDA, one of the most successful industrial initiatives was both regional and centralised: the Shannon Free Zone. The SFZ is a 600-acre business park where companies enjoyed special tax incentives on staff and profits until 2003, attracting many multinational manufacturing firms through the combination of low tax and integration with Shannon Airport. Today, though the tax incentives are gone, the site still retains about 100 international firms, with 6,500 people employed there.

Upheaval and change

The dramatic economic upheavals of the 1970s were deeply felt at the IDA offices. Multiple economic crises centred on oil prices and inflation had a depressing effect on inward investment, particularly from US companies. As White writes, selling burgeoning Silicon Valley tycoons and Wall Street executives on the benefits of investing in a country with 20% inflation was no easy task.

The increasing violence of the Troubles in Northern Ireland was also reducing international enthusiasm for the country. The IDA itself became involved in 1975 when Dr Tiede Herrema, managing director of Ferenka Ltd, the largest foreign employer in the midwest, was kidnapped by the IRA. Ferenka's plant in Limerick, which employed 1,400 people in the manufacture of steel cord, closed two years later, with White writing that the closure "gave foreign investment a bad name for years in Ireland".

Accession to the EEC brought with it changes to taxation policy, which meant the end of the long-running tax-free export profits. After much negotiation, at home and in Brussels, this was replaced with a general 10% tax on all profits, domestic or exported, guaranteed until the year 2000. White writes that this exceptionally low tax rate (and its long-term lock-in at that rate) allowed Ireland to remain competitive in the increasingly cut-throat job of attracting foreign capital, at the expense of some discontent from their new European compatriots. The IDA remained heavily involved in the construction of tax policy right up to the new millennium and the introduction of the 12.5% corporation tax, which remains in place today.

Donnelly writes that the 1970s were capped by a progress report citing a litany of achievements, including "an expanded, autonomous organisation employing almost 700 highly-skilled staff, client company investment of £2.7bn (compared to £130m in the 1960s) for a total grant commitment of £831m and job approvals of 192,000 (compared to 45,000 for the 1960s), with 99,000 in domestic industry".

At the same time, questions were beginning to be raised about the efficacy of the IDA's approach. The authority absorbed the equivalent of 2% of GNP, and despite its headline figures, little of the growth appeared consistent or sustainable. Jobs came and jobs went with a high degree of unpredictability. Ireland was still prone to high inflation and periodic recession. The early years of the 1980s brought several reports on the state of the economy and the IDA's role within it. None were to have a greater impact than the Telesis Report of 1982.

While the Telesis Report was complimentary of the IDA's activities, calling it "arguably the most dynamic, active, efficient and effective organisation of its kind in the world", the broader picture was less positive. According to Bielenberg and Ryan, the report argued that "the long-term economic value of FDI-based industries was questionable given their lack of R&D activity and the high levels of profit repatriation". It insisted that foreign industries establish R&D facilities in addition to the development of closer links with Irish businesses, and that grants to foreign companies should be reduced. On the home front, grants should favour export-oriented business over non-traded sectors, with select companies marked out for development into "world-class" businesses.

Arriving at the beginning of a recession that would linger throughout the decade, the Telesis Report had an immediate and lasting impact on both public and government thinking about the IDA, with all sides eventually agreeing on the need for more intensive investment in indigenous Irish business. With traditional multinational manufacturing industries (the bread-and-butter of the IDA up to this time) facing tough trading conditions throughout Europe and the US and increased competition from the Far East, the focus on home-grown business came at a time when there were few other options on the table.

"High real interest rates, depressed domestic demand and unfavourable exchange rates created a generally difficult environment for industry in 1986," writes White of this period. "In the face of such a gloomy consensus, the IDA version of Ireland sounded like a fairy tale. It was a tough time."

Computer world

The IDA was, however, already working on what would become its next great success story. The IDA Strategic Plan for 1982-92 called for a focus on high-output growth using the best technology available. A highly regarded Silicon Valley company, Apple, not widely known in Ireland at the time, had been convinced to set up a plant in Cork in 1980. It was followed in the forthcoming years by other companies at the forefront of the personal computer boom, most notably IBM, Microsoft and Lotus. These companies weren't as capital-intensive as the manufacturing or chemical companies, but their commitment to their staff was generally more long-term, with a greater investment in training and development. The IDA responded to this change by offering employment grants rather than the traditional capital grants, making it easier for companies to hire people when they first arrived and accelerating their commitment to the country.

This approach peaked in 1990 with the dramatic capture of Intel, which set up its European base just outside Leixlip in Kildare. The deal, in the face of intense competition from other EU countries, came at an unprecedented cost: a grant package of £87m spread over ten years, a figure equivalent to 80% of the government capital grant to the IDA in 1989. It was a significant gamble, but with 2,600 high-quality jobs on the line, the authority and the government both felt it was worth the risk. Within a few years the evidence would suggest the gamble paid off: between 1990 and 1994 Ireland attracted 40% of US electronic investment in Europe, with companies like Dell, Gateway 2000, Compaq, HP, Xerox, Ericsson, Matsushita, Philips, Siemens and Hitachi all arriving in the country.

For the first time a significant number of Irish companies emerged to supply these new companies, providing technical support, sales, packaging and manuals. The importance of electronics and computers during the 1990s was evident from the fact that according to Bielenberg and Ryan, "the employment share of electrical and optical equipment in total manufacturing employment rose from less than 17% to over 27% between 1991 and 2000, while its share of gross industrial output rose from less than 19% to almost 34%".

By the late 1990s, roughly a third of all European PC production happened in Ireland. The IDA's strategy of focusing on high-growth, high-tech industries, formulated in the 1970s, seemed to be prophetic: chemicals, computers and electrical engineering collectively accounted for 40% of Irish GDP growth in the 1990s.

However, despite the warnings of the Telesis Report, there remained an immense and growing gulf between indigenous and multinational business: by the late 1990s 84% of Ireland's industrial exports, worth roughly £50bn, were produced by foreign-owned companies. "At the time of EEC entry, half the employment in indigenous firms was in sectors facing full free-trade competition, like textiles, clothing and footwear," trade unionist and academic David Begg writes in his comparative study *Ireland, Small Open Economies and European Integration: Lost in Transition.* "By 1980, one out of four jobs was lost and in the bigger companies with over 500 employees, the losses were even more devastating – one out of two jobs disappeared." While Irish and multinational industrial firms employed roughly the same amount of people in the 1990s, native industry was increasingly dependent on meeting the needs of the foreign companies.

The foundation of the Irish Financial Services Centre in the late 1980s was a significant development with lasting consequences. The IFSC was designed to provide a low-tax hub for firms involved in "global money management, foreign-currency dealing, equity and bond dealing and insurance activities", and over the last 30 years it has attracted many of the most significant names in international finance. The IDA began working on attracting companies to the centre in 1987, but the idea of developing Ireland's viability as a financial services location took hold much earlier. In the mid-1970s the IDA enlisted Wall Street lawyer Bob Slater to produce a study of offshore banking centres. Slater's report examined the success of Bermuda, and found Ireland to be favourably compared with the Caribbean island.

When the Fianna Fáil government of 1987 took power, led by Charles Haughey, the time was right for implementation of these earlier plans. The scheme to build the IFSC coincided with a desire to redesign and repopulate Dublin's poor and largely deserted Docklands, and with the Taoiseach fully behind it results were quickly achieved.

White describes a steep learning curve for IDA staff as they pivoted from meeting the heads of industrial firms to entreating bank executives, attempting to convince them that Ireland, despite its proximity to the City of London and lack of history in the field, was the next big thing in international finance. Once again, the combination of EU access and guaranteed low taxation proved telling. Though far from an overnight success, the growth of the IFSC and the Irish banking sector throughout the 1990s was startlingly rapid, and a key element in the Celtic Tiger boom and bust cycle.

Since the late 1980s the growth of financial services has been paralleled by a growth in ancillary technological industries around the manufacture and service of software. Irish employment in computer component manufacturing peaked in 1998, even as the majority of multinational electronics firms were moving operations to the Far East. The computer hardware sector lost one third of its employees between 2000 and 2004, but it remained an important part of the Irish employment landscape right up until 2007.

Since the turn of the millennium, the lines between industry and service activity have blurred significantly, a factor which Bielenberg and Ryan describe as "disguising the successful emergence of multinational and indigenous information technology services including software, R&D and support services". In practical terms, this has meant that traditional manufacturing jobs have largely been replaced by service roles: shared services, inside sales, customer support, enterprise support, sales, technical writing, research, and so on.

Ireland's timezone means it can function as a global technical support hub, with a particular focus on Europe and the Middle East, though a historical deficiency in foreign-language education has meant that up to 27% of the employees in this area are themselves foreign-born. An increasing number of technology companies are also undertaking high-value engineering functions in Ireland. However, Ireland has proved extraordinarily attractive for high-value, highly regulated, zero-defect manufacturing in bio-pharmaceutical, medical devices and micro-electronics.

In 2007/08 Ireland faced the twin challenges of a global banking crisis and a self-made property bubble. The IDA under the leadership of Barry O'Leary continued to win investments. FDI, following an initial decline, proved extraordinarily resilient, with FDI investment increasing in response to improving competitiveness as the Irish economy restructured.

IDA Ireland's current strategy was launched in 2015, covering the 2015-2019 period. The strategy continues to target the technology sector (which in its broadest terms includes business services) that has changed utterly from when the IDA first identified it. While companies such as Apple, Intel, Microsoft and IBM have continued to invest, others such as Google, LinkedIn and Facebook have also invested and expanded as have the next wave of sharing economy companies like

Airbnb and Uber. The pharmaceutical sector has also transformed with significant bio-pharma investments in addition to traditional pharma sites. Companies like Alexion, Regeneron, BMS and Shire are all making significant capital investments. This is complemented by a well-developed medical technology sector, which has also moved up the value chain. The financial services sector, engineering and food remain. The IDA also identified convergence as a key opportunity based on the all-pervasive impact of technology.

As ever, the IDA continues to set its jobs and investment targets in public: its latest five-year plan, from 2015, aims to create 80,000 new jobs in client companies, and win over 900 new investments for Ireland. In its strategy, *Winning*, the IDA under the leadership of Martin Shanahan for the first time in its history set regional targets for investment.

This may prove to be one of the most challenging tasks yet for the IDA given the international flows of investments towards larger urban areas. Having said that, the first two years of the strategy saw remarkable results in overall terms with some of the highest growth rates in job creation in the authority's history in 2015 and 2016. Today, the IDA can boast of almost 200,000 jobs in foreign industry in Ireland – the highest in its history, providing over 70% of the country's exports and almost 10% of national employment accounted for directly by IDA client companies, and a much greater indirect impact.

The IDA today is quite distinct from the "super-sized" organisation that developed under Michael Killeen in the 1970s. Following on from the recommendations of the Telesis Report, the merger of the IDA with Foras Tionscal was essentially undone in 1994 when the old IDA was split into three separate organisations. Enterprise Ireland is now charged with the development of indigenous industry, while the IDA focuses entirely on foreign investment. Forfás, the third branch of the split, was the national policy advisory board for enterprise, trade, science, technology and innovation in Ireland, and has since been re-integrated back into the Department of Jobs, Enterprise and Innovation.

Ireland's proposition to investors continues to evolve. While a consistent, competitive and transparent taxation regime remains important, availability of talent both Irish and international, ease of doing business, an innovative eco-system that has been developed through State support for R&D, and access to the European market are also key features of the sell.

The world IDA Ireland operates in is now changing at a faster pace than ever – a new political global order, the questioning of globalisation, global tax reform and Brexit are but some of the challenges that it will face over the coming years.

Above:
Entrepreneur, engineer and philanthropist Martin Naughton, pictured in 1985 built Glen Dimplex into the world leader in electric heaters. Below: ringing the opening bell at Ireland Day London in 2014.

Above: Dr Pearse Lyons (Alltech), Terence O'Rourke (KPMG), Duncan Niederauer (New York Stock Exchange), Ian Hyland (*Business & Finance*), Dermot Desmond.

Below: Early plans for the IFSC, which transformed Dublin's Docklands.

The IFSC was the brainchild of stockbroking pioneer and financier Dermot Desmond, **above,** who built up a close relationship with Taoiseach Charles Haughey, a key supporter. They meet Coleman Lydon of Bank of Ireland at the launch of a Desmond project in 1991, **below.**

Above: Margaret Heffernan, CEO of Dunnes Stores, who took over from brother Ben Dunne in 1992. **Below:** American Ireland Fund leading lights Kieran McLoughlin and Loretta Brennan Glucksman with President Michael D Higgins.

Above: Arthur Ryan of Primark and retail magnate Galen Weston, whose family portfolio includes the clothing giant. **Right:** NYSE president Thomas Farley with Ian Hyland, publisher of *Business & Finance*.

Christine Moore
Freshways

Above: Feargal Quinn of Superquinn and Christine Moore of Freshways, 1993. **Left:** Don Keough, Coca-Cola boss and prominent Irish-American.

Herb Kelleher, founder of Southwest Airlines. The carrier provided crucial inspiration for Ryanair's low-cost model, and Kelleher remains a legendary Irish-American figure in the aviation industry.

Pádraig O hUiginn: the lynchpin former Department of the Taoiseach civil servant is closely associated with Charles Haughey and the IFSC project.

Right: Beef baron Larry Goodman, 1991, with his acting finance director Bernard Somers. **Below:** Edward Haughey, Lord Ballyedmond, built Norbrook Laboratories into a billion-pound cross-border enterprise before his untimely death in 2014.

98FM, Esat Digifone and Digicel founder Denis O'Brien. Telecommunications made the Dublin entrepreneur a billionaire, and he expanded his interests to encompass Communicorp, Independent News & Media, Topaz Energy and Actavo.

Clockwise from top left: Airtricity/Mainstream Renewable Power founder Eddie O'Connor, Peter Sutherland, Denis O'Brien. International corporate financier Paul Connolly pictured with Kofi Annan, and **below. Below left:** The Esat Digifone licence application, 1995.

Above: Richard
Burrows, chairman
and chief executive,
Irish Distillers Group;
Patrick Ricard, chairman and
chief executive of Groupe Pernod
Ricard; and Leo Crawford, chief
executive of BWG, 2000. **Left:**
executive and board director
Baroness Detta O'Cathain
with Ian Hyland of
Business & Finance.

Above: Maurice Pratt, 2006. The Quinnsworth boss was one of the country's most familiar business faces in the 1980s and '90s, and Quinnsworth would be taken over by Tesco.

Right: The six-word headline on this 1986 front cover says it all.

25th December, 1986, £1.20 (Incl. Tax)

Business
&FINANCE

Women in Business- gimmick or reality?

Mairead McEntee of MEK Foods

US senator George Mitchell, a key figure in the Northern Ireland peace process, at the Business & Finance Awards and at Ireland Day in New York.

Above: Former Bank of Ireland governor Laurence Crowley with John Major, UK Prime Minister 1990-1997. **Right:** Richie Boucher, CEO of Bank of Ireland from 2009 to 2017.

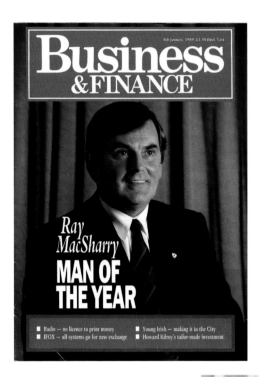

Left: Recently-departed Minister for Finance Ray MacSharry, Man of the Year in 1989, is remembered for stabilising the public finances via cutbacks and reforms that earned him the nickname Mac The Knife.

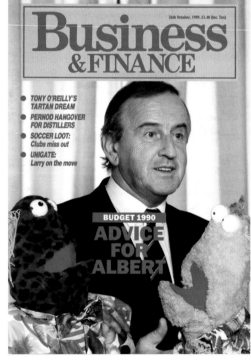

Right: MacSharry was succeeded by Albert Reynolds, who was ambushed by Zig and Zag on one of the zanier covers enjoyed by *Business & Finance* readers over the years.

CHAPTER 23

Enter the Entrepreneur

A CULTURE OF ENTREPRENEURSHIP TOOK TIME TO ESTABLISH ITSELF IN IRELAND – BUT RECENT YEARS HAVE SEEN THE COUNTRY PRODUCE MEMORABLE CHARACTERS AND IDEAS.

The entrepreneur has become a pivotal figure in the global business scene. The idealised figure of the lone businessman with energy, inspiration, tenacity and charm has, over time, become more and more ingrained in the general understanding of how business works, and what success in business looks like. The reality is rarely as clear-cut: entrepreneurs are part of a network of actors, from government agencies to financiers to corporations, who all contribute to the success, or otherwise, of any given venture. However, the nature of modern, globalised, networked business often means that an individual with an idea can seem mercurial. Today's young Irish entrepreneurs are savvy marketers, of businesses and themselves, but they're building on a legacy of innovation and disruption that stretches back, at the very least, to the arrival on these shores of Henry Ford.

That said, the early days of the Irish Free State were not exactly an ideal environment for the entrepreneurial spirit to flourish. Ireland's economy was small, with a deep-rooted agricultural focus. The export of live cattle to Britain, while certainly a staid industry in need of disruption, was both capital- and labour-intensive; not an inviting prospect for budding businessmen. Lean years of trade wars with Britain, the rationing of the Emergency, and expensive credit due to the Irish pound's link with the British pound, meant that there was little or no culture of self-started business. Even as the economy began to be liberalised in the 1950s, government policy was increasingly focused on securing foreign direct investment in the manufacturing sector, and companies that could provide large numbers of jobs for unskilled or semi-skilled workers.

This remained the case right through to the 1990s at least, with foreign firms growing in importance to the economy, backed by official policy such as export profits tax relief, while indigenous Irish industry tended to contract. In an IDA report from the mid-1970s, entrepreneurs of the time spoke about the divide between themselves and the newly-arrived foreign firms which they saw as likely to be given far more resources – land, facilities, staff and credit – at far lower prices than themselves. Between 1973, when Ireland joined the EU, and the end of the century, there was an actual drop in the number of people employed by Irish businesses. Padraic White, former managing director of the IDA, has said that the effect on Irish industry of exposure to globalised free trade after EU accession was "horrendous".

Despite the unwelcoming environment, a number of factors came together in the 1960s to accelerate the emergence of an indigenous entrepreneurial sector. Firstly, the population was becoming younger and more urban, with agriculture slowly beginning to decrease in economic importance for the country as a whole.

Secondly, unemployment was dropping, and more people had more disposable income to spend on consumer goods. Finally, and perhaps most importantly for Pat Quinn, society itself was becoming a touch more liberal.

Quinn was born in Leitrim in 1935, the son of a grocer and a garda. Aged just 23, and with experience as a store manager for Woolworths in Limerick, Quinn and his uncle opened Quinn Co, a grocery store on the main street of Longford town. The young Quinn quickly became involved in promoting events, bringing the likes of Joe Dolan, the Drifters and the Royal Showband to the midlands. After marrying in 1961 Quinn moved to Canada, where he again worked in department stores and promoted, among many pop acts, the first Rolling Stones concert in North America.

Returning to Ireland in 1965, Quinn had clearly learned a little something from the entertainment industry and he quickly applied that knowledge to retail. He was employed as general manager at H Williams and Co, an 11-store supermarket chain in Dublin, when the company decided not to participate in the new Stillorgan Shopping Centre. Quinn decided to strike out on his own and open a store there himself. Quinnsworth was born in December 1966, and the first store was opened by Seán Lemass. Five years later, Quinnsworth had grown to six stores, and boasted a turnover of £6m.

Quinn himself was central to its success, taking a very active and present part in the chain's advertising; he regularly appeared in different coloured polo necks (quite a fashion statement for a businessman in 1960s Ireland), he put a photograph on himself on all the advertisements, he opened on Sundays, and even gave away a car every week at a time when most people couldn't afford one (Quinn himself owned two Rolls Royces and a Mercedes, along with some racehorses). One month he gave away a semi-detached house – it was all good publicity, and it all fed back into the chain's success.

In 1973 Quinn sold Quinnsworth to the British supermarket operator Galen Weston, emerging with no debts and £500,000. He bought the Mooney chain of 13 pubs in Dublin and the Kilternan Sports Hotel on the Dublin-Wicklow border. In the major recession of the early 1970s, the business quickly folded and took the chain of pubs with it. He opened several pool halls in Dublin, Bray and Drogheda, before another budget supermarket venture, Shoparound, went bust in just three months during another recession in 1986. After this disappointment, aged 50, Quinn and his family moved back to Canada, where he eventually found success running Irish restaurants and pubs.

Woodchester watershed

Of course, not all entrepreneurs have been as publicity-friendly as Pat Quinn. Craig McKinney came to Ireland from Scotland in 1970, aged 22, to work for Hamilton Leasing, a company then owned by the British venture capital company 3i. After failing to secure the funding to buy out the company from its British owners in 1977, McKinney and his brother Jack subsequently set up a rival leasing company – Woodchester. The company specialised in leasing office equipment and cars, becoming one of the primary providers of forecourt finance in the country. Favourable tax arrangements in the leasing sector at the time allowed the company to expand quickly, and within ten years it was making profits of more than £36 million. With McKinney at the helm Woodchester expanded into the UK market, taking a 29.9% stake in Lookers motor finance group in 1985. Woodchester relied on equity partners to provide the necessary financial backing for its rapid growth, and its two of its most important partners were AIB's venture capital fund ACT, and British and Commonwealth, which financed Woodchester's £20 million takeover of Hamilton Leasing's Irish wing in 1986. At the time, Hamilton was Ireland's biggest non-bank leasing company.

In 1987 Woodchester expanded into the banking sector proper with the acquisition of Bowmaker Bank, followed by Trinity Bank in 1988 and Mercantile Credit in 1991. The French bank Credit Lyonnais acquired a 29.9% stake in Woodchester in 1989, later increasing to a majority share. This provided Woodchester with a greater freedom in terms of available capital, but the French bank's own troubles also led to some tough times for Woodchester, with profit-warnings and constant rumours that the bank would be sold during the 1990s.

By 1997, with McKinney still leading the day-to-day operations of the company, Woodchester could boast of a huge motor leasing operation, an insurance brokerage and a bank, with business in Ireland, Northern Ireland, Britain, Portugal and Denmark. That year the US-based General Electric Capital bought Woodchester in a deal that valued the company at £591m. McKinney retired from the company shortly afterwards, and now spends most of his time in South America where he owns a ranch outside Buenos Aires and concentrates on his polo team, also named Woodchester.

McKinney and Woodchester moved into commercial finance at the end of the 1980s, at a time when the deregulation of the credit markets across Europe and the US had increased both demand and supply considerably. The effects of this were felt in Ireland as much as anywhere else, perhaps most visibly in the foundation of the IFSC, but truly across the entire business spectrum.

This period was the first time when the figures of the banker and the financier became paramount in Irish business, in part because banking and financial services themselves were now major growth industries within Irish business. The greater availability of capital was made possible by the international banks and fund managers now using Dublin as a base, which created significant new business opportunities for Irish banks and other financial institutions. All that resting capital had to be put to work, and Irish entrepreneurs were stepping up to make that happen. McKinney himself was at the heart of this, with Woodchester providing finance to some of the most exciting prospects in Irish business. One of these was Richard Murphy, whose Xtra-Vision brand of video rental shops had blossomed from a single outlet in 1982 to over 300 across Ireland, the UK and the US less than ten years later. Murphy was seen as one of the new wave of Irish entrepreneurs, known for the brash and sometimes highly-sexualised branding of his stores, his fast cars, and his party-filled lifestyle. Xtra-Vision was launched on the Irish stock market in April 1989, with the stock price opening at 48p before later peaking at 107p. At the height of his success, and at just 30 years of age, Murphy was worth a reputed £25m.

Xtra-Vision's expansion was fuelled by investor money, but the fundamentals of the business were soon discovered to be unsound. According to a profile in *Business & Finance*, the profits the company was making ignored its depreciation policy that wrote off video tapes, most of which had a useful economic life of six weeks, over three years. It quickly became obvious that the company was losing cash at an alarming rate. Within a year of going public Xtra-Vision had debts of £18.3m and losses of £20.3m. Cambridge, a fast-growing financial services group led by Colm Menton and Liam Booth, bought a 61% share in Xtra-Vision in 1991, and Murphy left the company. Cambridge itself collapsed just two years later and the brand was later run by Paul O'Grady Walsh and owned by Blockbuster Entertainment, the American video-rental giant.

Murphy wasn't finished with video rental though. In 1993, after seeing out a two-year non-compete clause, he founded Chartbusters. Backed by property developers Paddy Kelly, John Walsh, John McCabe and Jarlath Sweeney, Murphy eventually opened 54 Chartbusters stores around Ireland, using a similar model to Xtra-Vision but incorporating tanning beds and internet cafés, before it entered receivership in 2009. "I was offered £30m to sell out to Blockbusters but refused it," Murphy later said of his Chartbusters experience. "At least three times a day I kick myself for saying no."

The increasingly volatile markets of the 1980s were visible in the quick rise-and-fall of Murphy's Xtra-Vision, and they played a major part in the story of Robin Power too. Power, a dentist by trade, got his start in the property business after the "accidental" purchase of a restaurant in Cork in 1973. He renovated the property, turning it into three shops before renting them out.

From there his property dealings expanded, with the *Irish Independent* calling him "the most audacious Irish property player of the eighties." During that decade Dublin was still a city in some level of disrepair, and Power took full advantage. He developed the Powerscourt Town Centre and Stephen's Green Shopping Centre, transforming the south inner city in the process.

By the time Power Corporation went public in 1987 the company was worth £50m. Power expanded into the UK and the US, getting involved in deals with Donald Trump (with whom he planned to redevelop the Ambassador Hotel in Los Angeles, where Bobby Kennedy was assassinated) and British boxer-turned-property-developer George Walker.

It was a project undertaken with the latter that would prove Power's first major downfall. In 1984 the pair had begun redeveloping the Trocadero building in London's Piccadilly Circus as a tourist-oriented entertainment, cinema and shopping complex but booming property prices during the eighties had slumped by the decade's end. Heavily indebted through its aggressive expansion, Power Corp was pushed into a precarious financial position and its partners ran into difficulties. The company's shares, which peaked at 215p in 1990 (giving it a stock market value of about £230 million), had fallen to 27p by late 1992, when Power resigned from the company to allow for its restructuring. Power himself had personal debts of up to £8m at the time.

However, much like Murphy, Power remained involved in business, though on a much smaller scale. From the mid-nineties he began buying houses in the affluent areas of south Dublin, concentrating on Killiney, Glasthule and Dalkey where he and his wife, fellow property developer Michelle Kavanagh, live in Sorrento Terrace. During the Celtic Tiger years, these investments began to pay off as property prices in the area skyrocketed. During these years property development became one of the prime drivers of the Irish economy, with the construction industry and banking sector ballooning in size until they rivalled traditional manufacturing industries for capital investment and job provision.

One figure who has expertly navigated the shifting sands of the modern Irish economy is Paul Coulson, chairman of the Ardagh Group. Coulson, a graduate of Trinity College Dublin, spent five years at Price Waterhouse Cooper before founding Yeoman Investments, a private investment vehicle, in 1980. Yeoman based itself in Shannon to take advantage of the area's Special Development Zone and low tax rates. In 1988 Yeoman acquired British company CLF Holdings for over £100m, saddling the group with significant debt. As Robin Power would also experience, the British economy slumped dramatically in 1990, and a major division of CLF posted large losses. The Yeoman share price also plummeted.

After this chastening experience, Coulson sued his former advisors to the tune of £44m, paid down the debts and began investing again in earnest. He acquired Tipperary Crystal from a receiver and invested in CityJet, but most importantly he acquired a 15% stake in Ardagh PLC, recently renamed from the Irish Glass Bottle Company. By 2000 he had 23% of Ardagh and in 2002 moved to delist Ardagh from the stock exchange and spin-off the overseas glass manufacturing operations into a new entity, Ardagh Glass. A new company, South Wharf, was established to hold the remaining assets, consisting of the leasehold interest in the Irish Glass site in Ringsend. Reflecting the changing economic times, Coulson recognised that the Ringsend site was worth more as a potential development site than as a manufacturing base.

Using a little-known loophole that allowed tenants with a lease in excess of 50 years to acquire the fee simple of the property, South Wharf was able to take control of the property for a very favourable price. Just over a year later the site was sold to the Becbay consortium, headed by developer Bernard McNamara along with the Dublin Docklands Development Authority and funded in part by a €288m loan from Anglo Irish Bank, for a fee of €412m. It is thought that Ardagh received about €273m from the sale of the site. In 2012, after the property market crashed, the still-vacant site was valued at just €45m and the *Irish Independent* would later call the deal "one of the signature events of the madness of the Celtic Tiger years".

Since then Coulson has steadily expanded Ardagh's global operations, acquiring assets from major European glass manufacturers Ball Corp and Rexam for €3.2bn, and buying global metal packaging group Impress Coöperatieve UA for €1.7bn. The company, now split between glass and metal manufacture, has annual revenues of over €7.7bn and employs 23,000 people in 22 countries, making it one of the largest companies to emerge from Ireland in recent times. An IPO on the New York Stock Exchange in 2017 valued the company, of which Coulson owns roughly 36%, at about €5bn.

Taking notice

As evidenced by the remarkable sale of the Glass Bottle site, the links between property developers, bankers and State bodies grew increasingly complex over the course of the Celtic Tiger years. Gillian Bowler found herself straddling the different sides of that divide over the course of a business career that made her, as Kathy Sheridan put it in *The Irish Times*, "the first successful businesswoman many of us actually noticed". Bowler was born in London in 1952 and raised in the Isle of Wight, where her childhood was interrupted by a near-fatal kidney disease that would linger for the rest of her life. She moved to Dublin when she was 19 and in 1975 she and her husband, Harry Sydner, founded the travel agency Budget Travel. At the time, foreign holidays were far from commonplace in Ireland. At the end of the first year of trading from their basement office on Baggot Street they had sold 200 holidays. By 1983 they were selling 25,000 holidays out of a total annual market of 200,000. Bowler was known for being an outspoken and sometimes controversial marketer, with refreshingly honest sales pitches and a cheeky approach to advertising.

Bowler sold Budget Travel to the Granada Group in 1987 for £4m, in a deal that included a continuing role as joint managing director with Sydner. A decade later Budget Travel had become Ireland's largest package holiday company, and by 1999 was flying 400,000 people to holiday destinations, operating 30 shops in Ireland and employing 400 people.

Bowler had an active and varied career outside of Budget Travel too. She was the founding chair of Fáilte Ireland, the State's tourism board, and founding chair of the Irish Museum of Modern Art. However, she was better known for her position with Irish Life. Bowler became a board member of Irish Life in 1998, and became the chair of Irish Life and Permanent in 2004, becoming the first woman to chair an Irish public limited company in the process. She remained in the position through the crash and ensuing economic crisis, a series of events through which IL&P did not come through unscathed, before stepping down in 2010.

After leaving IL&P Bowler concentrated on clickandgo.com, an online venture that attempted to modernise the failing travel agent sector she had so successfully built up 30 years previously. Bowler died in December 2016 from complications related to her long-standing kidney disease.

Despite the overwhelmingly male environment that is Irish business, Gillian Bowler was not the sole female presence at the top of the pile. Anne Heraty has been one of the most respected businesspeople in Ireland since co-founding specialist resourcing/placement company CPL in 1989. After working for Grafton Recruitment for several years, Heraty and her co-founder Keith O'Malley recognised a growing need for staff with particular skills at new technology companies then setting up in Ireland. Computer Placement Ltd set out to connect those companies with the people they needed, and quickly expanded to service other sectors: finance, industrial manufacturing, engineering, construction and sales.

In 1992 Heraty bought out her co-founder and took sole control of the company. Her husband, Paul Carroll, joined as director of business development in 1996 as the company was being restructured to better manage its continuing expansion. The company listed publicly in 1999, on both the Irish and London stock exchanges, making Heraty the first female CEO of a PLC. CPL has since acquired a number of recruitment and human resource solutions companies across Ireland, the UK and eastern Europe, though its core business remains in servicing multinational technology companies in Ireland. Heraty remains head of the business she founded almost 30 years ago, and has won a number of Businessperson of the Year awards for her work. In 2016 she became president of business representative body IBEC.

It was only in the 1990s that specific government efforts were made to encourage indigenous entrepreneurship, with the Industrial Development Act 1993 acting on the Culliton Report of 1992 which urged a renewed focus on indigenous industry. For the first time in Irish history policy moved towards encouragement of micro-enterprises, or those with fewer than ten employees. A system of local enterprise agencies was set up, devolving decision-making to boards representative of local business interests, local government and social partners. By the year 2000 the Global Entrepreneurship Monitor, an international think-tank, would claim that there were around 200,000 apparent 'entrepreneurs', or people running their own business, in the Republic. GEM did concede, however, that only a very small proportion were involved in anything innovative – most were simply replicating existing services to exploit a perceived gap.

Tech revolution

The most common business sectors for Irish entrepreneurs in the year 2000 were business services, retail, consumer services and construction, but the rapid economic growth of the 1990s and early 2000s was generated by a wave of new, foreign-owned computer manufacturing firms. Gradually a number of successful Irish firms emerged in ancillary areas, mostly based around software, services and internet technology. One of those firms was 123 Money, the first online broker in Ireland, selling motor insurance, home and pet policies under-written by the Irish office of US Travelers Insurance. Derek Richardson, the company's founder, had followed his father Herbert into the insurance business. Recognising the potential of online trading early on, 123 quickly captured the space through price competitiveness and colourful, earworm-driven advertising. When the company was sold to British insurance giant Royal Sun Alliance in 2010, Richardson made some €39 million from the sale.

Since then Richardson has maintained interests in some Irish businesses, including Hello, an online financial services business; and Insurance Solutions, a corporate insurance broking business, but his primary interest has been in Wasps Rugby Club in the UK. The club was on the brink of bankruptcy: they had no stadium, just £65.16 in the bank, £3m in annual losses and £1m in debt. The head coach had to pay for buses to away games and strapping for his players out of his own pocket – until Richardson stepped in. Just four years later the club now boasts a 32,000-seater stadium with indoor conference and entertain-ment facilities, and the second-biggest turnover in European rugby.

Eddie Jordan is another Irish entrepreneur transcending business and sport. A former Bank of Ireland clerk with a unique personality, Jordan's early instinct for dealmaking is commemorated in legendary stories of him standing on the Naas Road selling carpets to rivals on their way to Mondello Park, or cars to bank customers who applied to him for loans. It was a crucial skill that enabled him to build Jordan Grand Prix into a Ferrari-beating, Formula 1 World Championship-challenging team. Jordan exited the sport – or business, if you prefer – as an owner in 2005, but the team he founded continues to punch far above its weight. It had been a close-run thing in 1991 or so, when 'EJ' was evading bailiffs and ringing his local bank branch to pre-approve cheques and prevent them from bouncing. Surviving from deal to deal, and discovering one Michael Schumacher in the process, the late 1990s were glorious days of Benson & Hedges-backed race wins and a knack for publicity and branding that made the Silverstone-based tricolour-flying Irish team one of the most popular in the paddock. The Jordan name is sadly missed above the garage door, but 'EJ' remains a familiar face as a TV pundit in the F1 circus and his business empire now extends across property, publishing, hedge funds and more besides – enough to keep him in Sunseeker yachts and loud open-necked shirts for the foreseeable future.

Another extraordinary example of determination and growth comes via the life of Edward Haughey, later Lord Ballyedmond, who died in a helicopter crash in 2014. According to his son's funeral oration, Edward Senior was a "renaissance man" who "lived the life of five men": Westminster peer, Irish senator, one-time emigrant to America, self-taught cross-Border businessman – and founder of veterinary pharmaceutical firm Norbrook Laboratories.

In 1968 Haughey set up business in Newry with "a briefcase and a price list", importing and rebranding products before manufacturing them himself. "What made Mr Haughey's enterprise different from others at the time was that these products were manufactured to strict specifications," wrote *The Irish Times* after his death. "This is exactly what put him ahead of his competitors – when new legislation governing veterinary pharmaceuticals was eventually introduced by the then European Common Market, Haughey was doing what few others were at the time – already complying with the legislation. It gave him a major advantage."

Manufacturing began in 1970, first at Bessbrook Mill and then, in 1972, at Greenbank Industrial Estate. The first of many patents came in 1974, and with it a focus on developing Norbrook's export business. Winning a major contract with Dutch company Philips Duphar in 1976 established the company as a leader in the international market for animal health, and by the late 1970s it was exporting to Europe, Africa, the Middle East and Canada, followed by further expansion into Japan in 1980. Norbrook was granted approval by the US Food and Drug Administration (FDA) to manufacture injectables for the US market in 1987 and remains one of the very few companies manufacturing outside the US to win FDA approval and authorisation to export this type of product to the States.

The milestones continued unbroken in the 1990s, with Norbrook opening its Armagh Road facility in 1990 and a Kenyan manufacturing plant in 1993, supplying the east African market. 1996 saw the company win its largest contract yet, supplying sterile antibiotics to a US multinational for $33m. By 1999, when it was preparing to enter the human medicines market, profits were over £10m, 35% of its business was in Europe and the company had over 7,000 licences or registrations to sell products around the world. "We haven't ruled out going public after the millennium," Ballyedmond said a year previously.

It never happened. Norbrook developed over 70 new products as the company remained firmly private, investing heavily in chemical synthesis facilities as well as sales and distribution in the US, Australia, New Zealand and Brazil. Its first product for cats and dogs arrived in 2001. Norbrook reached another landmark in 2009 with the launch of Closamectin, a pour-on solution to treat fluke, worms and parasites in meat-producing animals. It was the result of six years' work by 80 scientists and an investment of £3.5m. Despite the recession, that year alone Norbrook grew 12%, with Ballyedmond hailing the product as a "tremendous breakthrough". A fifth Queen's Award for Enterprise came in 2011.

Lord Ballyedmond valued his privacy, rarely granting interviews, but a 2001 interview with Nick Webb of the *Sunday Independent* provided a unique insight into a unique personality. "I have made several mistakes and I've learnt from my mistakes," he acknowledged. "The worst mistake I ever made was probably not doing something. On three occasions I didn't buy companies, because I thought they were too expensive and didn't think that there was anything there."

He also revealed his resistance to numerous takeover offers or flotation opportunities. "I find it difficult to work with other people. I don't know whether it's an insecurity on my part or whether I'm an autocrat or even a combination of both. But whatever it is, it has resulted in me not being able to work fruitfully with other people." That proved little impediment to success, of course: at the time of his death he was Northern Ireland's richest man, and Norbrook's growth continues apace.

According to the directors' reports after Lord Ballyedmond's death, the company took steps to strengthen its board and management team and appointed Lady Ballyedmond, Professor James Haughey and Edward Haughey to the board, and it was their intention that Norbrook would remain under the control of the Haughey family as an independent firm. Investment and innovation have continued: new laboratories at Armagh Road in late 2016, warehousing in Monaghan, and five new products launched in 2016 alone.

Today the privately-owned company now run by CEO Liam Nagle – who previously served as CEO of the Sisk group – has annual revenues of £239m. The company sells to 120 countries and has manufacturing plants in four continents; Norbrook employs over 1,500 people in Newry and a further 1,500 worldwide.

Lord Ballyedmond's legacy is comprehensive and extends far beyond business. The 2014 helicopter crash took place in heavy fog departing his 17th-century stately home in Norfolk, Gillingham Hall, and the aftermath saw tributes for the late Lord Ballyedmond pour in from associates in business and public life. A supporter of the peace process, the Christian Brothers Dundalk-educated businessman was reportedly the first person to serve in both the Irish and British upper houses since the Marquess of Lansdowne in the 1920s. Appointed to the Seanad by Albert Reynolds, he was also close to David Trimble and encouraged Unionist buy-in to the Good Friday Agreement in 1998. That brought his appointment to the House of Lords, where he supported the Conservatives.

He also assembled a prestigious property portfolio in Britain and Ireland, including Corby Castle in Cumbria and landmark residences in London and Dublin. He had a long-running interest in aviation, serving as the first chair of the Irish Aviation Authority, was a director of Northern Irish aircraft manufacturer Shorts and owned Carlisle Airport for several years – as well as proposing a circular air route linking regional airports in Ireland.

He will be remembered foremost among the business community as a pioneer in an industry that has since burgeoned in Ireland, paving the way for a thriving life sciences community that includes domestic start-ups and an impressive rollcall of foreign direct investment alike.

Tech and globalisation

Recent years have seen two major interconnected threads in Irish entrepreneurship. First is the booming tech sector, centred globally on Silicon Valley but with enough energy and capital to sustain significant bubbles all around the world. Dublin is no exception. The second thread is globalisation. By virtue of our increasingly connected world, the most successful Irish entrepreneurs are operating on a global scale from the start. Their expansions have been more rapid than ever before, perhaps using Ireland only as a base for an operation that was conceived and implemented on a worldwide level.

Dómhnal Slattery's success as CEO of Avolon, an aircraft leasing company, is an example of the latter. Slattery began his career in 1989, initially in marketing roles with Guinness Peat Aviation (GPA) and GECAS. In 1994, shortly after GPA was acquired by GE Capital, he established his own aircraft advisory and investment banking services company, International Aviation Management Group (IAMG). In 2001 the Royal Bank of Scotland Group acquired IAMG for £35m.

Slattery remained as chief executive of the new RBS Aviation Capital business from 2001 to 2004. In 2005 he founded Claret, a private equity management fund that ran into difficulties after the financial crash of 2008. In 2010 Slattery founded Avolon, a global aircraft leasing business which, in just four years, became one of the top 10 lessors in the world. Avolon has been a global business from the start, securing funding from many of the leading banks around the world, from Dublin to Singapore, from Germany to Australia. This global outlook was cemented in 2015 when the company was bought by China's HNA conglomerate, which owns over 20 airlines, in a deal valued at $7.6bn. Slattery made upwards of €30m from the sale, and continues in his role as chief executive from a new base in Hong Kong.

Where Slattery's success has come in a globalised version of an established business sector, Paddy Cosgrave has been at the heart of a new wave of internet-based industry in Ireland since the establishment of the Web Summit in 2010. In just a few short years the Web Summit has grown from a single conference of tech sector leaders in Dublin to a global brand with sold-out events in Lisbon, Hong Kong and New Orleans. The success of the Web Summit, first in Dublin and now around the world, has illustrated the appetite for access to tech industry executives, and the tensions that exist between this new era of internet-based entrepreneurship and the existing government support structures.

Cosgrave got his start in business shortly after leaving college in Trinity in Dublin when the late publican Hugh O'Regan, owner of the Thomas Read chain of pubs in Dublin, gifted him an office on Stephen's Green and €60,000.

From there Cosgrave orchestrated the Rock the Vote Ireland campaign of 2007, which attempted to increase the youth turnout at the general election of that year, and the MiCandidate site, which listed and detailed all the candidates running for the 2009 European election. In 2009 Cosgrave organised F.ounders, a small conference for the founders of companies – 150 people showed up. In 2010 the Web Summit proper began, attracting 400 including Jack Dorsey and Chad Hurley, co-founders of Twitter and YouTube respectively. By 2014 over 20,000 people were attending the annual conference, which was beginning to strain at the limits of its base in the RDS. In 2015 an increasingly bitter and public argument began between the Irish government and Web Summit, with Cosgrave to the fore. Cosgrave felt that the event wasn't getting the infrastruc-tural support it needed, despite receiving significant amounts of public funding, and that government bodies like the IDA weren't taking full advantage of the opportunities offered to them by Web Summit. Frustrated, Cosgrave moved the event to Lisbon in 2016.

The furore over the decision to move the event out of Ireland split both ways, with some seeing the government as inept for failing to retain a global-ly-recognised brand, while others lashed out at Cosgrave for turning his back on a country that had given him and his event so much necessary support. Two of Ireland's most successful recent entrepreneurs, John and Patrick Collison of the Stripe payments software firm, have made their own criticisms of the Irish environment for start-up businesses, claiming that credit and venture capital are much more difficult to secure for businesses, like their own, that are entirely software-based. This led the brothers to move Stripe's headquarters to Silicon Valley in 2010. Michael Carey, founder of The Company of Food, a specialist food sector investment business, and chairman of Bord Bia, has written in agreement with these claims.

Given that many of the most high-profile entrepreneurial success stories of the last ten years have been rapid-growth software or services businesses, it remains to be seen whether the official policy of government agencies and banks can adapt to this new environment.

PART

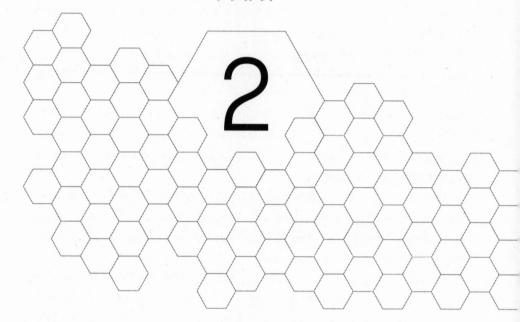

2

INTERVIEWS
2013-2017

CHAPTER 24

Interview: TK Whitaker
In conversation with Ian Hyland

THE LATE PUBLIC SERVANT TK WHITAKER HAS BEEN ACKNOWLEDGED AS A PIVOTAL
FIGURE IN 20TH CENTURY IRISH HISTORY, AND SHARED HIS OUTLOOK AND
MEMORIES SHORTLY BEFORE HIS DEATH IN 2017.

Dr Ken Whitaker is probably the most influential civil servant in the history of the State. He founded some of the institutions that have been key in shaping modern Ireland, in particular the Economic and Social Research Institute.

TK Whitaker was born in pre-partition Co Down in December 1916, to a father from Co Meath and a mother from Co Clare. Following his secondary education he joined the civil service in 1934. He gained first place in the entrance exams and would subsequently study for a degree in maths and a master's in economics part-time. His rise through the civil service was meteoric and he became the youngest ever secretary-general of the Department of Finance, in 1956, at the age of 39. It is a record that still stands.

The economic backdrop could not have been less favourable when Whitaker took over. Ireland was essentially a failed state: it was economically under-developed, with growth overwhelmingly dependent on agriculture. Emigration was rife and the standard of living was 60% of the European average. Two years after taking over at the Department of Finance Whitaker unveiled the seminal report *Economic Development*, which is generally credited as the single biggest factor that kickstarted the Irish economy. It aimed to diversify the economy and break down the massive protection barriers that were weighing on international trade. "I think what I was searching for really was some sort of arrangement of things that would work out well, because systems were elevating and I thought the Department of Finance had a particular responsibility in that regard," says Whitaker. "There had to be a foundation philosophy and a brave attempt to live by that. You can have an inverted pleasure in living a mess; you need to be a bit cold-blooded and sensible to offer any real guidance about policy."

Whitaker says that the Taoiseach from 1959 to 1966, Seán Lemass, fully supported the First Programme for Economic Expansion, which emerged from *Economic Development*. "I always had him in mind. He always picked the best way of dealing with things. He opened the way for people like myself who had some qualification to participate and be given the chance of being listened to on policy improvements and long-term policy methods." Whitaker says that one of his personal highlights from that period was changing the Department of Finance to an outward-looking "have a go" culture.

One of the central tenets of the First Programme was opening Ireland up to international investment. The Industrial Development Authority was a key part of this strategy. "It was very important. You know, governments need policy advice to keep them on the straight and narrow path. It is a tremendous advantage to any country if it develops a very good advisory body with advisory functions – there are so many countries and so many difficulties [to achieve] progress of a sustainable kind, you have to try and create a little idolatry of forwardness, of forward-looking care, the elements of good investments and good management."

The decision to join the European Economic Community in 1973 was another pivotal moment. Whitaker says that the move was just as important from a psychological perspective as it was in terms of economic development.

"I felt it was very important – actually vital. We needed all the stimulus we could muster because of the smallness of our economy, because [of the] agricultural economy mainly. We weren't sitting on any great goldmine – that we could see anything or induce policy action. I think all the while we got by and it was because people like [previous Taoiseach Éamon] De Valera realised that they themselves were at sea as far as their long-term policy was concerned, and it shifted the balance of interest of those who could see a way through what was then a very narrow gate. I think we've been very fortunate – I mean, luck has been on our side that an entity like the EEC evolved: that came at the right time when we realised we had to be competitive to make our way in the world."

The EU has experienced a number of crises over the past few years, so much so that there are concerns that the 28-member bloc could unravel. Despite ongoing problems, Whitaker says he is hopeful about the region's future and Ireland's role within it. "I'm that glad now and again some very deep thinking is done. I don't think we really have adopted any isolationist view about Europe. But of course it's still something to worry about because we have a lot of emigration and migration is becoming a huge issue."

Ireland has been very successful at attracting foreign multinationals, but the development of indigenous business has not always received the policy attention it deserves. Whitaker says that it is crucial to have a comprehensive strategy in place. "It is very important to have planning for the future, and that it is worked on by major public policy people. For a long time we were solving our problem by deserting our country. There has to be an integrated plan of action."

Since the economy crashed in 2008, emigration – the blight on economic development for most of the history of the State – once again became a feature of Irish life. Since then there has been a recovery, and key to this is the availability of a well-educated workforce. "We were fortunate in having quite a good number of factors working for us, education being one of the foremost. I think [that with] high grades, particularly at third level, I think we realise how beneficial it is. We can never go back to not being concerned about the latest information and guidance we can get from education."

Despite recent economic problems, Whitaker believes that Ireland has a bright economic future. "I am hopeful for Ireland, but I worry sometimes. I don't see that we're making enough effort to be highly competitive over a wide range of products. But I don't despair either. I don't think we've found enough underpinning for the old-fashioned production of agriculture. But I am heartened by the greater interest in education and particularly education of an industrial kind."

In changing that, what is the next step for Ireland? "I do believe it is time to refresh and judge again; things don't stand still. The outer world is changing all the time. I'm not sure we follow every phase of that; take the lessons that we learn."

TK Whitaker died in January 2017, leaving an indelible mark on the historical record – and his memory stands as an inspiration to all those in business, politics and public service.

CHAPTER 25

Interview: Pádraig O hUiginn
In conversation with Ian Hyland

THE FORMER SECRETARY GENERAL OF THE DEPARTMENT OF AN TAOISEACH DISCUSSES THE IFSC, ECONOMIC RECOVERY AND WORKING CLOSELY WITH CHARLES HAUGHEY.

Pádraig O hUiginn is among the most prominent civil servants in recent Irish history. He spent five decades in the public sector before retirement in 1993, rising to serve as secretary general of the Department of an Taoiseach between 1982 and his retirement.

He is perhaps best remembered for his close working relationship with the former Taoiseach Charles Haughey, and played a prominent role in one of the most successful public-private partnerships in the history of the State: the International Financial Services Centre (IFSC) in Dublin's Docklands in the late 1980s.

Pádraig O hUiginn went to school at St Finbarr's College in Cork. From school he went straight to the civil service, although he subsequently completed a master's in economic and social planning at the University of Edinburgh.

When O hUiginn achieved first place in the administrative officer exam he was assigned to the Department of Local Government. "When the government of which John Costello was Taoiseach was elected soon afterwards I was assigned to a special task," he remembers. "The government, if elected, had committed itself to abolishing the city and county management system. The secretary of the department, John Garvin, suggested to the new minister, Mr [Patrick] O'Donnell, that before deciding what to do he should go around the country and meet all city and county councillors and the chairpersons of urban councils to see what they thought of the proposal to abolish the management system. The minister agreed and I was given the task of arranging all those meetings, attending them and noting the views of councillors. When the meetings, which went on over a number of months, were over, the secretary asked me to report on the views of councillors and make any proposals I thought should be considered.

"I wrote a very short report to the effect that councillors generally did not want the management system removed as they were part-time politicians and had businesses and jobs to look after and could not do the work of managers. Their basic complaint was that managers paid little or no attention to their views. I suggested that to correct this situation councillors should be given the power by a two-thirds majority to direct a manager to perform a managerial function in the way they wanted. I argued that this would make the managers consult councillors more for fear of their two-thirds majority power.

"The secretary accepted this proposal as did the minister and the government, and the law was amended to give the two-thirds majority power to councillors. This forced managers to consult more fully with councillors and the dissatisfaction of councillors with the system disappeared. Local government has functioned now for over 60 years under that revised system, which as a young junior civil servant I suggested."

O hUiginn worked at the United Nations, first in Geneva and then in New York, between 1956 and 1964. "When I worked at the UN in Geneva I published a study on housing," he recalls. "In it I mentioned that rents in social housing should be sufficient to give funds to keep social housing in good repair. The Russian delegates wanted me to delete this recommendation but I refused. Two months later Khrushchev announced that he was adopting my recommendation by increasing rents so as to provide funds to keep social housing in good repair!"

Pádraig O hUiginn recalls the background to TK Whitaker's *Economic Development* and the First Programme for Economic Expansion, considered by many to be the biggest factor in shaping the modern industrial economy. The Industrial Development Authority (IDA) had been set up in the preceding decade, and an inflow of foreign direct investment was feeding through to economic activity, he says. Before Fianna Fáil took office in March 1957, Whitaker "had complained we were spending too much on social investment, particularly housing. He wasn't correct – we were spending proportionately more – but it wasn't that we were spending too much, it was that we weren't spending enough on economic investment.

"When the Fianna Fáil government came in he wrote the economic plan which emphasised much the same, and money was then found for the investment which had been lacking in the previous time. It was one of the reasons the government fell, because there was no money – yet when the Fianna Fáil government came in money was found."

O hUiginn says that the subsequent decision to join the European Economic Community was another important milestone in the development of the economy. "That was huge; we were now part of the EEC. The regional fund was coming in; that was an enormous benefit, and then the billions we got from the regional funds and subsequently the cohesion fund."

O hUiginn acknowledges that anti-EU sentiment has risen over the past few years, particularly in the wake of the 2010 bailout, but Ireland has been a huge net beneficiary from Brussels since accession in 1973 and that should not be forgotten, he says. He went to Brussels that year as a director of regional policy in the Council of Ministers. In this role, O hUiginn had responsibility for setting up the original framework of the regional fund.

"I published a report on the extent to which the civil service was centralised in Dublin," he remembers. "Two-thirds of civil servants were centralised in Dublin, whereas the proportion in other EC countries was 30-40%. In the light of this study the Council of Ministers agreed to loan me back to the government for two months to assist in developing a programme for a more decentralised civil service."

O hUiginn also demurred at the appointment of Professor Colin Buchanan to advise on regional strategy as he came from the most urbanised state in the EC whereas Ireland had the highest rural population. "I published a study that showed how successful industry was in the county towns and that this should be a focus of development strategy. The IDA backed that view."

After a few years in Brussels he decided to return to Dublin and go back to the civil service. He joined the newly-minted Department for Economic Planning and Development, where Noel Whelan was the secretary general.

"I was there only a few months when Charlie Haughey abolished it," he says: at the time this was seen as a power grab by the Taoiseach as he set up an economic policy group, under his control, to replace the department.

"Haughey abolished the planning department for the simple reason that you can't have two ministers in parity to each other. The minister for finance has no special ability to take down the minister for planning. There was a basic conflict of two ministers of equal standing trying to run the economy. And that was why, partly, Haughey decided: he was acting as a managing director, when somebody at the centre has to make the decision and he decided to be that person. But that was normal at the time: even Margaret Thatcher set up an economic policy group in order to cut through the red tape and the slowness with which policy development goes through the cabinet system.

"The cabinet system works OK in normal times, but not when you want speedy decisions. A policy originates in a department and it has to circulate a draft memorandum around the place and it has to deal with copious notes being written and replied to and so on, and months pass – and eventually a memorandum incorporating everything goes to government and they all have to understand this and so on."

Haughey set up his own economic policy unit in the aftermath of the oil crisis – which was standard procedure among OECD countries, says O hUiginn, because prime ministers all said: "We have to take charge, we've to run this like a business – we can't be waiting for memos to go around."

Perhaps one of O hUiginn's earliest and most significant contributions to public life came when he was the head of An Foras Forbartha, the National Physical Planning Institute, between 1964 and 1973. During this period he broke the marriage bar on employing women.

"I recruited a girl who was an expert – some qualification she had obtained in London on the protection and preservation of sand dunes; very important to us. We have so many sand dunes: we're an island with sand dunes all over which are very dangerous if they are not treated.

"There are historical records of whole villages being consumed. The big threat at the time was the sand dunes in Brittas Bay [Co Wicklow] and this girl was working on this and laying out a plan for it and so on, when she came to me one day and said 'I'm leaving you' and I said 'oh why?' and she said 'I'm getting married'.

"I said 'congratulations', but I said 'you don't have to leave'. 'What do you mean?', she said, 'I have to after the marriage bar'. I said 'no – are you prepared to come back as a consultant?' and then she said yes, and I said 'same terms'. 'Yes,' she said, 'I'd be delighted and my husband will be even more delighted', so she came back. I went to the board, and we had a mixed board of civil servants and they agreed without any thought that it seemed like the natural thing to do.

"I got a call from the head man in [the Department of] Finance, and he said 'Pádraig I hear you have re-employed a girl who got married' and he said 'you can't do that', and I said 'why not?'. And he says: 'you know the marriage bar?' and I said 'I know, but we're a private company and I have a mixed board and this girl is invaluable, I can't let her go'.

"He says 'you're insisting on it', and I said 'yes I am, my board has approved it' and he said 'you'll hear from us'. Within six months, Finance was in a similar case where a girl went to get married – she had come in as an administrative officer – and was going to retire upon marriage, and they said 'no, you can stay on'. They ended the marriage bar six months after I broke it. It was the end of 1964."

However, the two key events for which O hUiginn will be most remembered are his role in the blueprint for economic recovery written in the mid-1980s, and the subsequent development of the International Financial Services Centre.

When Charles Haughey formed a minority Fianna Fáil government in 1987, the country was on the precipice. Unemployment was running at 18% and debt was at 122% of GNP. There had been calls for the International Monetary Fund to take over the running of the economy.

Haughey was implacably opposed to the idea, says O hUiginn. "If we bring these guys [IMF] in we're gone. This is a parliamentary democracy and we have to run the country; we're elected to do it, he says. If these guys come in, civil servants are going to run the country." O hUiginn had been responsible for coming up with the seminal *Strategy for Development* document in 1986 through his chairmanship of the National Economic and Social Council. It called for much tighter control of public finances in order to rein in the ballooning levels of debt. He says that he told Garret FitzGerald, the then Taoiseach, that he should adopt the programme because "even Fianna Fáil will have to support you.

"He said no – I'm going to set up a committee, which included Professor [Brendan] Walsh from UCD and Tom Hardiman [former director general of RTÉ]. But I said this is urgent; I said how long will it take them to produce this report? I said that those people will not agree to produce a report in six months and in the end I think it took them a year and a half.

"I think MacSharry points out in his book that the delay was fatal. Of course Garret had the problem of the Labour Party, who wouldn't compromise. But the reality of Garret FitzGerald is that he was not really interested in the economy; his interest was Northern Ireland."

The Fine Gael-Labour coalition government fell because it could not agree spending cuts. Fianna Fáil formed a minority government in March 1987 with Haughey as Taoiseach and Ray MacSharry as the minister for finance. They quickly set about the *Strategy for Development*, which stabilised the public finances in the early 1990s and formed the basis for the Celtic Tiger.

O hUiginn says that MacSharry was "wonderful" as minister of finance. "I can remember he was unyielding in refusing extra expenditure and in cutting expenditure. I remember once pleading with him on behalf of some poor devils in Sligo, which was his own constituency, involved in something to do with rivers, and I said it wouldn't cost much and he said 'I'm not giving way to anybody, not even people in my own constituency'."

One of his more colourful encounters with Haughey was when the Taoiseach came back from a weekend away in Mayo. "He said 'do you know Monsignor [James] Horan' and I said 'well I know who he is but I don't know him'.

"Well he said 'he's the parish priest of Knock and he wants to build an international airport in Knock. What do you think?'" O hUiginn said that it would cost roughly €12m, which alternatively would only pay for a few miles of motorway.

"And he said Maurice Doyle [former secretary general in the Department of Finance] will never agree" – and O hUiginn told him to ignore Doyle: in no uncertain terms he told Haughey that he was in charge.

Support for the creative industries was another high-profile Haughey-era policy, as O hUiginn recalls. "I suggested to Mr Haughey that we should stimulate filmmaking by giving tax relief on investment in filmmaking. The industry now employs 6,000 in filmmaking. I also suggested to Mr Haughey the tax incentive for rental housing, which was highly successful, employing 10,000 at one stage."

Perhaps O hUiginn's most enduring legacy is the role he played in setting up the IFSC. It was originally the brainchild of Dermot Desmond, the founder of NCB Stockbrokers, who approached Haughey about the idea. The then-Taoiseach approached O hUiginn about setting up and chairing a meeting with a number of vested interests from the public and private sectors.

"I was given the task by Mr Haughey of establishing the Financial Services Centre and succeeded in doing so. It now employs 30,000 people," reflects O hUiginn. "Dermot and I knew each other; we played golf and so on. So we had a meeting and we called in all the experts both public and private, all the banks and so on, and they were all at a loss – the one question they were all asking, except the IDA who were very positive, was: what services are you talking about?

"Well I said 'you're bankers; you must know'. And they said 'what financial services could we be attracting here?'"

Haughey heard about the lack of progress at the meeting and summoned Desmond and O hUiginn to his office. He put O hUiginn in charge of the project, with the full authority to make decisions. He then went about setting up a committee that would be responsible for selling the concept of the IFSC abroad. "Then the problem was that we were very slow at getting any takers, although I remember making a speech in London that said if you want to set up in Dublin we'd give you a decision in two weeks; I think it was six months in Luxembourg. But we weren't getting the applications.

"The IDA were the people to promote it so I said to Haughey that the IDA are very supportive but they are not into banking." The special committee set up to promote the IFSC included Tomás F Ó Cofaigh, former governor of the Central Bank; Séamus Paircéir, former chairman of the Revenue Commissioners; Kieran McGowan from the IDA, and Mossie Horgan from the Department of Finance.

"I said if anyone can open the doors of the bank it's Ó Cofaigh. And so we sent them all over the world, and Ó Cofaigh was able to get in to central banks all over the world.

"Then they started to flow: Dresdner [a German investment bank] came in; once you got one bank from a country the other banks followed." The IFSC is now host to about 500 of some of the biggest financial institutions in the world; it directly employs over 35,000 people and contributes about €2.1bn every year to the exchequer.

And while the IFSC has played a hugely important role in the development of the economy, the domestic banking sector has not fared so well. Banks were a vital cog in the credit-fuelled property bubble of the 2000s, which resulted in the collapse of the financial system in 2010. O hUiginn says that the problem with the Irish banking system over the past few decades is that it was inefficient.

"The banking system was staffed by people who came in at the bottom of the rung a bit like the civil service – they had no real capacity; they just learned the business, they just knew the money came in and came out." He believes that the recruitment process across the Irish banking system has to be reviewed.

He is also very critical of the State guarantee of the banking system introduced on the night of September 29th, 2008. The government should have gone to the EU Commission and European Central Bank before introducing the wide-ranging guarantee that eventually undermined the sovereignty of the State, he says.

"They should have gone to Europe the next day and said 'we have a problem and it's your problem'. By the time they did go to Europe, the guarantee was already in place so it was too late."

In addition, O hUiginn would like to see a major reform to the institutions of government. "We have 15 government departments in a population of 4.4 million, and there are 15 sub-ministries and sub-departments and I am quite sure this is not necessary. I said this to Leo Varadkar before he became minister [for health, at the time]. I said you could run an empire with 15 government departments and he said the British did it with seven."

Upon retirement he joined the board of Esat Telecom, which was owned by businessman Denis O'Brien. O hUiginn says that O'Brien is one of the most able businessmen the country has produced.

He also says that Charles Haughey was a complex person with many different facets to his personality, and is well aware of his faults. "He had that ability to make decisions: he was a different politician. Johnny Ronan [the property developer] tried to buy his estate, and he said to me it was terrible negotiating with Haughey. I said to him: 'you forget you're negotiating with three people – he was a politician, a lawyer and an accountant. You rarely meet that.' 'Jesus', he said, 'that's what it was'. But when I would have one argument Haughey would come up with another."

O hUiginn has worked closely with some of Ireland's most influential figures in business and in the civil service – and become a figure of immense historical impact in the process.

CHAPTER 26

Interview: Michael Smurfit

In conversation with John Walsh

ONE OF IRELAND'S MOST SUCCESSFUL GLOBAL BUSINESS FIGURES DISCUSSES HIS CAREER, THE ORIGINS AND DEVELOPMENT OF WHAT WOULD BECOME SMURFIT KAPPA, AND HIS OUTLOOK ON LIFE AND ON BUSINESS.

Michael Smurfit was one of the very few success stories among Irish business executives in the 1960s and 1970s. Indeed, he took a small Irish box-making company and made it into one of the biggest in the world in its sector. Today Smurfit Kappa employs 45,000 people across 34 countries, with revenues of over €8bn.

Smurfit was born in St Helens, Lancashire in 1936 to an English father and an Irish mother. The family soon relocated to Ireland and the young Smurfit was educated in Clongowes Wood boarding school in Co Kildare, although he left aged 16 to join the family business. "My father said: 'you buy brains and you make businesspeople'. My parents had eight children and the four sons all left school at 16 and started in the business.

"For me it was a gradual take-off. I was a member of the ITGWU [Irish Transport and General Workers' Union] for a number of years. I don't think a chief executive of any Irish listed company was ever a member of a trade union. I was a bit of a socialist; 'up with the working man, down with the boss'." Smurfit worked for a number of years in all parts of the business before being elevated to a management position. "There was no support. My mentor was my father. I had hardly any friends. The only real outlet for my energy was golf. I played a lot with my later brother Jeff."

His early years in the business were characterised by trial and error, he says. Among the mistakes made along the way was a big investment in a machine that turned out to be unsuitable. "Money was really tight back then. That really taught me a lesson about doing homework instead of believing salespeople. From then on I always went to the factory to make sure it was the right one. I was 25 when that happened and it never happened to me again. It is OK to make a mistake, but you must make sure that you never make the same mistake again."

Although Smurfit left school at 16, he subsequently undertook night classes. The most important of these was accountancy. He became very good at reading balance sheets, which was to prove an invaluable advantage as the company expanded. The pivotal moment for Smurfit was the signing of the Anglo-Irish Trade Agreement in 1965. "I recognised immediately that it was going to be the deathknell for us. Not because we were inefficient, but because our customers were going to go to the wall. These were shirtmakers and shoemakers, and they did go to the wall.

"I looked at the strengths and weaknesses for Ireland. I didn't see many strengths. I decided the only way forward for me was to take over and rationalise the entire paper industry in Ireland and redefine it. Dad said 'how are you going to do that?' I said I don't know but I will find a way, and I did."

Consolidation in Ireland provided Smurfit with the platform for international expansion. "I was very fortunate that I could think in a way that was different to other people in the business. I found my competitors up to then to be inept. I took over companies in Ireland that were old boys' clubs – mainly Protestant ascendancy with a 'them and us' attitude.

"I didn't fight with them. I just ran the companies in a different way. I found my competitors hidebound by tradition. They did business in an old-fashioned way. We were one of the first to use computers and one of the first to innovate."

Access to credit during the 1960s was difficult. The banks were dominated by old boys' networks. Smurfit eventually joined the board of AIB and hired the Investment Bank of Ireland on an advisory basis. "Because of that I was able to get credit from Bank of Ireland to do deals. When I was able to prove I could do deals and make money from them, banks were more willing to lend."

The first company that Smurfit took over in the UK was WJ Noble in 1971. "The way they treated profits was totally false. It was misleading, but when you do a takeover as opposed to a merger you do not get to see the books. You had to rely on public information."

However, Smurfit had a very prudent policy on cash reserves. In the early 1970s the company's assets were roughly IR£3m and he had £3m in reserves. "I had reserves on reserves. Dad nearly went bankrupt because he had a hole in his accounts. He was let down badly by one of his accountants and it took a few years to get out of that. I swore that would never happen to me. You cannot do that today. The rules have changed over the last decade."

Moreover, because of accounting rules during the 1960s and 1970s, Smurfit could take big writeoffs during good years and could take these writeoffs back during bad years. This enabled him to grow in a managed way, which in turn ensured a healthy relationship with shareholders.

During the 1960s, Smurfit says, he had very little interaction with politicians, although his father had a close friendship with the then-Taoiseach Seán Lemass. "It came later for me when we became a bigger company. We needed to get laws changed and we did. When the double-taxation treaties were drawn up in the 1930s nobody on the Irish side thought Irish companies would be going to the US. They thought it would be all one-way."

Possibly one of the most important encounters of Smurfit's business career was a chance meeting with Don Hindman in Dublin's Shelbourne Hotel in early 1974. Hindman was the chief executive of Time Industries and was in Ireland to put the finishing touches to opening a sheet plant in Sligo. "He was going to make his own boxes. I didn't like that idea because I had control over the market. I got to know him and I went to see him in Chicago." Smurfit suggested that instead of going into competition with each other, they should form a partnership.

In September 1974 Smurfit bought a 40% stake in Time Industries for IR£2m. It was the company's first foray into the US market. By 1977 it had acquired the remainder of Time Industries. However, the transformative deal would come a decade later through the acquisition of Container Corporation of America (CCA). "It was a beautiful deal. I knew about them [CCA]. They had a system of producing boxes that was better than anybody else. It was owned by Mobil. I always wondered what Mobil was doing with a box company."

In 1986 Smurfit was in Los Angeles having lunch with investors. One of the investors, from Colony Capital, asked him whether he had ever thought about buying CCA. "I said it was too big and that Mobil would not be interested in selling." Smurfit was at his Los Angeles home when a call came through from Don Brennan at Morgan Stanley: "I didn't know Don Brennan from Adam." Smurfit had been brought to the attention of Morgan Stanley through the company's US chief executive, Jim Molloy. Brennan wanted to know would Smurfit be interested in a joint venture with Morgan Stanley to buy CCA.

"I nearly fell into the swimming pool. I went down to the airport and flew to New York that night. I was in his office the next morning." Brennan had made contact with Mobil and knew that it was willing to sell CCA. "I went to see the chairman of Mobil, who was of Irish descent, and we really hit it off. Tony O'Reilly was also on the board." Smurfit acquired 50% of CCA for $1.2bn.

"It was a hidden gem. Every time I kicked a stone it was a diamond." He subsequently bought CCA's Venezuelan operations for $19m. "It had $29m in the bank, which didn't count in those days because of accounting rules. It was a fantastic deal. For the entire Latin American operations, I paid Morgan Stanley $100m for their stake. That company makes over $250m today."

Assembling a team

Having a good leadership team is an essential component of building a successful business, he says. "I was very good at spotting talent. You need a good team around you. You can be a brilliant footballer, but if you don't have a good team then you will not win anything.

"I was very fortunate in having very good executives: Jim Molloy and Howard Kilroy, among others. We had an excellent finance department. They were all employed by me and I had to woo all of them. We were a small company at the time and it took a lot of persuading."

The corporate governance landscape for companies has changed quite considerably over the past few decades. "If institutional investors had their way, we would be living in an era of faceless CEOs. I ran my company a bit like a dictatorship. You had to do this to be successful. Look at [Apple founder] Steve Jobs – he was renowned for his dictatorial style.

"There is now too much focus on governance issues and too much focus on pay." Smurfit says that for most of the period when he was chief executive, if he had proposed to institutional investors "'I will make millions for you; do you mind if I make millions as well?' they would have taken my hand off."

He argues that Gary McGann should have been paid a lot more than €5m in 2013 when more than €2bn was added to shareholder value during the year. "I think shareholder activism is a bad thing. You need a certain amount of everything but I think the pendulum has swung too far the other way."

During the 1980s and 1990s Smurfit played a prominent role in Irish life, most notably spending nine years as chairman of Telecom Éireann. "All for no pay and for quite a lot of work. It was losing hundreds of millions and it was a monopoly. It was really badly run; it took 27 bits of paper and two years to get a phone." However, in 1991 Taoiseach Charles Haughey asked Smurfit to stand down as chairman of Telecom Éireann in controversial circumstances. Smurfit has always strenuously denied any impropriety in the affair. Moreover, it was the end of his friendship with Haughey.

Meanwhile, Smurfit's advice to emerging entrepreneurs is to not be afraid of risk. "The fear of the unknown holds a lot of people back. Unless you go to the unknown, you will never get anywhere. You have to be prepared to take risks and not to be put off by failure. If in doubt then don't do it, but try not to have doubts. You have to try and focus on making it work. Go on the field of play to win." Moreover, he advises entrepreneurs to take "drop dead money" out of the business when it becomes successful. "Always have your backstop. I have it myself and that is one of the reasons I survived the crisis."

Smurfit has six children from two marriages. "When I was chief executive I worked 14-hour days and weekends were for travelling. I hardly ever saw my family. I regret that now, but to achieve what I achieved the easiest thing to do was give up the home life."

CHAPTER 27

Interview: Martin Naughton

In conversation with Ian Hyland and John Walsh

ONE-OF-A-KIND ENGINEER AND BUSINESSMAN MARTIN NAUGHTON LED IRISH INDUSTRY FROM INSULARITY TOWARDS INNOVATION – AND PICKED UP MORE THAN A FEW STORIES IN THE COURSE OF A FASCINATING CAREER.

With origins in rural Ireland – Dundalk – Martin Naughton, an engineer by profession, is an entrepreneur and philanthropist responsible for the world leader in electric heating, Glen Dimplex.

Naughton was born in Dublin in 1940, but his family moved to Dundalk following the bombing of the capital by German warplanes in 1941. His father was from Mayo and a member of An Garda Síochána, while his mother was originally from Galway. She had emigrated to the US as a young woman, but met Naughton's father when she returned on holiday. He went to the De La Salle school in Dundalk for primary and secondary education.

"I know it is not politically correct – however, I believe as a country we owe an enormous debt to religious brothers and sisters who sacrificed their lives to educate generations of Irish children," he says.

Upon finishing second-level education in 1956, the popular career choices in Ireland were the civil service or banking. Martin Naughton chose neither; instead he emigrated. Studying engineering in England for five years before returning home, the latter stages of his third-level education focused on industrial engineering. "I witnessed at first hand the horrors of emigration. On the mailboat from Dún Laoghaire to Holyhead,

I saw distraught fathers leaving their wives and families," he remembers. The reason for Naughton's return? Ken Whitaker, Seán Lemass and the change in policy.

The Shannon Industrial Zone had been established, and upon his return Naughton worked for an American company called SPS, starting in 1961. It was the first American investment in Ireland since Henry Ford arrived on Irish soil, and so this caught Naughton's eye. Ireland, he recalls, was a different planet completely. SPS chose to invest in Ireland because of incentives and cheap labour: "We had a fantastic labour force; it was as good a labour as I have ever seen," Naughton says.

At that time SPS and other companies locating in Ireland brought their own management team with them, including supervisors. "In those days there was no managerial class," Naughton recalls: Ireland merely offered these companies cheap, willing and hard-working labour. The families of those who worked in these factories felt shame. "They felt like second-class citizens and were ashamed their children hadn't been educated" – working in a factory, Naughton says, had a stigma attached to it. However, he acknowledges that some who stayed in these jobs developed as the company did, and promising careers ensued.

Nowadays, American companies that choose to establish a European base in Ireland enjoy an infrastructure of lawyers and accountants from within Ireland who can advise them. "They can get Irish guys to run operations in Ireland, and can then get Irish guys to go back to America and run the parent company," he says. "It has changed dramatically in my lifetime." Ireland, he says, is a pro-American country and it is now a pro-business country.

Furthermore, he adds that America has a very good image of Ireland. "There are 44 million people in America who say they are Irish, and of course most of them have never been here," he says. Why do they identify themselves as such? He believes it is popular to be Irish. Nowadays, when American companies establish themselves successfully and look to invest overseas, they look to Ireland. "It became a vogue, the natural thing to do," Naughton says: other companies have used Ireland as a base, and so it is seen by many Americans as a safe bet.

After a year and a half in Shannon, Martin Naughton left to work in AET in Dunleer, which was subsequently bought by GEC, an appliance company in Ireland – earning the title of chief industrial engineer in his twenties. It employed 1,800 at its peak and built products for other companies such as Electrolux and AEG.

Coming from an advanced American technology company, Naughton thought AET to be behind the curve and played a role in the modernisation of the company. "I brought in conveyers and set up a payments-by-results scheme," he recalls.

Naughton was then headhunted back to Shannon, where a new company was being established in the field of capacitors and electronic components for televisions and radios. Returning to Shannon as services manager, an engagement to his wife Carmel ensued. It was then that the phone rang from AET.

"I got a call from the managing director back in Dunleer asking would I consider the job as deputy works manager in the company" – and in Martin Naughton's mind the answer was simple: no.

"Absolutely not, I said; I'm happy in Shannon, I'm getting married, we're going to build in Cratloe, Co Clare," he told the managing director. He understood Naughton's reasons, but invited him to Dublin to have dinner with himself and Seán Lemass to discuss some plans they had. "I was young and hugely flattered to meet my hero Seán Lemass, who had left government and this was his first board appointment with GEC," Naughton recalls.

During the course of a dinner in the Shelbourne Hotel, Lemass documented what Ireland needed – and in his mind that involved building Irish-based multinationals. Lemass spoke of sending Naughton around the world to study the best practice in appliances. At the end of the dinner an offer was made. "I heard myself accepting it," Naughton adds.

Enticed by his hero, Naughton found himself in Dunleer once more – this time as deputy works manager. However, the business of operating behind tariff barriers and quotas created a difficulty for AET, and so Naughton put forward a rescue plan. "I thought we should cut back the business dramatically: here are the good products, here's where the future is, let's kill these, get out of that, keep the best of it and build on that," he says. The rescue plan was turned down.

Ireland's entry to the EEC in 1973 opened up the country to competition, which was a deathknell for AET. Although dreaming of starting your own business is "lovely talk over cups of coffee or a glass of beer", Naughton says it is a different matter actually giving up a job to do so.

"I put together a small team of people then and we all put some funds in it. We started for better or worse," he says. In order to receive financial assistance Naughton decided to locate in Newry: "We were handed a small advanced factory in Newry and things started from there."

The culture of a small company served as a learning curve for Naughton, who quickly realised what you have to do without. It's a bold, brave thing to go out on your own, he says.

With a five-year plan in place, and because the Irish market for electrical appliances was deemed too small for the company to design, develop and tool products, the UK market was chosen as their home market – a market with 60 million people. Even so, there were salespeople both north and south of the Border, covering Northern Ireland and the Republic of Ireland.

Glen began in 1973, and the emphasis was on well-designed, quality products. There was no financial director at this time – instead there was an industrial designer from day one, as the company's priorities lay in this area.

Lochlann Quinn joins the Glen Dimplex family

Before joining forces, Naughton had previous business interactions with Lochlann Quinn during the latter's time with Arthur Andersen. "In dealing with Lochlann from the other side of the desk I found him to be a very sharp guy; he was as bright an accountant as I'd ever come across," Naughton says.

Upon establishing his own company, Naughton approached Arthur Andersen asking for help with the business proposal. They agreed on the condition they would get to audit the group. Upon acquiring Dimplex, Naughton asked Quinn to join the business. "He took a gamble. He was heading to be partner in Arthur Andersen. We were great partners – we were almost blood brothers; real buccaneers around the world," Naughton remembers of his relationship with Quinn. He credits their success to their combined skillset: Lochlann Quinn had the financial knowhow, while Martin Naughton had expertise in the realm of engineering, manufacturing and design.

They quickly learned about the potency of branding. With Glen, Naughton's focus had been on quality products. Admittedly, he says, if you haven't got a brand you are merely selling a price. In buying Dimplex, they also bought a brand. "It opened doors for us. Suddenly we were an establishment," he says.

And so in 1977, after four years in business, Naughton wrote a cheque for IR£1 million to buy Dimplex. "Lochlann tried very hard to talk me out of it," he adds, recalling discussions on the Dimplex acquisition. However, Naughton's gut instincts told him otherwise. After the purchase of Dimplex the company acquired a number of brands. The recession, Naughton says, was great for their business: "It shook the weak men out of the pack; we became skilled at being turnaround merchants quietly."

The philosophy of Glen Dimplex has been – and still is to this day – to do "clean deals" when acquiring new businesses. As a private company, Naughton explains, they only do cash deals. "It is not just a game, or shuffling paper around: it becomes very real money."

Acquisitions, for Glen Dimplex, tended to be opportunistic – whereby a company gets into difficulty and so becomes available – or strategic, whereby the group wishes to locate in a new country or area and so goes after a business. To Naughton's mind, every deal is a serious contract and in the event a contract has to be checked it means something has gone wrong.

A fair deal is integral in any acquisition or dealing. "I don't like to squeeze the last bit out of any deal. I'd like that at the end of the deal both sides say 'I didn't get what I wanted but I think it's fair'," he adds.

It's not for sale

Upon becoming a successful player in the UK, the company wanted to broaden its horizons – and so it prepared to focus its efforts on the international market. It began with another company's attempt to acquire

Glen Dimplex when a merchant bank in London phoned expressing their client's interest in a possible acquisition. Naughton's response was simple: "It's not for sale."

Despite the offer of an attractive price, Naughton had no interest in selling the company. He subsequently enquired who the company was: it was Siemens, and he asked to meet with them for a discussion. "We met Siemens in their offices in London, and we agreed we'd set up a study between us to see what would happen," he says.

With Siemens, Naughton recalls, their policy was such that if they weren't in the top two globally in a certain sector, they left it. At the time, Siemens had three electric heating businesses in Canada, Germany and Norway, but they weren't the global leaders; acquiring Glen Dimplex and another French company would ensure that they were market leaders worldwide.

Meeting with the managing director of the electric heating division in Cologne, Naughton's opposite number began: "Martin, you're not going to sell Dimplex to me, are you?"

The answer quite simply was no. In that case, he informed Naughton: "It makes sense for you to buy us." Glen Dimplex eventually bought the Siemens division, and with the acquisition received the Siemens brand name for ten years on electric heating across the globe.

"Talk about opening doors for us. Siemens, wow!" Naughton exclaims. In Israel, for example, customers would pay 10% more for a Siemens brand than any other; such was their respect for German technology.

Naughton recalls the small press release that followed the purchase: as a private business they chose a small statement that simply read that Glen Dimplex had acquired Siemens' electric heating division. Soon after, while at a trade show in Germany a journalist from a prominent Frankfurt newspaper approached him to enquire if there had been a mistake in the press release.

"Siemens have bought you, yes?" the journalist probed. Naughton set him straight, much to the confusion of the German journalist who was insistent that Ireland was merely a place for growing cattle, as opposed to engineering products. In 2003, after 30 years in business, the group broke the €1 billion sales barrier. It is now a global company with established brands and manufacturing operations in Germany, Holland, France, Norway, China, Australia, New Zealand and the USA, as well as Ireland and Britain.

According to Naughton, if a company is to succeed then it needs new products, markets and acquisitions. In 2016, Glen Dimplex made five acquisitions: two in Australia, one in the UK, a distribution company in Ireland and a manufacturing company on the west coast of the US.

In April 2016 Naughton stood down as president of Glen Dimplex and was replaced by Seán O'Driscoll, who had been chief executive of the company for the previous 27 years. Naughton now chairs a supervisory/shareholder board, which consists of the three Naughton children – Fiona, Neil and Fergal – as well as Lochlann Quinn and two outside non-executive directors. This board meets four times each year to review performance and plan for long-term strategic growth.

The board is separated by a fence from the executive board, which runs the business on a day-to-day basis. Martin McCourt is the chairman of the executive board, while Neil Naughton is deputy chairman and Fergal Naughton is the chief executive.

"I am convinced that the best days of Glen Dimplex are yet to come," Naughton says.

The Fighting Irish

Outside of Glen Dimplex, Naughton has been a trustee of Notre Dame, one of the top universities in the US, for the past couple of decades. "People often ask me how I got involved with Notre Dame. It all started back in 1996 when Notre Dame came to Dublin for the first time to play a college football match against US Navy," he recalls.

"Mike Wadsworth, who was the Canadian ambassador to Ireland, and had been a quarterback for Notre Dame, invited Carmel and I to lunch in Newman House to meet the senior officers and some trustees of the university. Over lunch I asked how did it take the 'Fighting Irish' so long to visit Dublin and Ireland. I said 'if you were Jews you would have visited Jerusalem and Israel long before now'. One of the Irish-Americans present said: 'I can answer that. Our parents were so busy rearing their children and educating them, they never wanted to go back or could afford to go back. We are the first generation of Irish to have succeeded and we both want to go back and can afford to go back.'"

It was at this lunch that Naughton met Don Keough, the former chief executive and chairman of Coca Cola. Together they established the Irish Studies Programme and founded the Keough Institute, which later became the Keough-Naughton Institute. Some 100 students arrive from the US and spend a semester at either University College Dublin or Trinity College, studying and interacting with Irish students.

"He [Keough] was one of the wisest and most generous men I have met. He was very proud to travel on an Irish passport. He called me his baby brother.

"Notre Dame is the heart and soul of Irish America. It has Irish DNA and is unapologetically Catholic. I was a trustee for many years and now I am a trustee emeritus." His wife Carmel is on the performing arts committee of Notre Dame, his daughter Fiona is on the Irish council, his son Neil is on the business council, and his other son Fergal is a trustee and chairs the Irish council with Don Keough's son Michael.

In 2012, when Notre Dame returned to take on Navy in the Aviva Stadium, the atmosphere was different. People engaged with the event, which was coined 'Welcome Home Notre Dame.' Laden with emotion, Irish-Americans toured the country for a further two weeks after the football game. With an influx of 35,000 people to the country, it was deemed a tremendous success.

Martin Naughton thinks we can welcome Notre Dame home again. "These people who come here are graduates from these universities and their alumni are leaders in America; if we can grab this college football space it would be most valuable," he says.

Croke Park played host to the Penn State versus Central Florida college football game in 2014, again yielding positive results. "Penn State has the largest alumni of any university in the world, and Central Florida is one of the new universities, which is heavily involved in NASA," he explains. As a result of these games, many universities want to take American football global and expand the sport; some are thinking of playing in China. Naughton believes that many feel it may be safer to trial a game in Ireland: "If we grab this space we can do more in Ireland than you can imagine."

College football is a family affair, and in many instances generations will travel together – from grandparents to grandchildren. Notre Dame will definitely come back, Naughton says, adding that Navy also wish to return.

Education and philanthropy

Martin Naughton believes very thoroughly in third-level education: "Universities are ranked whether we like it or not, and rankings are important," he says. Irish universities need to be competing with top universities for those rankings.

The current situation in Ireland means that universities cannot cut their staff because of the Haddington Road Agreement. Naughton cites an example, saying that Trinity College have approximately 120 surplus staff and cannot let them go despite acquiring computer systems that rendered these 120 jobs superfluous. So while universities in Ireland are putting money into new systems to better themselves, there is no return.

In the field of philanthropy, Martin and Carmel Naughton set up the Naughton Foundation in 1994. It is a private family foundation and its goal is to support worthwhile causes in the arts and education. In 2008 the foundation created the Naughton Scholarships, a programme to support Leaving Cert students who would like to study science, technology, engineering and mathematics at third level on both sides of the Border. Originally the programme was only available to pupils from Louth, Meath and Monaghan, but it has now been expanded nationwide. In the arts, the Naughton Foundation recently supported the Royal Irish Academy's publication *Art and Architecture of Ireland*.

Naughton says that making money was never a motivating factor or priority in his career: "As the man said, it just keeps the score. Making money is a useful by-product of running a small business. I regard money as a commodity which when used properly can do great good, but it is also destructive. I have seen money destroy a lot of families. I always planned in giving a proportion of my income to good causes."

"To date we have spent or committed approximately €40 million on deserving causes such as the Naughton Scholarships. A member of the family reads every application and we come together to select the winners. We try and make an occasion of the award ceremony. The prize is a gold medal and €5,000 per year for four years.

"This is one of the most exciting days of the year for me. I am proud of the country and believe it is in safe hands with these awesome young people who are achievers not just academically, but in sport, music and everything they set their hands to.

"Our young people deserve world-class facilities and teachers. Investment in education is a top priority if we want to build prosperity and an economy that can support social justice."

We don't forgive failures

Upon reflection, there are two Irish business leaders for whom Martin Naughton has great admiration: Michael Smurfit and Tony O'Reilly.

"Michael went global," he says, and so he serves as a great example of a businessman who stood out. Naughton also pays tribute to Smurfit's philanthropy in particular. Tony O'Reilly is in his eyes a patriot and was a role model for many people.

Another businessman worthy of note is Seán Quinn. Naughton describes him as "a gambler", one who gambled and lost, destroying everything he'd built up. However, Naughton credits the role he played in the landscape of Irish business: "As a local patriot he brought in businesses that would never have been in Ireland; an extraordinary guy." He acknowledges that society has not been kind to Seán Quinn. "We don't forgive failures," he says.

In 1992 Naughton and his wife Carmel bought Stackallen House in Co Meath, which was built in 1712 and is now the family home. "To be honest we are only caretakers, and hope to leave it a little better than we found it."

Outside of Glen Dimplex, Naughton's other main business interests are the Merrion Hotel in Dublin and Restaurant Patrick Guilbaud. He also sits on the advisory board of Citi Private Bank for Europe, the Middle East and Africa and served on the Council of State during one of Mary McAleese's terms as president.

Humility is a trait that Martin Naughton embodies: when asked about his personal highlight he simply says "I don't do pride."

CHAPTER 28

Interview: Niall FitzGerald

In conversation with Ian Hyland

THE FORMER UNILEVER CEO DISCUSSES LEAVING IRELAND TO FURTHER HIS CAREER, DEFYING APARTHEID IN SOUTH AFRICA, AND LESSONS LEARNED FROM HIGHLIGHTS AND LOWLIGHTS ALIKE.

With a globetrotting career spanning over 30 years in one of the world's biggest multinational companies, Niall FitzGerald is renowned for his various roles – including those of chairman and chief executive officer with Unilever.

In the late 1960s, the landscape of Irish business did not afford Niall FitzGerald the freedom he desired. To his mind, Ireland was at that time claustrophobic and narrow, and it was for these reasons that FitzGerald decided to pursue his career outside of Ireland.

"I could have written on the back of an envelope the names of the 20 people who would matter, in my view, if I were to pursue a career in Ireland," he says. Due to differing views and values on which he was not prepared to compromise, he did not see the scope for doing things his way in Ireland – and so he left.

Following his departure from Ireland in 1971, FitzGerald's career spanned across three continents as he worked in the UK, US and South Africa during a 15-year period. Such was the global reach of his career that Niall FitzGerald's day-to-day detailed observations of Ireland were minimal. However, despite this he recognised the importance of Ireland's entry into Europe.

"This was perhaps the single most important positive thing that happened to Ireland, because it lifted Ireland out from underneath the shadow of its bigger neighbour," he says. The notion of equality was of great significance, as Ireland was now an equal member of a group of nations regardless of its size. This, FitzGerald believes, gave a greater confidence to Irish business.

"They [Irish businesses] could get out there and compete, without always wondering whether they were a second-class version of their UK counterparts," FitzGerald adds.

For Niall FitzGerald, being Irish has never been anything but an advantage. The ability to seamlessly integrate into any society is something with which he credits Irish people: there is an expectation that the Irish will be slightly different, maybe even a little eccentric. FitzGerald explains: "Because your background is different and not definable, you get away with doing things in different ways, which you wouldn't if you came from somewhere more conventional." And herein, for FitzGerald, the advantage lies: the possibility of getting the job done his way.

"This allows you to push harder in the business context to do things differently, to do them your way. They are not expecting you to behave in a particular way," FitzGerald says.

Perhaps his determination to do things his own way is best illustrated by his handling of the knighthood received from the Queen in 2003. He refuses to use the title but acknowledges the honour by putting the initials KBE after his name together with the DSA (Distinguished Service Award) received from President Higgins. "I don't feel like Sir Niall, so why would I want people to address me as such!"

Irish-British relations

The relationship between Ireland and Britain has changed much since Niall FitzGerald first arrived in the United Kingdom in the 1970s. "When I came here in the 1970s, the Irish were still second-class citizens," he recalls. However, he describes the relationship now enjoyed by the two nations as one of equals. He credits the Good Friday Agreement with alleviating tensions that underscored the relationship for many years.

As Ireland and its people became more successful on the global stage, FitzGerald noted a change in the way the British looked at their Irish counterparts. "Ireland was seen to be very successful within the European dimension.

We very quickly got more than our fair share of influential roles in Brussels, and those who went into those roles were high-quality people," he says.

If Britain is to leave the European Union, FitzGerald believes that the most important role Ireland could play is to act as the mediating party. "I think Britain without Europe would be seriously weakened," he adds. While he believes it would be an undesirable outcome for all concerned, he notes that the body of opinion in Britain differs.

"It is currently the majority opinion that Europe has been a doer of great evil to us [British] and we would be better off economically outside it," FitzGerald says. Niall FitzGerald may be pro-European, but he is equally critical of certain aspects of the way the European Union operates. Reform, he says, is desperately overdue, and he thinks Britain seeking to renegotiate will be the catalyst for reform.

The fundamental issues of the eurozone crisis have not been dealt with, he adds. In economic terms, the enlargement of the eurozone, to his mind, was not wise. Some economies were too different, he says. "I think it made countries such as Greece and Portugal uncompetitive." From a political standpoint it made sense, but when measured in a purely economic view, he believes it does not. For the moment, however, FitzGerald is of the opinion that the issues have not yet been grounded out. "I think we can solve debt issues for the time being, but the fundamental economic imbalances will not be resolved," he adds.

Foreign direct investment

FitzGerald believes that our reliance on foreign direct investment is a byproduct of the 12.5% corporate tax regime. "Would that still be the case if it was a 40% tax rate?" he asks. There is no doubt in his mind that many countries internationally are deeply concerned about their lack of ability to appropriately tax international companies. Ireland, he says, is very exposed: things will happen that will make people re-examine the financial fundamentals of operating in Ireland. "If the reliance has been too great on continuing very aggressive tax regimes, that is a problem," he says.

FitzGerald recalls his appointment as finance director of Unilever in 1985: "I was a young finance director in my 30s and it was my view that we were not managing our tax line appropriately." But it was his then-chairman who took FitzGerald aside; what he said influenced much of his thinking from that day forward. "He said to me: you as a finance director have a responsibility to minimise our tax cost, but equally I want you to remember that we depend for our business on the consumers in the 200 countries in which we operate," he recounts.

With this in mind FitzGerald adopted a hybrid model that ensured that Unilever worked actively to minimise its tax cost, but never allowed tax payments to drop below 70% of the standard rate in the country in which they operated. His justification: "We have to make a minimum contribution to justify our freedom to operate in that country," FitzGerald says.

If there are no fish, there are no fish fingers

As Unilever chief executive Niall FitzGerald travelled extensively, spending around 70% of his time on the road. When visiting a country, FitzGerald always made it his priority to meet with the youngest and latest members of management teams. He would engage with them, listen to their views, and relay to them the standards and values that prevailed at Unilever. FitzGerald had a standard opening line: "There is something you need to understand from the beginning: Unilever does not own the brands. The consumer owns the brands, every one of our consumers is a citizen, and every one of those citizens lives in a community," FitzGerald explained.

It was his belief that if as a business Unilever was not an engaged, constructive and active member of the community in which it operated, it would lose the respect of the citizens. Losing the support of the consumers would then follow.

It is for this reason that corporate social responsibility, a phrase FitzGerald detests as it sounds like a mere add-on, is integral to the manner in which Unilever conducts business. One example of such behaviour is a partnership between Unilever and the World Wildlife Fund during his term as chief executive, a result of which was the creation of the Marine Stewardship Council. It was a body that certified that fish being used had been caught in a sustainable manner. There was a time that Unilever was the largest producer and seller of frozen fish products in the world, and FitzGerald recalls that people within the business questioned the reasoning behind such a partnership. As the chief executive, Niall FitzGerald felt he needed to be the advocate – and so he explained to employees why as a company they were committing large sums of money to an NGO to establish the Marine Stewardship Council, which may ultimately restrict their ability to source fish in the most financially effective manner. To aid employees' understanding of why this was aligned to the business, he told them quite simply: "If there are no fish, there are no fish fingers. Unless we are part of ensuring that the supply chain can be sustainable our whole business will vanish."

Another such example resulted from a conversation with Barbara Stocking, the then-chief executive of Oxfam GB. According to FitzGerald, she told him: "There is very little multinational companies do that is any good." In response, FitzGerald offered Oxfam unfettered access to Unilever in a developing country, and subsequently the opportunity to pen a report on their behaviour. Oxfam chose Indonesia, a country where Unilever was dominant.

Why did FitzGerald propose this? "Firstly, I believed very strongly that we behaved in a very responsible way. But secondly, I knew that once we engaged them inside they will find much more good than they think," he says. After a period of 18 months the report was complete, and admittedly FitzGerald did not like every part of it. However, he did feel it showed that not just Unilever, but other multinationals, can on balance do much more good than damage. "Did that change the way NGOs perceive companies? It was the start of a very appropriate change of perspective," he adds.

The American dream is fractured

When discussing his biggest macro concerns, FitzGerald looks to the US model. "The American dream is fractured," he says. The American dream is comprised of two parts: that every generation will be better off than their parents, and that within each generation the barriers to progress for individuals are eliminated. FitzGerald identifies how it has changed in the past 20 years.

"We are looking at the second successive generation who are worse off than their parents, and it is no longer that easy for a person to work your way through the societal barriers of the United States," he says. He points to the facts: 95% of economic growth in the US in the 20 years previous has gone to 1% of the population. Society, he believes, will begin to withdraw its support from the economic free-enterprise model if there is not a more equitable distribution of the proceeds from the model – and this observation was formed some years before the Trump phenomenon.

FitzGerald applies this to the Irish context – and in doing so he says that it is exactly the same, but in a more extreme form. In stabilising the debt issue, he believes it is important to translate through to people that there is a prospect of being better off. FitzGerald thinks the following needs to be conveyed to the Irish: that they don't have to do as people did in the 1950s and early 1960s; to get out of the country to succeed. "There still is a prospect of the dream within."

In FitzGerald's view Ireland is extremely lucky that it came through the crisis without riots in the streets, as other countries experienced. "People got on with it without making too much fuss," he says. In behaving in such a manner, to his mind there is now a higher premium on ensuring that there is hope that the benefits of the economic approach will spread throughout the population.

Prospects of the Irish economy

Niall FitzGerald feels he is not sufficiently close to the workings of the Irish economy to comment on its prospects. However, as a small economy, he notes the following: "For a small economy like Ireland to function competitively in the world, it has to be very clear as to what the limited number of competitive advantages it can have are."

It is his opinion that Ireland must therefore focus its priority and resources on being globally competitive in those areas. "One of the areas which I think Ireland has missed so far, where it could have been extremely competitive, is education," he says.

The world, he says, desperately needs an educated and skilled workforce. The view from the east is that the western education system is better. To Niall FitzGerald, herein lies the opportunity. The UK and the US have made it more difficult for overseas students to be educated in their countries. Meanwhile, he believes that Ireland has both the infrastructure and the capability to sell its education product, and equally important, we are a welcoming people.

"There has been no coherent effort to do that as a nation," he says. The government, he feels, should give a small number of areas of competitive advantage all their support, to the exclusion of other areas. Admittedly, though, he acknowledges: "That's easy to say, it's not that easy to do."

Emigration: we're good at exporting things

To Niall FitzGerald, emigration is not at all wrong in principle. Speaking from experience, he says that there are a lot of opportunities for those who choose to pursue their careers elsewhere. "I think for a small nation to assume it can provide all the opportunities for a smart, hard-working population is unrealistic," FitzGerald says.

The trick, he says, is to keep those who have emigrated connected with Ireland so that they return at later stages in their lives. "We're good at exporting things that look like Irish pubs and Irish music and dancing; we make that connection," he says.

But FitzGerald alludes to a valuable point: until recently he has never been aware of any attempts by Ireland, through its embassies, to keep connected with Irish people who are based abroad. The Irish embassy in the UK has a number of events to keep people engaged. Yet he believes that there is an informality to them that doesn't actually work.

"It needs to be more structured," FitzGerald adds. Never, until recent times, has Niall FitzGerald been approached to do anything. He touches on a simple example: the school that he attended – St Munchin's in Limerick – contacted him asking for help when he became CEO of Unilever. It was an offer he declined, informing them that he had a difficulty with their apparent lack of interest in staying connected over the 30 years since he had left school. "Networks are built from the ground up, continuously and consistently, and if you haven't done that you aren't going to get any benefit I can give you," he told his former school.

Herein lies a message FitzGerald applies to the Irish context: Ireland cannot suddenly ask its émigré population for help. "We haven't spoken to you for the last 20 years but we now need you. There has to be a more structured, robust well-thought-through plan of continuous and consistent engagement with people."

Redefining banking

FitzGerald thinks that banks have departed from their understanding that they exist to support businesses and individuals; that is why they are here. He acknowledges that banks also need to make a profit because their clients and customers are successful. However, FitzGerald believes that banks began making money not from supporting their clients, but from moving that money around and trading it.

"In the end you only have a sustainable economic model if you are building; you have no sustainable economic model if you are trading all the time," FitzGerald says. In his view, that is what went wrong – and it is quite difficult to fix it. There is a second aspect to the redefinition of banking that is needed, and he feels his thoughts may sound slightly bitter.

"There are an awful lot of people in banking who have an extraordinary and excessive view of their own competence, which actually the reality belies," FitzGerald says. Many in the banking industry still believe that they should be paid substantially more than others who are building a wonderful business that creates employment and grows wealth, not one that trades wealth.

While FitzGerald acknowledges that there are exceptional people in every sector, he feels that in banking the exceptional reward has been given indiscriminately. There remains no great depth of understanding in the banking community, he says, that someone has blown the whistle on this.

Personal highlight

The day that Niall FitzGerald met the late Nelson Mandela is undoubtedly the personal highlight of his career. Mandela later asked him to chair the Nelson Mandela Legacy Trust (UK). "It was an extraordinary privilege," FitzGerald says.

He describes Mandela as a man who could walk into any arena or a small room and instantly communicate with everybody. "This was someone who had a talent that few could even aspire to," he adds. FitzGerald recalls one occasion when Nelson Mandela came to his home in Sussex for lunch.

Some 30 minutes before Mandela's arrival, FitzGerald informed his two gardeners of the impending arrival. Mandela was due to have lunch with "self-important" people, but upon his arrival the two gardeners were singled out: "He stopped and he said: 'are you the geniuses that have created this beautiful garden?'" In those short seconds, FitzGerald said, "You could see these two men grow ten feet tall: on a very personal level that was a huge highlight".

Career highlight

The Mandela connection arose because in the 1980s FitzGerald was asked by the then-chairman of Unilever to run its businesses in South Africa. Admittedly, he was appalled by such a suggestion. It was explained to FitzGerald that it was integral to Unilever to deal in everyday products to everybody in the South African community, but in particular the black community. It was their aim as a business to stay in the country as long as they could operate by their own principles, which were at that time increasingly contrary to the law of the land.

FitzGerald took the job, but on the condition: "If there is any time in the first six months that I ring you [the chairman] and I say I want out of here, you must make it happen. No discussion." Upon taking up his role in South Africa he met with President PW Botha; a deeply unpleasant encounter as he recalls. "I explained to him what I was there to do with Unilever and he said 'I'll put you in jail if you break the law'." To which FitzGerald responded: "'You just need to know we are going to run our business by our values. We don't believe in segregation of any kind' – and that's what we did."

At first some colleagues in Unilever's South African business did not agree with him, but FitzGerald explained to them that society was going to change. It was a political statement about fairness and human dignity. He wanted to demonstrate to others that you could run a business by having the appropriate values in place and be hugely successful in the marketplace. He felt that others would follow – and that, he says, is exactly what happened.

He recalls Unilever building a new factory in Johannesburg, and upon seeing the plans he instructed for the ablution blocks to be redesigned to include only male and female toilets without segregation. Upon the factory's opening he was approached about the illegal ablution facilities. FitzGerald refused to change them. "If you do anything to make us change anything we will not be operating in this country next week," he said.

This changed FitzGerald's view on how you changed things fundamentally. "If you really want to make a difference," he says, "you must be prepared to get inside and make the changes and convince people – which may make you unpopular, and may even put you in personal danger. You can't drive changes from observing from the outside," he says.

The man who shredded your underpants

Juxtaposing a career highlight and lowpoint, FitzGerald recalls a time in the 1990s when he oversold the launch of a Unilever product. It was a new piece of technology: a molecule for a cleaning agent that cleaned clothes more effectively than anything that had ever been deployed before.

"My reputation in the business was as a risk-taker, and so far every risk I had ever taken, it had worked," FitzGerald says. With this in mind, he launched the product simultaneously in every country in Europe with vast sums of money supporting the marketing drive. Within a matter of weeks, the market share had increased by 10-15 points, something FitzGerald says had never happened before. Alas, a problem emerged. The molecule, if not used precisely as the instructions said, not only removed dirt but also removed the clothing. It was then that FitzGerald featured on the front page of the *Financial Times*.

"My picture was on the front of the *Financial Times* and underneath it a picture of a clothesline with tattered clothes, with a headline which read 'The man who shredded your underpants'," he says. And so a battle between Unilever and the media ensued. Eventually, Unilever withdrew the product.

"We'd lost many hundreds of millions – the biggest product disaster Unilever ever had," he adds. The company's best marketing and science brains gathered to solve the problem, and were unable to do so. It was then that FitzGerald realised the error of his ways. Of the 31 people he had assembled to deconstruct the problem, nobody had washed their own clothes in the last six months.

"We were talking about a consumer problem and we were not acting like a consumer. We were so distant in a corporate way from the experience of people using our product day in, day out," he says. It was an incident for which Niall FitzGerald took entire responsibility. He went to see the CEO to tell him that he had to resign. However, the reaction of the CEO was not one he had anticipated. "He said: 'Look young man, we've just invested millions in your education – if you think you're going to go off out of here and give the benefit of it to someone else you've got another thing coming.'"

Niall FitzGerald remained with Unilever, and in terms of his growth as a businessperson this was the single most important time in his whole business life. "It was the biggest failure I had. I learned more from that than anything else in my career; any combination of things," he says.

Do unto others as you would they do unto you

Following the banking collapse, FitzGerald was asked to deliver the annual Tyburn lecture on a subject of his choice that related to the role of humanity in the world. He decided to focus on the role of business in society. While researching for the lecture he stumbled across his philosophy in life. "Corny though it may be, it is written very clearly in the Bible. Do unto others as you would they do unto you," he says.

Upon researching other religions, he found that the same sentiment can be found in all other religions: Hinduism, Islam, Judaism and Buddhism. FitzGerald made this point in the lecture: "Whether you lead your life whether it is in business, or just personally, and you would not take any action onto others which if it was done to you would be harmful, unpleasant, and unacceptable, then you are likely on balance to get things right." That is what works, he says, and that underpins how Unilever works.

For Niall FitzGerald, there is somebody who stands out as a business leader and has managed to combine being a very effective hard-nosed businessman while never departing from his own humanity. That person was the late Coca-Cola Company president Don Keough.

"People would have walked through fire for Don Keough," FitzGerald says. In his view Keough was a very special human being who retained that ability to influence people. "People today who never worked with Don directly, and have only encountered things that Don influenced many years ago, still have the same respect for him." And that, Niall FitzGerald says, is very rare.

The Irish-American Keough is remembered for a career of achievement at the highest level of international corporate life – something that could also be said about Niall FitzGerald, one of the most influential executives that Ireland has ever produced.

CHAPTER 29

Interview: Peter Sutherland
In conversation with Ian Hyland

A SEASONED FIGURE IN THE CORRIDORS OF POWER, PETER SUTHERLAND OFFERS AN INSIGHT INTO HIS MANY ROLES AND AN ASSESSMENT OF IRISH POLITICS AND ECONOMICS.

Attorney general, European commissioner, director general of the General Agreement on Tariffs and Trade (GATT), director general of the World Trade Organisation (WTO), chairmanships of BP and Goldman Sachs... Peter Sutherland has undoubtedly enjoyed an illustrious career. In fact, he was described by one newspaper as possibly having the best CV on the planet.

Prior to embarking on an international career that straddled politics and business, the Gonzaga- and UCD-educated barrister served on the board of a number of Irish businesses, becoming chairman of Allied Irish Bank and the first chairman of Shannon Aerospace, as well as joining the boards of CRH and Guinness Peat Aviation (GPA).

Needless to say, the Irish business landscape has changed substantially since the beginning of his career. "My recollections of those times are that they were a time of both extreme economic difficulty and transition of attitude from closed to open, in terms of our future," recalls Sutherland.

Sutherland served as attorney general under Garret FitzGerald's two governments during a period of straightened economic times in the early- and mid-1980s. However, it appeared to him that a significant economic transition was underway. The import substitute economy and the protectionist attitude that Ireland had adopted following independence was rapidly losing favour.

Instead, the Irish economy was becoming increasingly plugged into the international trading system. Sutherland's role within the European Commission (1985-1989) was of huge relevance too. He was part of a triumvirate of commissioners who were responsible for the 1992 reforms, which included free movement of goods, persons, capital and services. "I had learned through my experience in government that this was nationally extremely important," Sutherland says. On the request of Jack Delors, president of the European Commission, Sutherland was asked to devise a method through which the 1992 Programme could be implemented. The result was the Sutherland Report.

"This has been transformative in the Irish economy ever since," he adds. At this time, it became evident that there had to be a focus on attracting inward investment, since Ireland lacked the industrial skillset to establish its own industries. He points to some pioneers – Smurfit, CRH and GPA – that were innovative. Combining these companies and a rapidly developing banking industry provided the basis for solid growth. But he was under no illusions – another leg to Ireland's growth strategy was needed.

"We didn't have enough of indigenous industry to present a future for our young people," Sutherland says. Creating employment and the generation of growth depended on attracting large volumes of foreign direct investment.

Good Europeans

Given Ireland's dependence on the United Kingdom, Europe was of exceptional importance in this context. "Europe was at that time the crucial element in providing us with a future," Sutherland says. The old Anglo-Irish Trade Agreement generated opportunity but ultimately an over-dependence on the United Kingdom. Therefore Europe was perceived as the vehicle for industrial strategy as well as political advancement and engagement, he says.

Proclaiming that we are "good Europeans" is a position with which Sutherland does not agree. While he questions the necessity for some of the nine referenda that were held on various EU treaties over the past four decades, he points to the fact that Ireland has on a number of occasions stopped Europe in its tracks. "I believe we were unduly sensitive and have been on the issue of neutrality over a prolonged period of time," he says.

Britain voted to leave the EU in 2016, posing huge challenges for Ireland. Sutherland says that a new trade deal between the EU and the UK must not disadvantage Irish products. The free movement of goods and people between Britain and Ireland must be maintained, he says.

"Paradoxically it could have the effect of stimulating further foreign direct investment into the Republic of Ireland," he adds. Britain will be a huge loss to the EU because it has always been one of the members most committed to open borders and free trade. Even though Brexit will be bad for both Britain and the EU, "it will not be a fatal blow to the Irish economy".

Prospects of the Irish economy

While he believes that the Irish economy is in a good position, following a catastrophic down, he errs on the side of caution. "I think that we must be careful not to get carried away, because there are dangers still out there," Sutherland says.

The eurozone still faces huge challenges, particularly high debt levels among periphery member states. Sutherland feels this may lead to further traumas in the future. He also points to Ireland's heavy debt burden. "This is going to mean a continued need to be very cautious and prudent," he says.

Yet in terms of the outlook for foreign direct investment, the future for Ireland is bright because of a number of advantages: an English-speaking country, being in the EU unlike the United Kingdom after Brexit, access to a vast market, and a demographic profile that is positive in terms of youth and education.

"I think Ireland should have a positive view of its own future," Sutherland says. In relation to underpinning Ireland's position as an open trading economy, he has a simple message: "Competitiveness will determine investment."

It is important that this level of competitiveness is maintained, Sutherland says: "We're in an open market, and we absolutely need an open market in Europe to provide employment, so it is in our own hands to remain competitive."

With regard to emigration it is a personal choice based on opportunity that young people must have. "For some it may be an appropriate thing at an appropriate time. For others it may not be, but it is a personal choice," he says. The common refrain that those who emigrate will gain experience and come home is not self-evident, he says – many will not come back. With this in mind, he believes that the government should instead harness the efforts of the global Irish. "The experiences of the people outside the country may be valuable to those inside it," he adds.

There are opportunities for investment into Ireland that can be stimulated abroad. Sutherland draws on one example: the connection between Silicon Valley and technology companies in Ireland, a relationship that he believes has been immensely valuable. "Every company I've ever served on, we've had significant Irish input," Sutherland says.

Within the banking sector, according to Sutherland, the fundamental issue is the skillset of risk analysis. It is his opinion that capital will be available to lend if there is sufficient confidence in the capacity to evaluate risk. However, if the skillset necessary to effectively evaluate the entity to which you are lending is absent, he believes, there will be a reluctance to lend such capital.

Looking at Ireland's future, he cites pioneers of Irish business who have enjoyed phenomenal success such as Tony Ryan in the aircraft leasing business. It is these accomplishments, he believes, that we must nurture.

For a small open economy, it is essential that all the arms of the State are working together for the benefit of the economy. It also means that there should be clear and open lines of communication between the civil service, the government and business. "I think one of the dangers of the current toxic environment is that communication may be limited because of fears of contamination," he says.

Anglo-Irish Relations

As a man who describes himself as "intensely Irish", Sutherland has never experienced any negativity towards the Irish people while based in Britain. He thinks there is an immensely positive attitude from Britain to Ireland, and British people to Irish people. He recalls an occasion where as attorney general he travelled to Britain to visit his opposite number Michael Havers, the UK attorney general in the early 1980s. Having spent three hours talking to Havers and conversing over lunch, the UK attorney general casually said: "Did you not hear they blew up my house in Wimbledon last night?" Yet while the memory of mortar bombing Downing Street is recent history, he has never found the slightest degree of antagonism towards the Irish.

He also says that many Irish people have accomplished much in Britain, and have been accepted at the top of British industry. "I have no doubt that a properly managed independence is the best way for us in terms of our relationship," he says. Britain, according to Sutherland, is good for Ireland.

Interestingly, the two most distinguishing moments in Sutherland's career are in the fields of politics and economics, rather than business as such: his role with the World Trade Organisation and his appointment to the European Commission. The creation of the World Trade Organisation was undeniably a pivotal moment for him. "It defined everything for me," Sutherland says of becoming its first director general.

The pinnacle of his time with the European Commission was the Competition Directorate, which opened up competition in air transport and telecommunications across Europe. As commissioner for education, he is most proud of the establishment of the Erasmus (European Regional Action Scheme for Mobility of University Students) programme.

"My emotional connection has most been to Europe and that has remained as fervent when I was a commissioner as it is now," Sutherland adds. While acknowledging the pride he felt while serving as the chairman of BP for a 13-year period, the credit for the business's successes, in his mind, rests with the executive rather than the chairman.

For Peter Sutherland, there is no one person within the realm of Irish business to be highlighted. Instead, he asserts that it is the collective efforts of many influential Irish businesspeople who have had a significant impact on shaping Ireland as it is today. "It is invidious to pick one, because there were a number of great Irish businessmen," he says – an observation itself formed throughout a unique career as an Irish businessman on the international stage.

CHAPTER 30

Interview: Leslie Buckley

In conversation with Ian Hyland

THE PROMINENT CORKONIAN DISCUSSES AER LINGUS, IRISH STEEL, SMURFIT – AND HIS CLOSE ASSOCIATION WITH DENIS O'BRIEN AND ESAT, DIGICEL, INDEPENDENT NEWS & MEDIA AND HAITI.

Leslie Buckley is one of the country's most successful businessmen; a business associate of Denis O'Brien who has been involved in some of the most profitable companies in the history of the State.

Buckley was born in Cork in 1945 and educated locally at Presentation Brothers (Pres) and University College Cork. Business was in his genes and his earliest mentor was his father.

"My dad had a floor-covering business off Washington Street, almost in the centre of Cork city. In his own way he was an entrepreneur, because he actually changed it from an outfitting shop for farmers from West Cork to a floor-covering business. From the age of eight or nine I worked there on Saturdays, and during the summer holidays – from the time I could look over the counter."

Buckley's maths teacher at Pres was a man named Freddy Holland. He was less than flattering about his student's abilities and advised him against going to UCC. "He'd say to me 'Buckley, they don't need guys like you in UCC'. In many ways, he was probably right."

Buckley ended up doing a science degree, which included a number of modules on maths. "I decided I was going to take really good maths notes, and even if I couldn't attend I'd get a copy of the notes, so I ended up with the best maths notes in UCC. Whilst Freddy was probably right about my ability at maths, he taught me one thing – that I was a really tenacious guy who wanted to prove him wrong.

"He spurred me on in such a way that I was able to make a fortune from giving maths grinds to any student who came into UCC in the next four or five years. In many ways, UCC kind of kickstarted my business life.

"Then I decided that it probably would break my good relationship with my dad if I continued working with him, so I started to earn money by selling women's make-up. I firmly believe everybody should have a job selling; you experience great highs and awful lows.

"Six months into selling make-up, I knocked on a door. The woman of the house said she needed such-and-such so I went out to the car. The back seat was empty. All of the stock had been stolen. It was actually quite difficult to make a call, because there was no such thing as a mobile phone. I drove to the nearest telephone kiosk and I rang my boss. There and then I got my first P45!"

After completing his master's in UCC, Buckley took up a graduate trainee position with Waterford Glass – at the time one of the biggest and most successful companies in the State.

"The owners of Waterford Crystal were Paddy McGrath and his family. It was a company with quite a republican culture. It was a very interesting period, as it was the same time as the Arms Crisis. I was always very interested in Irish politics and was a great admirer of Seán Lemass.

"Waterford Crystal was a great training-ground, absolutely fantastic, but at that stage the unions were very much running the company. Within a couple of weeks I had my first union meeting and it was actually a turning point in my life.

"When I look back at my first union meeting, and I had no involvement in unions prior to that... I remember ringing up my boss and he said 'listen and don't say anything else'. I would spend a lot of my life over the next 40 years working with unions and those initial days were of immense value."

Buckley then took what was an almost unprecedented move at the time and left the company after five years. "I was the first manager to leave Waterford Crystal, because at that stage it was the job to get. I got a 10% loan on my house simply because I worked in Waterford Crystal."

He decided to take up a more senior position with a smaller company, but after a few years another blue-chip Irish corporate would come calling. "Smurfits was just an absolutely incredible experience," he says – the box-making company set up by the Smurfit family, and run at that stage by brothers Michael and Dermot, was on its way to becoming the biggest in the world in its sector.

However, again it was heavily unionised – which caused many serious problems for the production manager. "I think I was the 14th or 15th production director, so it was a really high-risk role. But I decided to go for it and I really enjoyed it. There were about 14 work stoppages in one form or another in the first two years."

A meeting with Dermot Smurfit about the number of strikes led to a difference of opinion on management styles. "The meeting ended fairly abruptly and I then decided that whatever Michael [Smurfit] wanted me for, he didn't want me for any more.

"A couple of days later I get a phonecall asking me would I attend the first board meeting of An Bord Telecom, set up in 1979. Michael [Smurfit] asked me to be his PA.

"Michael was ahead of his time by defining the role of a PA because it was an executive role. An Bord Telecom was set up at that time as a semi-state business to take communications out of the civil service. Michael was an incredible chairman and revolutionised the business. We went from really old-fashioned technology to really modern technology – and Michael drove that."

It was following his work with Bord Telecom that Buckley set up a consultancy business. One of his biggest achievements during that period was saving Cobh-based Irish Steel from closure in the early 1990s.

"I was asked by Pat Dineen, who was then the chairman of Irish Steel, would I come in and assist and I eventually took over as acting CEO. Again, it was very challenging and interesting industrial relations with a lot of union negotiations. We managed to save the company and then we sold it. All of the employees were retained for a five-year period, and it was then closed.

"I had two arms to my business; one was a small entrepreneurial side and the other was for larger companies: Irish Steel, Aer Lingus et cetera. I got a call from the late Bernie Cahill, the then-chairman of Aer Lingus, asking me would I assist with the cost-reduction programme. I put together a plan with a very good financial director called Sam Young, who still remains a very good friend of mine and who now lives in the States. We achieved in taking IR£60m out of the business at the time. More recently I was fortunate enough to be asked to serve on the board of Aer Lingus for a three-year period."

Meeting Denis O'Brien

In the early 1990s a mutual acquaintance introduced Buckley to Denis O'Brien. It would be the start of a very successful business relationship between the two.

"I met with Denis – I was hugely impressed with his charisma, with his tenacity in business, but then I got to know him as a person. He is one of the most visionary and most generous people that I have met. He has really proved himself capable of building different teams of people around him who are so dedicated to him, because of his driven personality, ambition, and his generosity to people and good causes. It is a combination of that that just gives everybody the appetite to keep supporting him.

"Anyway, I was particularly lucky to meet with him and I remember saying 'Denis, I'll give you one day a week for the next six weeks and then I'm gone', as I was involved with Irish Steel and other businesses at the time. However, we've more or less been joined at the hip ever since and it's been a fantastic rollercoaster."

When the pair first met, O'Brien had just set up Esat Telecom Group. He would subsequently set up Esat Digifone, which would tender for and win the State's second mobile phone licence. It was a bumpy ride before success eventually arrived.

"Yes, there were a lot of scary moments: Denis used to be out in the States raising funds and he would ring me every evening to see how the sales were doing because we were fairly frequently on a knife-edge. There was a guy called O'Gara; I used to break his heart because I'd do the cashflow three times a day and you know what I learnt? The more often you did it, it didn't get better. We used to run the international traffic through the Esat lines, and we used to lease them from a company called Sprint. We owed them a lot of money and they called Denis and myself over to an office in London one day, and Denis was telling them the whole visionary story about Esat.

"But all they wanted to know is: are we going to be paid? And Denis wasn't quite getting there, so I eventually interrupted and I said 'in relation to the payment...' and Denis would interrupt again, and this went on for another half an hour. We told them we didn't have any money, but asked if we could agree a schedule going forward.

"The guy we were dealing with had a very bald head but he'd a big pimple on the top of it and as we were talking he just sank lower and lower into the seat, and eventually all we could see was the two eyes, the bald head and the pimple. And I'm sure what was coming out of the top of his head was 'these guys have just f**ked me; I'm probably going to lose my job'. But the night we won the licence Denis came to me and he says 'Leslie, are you available in the morning?' He knew the difficulty the guy was going through and the following morning Denis was on a plane over to pay him."

Esat was eventually sold to BT in one of the biggest transactions for an Irish-owned company at the time.

Joining the team

Following Esat, Buckley became a key member of O'Brien's team that set up mobile phone company Digicel. In just over a decade from when it was established, in the early 2000s, it has revenues of just under $3 billion.

"Here we are now, 14 years later: we're in 32 different countries, the Caribbean, Central America and the Pacific Rim – and again here's a business where the market is changing, so therefore the product is changing. We were, up to three years ago, a voice-centric business and now we are changing to a data-centric business and also developing into TV."

There was a planned flotation of Digicel on the New York Stock Exchange in September 2015, but the management team postponed it because of choppy market conditions. That will not limit plans for expansion in the future, says Buckley.

At the same time that Digicel was developing its business throughout the region, it was also putting together a large corporate social responsibility programme – one of the biggest of any company operating across the Caribbean.

"From a very early stage it started in Jamaica: there was one of many hurricanes to hit the Caribbean. Denis O'Brien, because he is an absolute philanthropist, decided: 'you know, we are going to set up a foundation in Jamaica and help'. It started in education and branched out from there. And similarly in Haiti, even prior to the devastating earthquake in 2010 Denis had launched the Haiti Digicel Foundation and he said we are going to build 20 schools in the first 12 months and the government are going to train the teachers.

"Everyone thought that this was going to be an impossible task. But fair credit to Denis and the management team: 20 schools were built. Unfortunately the teachers weren't trained, but we've found a formula to overcome that. I think at this stage we have certainly over 100 schools built in Haiti alone. There's also a foundation in Papua New Guinea. So when you actually stand back and forget about the business part of Digicel and see the number of lives Denis and Digicel have touched it is absolutely incredible."

Building a Haven

Buckley and his wife Carmel set up a charity in Haiti 12 months before the January 2010 earthquake that would eventually claim 250,000 lives. Haven would go on to do invaluable work in the aftermath of the tragedy. "I went up to a place on the border of the Dominican Republic in Haiti – a very poor area, and I was speaking through a translator to the headmaster of one of the Digicel schools.

"I thought then: I'm going to set up this charity. I told the headmaster I wanted land and I didn't want to pay for it. I wanted to build houses for the very poor of Haiti and he said "my family own some of the land here", and he asked "how much do you need?" I replied 14 acres. He said fine. Long story short, about three months later it transpired he didn't own the land; he hadn't paid any of the rent on it for ten or 12 years. I paid all the rent and hope now that Haven will eventually be the owner of the land. But it got us started.

"Then we decided we would bring volunteers out to Haiti. The first Haven Build It Week was in October 2009. We brought 300 volunteers over from Ireland and built approximately 300 houses. Then on January 12th 2010, the devastating earthquake hit Haiti. Here is a country that is the poorest in the western hemisphere and to be hit by an earthquake was the worst thing that could have possibly happened to it and its people.

"No country is ever prepared for it, but a country like Haiti is very ill-prepared. Denis, myself and a few others went out to Haiti a few days after the earthquake.

"It was just unbelievable, indescribable: there were people sleeping in the open parks. I was in a campsite that was just developed; it was part of a golf course and there were about 2,000 tents there. I said 'what type of toilet facilities have you?' and they had none.

"There was a guy who had one and I said to him 'do you know anyone who can build latrines?' and he said 'I can', and I said 'you better be sure of this'. Anyway, we ended up being the second-biggest builder of latrines; we weren't equipped to do it, but necessity is the mother of invention. We built 1,500 latrines and we trained people in how to clean them, which is a very important aspect."

Alongside his career with Digicel, Buckley is also the chairman of Independent News and Media (INM), Ireland's biggest media group. It is a sector that has been hit hard by the advent of the internet and free access to abundant sources of information. Media companies have had to cut costs to compete in this new environment.

"But there is only so much costs you can take out of a business like this before you damage the product itself. That's the balance that one continues working with on a daily and weekly basis – to ensure that the product is attractive to the customer, the reader.

"We have to do everything to continue to run the traditional business as efficiently as possible and manage that really tightly whilst ensuring the quality of the product – and at the same time concentrating on building the digital business. We've built a team of people in the business who have really good digital and information technology skills but we must now be able to convert the content we have into revenue."

The future

How does the future look for the Irish media sector? "I would say that there needs to be and will be consolidation of the traditional print business that we see today, and there will have to be closer synergies between radio, television, print, the entire media sector – because in five years' time there should be a central hub for all print business, another hub for the radio business and a subset of the two merged together.

"To be quite honest, people will continue to read newspapers and we're going to have to do more to get young people involved in the newspaper industry. In France there's a company that gets kids to edit a children's newspaper on a daily basis. Now kids that are involved at that age will then continue their interest in reading newspapers and you rebuild the audience. So I think there's a much greater opportunity for the newsprint business, but we have to think outside the box and see internationally what other countries are doing today."

Buckley agrees that he is very bullish about the prospects for Ireland in the future. "Oh I am; I think one of the great assets Ireland has is the corporation tax and I strongly urge that it is retained – and it would be fantastic for Northern Ireland to have a similar tax level, and hopefully we'll see that come.

"One of the best decisions Ireland ever made was to join the European Economic Community in 1973, and that has had a major impact in the development of Ireland.

"If you look back over the 50 years – and I know there have been certain questionmarks about it over the years – but it has to be one of the most positive decisions that an Irish government has ever made."

CHAPTER 31

Interview: Willie Walsh
In conversation with Ian Hyland

THE IAG CEO ON THE AVIATION INDUSTRY, THE IRISH ECONOMY, AND HIS CAREERS
AS PILOT AND CHIEF EXECUTIVE AT AER LINGUS – AN AIRLINE ON WHICH HE HAS
LEFT A CONSIDERABLE MARK.

From his beginnings as a trainee pilot, Willie Walsh has enjoyed a varied career in the airline industry, serving as chief operating officer at Aer Lingus before rising to the role of CEO. Walsh subsequently left Aer Lingus to take up the role of CEO of British Airways in 2005 and is currently the chief executive of International Airlines Group, the parent company of British Airways, Iberia – and from May 2015, Aer Lingus.

Walsh arrived into management by an unusual route. "I started in Aer Lingus as a trainee pilot, and most of my early career was as a pilot," he recalls. At that time, big players in business had come from Aer Lingus. "David Kennedy, former chief executive, was a very high-profile individual, and was for many years even after he left Aer Lingus."

As Walsh became more involved in the business side of Aer Lingus, Tony Ryan had come to the fore with aircraft-leasing firm Guinness Peat Aviation (GPA). Walsh cites Ryan as one of the pioneering figures in the aviation sector and describes Ryan as a "maverick" because of his tendency not to comply with what was expected from business leaders. Instead he was known to be tough but fair to those who worked with him.

"He had a reputation for being a workaholic, for being a strong achiever, and the stories about him at the time were legendary," Walsh remembers.

Ryan's uncompromising style and success in what is a tough business made him a target. "It was the old begrudging attitude in Ireland. I can remember when the [GPA] IPO collapsed so many people said they knew it wouldn't work; all the negatives that were positives about him emerged."

Walsh recalls the collapse of GPA in 1992 and the impact it had on Aer Lingus. "The Aer Lingus balance sheet was in effect being propped up by the stake Aer Lingus held in GPA. So when the GPA flotation collapsed, the Aer Lingus financial situation became perilous." During this time, his interest became more focused on the business than flying.

"I found flying to be interesting, but if I'm honest not that challenging. I just found the business side of the industry so much more interesting and challenging, so it was an easy transition for me to move from full-time flying into management and then into full-time management."

When an opportunity with Aer Lingus's troubled Spanish charter airline business Futura presented itself in 1998, Walsh had made a conscious decision that he would stop flying. "The challenge for me at the time was posed by people who I respected within Aer Lingus. To be considered credible as a senior manager in Aer Lingus, I had to commit to be a senior manager rather than a pilot who happened to be involved in management as well." Taking up the CEO role at Futura was a fantastic opportunity, he acknowledges: in 1998, at only 36 years of age, he was given the chance to run a business in a different country.

However, the government-backed Cahill Plan, which was unveiled in 1993 in an effort to rescue Aer Lingus, recommended the sale of non-core activities. When Aer Lingus then received a government bailout, under EU rules on state aid Aer Lingus had to divest all non-core activities. It eventually offloaded Futura in 2002 for IR£39 million.

Walsh learned one big lesson during his stint at the helm of Aer Lingus from 2001 to 2005: he believes you're better off facing up to challenges as soon as you see them, rather than being forced to face them by virtue of a crisis. "Crisis will always get you to act, but you have more options if you try to respond to the crisis as early as you possibly can."

His leadership of the airline was eventful, turning it away from post-9/11 disaster via cutbacks and reforms. Walsh left Aer Lingus in 2005 following a management buyout proposal that ignited political controversy. He became CEO of British Airways – and, as head of International Airlines Group, in time led a more successful attempt to acquire the former State airline.

In July 2015 the European Commission gave the formal approval for IAG to complete its €1.4 billion takeover of Aer Lingus. "It will remain an iconic Irish brand with its base and management team in Ireland but will now grow as part of a strong, profitable airline group. This means new routes and more jobs benefiting customers, employees and the Irish economy and tourism," Walsh said at the time.

Irish-British relations

Walsh undertook his flying training in the UK in 1979 over a 14-month period. "I remember what it was like being Irish in the UK. I went to Oxford in October 1979 and Lord Mountbatten had been murdered a few months before." The Troubles in Northern Ireland created huge strains in the British-Irish relationship at all levels. Throughout the 1970s and 1980s life was difficult for many Irish people living in the UK. But that has changed over recent times.

"Irish are welcomed; if anything it is a positive," Walsh says. This benign view of Ireland extends to how the country has successfully come through the financial crisis. "I think there's been great admiration for how Ireland has been restructuring itself; my experience has been very positive. I think we fit in very well; the way we think, the way we act, I think suits business."

Walsh also says that because Irish people in the UK have no interest in a knighthood, they are much freer to speak their mind on political topics. "I can be naturally critical of the [British] government. I know some British people in business tend to hesitate a little before they say critical things of government, whereas I find it easy and I think journalists and public business people enjoy that I do that.

"Under the Labour government of Tony Blair, Alistair Darling was the first secretary of state for transport that I met. During his time as chancellor of the exchequer I had many conversations with him; they are very accessible in the UK and if you want to talk to senior politicians you can do so," Walsh says. In some instances senior politicians contact him to obtain his opinion on certain matters. His experience during his time with Aer Lingus differed. "I don't think I had any dealings with any politicians other than appearing before the Oireachtas Transport Select Committee. I never had a conversation with the Taoiseach in my whole time there," Walsh recalls.

Instead, the first time he met the then-Taoiseach Bertie Ahern was after the announcement of his new role in British Airways. His interactions with members of the Irish government were limited and merely involved attending a small number of meetings with transport ministers. "I don't know whether that was just me or if it was the way it [the government] operated in business in Ireland at the time. If you need to talk to a politician here [the UK], it's easy to do so."

Irish diaspora

The attempt made in Ireland, through the Global Irish Network, to tap into the Irish diaspora was a very good initiative, Walsh says. However, there is an argument that the initiative could have been established earlier, as opposed to during difficult economic times. "The diaspora is hugely important to Ireland. When senior people in business are looking for investment abroad, they are more likely to consider a country they have a relationship with – and so for this reason, the more Irish business networks available the better.

"I think it's good business. If you've had an experience with a country you'll be familiar with it; you'll know the pluses and the minuses." Engaging with the diaspora must be done in a businesslike way, he says. "Having a party is fine but I've no interest in attending social events."

Walsh also acknowledges the work of Enterprise Ireland and the IDA. "These are very professional and well-organised support structured settings that exist in Ireland" – other countries see going up against the IDA as a real challenge, he says. "When they are competing for investment, they know they are competing with an organisation that does a really good job." Overall, in terms of the diaspora Walsh believes the pitch needs to be structured in a manner that appeals to a business decision, rather than having "a bit of craic in Ireland".

The corporate tax rate is absolutely critical for Ireland, he also says. "Ireland has got to have a business environment that is conducive to foreign investment if we are going to depend on foreign investment." The attractiveness of Ireland's corporate tax regime is that it is low and relatively straightforward by international standards. But what is crucial is stability, he adds. Investors need to know that in ten years' time the rate will still be 12.5%.

"That is as important as the fact that it is lower. Other jurisdictions have complex tax regimes where you could do better than that if you wanted." Well-educated people, a flexible workforce, flexible labour laws and good infrastructure are components in the country's investment package.

Access to Ireland by air through Ryanair and Aer Lingus, Walsh believes, is extremely important. Research at IAG reveals shows that 20 times more business is done where there is a direct flight connection rather than an indirect one. "Having direct connectivity is an opportunity and a challenge for Ireland," Walsh says.

Other areas such as a visa regime benefit Ireland, facilitating people who want to visit the country and do business here: "Ireland ticks a lot of those boxes". Walsh believes that if the country wants more investment then the government needs to show that it is responsive to the needs of business. "When people in business give an opinion they want to see progress on issues raised, and if improvement has been made that creates a good impression."

Although Walsh has no political affiliation, he admires Enda Kenny. "You can be critical of government policies, but I think having somebody who has portrayed Ireland positively is important. I think he has done a good job. Being available and accessible for people who are investing is also important."

He says he had a lot of admiration for the Fine Gael-Labour Party coalition elected in 2011 and the policies they introduced. "They didn't really have a choice. If you're in a crisis your options are very limited. You could re-write history if you wanted to; it's not going to make any difference today."

Restructuring in Ireland

The reforms that have taken place in Ireland over the past few years are deep-rooted and will be much more beneficial than what has happened in southern European countries, Walsh says. "I think Ireland has gone about this in a much more determined fashion than I've seen in Spain." However, he observes that some aspects of the restructuring process are cyclical, and there is evidence of this in terms of property prices. Walsh also says that the inability to fully control currency and interest rates means there was no alternative to an internal devaluation to restore competitiveness.

Given his position, Walsh has had the opportunity to meet with finance ministers from a number of countries. In recent years he met with the Portuguese finance minister during a lunch to talk business. "He was more interested in talking about what was happening in Ireland than what was happening in the airline industry," Walsh says of their encounter. The Global Irish Network was perceived by the Portuguese finance minister as a fascinating development.

Opportunites and reforms

There are lots of challenges for Europe yet, Walsh believes. While he describes himself as "pro-Europe", Walsh says his experience of first-hand dealings with the EU Commission has generally been very negative.

"I've met José Manuel Barroso [former president of the European Commission] on a number of occasions and I've had dealings with transport, competition and a few other areas, such as environment," he says.

There are huge challenges ahead for the region. "I worry about Europe being competitive on a global scale, when we're far too inward looking," he says. Such anxieties also trigger thoughts of Ireland in Europe. "If you're worried about Europe, you have to be worried about Ireland in Europe." Europe, he says, is at risk of being left behind.

"I think there are big challenges for Europe unless we face up to some fundamental reform and start thinking about Europe's competitiveness globally, rather than looking at how we compete with one and another within Europe."

The agri-food industry has great potential for Ireland and the Irish reputation in the sector has been enhanced in recent years. While many believed the country should have moved away from the industry ten years ago, Walsh has a differing viewpoint. "I think it is definitely an industry that represents a massive opportunity, particularly if we can expand our reach into markets outside of our traditional focus in the UK." Walsh references exports from the UK to Ireland to illustrate his point: "I think 2012 was the first year when the UK exported more to the BRICs [Brazil, Russia, India, China] than Ireland, and that was only marginally ahead of it. This tells us a lot about the UK's reach in terms of international trade."

Another challenge for indigenous Irish industry, and the wider economy, is to have a functioning banking system that supports businesses. "I think Ireland is getting there," Walsh says.

Learning from mistakes

Making a mistake is something you should not fear, according to Willie Walsh. "Some of the best things you will ever do will be learning from mistakes you have made; the critical thing is that you don't keep making the same mistake," he says.

Walsh considers Michael O'Leary to be one of very few people who could have made Ryanair work, as he was determined to succeed. "Michael O'Leary, being the genius he is, extracted a good deal from Tony Ryan to share in this success," he recalls.

The letter that documents the opportunity Aer Lingus had to purchase Ryanair for £29 million still remains in Walsh's home in Dublin. "Had Aer Lingus bought Ryanair for £29 million it would have been wasted. They wouldn't have turned a £29 million business into a €10 billion business that it is today; it would have shut it down," he says. To Walsh's mind, Michael O'Leary and his team are deserving of admiration for what they have achieved with Ryanair.

Walsh credits former Aer Lingus deputy CEO and acting CEO Larry Stanley with unconsciously mentoring him as he worked his way up through management. "I hadn't realised that in my meetings with him over the years I was unconsciously learning from this guy, watching how he operated, listening to the things he would say and focus on," he recalls.

As his career developed Walsh was asked to mentor others, and has done so on occasion. However, he now errs on the side of caution when requests are made for him to mentor employees within his organisation.

"I think when you're CEO mentoring someone in your organisation can be a challenge. It can develop a bit of unease around an organisation if someone is seen to be mentored by the CEO," he says.

Herb Kelleher, former CEO of Southwest Airlines, is another business person who is greatly admired. "I remember reading the book about this guy back in the 1980s and I was thinking there's no way somebody can be like this," he recalls. Upon meeting Kelleher, Walsh's thoughts were much altered. "He's truly inspirational; he's unlike anybody I've ever met in business – he's a complete maverick."

While Walsh admires many, he does not have role models. "Pick on aspects of what people do that you admire, what you think is good, and develop your own style – it's advice that I pass on," he says. In the past he has observed others attempting to mimic the styles of other business leaders, something that disappears under pressure as people tend to revert to their own natural style. Many people attempt to mimic the style of Michael O'Leary, but Walsh considers it unique to him – and, as such, has never seen anybody else succeed in adopting the O'Leary style. "I have learned a lot from watching other people; you build a style you're comfortable with, recognising that there is always something you can learn from people."

The other piece of advice that he believes has served him well in his career is to learn from your mistakes. "I think it's great when you hear business leaders acknowledge that they've made a mistake," he says. One example that Walsh points to is the troubled launch of Heathrow's Terminal 5. At the time of its opening, Walsh undertook an interview for TV and when a reporter said to him "this is a disaster; whose fault is it?" Walsh responded quite simply with the word "mine".

The business community does not have a reputation for being honest – and for this reason acknowledging mistakes is invaluable, he says.

For Willie Walsh there are a myriad of career highlights – some good, some bad. "I just love what I do. It's great to be able to get up in the morning, looking forward to going into work. I consider myself to be incredibly lucky in that I've got to where I've got to without ever planning a career," he says.

And it is for this reason Walsh believes he is not the ideal person to seek career advice from. Nonetheless, he urges those who ask advice to take every opportunity. "I've been offered great opportunities and I've always grabbed the opportunities as they came along," he says.

From Aer Lingus pilot to head of British Airways, those opportunities were grabbed with both hands.

CHAPTER 32

Interview: Gary McGann

In conversation with Ian Hyland

THE FORMER SMURFIT KAPPA CEO DISCUSSES HIS CAREER AT THE PACKAGING MANUFACTURER AND AER LINGUS, AND OFFERS BUSINESS ADVICE BORNE OF EXPERIENCE.

Gary McGann is one of the most high-profile and successful chief executives this country has produced in the past few decades.

After a brief stint studying medicine, he joined the civil service and completed a maths and history degree part-time. After a number of years in the Comptroller and Auditor General's office, where he studied accountancy part-time and honed his auditing skills, he joined the private sector by taking up the role of management accountant with the Swedish firm Ericsson.

In terms of the trajectory of the Irish economy, McGann is in no doubt that accession to the EEC in 1973 was a defining moment. "Instead of people coming to Ireland primarily for the domestic market like Ericssons, Rowntree Mackintosh and Cadbury et cetera, and that being the summit of their ambitions, Ireland became the jumping-off point serving the whole of Europe and eventually the Middle East and Africa.

"And that's because Ireland had a history of travel. It is an island nation where the idea of going abroad and foraging wasn't alien to us. The monks of old had established our adventuring and educational credibility. We were also extremely well-received, we were non-threatening, we were respectful of other people's culture. But more importantly, we were driven." From Ericsson, McGann joined the manufacturer and drinks distributor Gilbeys and then, in the late 1980s, he moved to Aer Lingus, the State-owned airline. When he joined the company it was struggling. In fact it was almost bankrupt.

"There were massive overheads, fares were coming down rapidly and we were replacing 25 year-old 747s with modern fuel-economic A330s. It wasn't that the people who had previously run Aer Lingus had necessarily done a bad job – the game had simply moved on in a dramatic way. The competition in the airline business had got significantly more difficult.

"At the time, Aer Lingus was in many diverse industries with a large number of different companies from robotics to computing, to pilot and cabin crew recruitment, to the hotel business – the Tara Hotel – and so on.

"The only business that was effectively making no money was the airline business. So in the first couple of years we had to attack the cost base aggressively and drive efficiencies. It wasn't pleasant or easy on the mostly very loyal workforce, but it was about survival." Joan Carmichael, who was the Congress of Trade Unions representative in the airport, told McGann that if Aer Lingus was to have a viable future then the problem of low morale had to be tackled.

"So we started a major programme of engagement with people, giving them a view of what success might look like, holding out hope that there would be success – and confirming that as a commercial business it couldn't be dependent on the State because we weren't going back for equity a second time.

"I remember a major meeting early in my Aer Lingus career: I explained to my colleagues what the vision was, how the financing was happening, how we'd get the equity. There were about 200 people at the meeting in the canteen and I got a question from this guy at the back of the room who said: 'sure if it fails can't we always go back to the government for more capital?' In my reply I said 'over my dead body' and he said 'sure that can be arranged too'."

From 2007 onwards, Aer Lingus had been fighting off a takeover attempt from Ryanair. Then in 2015 British Airways took over the partly State-owned airline. "Michael O'Leary [Ryanair chief executive] has stated that in his view the ideal situation for Ireland was a consolidated Irish airline comprising Ryanair and Aer Lingus. I don't think anyone could have worn such an outcome. The irony of it was that in my day, Aer Lingus had actually tried to buy Ryanair.

"In my view, the natural home for Aer Lingus was always British Airways. There's been a good relationship for many years between the two airlines – now consolidated under Willie Walsh. But even in the more difficult times between Britain and Ireland, British Airways and Aer Lingus had a lot of affinity and many things in common including high standards, world-class pilots, world-class cabin crew and a good understanding of the concept of service, which is not always practised in the Western world."

There were a number of senior executives and board members from Smurfit sitting on the board of Aer Lingus during McGann's time at the airline, including Martin Rafferty, Paddy Wright and David Austin. Following on from an introduction made by Wright, McGann met Michael Smurfit, the then-chief executive of the company.

"We hit it off well and Michael recruited me as CFO in 1998." Paddy Wright was chief operating officer at the time, but retired in 1999. McGann joined Smurfit on the same day it was announced that the company's US subsidiary was merging with the Stone Corporation to form Smurfit-Stone Container Corporation (SSCC), the largest paper packaging company in the US. However, in hindsight the backdrop to the deal was ominous.

"As the deal was being concluded the dollar strengthened and US manu-facturing declined. SSCC was highly leveraged and instead of deleveraging the company was leveraging and re-leveraging into a declining market... so it became clear by 2000/2001 that it was becoming a millstone around Jefferson Smurfit Group's (JSG) neck."

In 2002 JSG was taken private by the private equity firm Madison Dearborn, although a number of other options had also been looked at. As part of the consideration shareholders received the underlying shares in SSCC as well as cash. "This was undoubtedly the best value for sharehold-ers, so we eventually got the deal done." The initial reaction to the deal was mixed because of the prevailing image of the private equity industry. McGann says, however: "Madison Dearborn were very different – we believed they were different; they turned out to be different. They were progressive, they were supportive, they were honourable, they did exactly what they said they would do so we bought companies, we sold companies, we took costs out and we deleveraged – we effectively deleveraged every year from 2002 through the 2008/9 crisis.

"So from 2002 to 2005 we basically sold companies, bought some companies, took costs out and deleveraged. We optimised our business model and focused on east and west Europe and on Latin America, two of the three biggest growth markets for packaging in the world."

Then in 2005 a truly transformative deal loomed large when preliminary negotiations began with the Dutch company Kappa, which was the number-three company in the paper and packaging sector in Europe, with Smurfit being number one.

Initially, the management team believed the price for Kappa was too high. It was subsequently agreed that a merger was the best way to proceed. "The marriage of Smurfit and Kappa was superb in terms of complementary talents, complementary geographies, complementary origins – they were big mill and paper people, they were big R&D people; we were strong corrugated packaging, market-facing, commercially driven. If you designed it you probably wouldn't have gotten a better fit.

"And culturally – the 'marriage' of the Dutch and the Irish was fantastic. You could ask any former Kappa person and any former Smurfit person whether this was a happy marriage and to this day they would say mostly yes, notwithstanding the tough steps that had to be taken to optimise the integration.

"In going private in 2002 we were mindful of the old adage 'nobody ever shrunk to greatness'. So we knew we had to grow again if we were to re-enter the public market in order to have a proposition different to what we left the market with – the Kappa deal was it."

In the second quarter of 2007 Smurfit Kappa went public again at an initial public offering price of €16.50 and within a short time it reached €20.88. Then the global economy fell off a steep precipice and the company's share price plummeted to €1.09. Smurfit Kappa weathered the financial crisis through paying down debt and sticking to its core competencies. The share price has rebounded to well in excess of its pre-crisis level.

Moving on

When McGann retired in August 2015 Tony Smurfit took over as CEO. "Tony has done a superb job in taking over and has presided over the seamless transition of a number of senior roles [Ian Curley having joined Ardagh as CEO] and has continued to grow the company from strength to strength." Following his retirement, McGann took up the position of chairman of Paddy Power, the bookmaking firm. Rather than ease his way into retirement, however, McGann steered the company through the multi-billion euro merger with Betfair.

"The fundamental philosophy I've tried to live my life on is the concept of 'the team'. Tony Smurfit, Ian Curley and myself – and indeed three or four others, with the support of an excellent chairman and board – have been the architects of the strategy that Smurfit Kappa is working to, which has evolved over the years.

"In very simple terms the Smurfit Kappa strategy is to grow organically through differentiation, which is underpinned by an innovative digital-based activity with our customers to demonstrate to them, at the point of purchase, how we can sell more of their products. That is enhanced by a judicious expansion strategy through appropriate M&A.

"We have bespoke original software that does that. It's called ShelfSmart – it is a six-stage process. We have thousands of real supermarket images from all over the world we operate in, so we can go to any boardroom or any marketing centre for any big company and show them their product anywhere in this world, demonstrating its issues and opportunities.

"Secondly, we have a 3D visualiser that takes that shelf and in 3D can start to reorient the packaging and effectively redesign it before their eyes. Thirdly, we can take that outcome and actually test it in focus groups via the internet, with eye technology (facial recognition-type technology) using eye intensity on the screen to highlight the products that are most attractive. We have evidence-based research that shows that eye intensity converts into a high percentage correlation with expenditure."

Organic growth, differentiation, driving a big manufacturing company with 350 plants, unit costs and efficiencies and lean manufacturing are all on the agenda, as is "growth through acquisition in eastern Europe, southern parts of North America and Latin America. That's the gameplan," says McGann, having moved on in his career.

The wider economy

McGann takes an interest in the broader economy and has held several wide-ranging roles through his career. A former IBEC president, he is very positive about the Irish economy, although he has concerns about the country's competitiveness and education system. "First of all, Ireland, in trading and commercial terms, is in a good place. Obviously the balance sheet had been seriously damaged by the banking crisis, which I unfortunately have been very familiar with. It has been very tough on the country in general." McGann was a non-executive director of Anglo Irish Bank in the years before it was nationalised, and appeared before the Oireachtas banking inquiry in the summer of 2015.

Growth prior to the frothy years leading up to the crash of 2008 was based on compelling fundamentals such as a competitive economy with a leading edge in manufacturing sectors such as pharma, ICT and bio. "Now the critical issue for us is that we don't get ahead of ourselves on the cost side. We only have one thing in our favour apart from our native acumen and that is competitiveness. Our competitiveness has improved, but it is nowhere near the best in Europe, particularly for manufacturing. Manufacturing in Europe declined from about 20% of GDP to about 14% of GDP at a time when European unemployment went up to 12%. Do you think the two of them are related? Of course they are."

The greatest problem with persistent and long-term unemployment in Ireland and Europe is among non-graduates and lower-skilled workers, he says. "It is people who have no possibility of going abroad and who don't have professions – and they are dependent on the various levels of manufacturing-type industries that are indigenous to the countries they live in, and we have to be competitive to retain our appropriate share of that.

"It's not enough to be a service industry; we can see that in the UK outside the London area. We have to have a more mixed economy. We have done it in the past with some fantastic industrial companies such as CRH, Kerry Group, Glanbia, Smurfit Kappa, Glen Dimplex et cetera. They can do it;

there's no reason others can't do it. There are some really good SMEs; we have to get the money to them. There is no point in us having quantitative easing if that money doesn't get to the 'main street'; getting it to Wall Street, or the equivalent in Europe, doesn't get it to the market."

McGann says that having a well-funded third-level sector is crucial for the future health of the economy. He is critical of the restrictions imposed on universities in the very competitive education sector, such as excessive limits on what salaries can be offered to the teaching staff. "The concept of stopping universities finding a way of capturing the right talent and rewarding it appropriately makes no sense for an island that has historically led the education field. I understand the problem but there has to be a way around it. The day we stop recognising talent appropriately is the day we stop recruiting it. And universities and universities' positioning in the league tables is critical."

He also says there is a problem with the duplication of courses and specialities offered by universities: "I'll declare a vested interest; I'm a former director of the Smurfit Business School [in UCD]. It is ranked consistently in the top 100 business schools by the *Financial Times*, and now Trinity is raising money for a business school in competition with it. This duplication rather than single centres of various excellence makes no sense and is unaffordable."

Sage advice

McGann is generous with his advice and business insight, which often involves how to assemble the correct management team around you. "I think the chairman-CEO relationship is critical," he says. "Nowadays, by necessity, they spend a lot of time together because chairmen are required to engage a lot more, and CEOs – the good ones – use their chairman and boards as supportive challenging soundingboards.

"The other thing that I think is important – and it needs to be done with appropriate governance and compliance – is avoiding appointing people unknown from places unknown, often with fantastic reputations but who don't necessarily 'fit'. We all know that in business the interview is the crudest process of recruitment ever invented by man, with efforts to supplement it by psychometric testing and so on. But nothing is superior, to my mind, than a reference on behalf of a candidate by somebody you trust, whose style you understand and know, and who has an understanding of who would fit in your team. Because a board is a team at the end. Too often we see 11 or 15 'stars' defeated by more modest capabilities playing as a team."

McGann recalls how the board operated during his Smurfit Kappa days. "First of all, I think we've been very lucky in that we got the people that we wanted. Together with a chairman of Liam O'Mahony's calibre, we sought to have a variety of different cultures represented in the boardroom. We sought to have the major geographies in which we operated represented, with the various skills and backgrounds also present in the appointees that we would need in the world we live in, not just today but tomorrow.

"So for example we have international brand expertise, we have a number of industrialists, we have financial experts and we have successful retail and marketing skills. So the functionalities, the geography and the cultural representation – but most importantly the chemistry – make a great board, supporting and challenging management."

McGann also offers a word of caution about international expansion. "I'm not a great believer of the phrase 'I must be in China'. I know a lot of people who have been in the 'must be in China' mode, and within eight years in our case (and others more or less), sought to leave. So I don't think there is anywhere you should be, other than places where you can actually be successful in business because of either of what you are or what the opportunity is."

On the other hand, the company knows Latin America and McGann says it is critical to have people with local knowledge. "Who can train you how to manage in a society where a currency drops to a quarter of its value overnight? Who can train you how to survive an earthquake?" The answer is to find the correct local talent in the correct environment and nurture it.

McGann says that he has had many highlights during his career. "*Business & Finance* made me Business Person of the Year in 2007, which was a very interesting year to be given that award." Among other recognitions he was also honoured by the Colombian government for his services to industry there. Colombia is a country for which he has great respect and affinity.

"But most importantly is the success of Smurfit Kappa: the big highlight for me is that we went private, we did the biggest and best deal ever in the European industry, the biggest IPO ever in the industry, and we survived almost the end of the game, mainly because of 40,000 incredible people who dug deep, who took pay cuts, ran hard… they were shareholders in many cases. One minute the share was at €20 and next thing it was a euro, and we were asking them to work even harder and take paycuts. And drive the business. And they did – they are the highlight for me."

McGann has encountered many leading businesspeople who guided him on his way – Vincent Daly whom he describes as his "guru", David Dand and Ned Sullivan – consummate marketers who made Baileys famous; and Tom Keaveney, the ultimate salesman. "Bernie Cahill was an amazing character, but I've benefited enormously from working with Michael [Smurfit]. Michael has enormous talents; he's without a shadow of a doubt the best dealmaker I've ever met. Himself and Howard Kilroy were just two amazing people, a great complementary team. They never fell in love with a deal, and never looked back. And I keep reminding people of Michael's mantra – if it isn't criminal and it isn't terminal, it isn't a problem.

"Paddy Wright, who was one of the toughest operators you could meet but a charismatic leader for whom people always went the extra mile. Tony Ryan was another: I've spent a number of interesting hours with Tony. You know, what they all had, and Denis O'Brien and Dermot Desmond also – it was courage. Money is a commodity; brilliance – you're born with it or not. Michael used to say you can buy skills but you can't buy entrepreneurialism, you can have everything and if you haven't the courage to pull the trigger and take the consequences – and the consequences are never all positive – and get up and do it again and again and again, then you will have achieved nothing! So I think the one thing we really have to be better at in Ireland is forgiving failure – because failure is only the other side of the success coin."

CHAPTER 33

Interview: Denis O'Brien

In conversation with Ian Hyland

THE IRISH BUSINESSMAN DISCUSSES POLICY, ENTREPRENEURSHIP – AND HIS WIDE ARRAY OF ENDEAVOURS FROM 98FM THROUGH ESAT TELECOM TO INTERNATIONAL SUCCESS WITH DIGICEL.

Denis O'Brien is one of the most successful businessmen Ireland has ever produced. His interests have grown extensively and today include telecoms, media, hotels and leisure, healthcare and real estate property. Initial success came through the Dublin radio station 98FM, and then through the telecoms firm Esat.

But O'Brien's biggest success to date is his Caribbean-based telco, Digicel. From taking out a licence in Jamaica in 2001, the company now has a presence in over 30 countries. Moreover, it has taken on incumbents such as AT&T and Cable and Wireless in their own back yard, and won.

The Dublin-born entrepreneur took an early interest in business. "I went to High School [in Rathgar, Dublin] and in the library every week on a Thursday there would be the latest edition of *Business and Finance*, *Fortune* and maybe one other magazine. I would go up to the library and read those magazines every week. I was probably 15 at that stage but I had started reading a newspaper every day since I was 12. And so I had a real interest in what was going on in the world, particularly in the world of business.

"Plus, every morning between 8am and 8.50am my father would give me a lift to school and he would talk about everything to do with business – exactly what was going on in his business, what happened yesterday, fellas not paying him, orders not coming through, sales reps crashing cars, the situation with the bank. And then every evening around 7pm he would tell me what happened. So every evening I would race home after rugby to find out what happened and he'd be getting out of his suit and he would tell me what happened that day. Then we'd carry on the conversation. So it was a conversational education in business."

Denis O'Brien Snr ran a successful equine drugs business. He had a formidable impact on his son's future career. "You're either interested or you're not – I was particularly interested. At the weekend we [father and son] would go running in the mountains – and it would be an hour out to the country, an hour and a half running, climbing, walking and an hour back, so I'd get another four or five hours of what was happening.

"It was like a private education and that was a big advantage to me – I'd already listened to his experiences at a very early stage, so when I went to do my own thing I'd a lot of stuff in the ether that I'd already learned."

Michael Smurfit was also an early influence on O'Brien. The Smurfit Group was a truly international Irish company in the paper and packaging sector. "I think Tony O'Reilly becoming CEO of Heinz was another step in terms of Irish people doing extremely well overseas. Then there was Tony Ryan, who set up his aircraft leasing business, GPA, in 1976 – I'd just started in university at that stage."

O'Brien studied for an arts degree in UCD, followed by an MBA in Boston College. Upon graduation he worked for US-based Trinity Bank for a year. But his first big break in business was securing a role as personal assistant to Tony Ryan. The GPA founder, and later Ryanair founder, was an influential figure on the Irish business landscape.

He would leave an indelible print on O'Brien's approach to business. "Tony Ryan was different. His urgency about getting things done and his work ethic. I was never afraid of hard work – but you know he [Ryan] was a smart worker; he used time really efficiently.

He got everything done in a day. In fact, he'd probably do three days in one day – meetings led till late at night, and if he was in Ireland at the weekend he'd work all day Saturday from 8am until 6 or 7 o'clock at night. He used his time very efficiently, he worked on a basis of lists, and everything was fast – get it done quick. If you were selling something sell it quickly, get the money in the bank and move on – an urgency to get a deal. Tony Ryan had a vision that was global.

"My father used to go travelling at least ten days a month and that might include Trinidad, Australia or Japan. He'd go all over the world selling his products, for supplements for horses. He got to Trinidad before I did! My dad got me interested in the outer world, but Tony Ryan got me further interested in it."

From GPA, O'Brien set out on his own. Before hitting a winning formula with 98FM and then Esat, there were a number of not so successful ventures along the way – including an Irish shopping channel, which was backed by Michael Smurfit.

"In terms of failure... you learn so much with failure. You learn how to run out of money – and all the lessons associated with running out of money. For example, being too optimistic about what your revenues are going to be and are people paying you on time or what money you can raise. We effectively ran out of money – we were too early with The Shopping Channel.

"The big lesson for me from that project was that I don't believe in blue-sky plans. And I don't believe you should lose money for three or four years and look at discounted cash flows. I think a business has to make money quickly within a year or so, a year and a half maybe, without looking to five years to see if you can make a return."

O'Brien stayed within the media sector but switched from TV to radio. It was 1989. "98FM was the first successful business; it made money virtually immediately and that was a big surprise – that was great, but we said: what would we do next?

"Within six months of starting that business we were out looking for a licence in eastern Europe, initially in Hungary. It's like France, an extraordinarily difficult place to do business, but we eventually got a licence in Prague."

Financial backing for his radio assets came from Anglo Irish Bank. "One of the reasons why I'm thankful to Anglo Irish Bank is because they lent me the money to do that – and that would never have happened without

Anglo. And the process they put me through in 1990 was a really rigorous credit process and we borrowed about IR£1.8 million from them. I was interviewed by so many different people and they even brought me to dinner! I'd never had a banker bring me out to dinner. I remember [senior Anglo figure] Bill Barrett bringing me to the dogs to see if I had any vices, like did I own any greyhounds or was I a gambler."

O'Brien became a household name in Ireland when he won the State's second GSM mobile phone licence in 1995. However, the inspiration for setting up Esat Telecom came from a meeting at the Dublin Horse Show in the late 1980s with John Goeken, the founder of the US telecoms firm MCI.

In 1991 O'Brien, along with fellow entrepreneur Mark Roden, set up Esat. The Norwegian state telecoms firm Telenor were Esat's main partner in the Esat Digifone consortium. Following a period of tensions between the two parties and a hostile takeover bid by Telenor, O'Brien sold the company to British Telecom in 2000. At first he was reluctant to sell because he thought there would be a backlash from the staff. "Would they be pissed off at the dream ending of an Irish-owned company floating on the Nasdaq? But when it came to announcing the deal, they were cheering. The minimum payout for all staff was between €30-€40k, but 20-odd people got over €1million. In all, 10% of the proceeds went to the staff."

O'Brien himself made over €300m from the deal. The granting of the licence to Esat Digifone became the subject of the long-running Moriarty Tribunal. It ran from 1997 until March 2011. O'Brien has consistently and trenchantly refuted that there was anything untoward about the tendering process and the outcome.

Digicel

O'Brien is also critical of share options in business. "The tax implications of share options make them totally unattractive – as a way of incentivising people it's a disincentive, to be honest. Because the highest tax rate is what they get paid off – there have been so many different initiatives in Ireland to change this, but it has failed."

After a brief hiatus from business, O'Brien spotted an ad for a telecoms licence in Jamaica. He set up Digicel in 2001. It now operates in 31 countries.

In terms of its future expansion, the company will look at bolt-on acquisitions. "We're picking up businesses – we are adding to what we have. Up until three years ago we were a purely voice and text business and some data – now we're very much a data business, plus we've gone into fibre to the home, cable TV, and plus we're doing all the enterprise networking solutions for bigger companies and medium companies as well.

"We are now also providing content, we bought the biggest sports broadcaster in the Caribbean, we are setting up a terrestrial TV business in Papua New Guinea, we have set up a Sky-like platform in the Pacific so we're buying lots of content there – we initially had 30 channels. We now have 120 channels.

"We're becoming the 360 provider, so people will not have to buy tele-communications or communications services from anybody else – they can just come to us as a one-stop. And that is the opportunity for the business, and that's where we see the real growth in the business: people are going to have smartphones, they are buying data and voice – but when they get to the office, the whole solution has to be Digicel as well. We have invested $2billion in capital expenditure over the last three years."

Even though Digicel has so far been geographically concentrated in the Caribbean and South America, a move in the vast Asian market could be on the cards at some stage in the future.

"There's a pocket of potential; obviously the last place is really North Korea. Myanmar is just done in the last two years – we didn't get a licence there, but that's life. The opportunity is now breaking out of your revenue stream and making more products and services for customers in every country that we're in."

The company pulled a planned flotation on the New York Stock Exchange in October 2015 because of turbulent market conditions. It will be at least mid-to-late 2018 before a Digicel initial public offering is looked at again, O'Brien has said.

Independent News and Media

In January 2006 O'Brien first started buying shares in the Tony O'Reilly-controlled Independent News and Media (INM). Over the next few years there were a number of acrimonious exchanges between the two camps over the strategy and direction the company was taking. O'Brien was concerned that the value in INM was declining dramatically. The status quo at INM didn't welcome his comments and at the 2008 AGM O'Brien was labelled a 'dissident shareholder'.

Throughout this time the INM share price was collapsing and borrowings were at an all-time high. Over the course of 2012 the battle reached a climax with O'Brien emerging victorious. Gavin O'Reilly resigned as chief executive in June of that year.

O'Brien's long-time business associate Leslie Buckley was installed as chairman. Following an intense bout of negotiations with the company's creditors, the crippling €432m debt obligation was restructured and reduced to a more manageable €118m. Following the sale of INM's stake in APN in 2015, the company became debt-free.

However, like any other media company it is facing a challenging landscape. "I think the media business is becoming more fragmented and brutal," says O'Brien.

"It's becoming more challenging for management teams; unless you can reinvent your management team it's going to be hard. And we've had to reinvent management teams in nearly all our businesses in the media area, and that has been a very difficult task. There is a big surge in work going on online that takes money to build revenues, but revenues will be there in two or three years' time – you just have to swallow the costs at the moment, which we're doing."

O'Brien also owns Communicorp, which controls Newstalk and Today FM as well as 42 other radio stations in Ireland and across Europe. He has some advice for the regulatory regime in this country.

"I think the BAI [Broadcasting Authority of Ireland] need to really re-look at themselves and say: 'Are we helping the industry, or what can we really do to help the industry?'" He questions the rationale surrounding separate news teams and separate overheads for every radio station.

O'Brien claims that two-thirds of Irish radio stations are loss-making, which makes a review of the regulatory regime all the more pressing. "We're [Communicorp] doing more public-service content in Newstalk than RTÉ Radio 1 are. And they have a massive featherbed of money coming at them every month from the licence fee – and the problem now is that every minister for communications is completely conflicted, because they are given a platform by RTÉ for themselves and their cabinet colleagues on a daily basis on television and radio. I think the BAI needs to be tougher on RTÉ. We pay fees to the BAI; they need to say 'we need to overhaul this industry dramatically'. There's going to have to be mergers of, maybe, clusters of six or seven local radio stations across the country or they'll go out of business."

Education matters

On the wider economic front, he has concerns that the Irish education system is not up to the standards needed to service a knowledge-based economy.

"I think we have lost our way over the last five years in terms of education. I think there is ambition within the university sector, but to be ambitious you have to attract investment and philanthropy.

"When you read about Ireland's falling rankings I'd say all the donors to all the universities are increasingly unhappy and saying: what is going on? I think the universities here need to do another divide-up – and UCD should specialise even more in some areas, and Trinity should do the same. We should be much more strategic in putting money behind universities to specialise in particular areas.

"The second thing is that the Department of Education has capped the salaries for academic staff to bring real talent into that sector. The single biggest problem is attracting talent. There are appointments open in UCD because they can't attract talent because the Department of Education says the pay guidelines are capped and that's all you can pay. You can't do top-ups, you can't do anything. We'll go down another 30 to 50 notches in those rankings in the next 18 months. I think we need to focus on fourth-level as well – we need to focus on research; there needs to be a massive overhaul. Peter Sutherland has been beating this drum; everybody is really upset – it's one of the most negative things over the last few years that our universities have not moved up another gear." We need to set up centres of excellence in artificial intelligence (AI) and other areas where our 'new' economy is moving towards, he says.

According to O'Brien, the solution lies with more private-sector funding of universities. "The private sector should contribute towards the top-up payments, but adding to the salaries of these professors and other academics who are coming to run these major schools in universities. We should be paying €250k, €300k, €400k or simply whatever it takes to get the best talent, just like in the US. They do 'chairs', or whatever, to subsidise a salary – that should be also allowed. But unfortunately the Department of Education won't allow that."

Moreover, privatisation could be a more viable option for some of the universities. "There is a potential for some of the universities to be privatised. One great example is the Royal College of Surgeons – they have been able to survive through private philanthropy, but also by being very commercial. They are one of the best medical schools in the world. I think UCD and Trinity need to be unshackled – and maybe DCU. Hibernia is a great example of where they've been able to make a niche for themselves in teacher training – they've done a magnificent job."

Going multinational

Overall, O'Brien is enthusiastic about the prospects for the Irish economy and Ireland as a hub for new business ideas. However, over the past few decades this country has a lamentable record in developing small successful companies into large caps.

"The great difficulty we have is that people have great business ideas, they set up the business, it makes €1m or €2m and goes on to make €5m. But they then get a tap on the shoulder from a big multinational saying 'sell us your business' and they then sell it. Instead of saying 'maybe I should be the acquirer and become a big multinational'. When I see Irish businesses being sold when they have a global product, looking to sell globally... if you're not thinking of selling globally, you should sell your business when you get the tap on your shoulder. But be the acquirer, not the person being acquired."

He argues that for management teams to persist with companies as they grow in scale, there has to be specific funds in place that cater for these type of firms. "If you take Enterprise Ireland, if I rang Julie Sinnamon, CEO, she could tell me about 10-15 companies who are the ones who could go global. We should have a fund for them – so the entrepreneur can take a bit of money out, pay off their mortgage, and let them go on. I actually did that when we did our first institutional round in 1996 – I took money off the table. I paid off my mortgage – put some money in the bank. I felt much better about myself. I could then go to work every day and not worry that all my eggs were in one basket."

O'Brien invested heavily in this country during the downturn. "We've probably tripled our employment in the last four years in Ireland. It's a great time to invest if you believe in the opportunity. But I'm worried about the property market – because basically NAMA have sold loans, banks have sold loans, Anglo have sold their loans to all these hedge funds who are wholesaling these loans now and trying to sell off these properties.

"If you look at the paper, there are hundreds of properties for sale, whereas two years ago there may have just been 20 advertised for sale. It's just gone through the roof again; I'm concerned about that. I'm concerned about the way these hedge funds are treating Irish borrowers; there was no duty of care to these people. I thought the way Michael O'Flynn was treated was appalling."

Cork developer O'Flynn had a high-profile legal wrangle with Blackstone over the summer and autumn of 2014 when the US private equity firm tried to take control of his companies.

"If you're a performing borrower you should not be thrown to the wolves; he was a performing borrower and was thrown to the wolves. There was no duty of care from NAMA as to what would happen when Blackstone bought those loans. If someone is a good borrower – and is honest in their dealings with them – you should have a duty of care to them."

Outstanding business leaders

O'Brien nominates several figures who come to mind as the outstanding Irish business leaders of recent decades. "There's all sorts of people that you pick out from different sectors: in the financial area and risktaking I'd say Dermot Desmond. In technology I'd say Pat McDonagh." He cites Coolmore Stud as a major international success story. O'Brien also points to Aidan Heavey (Tullow Oil), JP McManus, Martin Naughton (Glen Dimplex), Barry O'Callaghan (Riverdeep) and Dómhnal Slattery (Avolon).

He argues that the Irish diaspora needs to be leveraged more effectively. "We need to be as strong as the Israeli lobby is in North America. It's been haphazard. The Israelis have been very strategic and we need to be the same. We need to have a proper lobbying unit in Capitol Hill. At the moment we've a one-man lobbying effort in Niall O'Dowd – he's on his own; he deserves a lot of support. The Australians can get a bill for their illegal immigrants, we can't – I mean that's ridiculous. We need government and the private sector people putting money in hiring really smart people as lobbyists for the Irish cause. We need to create a deeper network effect.

"It should be a collaboration between the Department of Foreign Affairs (DFA) and the private sector and the Ireland Funds. The DFA needs to be given strategic money – how do you push Ireland's position in North America in the US, and how we can be a much more powerful grouping and lobby like Israel has been able to do? You need to write cheques, on a multi-annual funding basis."

What are O'Brien's personal highlights from his business career so far? "What am I proud of? What Colm Delves and the team at Digicel have done has been fantastic. Leslie [Buckley] as my partner in a whole array of businesses has been unbelievable. I'm particularly bullish about Actavo (formally known as Siteserv).

"Topaz was an excellent business. We had fully intended growing it but when Canadian company Alimentation Couche-Tard came along with an offer of €258 million cash it was really impossible to turn down. I think INM would be out of business only for Leslie.

"Esat Telecom was a highlight as it was an interesting phase. But right now you don't want to be caught in a timewarp, you want to reinvent yourself – and for the next two years I'm looking at the reinvention. Everything is being disrupted."

CHAPTER 34

Interview: Dermot Desmond

In conversation with Ian Hyland

THE INVESTOR DISCUSSES IRISH ENTREPRENEURSHIP, POLITICS AND PUBLIC LIFE, HIS CAREER AND MOTIVATIONS, AND THE WAY FORWARD FOR BUSINESS AND THE IRISH ECONOMY.

"I wanted to have money in my back pocket and I wanted to be independent. That was my whole thing," says Dermot Desmond. A regular fixture on *The Sunday Times* Rich List, Desmond is among the top ten wealthiest people in Ireland, with a personal fortune estimated at over €2bn. He has certainly achieved his aim of independence, and a lot more besides.

"I started working early, picking strawberries at 11 years of age. Every summer I had a job to be independent and I enjoyed it immensely. And if you said my hallmark today is to be independent, my hallmark was to be independent when I was 11. Independence is doing exactly what you want to do while recognising that there are constraints in life with what you can do, but having the freedom in general to be independent," he says when asked about what he thought the future had in store for him when he was younger.

Desmond is one of Ireland's best-known and most successful entrepreneurs. He is associated with some of the most important developments in the Irish economy, particularly Dublin's International Financial Services Centre (IFSC). Born in Cork, he grew up in Dublin and left school at 18 to join Citibank in Dublin in 1968. It was there that he developed a taste for business.

"I joined Citibank in the late sixties. In the late sixties and the 1970s a lot of the premier businesspeople in Ireland banked with Citibank – especially from 1970, when there was a bank strike. It brought in the Tony O'Reillys and the Michael Smurfits of the day, and the other people who needed to use foreign banks in Ireland. I moved through the various operations. I moved to the Credit Department and that is where I first got to interface with the businesses that were growing in Ireland; businesses that Citibank were lending to."

From the foundation of the State to the 1960s, the Irish business landscape was dominated mostly by an Anglo-Irish elite. However, throughout that decade a number of Catholic entrepreneurs started making their mark both at home and abroad, and home-grown companies like CRH were expanding.

"Tony O'Reilly had developed an international focus from his experience working in the UK and then with Heinz, where he had been engaged in multiple cross-border acquisitions. Smurfit had made acquisitions in the UK and also had investments in Nigeria, so he understood exactly what factors were influencing paper and pulp prices and that they were internationally dictated. He also knew that innovation was a key element in the paper industry and that he had to continually search internationally for innovation. CRH also understood that the path to growth was through acquisitions. Tony Ryan came to the fore a little bit later, in the early eighties.

"In the mid-seventies I joined the Investment Bank of Ireland, and they were doing a lot of corporate finance work for Smurfit and for CRH. I was on the lending side. The lending side interfaced with corporate finance because every acquisition needed funding. IBI was doing a lot of syndicate lending, and I was fortunate to be involved even as a very junior banker.

"I was pushing the numbers, analysing the figures and looking at the acquisitions. This gave me an understanding of how value was created through acquisitions, how costs were cut out, how your income was generated, and how synergy was created – using that fantastic word that's used when people are buying businesses and are suggesting how value can be created. Fitzwilton was at the fore at that time as well; coming into IBI at that

The mischief-making, headline-grabbing Michael O'Leary would turn Tony Ryan's Ryanair into Europe's largest airline through a combination of ultra-low fares and mass-marketing.

Peter Sutherlan...

Peter Sutherland and Gary McGann, 1994. McGann, seen here representing IBEC, would succeed Michael Smurfit as CEO of the eponymous packaging firm in 2002, and his tenure was marked by exponential growth for the company.

Above: Anglo Irish Bank's Seán FitzPatrick was CEO and then chairman until its dramatic collapse in 2008. **Left:** Property developer Johnny Ronan was one of the most recognisable faces of the Celtic Tiger property bubble.

Above left: Daniel Tierney of veterinary pharma firm Bimeda. **Above right:** Alexander Mann Solutions founder Rosaleen Blair. **Below:** Lucy Hyland, the late Albert Reynolds' wife Kathleen, Sir John Major and Ian Hyland.

Stud owner John Magnier is one of the pre-eminent figures on the international horse racing scene, and helped to turn the Irish industry into one of the strongest in the world.

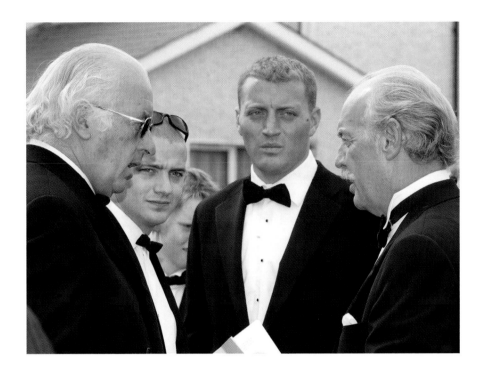

Above:
John Magnier
with Dermot
Desmond, 2006.
Right: Desmond with
businessman and
horse owner
JP McManus.

As Minister for Finance under Bertie Ahern, Charlie McCreevy's tenure was one of tax cuts, public spending hikes and deregulation. He meets Peter Sutherland at the launch of *The Best is Yet To Come* by Marc Coleman in late 2007 – just before the crash.

McCreevy
and Dermot
Desmond.

Clockwise:
resources and
distilling magnate John
Teeling. Neville Isdell served
as chairman and CEO of
Coca-Cola and became a global
Irish leading light. Gillian Bowler
founded Budget Travel and blazed
a trail for female entrepreneurs
and executives. Breege
O'Donoghue, long-
serving former Primark
executive.

Above: Prominent ESRI economist and director Frances Ruane with Progressive Democrats leader and Minister for Health Mary Harney. **Below left:** Neil McCann of the ever-growing Fyffes, and son Carl **(right)** of Total Produce, which separated from Fyffes in 2007.

Jim O'Hara headed up Intel's Irish operations at a time of enormous high-tech growth, the Leixlip campus becoming a prized asset in Ireland's foreign direct investment reputation.

Eamonn Sinnott became general manager of Intel Ireland in 2010. In 2014 the company announced that it had invested $12.5 billion in its Irish operations since setting up in 1989.

Above: Rugby legend Brian O'Driscoll, Senator George Mitchell, boxer Katie Taylor and Shaun Murphy of KPMG. Right: Businessman, New York City mayor and Ireland Day attendee Mike Bloomberg.

Above: Mould-
breaking Kerry
Group founder
Denis Brosnan.
Right: Michael Maughan
of Gowan Group with
media and PR expert
Mary Finan.

stage to visit [IBI head] Richard Hooper you again had Tony O'Reilly and Michael Smurfit – and these were great men who were pioneers at building new business and were globally focused. I really devoured what they were doing. From them I learnt that to be a success you had to look outside your own pond. You had to look at the ocean to find the bigger fish."

Following Citibank and the Investment Bank of Ireland, Desmond went to Kabul in Afghanistan to work for PwC. However, it was when he returned to Ireland that the template for his future career would take shape. In 1981 Desmond embarked on the major solo business initiative that would lay the groundwork for his future success. Stockbroking, in the preceding number of decades, had been mostly dominated by stuffy Anglo-Irish operations. Desmond set up National City Brokers (NCB) with an eye on the expanding financial services sector.

"What I recognised was that the two predominant qualities going forward, starting in the early eighties, were always going to be people and then technology, especially in financial services. So the hallmarks of NCB were quality people and technology. I specialised in looking for the best possible people, and I got some great people in Eamon Rothwell, Kevin Barry, Michael Buckley and Dan O'Donovan."

How Ireland should be run

Desmond also took a keen interest in how the country was run. In the early 1980s the economy was mired in a deep recession. "I think we all had a national interest in what was best for Ireland, and what was best for Ireland was naturally going to be best for us as we were living in that microcosm. We were a group that had a view on how Ireland should be run, the mistakes that were being made and what should be done – we were totally apolitical in that view.

"There was no party political broadcast; it was just 'this is the professional way to run the business'. We had views on how Ireland should be run irrespective of the IFSC, which is a story of its own. We met with a lot of politicians and we gave our view. One of those politicians was Charlie Haughey. They came to our office and we told them the mistakes we felt they made. We told them that they really had to manage the country's liabilities and this had to be done outside the Department of Finance. I went particularly to Charlie and said he had to separate the specialist debt management from the generalist to maximise the value to the State, because if you saved even a small percentage point on the national debt it turned into a huge saving. So the setting up of the National Treasury Management Agency was at least partially an NCB creation."

The late Charles Haughey remains one of the most divisive figures in Irish life. When the former Taoiseach resigned, it emerged that he had received hundreds of thousands of pounds from businesspeople including Desmond. How did he view Haughey?

"Nobody who knew Haughey could disagree that he was a highly intelligent man. He was highly independent as far as his viewpoint was concerned: if he saw the value of a concept or idea, he was able to implement it. Some people can see value but they can't implement; Charlie had the ability to do both – he saw the idea, and he also saw through the implementation. If he believed in something, he was steadfast in his deter-mination that it would happen. There were so many initiatives that he got across the political divide. He saw the logic. Now I'm not advocating that Charlie Haughey is the greatest politician of all time, but I always wanted to deal with a politician who was smart because at least they understand what you're talking about, irrespective of whether they support your idea."

Booms and bubbles

The 1990s was an interesting time for the Irish economy. A number of far-reaching reforms introduced by the Haughey government in the late 1980s and early 1990s stoked economic growth. Indeed, Ireland became a magnet for mainly US foreign direct investment, particularly in the technology sector. In the mid-to-late 1990s the emergence of the internet helped to create an investment frenzy.

Baltimore Technologies was at the vanguard of the internet bubble in the late 1990s and early 2000s. The company, as well as its chief executive Fran Rooney, symbolised the seemingly limitless potential of corporate Ireland during that period. Desmond became interested in the area of online security during a business trip to the US in the mid-1990s. Upon his return he asked Rooney to look at any companies involved in encrypted digital security. "He came across a company called Baltimore Technologies which really appealed to me because it was a Trinity [College Dublin]-based technology company that operated in Fitzwilliam Square, and the founder and the man who created it was a lecturer in Trinity, Michael Purser.

"Michael had created the name Baltimore Technologies, and Baltimore was very important to me as I believe in a kind of serendipity in life. I had lived in Baltimore in Ireland; it holds a great place of warmth for me. My grandfather taught in an industrial school there in the 1920s and thirties."

Desmond acquired Baltimore Technologies and Rooney was installed as chief executive. Its growth was meteoric. As well as inclusion in the FTSE 100, the company was floated on Nasdaq. During 1999, Desmond sold around two million shares in Baltimore at a reported profit of about €70m. The timing could not have been better. At the dawn of the new millennium, the internet bubble burst and Baltimore was taken over.

"Baltimore went through the roof – which I did not really understand, and I came out publicly and sold shares and it hit the headlines. I think when you live in a bubble you can easily get caught by the bubble. People were caught in the tech bubble and a lot of people lost money in the tech bubble.

"Fortunately, I sold through the tech bubble: I sold because I didn't understand it – I wasn't clever enough to follow the tech guys, to understand what they were about. The bubble has two elements, and one is that it elevates people to guru status which nobody really is, and then when it collapses it crucifies them confidence-wise. But some people think they still have that guru ability and they go on and then they get crucified further. And I think in any bubble that's the case: you've guys that learn lessons out of it, the guys that are destroyed by the bubble and never recover, and the guys that come out of the ashes and become stronger and become liquid – and they are the guys you want to put money behind because they've looked down the black hole and are getting out of it, and won't go down the black hole again."

Desmond has some harsh words about Irish society and the way it treats business successes and failures. "I think we live in a world in Ireland where we are envious. We've come from a colonial history where everybody was hierarchical and everybody is watching each other's neighbour and how they've got on, so nobody ever likes to see anybody getting on.

"People in fact like to see people down. I don't think people in Ireland like to see people coming back up, or coming up in the first place. Other people's success should not affect our own happiness. When we fully understand that, then a lot of people will have freedom. Your or anybody's intellectual values or other talents should not impinge on my life because they are not integral to my life – my life is outside them, it's only that I'm making them integral by comparing with them, so why compare yourselves with them because there is no valid comparison? Whatever the criteria, whether you're superior or inferior to others, you are who you are."

However, Desmond is positive about the future of the country. "I'm very positive about the Irish entrepreneurial character and the creative team spirit. I work with some great Irish people. I'd prefer to have Irish people left and right of me going into battle in business than anybody else. I think they are supremely accomplished. I don't say that as an Irish exile, or with rose-tinted glasses, I take it from experience.

"I think it's proved by the success of our great universities as I call them: the University of Facebook, the University of Google, the University of Twitter, because they are operating in Ireland because we supply talented people. And of course we know with all these tech companies the average is only a small number of years before their graduates go out and create their own businesses or move to another multinational. So we've shown that we can be the leaders in the field; we have shown that we can embrace modern technologies and businesses. I believe that the best of Ireland is to come."

A quasi-public role

Desmond has always had a quasi-public role in Ireland and has advised successive Irish governments on economic development issues. Perhaps his single biggest contribution to the Irish economy was coming up with the concept of the IFSC.

"The best contribution I've been involved in has definitely got to be the IFSC," he confirms. "In addition to direct employment we must consider what the IFSC has done for confidence, for identity, for the recognition of the country, for the auxiliary businesses it creates, for the knock-on jobs… and when you create any business, people will tell you they always develop secondary businesses. The IFSC has created opportunities for us to be global, and maybe the IFSC has created the opportunity to bring in the Twitters, the Facebooks and the Googles, because they've seen that we are global in nature: the financial services centre is global in nature."

Desmond says that credit for the IFSC has also to be attributed to Haughey, who grasped the vision, and former secretary general at the Department of An Taoiseach Pádraig O hUiginn, the ultimate implementer.

"Ireland has benefited from having the IFSC, and it will benefit going forward – and what I like is that there's a section of the IDA that's focused on recognising how global financial services are changing, how we're adapting to change, and I love that. I hate complacency; I love the recognition of change."

Desmond believes that Ireland has shown a huge amount of resilience in coming through the recession. "I'm very proud of the way the government has led the recovery. I'm very proud of the way people have dealt with the challenges and the personal difficulties that a financial collapse creates; it is horrendous. I have had my own mini-financial collapses at different stages in my life, when there was no global collapse, and I looked down black holes. That probably saved me at later stages and that saved me from the tech collapse.

"But in earlier years I had a lot of debt. I had an agonising situation where my world was going to implode, and there was that awful worry and fear. So I have a certain understanding and a lot of compassion for people who went through difficult times in both personal and business terms. Because you can't avoid both of them; there's no separation… if you're whistling coming in from the office, it has a positive effect on your home life. If you're coming in worried and pensive, it does transfer into your home life. I have a lot of admiration for people who have come through these challenges."

If Desmond was to advise the government now, what would he say? "I don't believe that you can go along and say: what's the next big thing?

The next big idea is happening at the present time without us knowing it. I think the next big idea is us creating our own Silicon Valley. Bringing that reservoir of knowledge from around the world, from the Googles, the Twitters, the Facebooks, all these tech companies that are in Ireland, and what they are going to throw out. That is of such value that I think we should recognise it and harness it. That is the next big idea, that's what is happening, and that is going to grow exponentially over the next few years and we should feed into that. We should recognise that those businesses are contiguous to all our lives in every single business, and we should embrace the knowledge and the advantage that they will give us. We should recognise that they are the fulcrum that will herald us into future success."

His outstanding business person

Who does he think stands out in Ireland as an outstanding businessperson? "One person I love is Paddy Moriarty, god be good to him. He ran the ESB. But he ran the ESB as an international business; the ESB did work around the world. When there was a crisis they supported countries and they did it as development projects. I loved the way he found balance between the unions and the owners, which were the government. I loved his philosophy, I loved his Irishness, and I loved his humour. He would be one standing out there.

"Tony Ryan, Michael Smurfit, Michael O'Leary, Tony O'Reilly – all these – Martin Naughton, Lochlann Quinn... there's a slew of people. Dunnes Stores, the Kerry Group, Denis Brosnan. There's great men that have done a lot of things, and have been business explorers, financial explorers, and have left a wonderful legacy. Some of their businesses might have collapsed, but at the end of the day they each left a wonderful legacy.

"Denis O'Brien is out there; my friend John Magnier took a small business [Coolmore Stud] and made Ireland the absolute global leaders in it. JP McManus is one of the great financial traders in the world. So all of these people have made serious contributions to Ireland, contributions that people don't even understand or recognise. It's very hard to pick out anybody. But to pick out somebody that was not out for millions, or for themselves; somebody that made a difference, that was real Irish, that you'd be proud to say he reflects the Irish spirit – definitely Paddy Moriarty."

A key figure in the development of Ireland's financial services industry, Dermot Desmond's own presence on a list of outstanding business people is surely secure.

CHAPTER 35

Interview: Frances Ruane

In conversation with Ian Hyland

THE PROLIFIC ECONOMIST AND FORMER ESRI DIRECTOR TALKS ABOUT HER CAREER, THE THIRD-LEVEL SECTOR, AND HER PERSPECTIVE ON POST-WHITAKER ECONOMIC HISTORY.

The Economic and Social Research Institute is one of a handful of bodies that has been right at the centre of Ireland's economic story, through good times and bad, since protectionist barriers began to be dismantled and the narrative of postwar Irish business history began to crystallise.

Likewise, Frances Ruane – who would become the ESRI's director for just under a decade – has also played a central role in that narrative. And, as if to underline her unique perspective, she started out at another of those coalface bodies: the IDA, which she joined upon leaving college in 1971.

At that time the IDA that was preparing for EEC entry, actively engaged in promoting foreign direct investment and in allocating re-equipment grants to help existing Irish companies to adapt and survive in the transition from protectionism to freer trade in the common market. The IDA was also busy using financial supports to encourage new and small businesses to develop. Working for an organisation that was at the heart of Ireland's new strategy of internationalisation had an "absolutely formative effect on my interests in economics that have lasted over 40 years", she recalls.

"The IDA was a very dynamic organisation. Staff numbers were growing so quickly that within little more than a year I had become one of the longer-serving staff members. You've got to remember: in 1971 it was clear that we were definitely going into what became the EU. American companies were coming in with a view to servicing the common market from the inside, and German companies were investing because Ireland was seen as a very cost-effective location and had available labour. I worked on the planning side – and that involved, for example, looking at what kinds of sectors to promote, where to encourage companies to locate around the country, and what was the capacity of smaller towns to support those companies in terms of infrastructure and skills.

"I think that what the IDA was doing in relation to FDI at that time was very strategic and way ahead of its time. It took a highly methodical pro-active approach to identifying the companies it wanted to attract to Ireland. Then it had teams of people whose job it was to persuade those companies in sectors likely to want to service the European markets through FDI to consider locating their plants in Ireland."

As the IDA knows, it's a more competitive world these days. So is our approach robust enough to take us to the next level? "I think the biggest problem there is that the approach we used very successfully has now been copied by everybody," says Ruane. "So we were a first mover and today we have a lot of followers. I did some research a number of years ago comparing Ireland to Singapore, and we have both followed remarkably similar approaches. What Singapore does well is to take a very long-term approach and try to see early what the future steps might be and plan accordingly.

"It seems to me that to ensure that we're fit for purpose and remain competitive we must take a holistic approach – this is something I have recently worked on with Louis Brennan at TCD, and have been seeing in action in Scotland. A holistic approach means thinking about the full policy system as a chain along which business takes place, and recognising that the chain is as strong as its weakest link. This means explicitly identifying the links between research, higher education, different business types, life-long skills training strategies and labour market capacities. Put all these things together correctly and it will strengthen our hand – for example, a good starting point means recognising that training for the future workplace does not end at the age of 21 or 22."

According to Ruane, a holistic approach also means giving due attention to Irish businesses – the policy domain of Enterprise Ireland. "Its role is a much more challenging one and its success is even more dependent on having the right combination of policies than the IDA's is. Multinationals arriving in Ireland already have their international export markets, have access to parent company research and innovation, and have a capacity for skills development that is exceptional. Irish businesses need to grow their export markets, scale up their research and innovation to maintain and grow markets, and work hard to attract and retain skilled staff."

As for entrepreneurship, which is at the heart of developing more successful indigenous companies, it's often said that it is a matter of culture: the right environment to bring ideas to viability, and the right mix of risk and reward. "It is about culture," confirms Ruane, "and I'm sure this is helped by making sure to have a tax and welfare system that supports entrepreneurship. This means, for example, ensuring some form of welfare net for the entrepreneurs whose businesses crash, to reduce their risks. From an entrepreneurial perspective, the design of the welfare system may be a weak link in the Irish chain."

Academia

After the IDA and a stint at the Central Bank, and a PhD at Oxford, Ruane entered academia. She joined the economics department of Trinity College Dublin, where she is today an honorary professor, having spent almost 30 years there as a lecturer and professor. A long CV of achievements and memberships of academic bodies, committees and boards has been amassed. Close interactions with her colleagues in science and engineering brought her face to face with Ireland's urgent need to invest more in research, development and innovation.

"Serious support for serious scientific research to underpin the country's strategy as a base for high-tech businesses only began in the 1990s. There was a bit of funding coming into universities in the 1970s, and then it slowed down again in the eighties because of the economy's financial difficulties. The only serious source of funding came from the European Commission." Ruane recalls a famous – or perhaps infamous – anecdote about university officials meeting Charles Haughey seeking funding for research in the late 1980s. They argued that countries such as Denmark and the Netherlands had much higher rates of investment in R&D in higher education and that this left Ireland lagging behind – "and he supposedly said 'well tell me about Uganda'. In other words, the implicit narrative was that university-level research was a luxury we could not afford. In effect, no connection was recognised between this research and economic growth. So we ended up in the early 1990s with a lot of world-class businesses in high-tech sectors but many of these businesses were not really engaging in high-tech activities in Ireland. Why? Because we didn't have the skill base and the research base at the universities that is needed to support these activities."

Ruane witnessed a major change at close quarters in the 1990s as the single market gave a further boost to FDI, and the global narrative in economic policy began to focus more on how R&D influences productivity and growth. "Things improved rapidly in the late 1990s – but unfortunately what was put in place was not sustainable and the budgetary cuts and adjustments following the economic crash in 2008 had a terrible effect on the research community and on Ireland's research reputation.

"I would say that two of the most important elements in policy are consistency and sustainability, and in the case of the national research infrastructure (people and equipment) we needed to build in a steady, sustainable way. What we got was a reorientation in funding (which damaged the consistency element) and a sudden collapse in funding (which showed unsustainability). What happened was very bad for the universities in terms of attracting academic staff, postgraduate students and international project income that needed co-financing. It was also bad for companies that have been trying to build sustainable relationships with institutes of technology and universities. I think that it is better to have a steady pattern of investment at a lower level than to have a pattern of highs and then lows."

With this experience in mind, she highlights one area in which Ireland did have consistent investment in research starting in the 1950s. "The one area of research that Ireland has invested in consistently since the 1950s was agriculture and in food, through Teagasc (and its predecessors). I believe that this long-term investment contributed to the huge growth in the food industry in recent times and that this is the sector in which Ireland has grown major international companies. This demonstrates the importance of consistency – it was several decades before the food sector boomed and moved into higher-value products and services. So what that shows to me is that you need a consistent sustainable investment pattern over a period of time if you're going to reap the results."

In academia, she notes that there has been an "enormous change" in attitudes over the past two and a half decades. "Throughout the higher education system there is now a greater emphasis on the relevance of higher education research and skills to business and directly on research performance. In my experience, 25 years ago academics in universities didn't really connect with business: they saw it as a way of possibly getting some money for projects and to support students, but they really weren't engaged with what business was trying to do. Now they realise their graduates are going to work in the industry, and they need to have a greater understanding of it.

"Also, the supports from the EU and from the Irish government for industry-relevant research have put many academics in touch with the reality of entrepreneurship. Consequently entrepreneurship is much more highly regarded now than it was previously. Today Irish parents would be very proud to say their 27-year old had set up a small business – whereas back in the 1980s I think that this would rarely have really been the case."

Research performance, university rankings and third-level funding are inextricably linked. In 2011 Dr Colin Hunt published his report, *National Strategy for Higher Education to 2030*, that was intended to underpin the strategic development of the sector. "I think we need to revisit this area again," says Ruane. "I think that that report was done with a lot of good intention, but circumstances meant that it did not have the evidence base that was needed for such an exercise and it did not include the creation of a broad framework that could take account of the many dimensions of higher education in a globalised world."

Ruane expresses concern about the role that rankings have begun to play. "For starters, they relate to individual institutions and not to a country. It's possible for a country to have some institutions that do well on the rankings but not have a good education system, and it's possible to have a good education system and not have an institution that does exceptionally well on the rankings. But you can't ignore the rankings because everyone looks at them, from FDI companies checking out the quality of education in a country to students deciding where to do graduate work."

It is important to look closely at what has caused changes in the rankings, according to Ruane. "Clearly the recent cuts in funding and the rise in student-staff ratios have been key issues. There's definitely a need for more resources but I think it is important not to look at the funding issue as one of simply reversing the cuts that have come in the last number of years. In particular, we need to look at a new funding model and in particular how public and private money can jointly fund higher education. I don't think you can expect the exchequer to pay for it simply through taxation when there are so many other needs in society to be addressed. Private funding can come through fees, or loans that have to be repaid back, or philanthropy, or from business which is a major beneficiary of higher education investment in producing graduates with key skills."

Student fees were abolished by the Rainbow Coalition in the mid-1990s, and as Ruane recalls the education sector was under less pressure at the time. The government was putting more money in, and colleges were encouraged to see the State as the funder of higher education and didn't feel any great need to attract alumni funding, which they do now. "But remember, the future of the alumni money depends on the quality of student experience. And I think one of the good things that has happened in the last number of years is an awareness of the student experience." That got neglected in the early 2000s, when new money for research projects caused the undergraduate student experience to slip down the pecking order. Ruane says that this was a mistake, both because students deserve better and because colleges were not focused on different income sources:

"Alumni money tends to come from undergraduates so if students don't have a good experience they are unlikely to support their alma maters later. So there's a lesson for colleges in terms of taking care of the students."

Into the ESRI

The industrial development agencies and the university sector have changed much in the course of her career, but so too has the institution with which she is perhaps most closely associated: the ESRI. It was established in 1960 by academics and public servants, including TK Whitaker, who identified a need for an independent institute that would focus on research relevant to Irish policy. The institute, for its first 25 years, was primarily funded by the Department of Finance – research programmes were decided within the institute and subjected to approval by its independent council. The financial crisis in the mid-1980s led to the institute being told by the Department of Finance that if it wanted to grow it would have to raise its own funds. This meant looking for funding from other departments and agencies and from the European Commission, since these are the organisations that have a keen interest in policy research.

And so from around 1985 until the early 2000s the ESRI increasingly embarked on research funded primarily by the European Commission and particular government departments and agencies. "That actually worked very well, and most people will say the quality of the ESRI's work became even more relevant as researchers were dealing directly with the policymakers who were going to use the research results to inform policymaking," says Ruane. But when the Celtic Tiger economy took over around 2000 and there was a lot of public money potentially available for research, the appetite for research to inform policymaking diminished. As Ruane explains: "As economic growth seemed assured and the government's fiscal coffers were overflowing, there was reduced interest in the ESRI's research, and the development of what amounted to almost an evidence-free approach to policymaking for a period of time. This was the era of 'when I have it, I spend it' which fuelled excessive growth and economic imbalance in the economy."

The situation changed dramatically in 2008, according to Ruane, who by this time was director. "The downturn then suddenly made resources very scarce, but at the same time it made policymakers realise that research was more important because you want to be very clear on how you are spending money. The institute's research output became relevant across so many areas in the following six years and continues to be so today."

The range of areas the ESRI covers is very wide, she notes, and has been set out in the institute's two recent strategy documents. Because of the ESRI funding model, the precise issues being researched "reflect the extent to which individual departments and the agencies are intellectually curious about what works and what doesn't work, and that varies widely", she says. "In my experience, some departments and agencies were extremely interested, and usually it was down to the heads of departments and government agencies. Some of them were naturally intellectually curious about different things; they wanted to know what research could do for them and how using their own data they could learn about what is going on. Other heads were not curious or interested at all. So in relation to research evidence, the tone at the top is not uniform across the system."

Ruane served as director of the ESRI between 2006 and 2015. During this time the relationship between the institute and the government departments improved, primarily due to the development of a series of new multiannual research agreements promoted by Ruane and her successor, Alan Barrett, and supported by the new emphasis on skills in the civil service. "I think there's more engagement with research evidence with the build-up of skills in the civil service," she says. "The public service are now employing specialists as well as generalists. So those specialists are now working with researchers in the institute and in university departments, and I think that this will improve the quality of work and make it increasingly relevant to their decisions." For example, the ESRI's current work on the health sector feeds directly into decisionmaking in the Department of Health.

"These research programmes take the research questions out of the department, which means that they are open to fresh thinking, international reference points and to the latest methodologies. But the process involves continuous engagement with the specialists in the department. In this way knowledge transfers in both directions and best practice is assured by subjecting the research to peer review and external presentation."

Policy stability

Politics and economics overlap enormously, of course, all across the world. But Ruane has identified something unique about the Irish experience of political economy: its stability. "This is something that I've written about quite extensively in the past: Irish industrial policy has been more consistent than any other democracy in the world. Many people don't actually realise how exceptional that is. I started looking at Irish industrial policy in the 1970s when I was doing my PhD. I noticed, for example, that the UK changed its structures and incentives all the time – it was part of the annual budget process. In Ireland we've had a long-term industrial development policy that has been consistent across political cycles. So when we moved from a Fianna Fáil led government (or coalition) to a Fine Gael-led coalition, there were no abrupt changes in policy. From the viewpoint of foreign and domestic investors, this is very good as it gives them a degree of certainty in making plans and decisions."

This stability informs her analysis of the political environment. "I think the areas of policy where we have taken the long view, as we did with industrial policy, are the ones where we've been most consistent and most successful."

For example, Ruane notes that the policy of promoting exports started in the 1950s under a Fine Gael-led government with Taoiseach John A Costello. When there was a change in government, the same policy was adopted and strengthened by Fianna Fáil under the influence of Seán Lemass. "Lemass as minister for industry and commerce had held the country back by staying in a protectionist mode, preventing Ireland from benefiting from the post-war growth. But when push came to shove he made that change and instead of pushing to reverse the policy of reduced tax on corporate profits generated by exports introduced by Costello, he agreed to the introduction of a full tax holiday on these profits to incentivise export-orientated FDI and to encourage indigenous firms to start exporting. The commitment to move from protection to free trade was a massive shift. People link it to Ken Whitaker – which is true, but its support was much more widely based in the Department of Finance and certainly politicians and Lemass had a lot to do with the consolidation of this policy."

The close Lemass/Whitaker working relationship is one of the most scrutinised, admired and even mythologised among commentators. But their achievements were very real, says Ruane. "Yes, Lemass had been involved for a very long period in the Department of Industry and Commerce, and had been comfortable around the protection model which focused on our producing for ourselves behind tariffs and quotas introduced in the 1930s and 1940s. In my view, the very clever way Ireland managed the shift from protectionist to free trade is one of those great Irish stories.

"Before we started reducing the tariffs and quotas, we created incentives to export for Irish and foreign companies. This meant that new jobs were created in producing products that did not compete on the Irish market and gave a window for companies that were dependent on tariffs for survival to adjust to the coming freer trade conditions. This meant that Ireland had a steady evolution towards free trade over two decades and avoided a catastrophic collapse of employment that would likely have occurred had we simply reduced tariffs.

"The political and the administrative systems worked exception-ally well, in my view, in managing that transition. If you look at other countries where they had transitions, very often they did it quickly and ended up with very large numbers of people who never worked again. And in Ireland this transition in the industrial sector was managed alongside another major economic transition – the reduction in the proportion of the population that were employed in agriculture. The scale of that reduction was large and is another testimony to consistent policymaking which focused on new jobs in the industrial and service sectors to absorb generations who would not be employed in agriculture as their parents and grandparents had been."

With that vision and achievement in mind, could it be time to revisit – and even rewrite – the Programme for Economic Expansion? The thought occurs that not many people have even seen a copy of what is, after all, probably the most famous document in Irish economic history. But Ruane has, while working on a paper for a conference to mark the 50th anniversary of the publication of *Economic Development*. "I went back and re-read the copy in the ESRI library. It's a small little volume with a lot of text and a small number of tables and none of the fancy charts or pictures that we find in today's policy documents. *Economic Development* envisaged growth coming out of agriculture, which was seen as our natural economic strength. Actually it didn't [happen] – while there was growth in the food sector, most growth came more out of broader industrial development, greatly strengthened by FDI. The major growth in the food sector happened much later.

"But the success of the First Programme for Economic Expansion, published by the government shortly after Whitaker's *Economic Development*, was due to its giving people and businesses a reason to think that growth was possible. Call it 'hope', call it 'vision' or just call it the 'potential for things being different' – and I think that was the most crucial thing that these documents contributed. They put a focus on planning for the longer term and that planning gave rise to people seeing the potential for growth and what might be done to support it."

Timing worked in Ireland's favour with entry into the European Economic Community in 1973, according to Ruane. "The really big break for Ireland was that in marketing Ireland as a location for FDI it could sell our access to the common market. Effectively what we were doing was saying: 'come to this small country as an exporter; we don't want you selling in the domestic market and putting the producers in our protected markets out of jobs. We want you to sell into Europe, which is a big market'. Of course this policy of export-only production has had to change over the years as it was incompatible with EU competition law, but we were able to use it at a crucial time in our development."

The 'Ireland factor' is a somewhat unquantifiable commodity in multinational business: what is it that makes Ireland, its people and its environment so compatible with multinational investment? Cultural ties were identified by the IDA at an early stage, says Ruane. "Let me go back to 1971: the IDA had started identifying the sectors it wanted to develop – essentially sectors that had strong demand growth and which could function profitably on an island off the coast of Europe.

"This analysis led to the focus on high-tech sectors – chemicals, pharmaceuticals and electronics. A key marketing approach was to look for diaspora links into key companies in these sectors. It's easy to do this today – you can start with Google. But doing it back then was time-consuming: tracking down the market leaders in the key sectors, establishing where there might be an Irish connection and then working out how to activate that connection."

Change in Northern Ireland has been another part of the Irish development narrative over the years, the business angle of which is so often overlooked for understandable reasons. "I think that if the peace process had happened 10 years earlier Northern Ireland would be very, very different now. Unfortunately Northern Ireland missed that growth take-off that was coming out of the single market process in the early nineties," says Ruane.

"The region has more potential than it is realising and this has not been helped by its difficulty in reducing its dependency on Westminster. It's got tremendous strengths in some of the business sectors but it has not been as export-orientated as it might have been."

The North has looked with envy at the Republic, and has sought to have the same sets of policies introduced to support economic development, according to Ruane. "But from what I can see, I don't think that Invest NI is as self-critical an organisation as either IDA Ireland or as Enterprise Ireland. For example, even when it has had great successes, say with the ICT boom in the 1990s, the IDA wasn't the slightest bit smug. The executives knew that the ICT sector was so dynamic that there was no basis for assuming that patterns of investments would continue. In my experience the political and institutional arrangements here are more strategically focused than in the North and the level of engagement between businesses and the relevant ministers is stronger."

Highlights and memories

Over the years, one business dynasty in particular has impressed Frances Ruane – and it's rooted in a childhood memory. "In the early- to mid-1950s my family moved to live in Mount Merrion in south Dublin. It was a middle-class suburb and the fathers of children in the local national school were mostly civil and public servants, academics and various professionals. There was a weekly collection of waste paper, mostly newspapers, for recycling organised to help pay for the new local Catholic church. The papers went to Smurfits for their packaging business. The Smurfit family lived up the road from our house – they were unusual in that they were businesspeople. I remember hearing as I was growing up that the company had run into major financial difficulties but had survived and gone on to build a major business. This was the first time I heard of a business getting back on its feet and the memory stuck with me. Only years later did I realise how important what Smurfits developed was for Ireland's development policy – you absolutely need high-quality packaging for exporting."

The food industry is also particularly notable in her memories from the time she joined the IDA. Denis Brosnan, who established the Kerry Group, stands out. "A real superstar who saw the importance of producing more sophisticated products and of marketing and branding internationally.

"In other sectors, I guess Chris Horn was one of the first people to show that it was possible to develop an indigenous ICT company, coming from an academic research background. His success really helped people to recognise the potential of campus companies."

As for her own personal highlights, Ruane has several. "I went on to be on the board of the IDA in 1993, which was just 20 years after I'd left the IDA as a junior economist. It was an amazing experience – I knew a lot about the IDA because of my research over the previous 15 years or so, but I got a much deeper understanding, when I was on the board, of how policy was working on the ground and the importance of taking a holistic approach to industrial development policy. The experience also affected my research – it made me aware of how vital it was for researchers to work with data at enterprise level and not just at sectoral level, which was the norm at that time. Over the following 20 years when it became possible to work on these data, when they had been anonymised to guarantee confidentiality, I was one of the first researchers in that space."

Studying in Oxford in the 1970s was where Ruane developed her understanding of policy. As such, travel and outside ideas are, to her, valuable commodities. "I think every organisation, and particularly those in the policy sphere, needs to have external challenges, and these can come through academic research but also through hiring people with different backgrounds or having boards with members that would be seen as outsiders. The outside perspective provides a point of reflection and obviously helps to avoid groupthink." She points to the 2015 Academy Award Best Picture winner *Spotlight*, centred around the *Boston Globe*'s investigation into child abuse. "It's a great movie and provides a very clear example of the important role of the outsider. All of the journalists who were working in the *Boston Globe* were Catholic and from Boston. They were talented and committed to their jobs. Suddenly the paper appoints a new editor who was Jewish and had just come from Florida – no connection with Boston at all. He asked the simple questions that come naturally to the outsider and that triggers the journalists to look again at long-standing issues in the church. By the way, the movie also points to how valuable detailed and systematic research is in journalism.

"So it was my supervisors in Oxford asking questions about Ireland that made me realise how different Ireland was in a European context – I came to describe Ireland as a semi-developed economy because it had features of other small European countries but its large population in agriculture and the small numbers of people completing post-primary education made it more like developing economies." One Oxford academic – who subsequently won the Nobel Prize in economics – asked her to give a brief summary of the issues in the Irish economy soon after she arrived in 1974. Ruane did so. "And he said 'so all Irish economists are concerned with microeconomic issues', and I said 'well actually, almost all are concerned about macroeconomic issues at the moment' and I realised that there was excessive concentration among researchers on macro issues. By his listening to my description he had a view that said yes, there is a macro issue. But there's a huge economic development issue for which microeconomic analysis is essential."

And throughout her career at TCD and the ESRI, Ruane had people from outside Ireland asking her questions about Ireland and its policies. "The outside perspectives in their questions gave me many new insights into policy issues and solutions. The value of having the outside view to challenge you cannot be underestimated."

A different insight in a career full of them: throughout the various phases of her career, whether at the ESRI, IDA or TCD, Frances Ruane's work in Irish economics has been far-reaching.

CHAPTER 36

Interview: Herb Kelleher
In conversation with Ian Hyland

THE PIONEERING SOUTHWEST AIRLINES FOUNDER TALKS ABOUT HIS CAREER, THE INDUSTRY HE SO COMPREHENSIVELY CHANGED, AND THE HARD WORK AND RESILIENCE THAT CAME WITH HIS IRISH-AMERICAN HERITAGE.

One could be forgiven for assuming that Michael O'Leary was the trendsetter in providing low-cost airfares while courting high-profile media opportunities, but the title really belongs to an Irish-American who is widely regarded as one of America's greatest CEOs.

Born in 1931, Herb Kelleher was welcomed into a middle-class Catholic Irish-American family in the suburbs of New Jersey. His paternal grandparents are believed to have travelled to the land of opportunity from Cork and Kerry – with their grandson ensuring that their pursuit of the American dream was worthwhile.

Having originally studied English and philosophy at university, Kelleher decided to move to Texas in 1961 to pursue a career in law after graduating from NYU Law School. It was in 1966 – while living in Texas with his wife and working for the law firm of Matthews, Nowlin, Macfarlane and Barrett – that Kelleher met the business colleagues who were soon to co-found the only airline to be ever featured on *Fortune* magazine's top 10 list of the World's Most Admired Companies.

Starting with just three aircraft on three routes, Southwest Airlines planned to use a loophole to avoid the Civil Aeronautics Board by only flying in the state of Texas. While Kelleher and business partner Rollin King saw an opportunity to offer in-state flights at a cheaper price, competitors engaged in a legal dispute that would ground Kelleher's commercial plans for nearly four years. After three years of litigation the Texas Supreme Court finally upheld Southwest's right to fly in the state. With the Airline Deregulation Act of 1978 Southwest finally spread its wings outside Texas, claiming New Orleans as its first port of call in December of the same year.

Never one to shy away from a challenge (or a publicity stunt), Herb Kelleher famously plotted out his plans for Southwest Airlines on the back of a cocktail napkin during dinner drinks in San Antonio. His unconventional style and strategy hinted at the barriers he was willing to break in business – with one of favourite slogans being 'the business of business is people'.

Kelleher has never shied away from his employee-first mindset. Having previously credited his workforce as more important than either shareholders or customers, his approach to Southwest Airlines "was somewhat of an anomaly I would say, in terms of our humanistic approach to our employees", he recalls.

As well as providing total job security to all employees – which was unusual in itself in the airline industry – the company prided itself on "keeping track of their every joy and every grief and being part of it – you know, when they had a baby, or lost a parent, and we felt that that was the appropriate thing to do".

When it was once suggested that this was a strategy in itself, Kelleher quite simply clarifies: "No, it's not a strategy. It's morality and work and I said if it evolves into a strategy than it's just accidental". The side-effect? Kelleher was guaranteed a dedicated workforce who were willing to look past the remuneration to work for a balanced company culture.

"We would have people come to Southwest Airlines to take 25% cuts in their salary because they liked our people and our atmosphere and the freedom they had with us, compared to where they were. It wasn't designed to achieve that, but it did have that effect."

It hasn't always been plane sailing (pardon the pun) for the aviation entrepreneur, who was forced to defend his company and leadership to those who thought they knew better in its early days. "When I took over as CEO of Southwest Airlines full-time, some of the Wall Street analysts said 'we're dropping our recommendations on Southwest's stock, we think you should sell it'. They said the reason was that lawyers don't know how to run businesses. Well for 30 years, we produced a compounded annual return to shareholders of 25.99%. Not too bad, not too bad." In fact, during his tenure Herb Kelleher produced the highest return to shareholders of any company in the S&P 500.

Staying positive

While Kelleher claims to never mourn a bad day, he has made mistakes in the past. One such misstep was the company's attempt at acquiring Muse Air: lawyers persuaded the businessman not to blend the airline and its employees with his successful Southwest Airlines model, but to operate it as a separate company.

The decision, while it protected Southwest from debt and liability, proved fatal for the new acquisition. "I think that was a mistake in judgement," he says. "I listened too much to the labour lawyers that were involved and maybe a little too much to the financial people." The airline was eventually shut down, but Kelleher received three letters from union leaders who thanked him for the fair severance packages offered to the Muse Air workforce.

Not to be disheartened, Southwest went on to successfully acquire other carriers – but Kelleher made sure not to get carried away with experts and to trust his own intuition and accept his shortcomings. "But we correct mistakes quickly: one of the things I've always preached is never let your ego get in the way of rectifying a mistake that you have made – and I mean quickly."

Despite any number of successes or failures, nothing could prepare the aviation industry for the effects of 9/11. Surprisingly, Kelleher believes that the challenging time showed the importance of having heart at the centre of one's business plan. When asked for a personal highlight of his career, it wasn't the wealth, the awards or the honours bestowed upon him that came to mind. Kelleher happened to recall one of the darkest periods in America's recent history.

"9/11 demonstrated the kind of culture Southwest Airlines had, because if you remember – at least reading about it – the FAA said no flights could fly more than an hour. You could remain in the air for an hour after this happened but you had to put down somewhere. The upside of that was that a lot of our airplanes had to land in cities we didn't serve. We called a hotel in Flint Michigan, which we didn't serve at that time, and said we'd like to talk to our captain on that flight. They said 'we're sorry you can't'. Well why not? 'He's taken all of the passengers to a movie downtown at his expense to keep them entertained.'

"We called another hotel... and we were told the pilot had bought Amtrak tickets for all of the passengers on our airplane out of his own pocket to get them on to their destinations on the ground."

The culture of care is echoed in an old tale that Kelleher emphasises has always been at the core of his company's ethos. "When I was quite younger, a lot younger, in San Antonio, this friend of mine was talking to his mother and he said that she got a new automobile every year without fail. He said 'Mom, let me tell you something – I've talked to this other automobile dealer and he said you're paying about $1,500 or $2,000 more every year for your car'.

"She said 'dummy, don't you understand? When something goes wrong with this the owner comes out and fixes it.' Suddenly it hit me she wasn't buying the car, she was buying the care."

In the public eye

Kelleher has always been keen to toy with the public's interest. In 1990 he started using the phrase 'Just Plane Smart'. This was quickly disputed by Stevens Aviation chairman Kurt Herwald, who had previously been using 'Plane Smart' as part of their marketing plan. When he was challenged with a lawsuit for copyright over his use of the pun phrase in 1992, Kelleher decided to settle the legal matter by agreeing to an arm-wrestling match with his opponent at the Dallas Sportatorium in downtown Dallas. While he may have technically lost the battle, the public interest for Southwest Airlines was certainly spiked.

A characterful approach to dealing with the public brings to mind, on this side of the Atlantic, the entrepreneurial manner of Michael O'Leary. Kelleher isn't blind to the Kildare man's influence. "I think that Spirit Airlines in the US, at least intellectually and conceptually, was following Michael's model with Ryanair – so he's had a pervasive influence around the world. People say Spirit Airlines and other airlines of that get nature get a lot of complaints from passengers, and you just hear constant griping about them. But it's very interesting to me that they operate at a 90% load factor. So there is a market for a totally price-conscious market and they are appealing to it."

Recalling his own immigrant heritage, Kelleher has always been proud of his Irish ancestry – a bridge between his hard work and a strong resilience instilled in him from his parents. "Well, I think the Irish have a wonderful spirit and that's always inspired me and really buoyed me up during difficult times when things would not be going too well. Their feeling for fellow human beings has always inspired me."

From his perspective in an America that sees a wealth of Irish companies and individuals investing, Kelleher says that there is an opportunity to use the Irish spirit to show how business is a joint partnership between the company and the people it hires.

"That's a great story to tell about the Irish businesses in the US and all the value that they bring here. Of the hundreds and thousands of people that they employ in the US, I think it's important for America to realise that it's not just a one-way street."

CHAPTER 37

Interview: Liam O'Mahony
In conversation with Ian Hyland

FROM CRH TO SMURFIT KAPPA TO THE IDA, LIAM O'MAHONY'S CAREER AS ONE OF IRELAND'S LEADING EXECUTIVES HAS BROKEN NEW GROUND AND SEEN HIM TRAVEL THE WORLD.

It was a chance meeting while studying for an MBA that secured Liam O'Mahony his first role in the Roadstone Group. What the civil engineer didn't expect was that in a 40-year career he would go on to serve as its CEO for nine years until his retirement in 2008.

During his tenure at the building supplies company, CRH expanded its operations into 38 countries and became a world leader in its industry with annual revenues of €20bn. "I suppose I entered the business world not knowing an awful lot about it," O'Mahony recalls. "I started out as a civil engineer. I'd worked as a civil engineer for a few years... I did an MBA and there was a guy involved in the course, Bill Murray, who was a management consultant. He happened to be on the board of the Roadstone Group, which then became CRH and was involved with an exchange programme in the merged group."

During a time of depressed growth in Ireland, O'Mahony saw the opportunity to venture into new markets. "I joined a small development team that was really looking at anything except the core business, which was Ireland. It was there, it was solid, so my scope was anything beyond that: where it might go, what it might do. So I wasn't just looking at it from an Irish business [perspective]; I was looking at the opportunities for a young person – where it might take me." During his first five years with CRH, O'Mahony married and started his family while attaining a law degree in his spare time. He wanted to concentrate on building his career in an industry that saw emerging markets opening up in far-flung corners of the world. "I was mainly Irish-based but I got the opportunity to work on various projects.

"One of the exciting ones for a young guy in my late twenties was when things were slow at home in Roadstone: we got the opportunity to do a project in Nigeria. A Dutch company was building a port, and we got to supply stone material for the project to build a quarry. I was the young guy sent out to explore that. Obviously there was support from the background. It wasn't just the Liam O'Mahony show. It opened my eyes up to so many things though. It was fantastic."

The Nigerian trip provided a taste for growth and expansion – with the perfect opportunity presenting itself when CRH acquired a large US company in upstate New York. "In the mid-eighties we'd acquired a big company in the US – Callanan Industries in upstate New York. It was CRH's biggest acquisition at the time.

"Unfortunately, the guy who owned it and stayed on to run it – and his right-hand man – were dead within the year. CRH needed somebody to go out and run it for a period. Obviously there were good people inside, but the company wasn't quite sure who was going to run it. So I was asked to go out and run it for a couple of years and see who might take over internally and promote them. At least that's how I sold it to my wife. We had just done a major expansion on the house. She wasn't too pleased."

The experience was novel to CRH, which didn't have a policy of sending executives overseas to run a company. "I suppose it brought home to me, on the one hand, the goodwill in a company that has often been acquired towards the acquirer. There was great goodwill towards CRH. So that gave me a great entrée to Callanans."

Despite the warm reception from Callanans, O'Mahony was still reminded of the somewhat fledgling reputation CRH then held in the international market. "It also brought home to me how small CRH was and how small Ireland was.

"Here I was in upstate New York. Nobody gave a hoot about CRH or gave a hoot about Ireland. It gave me a grounding of the value of Irishness, the value of interesting people, the value of a sense of support, because we didn't bring any baggage like other countries that would have an imperial background or whatever else. There was an instinctive likeness of the Irish and that was a great plus. But we had to get out and earn our bread at the same time."

The success of the Irish was beginning to resonate in America, with Tony O'Reilly being appointed to the chief-executive role of a Fortune 500 company in 1979. "I think there would have been a great sense of pride in Ireland, quite honestly," says O'Mahony. "I think in Tony O'Reilly and particularly his achievements, of having gone off to be chief executive of Heinz... he was one of the few non-US nationals at that stage running a Fortune 500 company.

"I think there was a sense there of Irish people and Irish connections helping each other out. So I've no doubt that the Irish network would have opened doors for CRH. But I suspect there would have been a number of friends throughout the Irish network that would have been helpful."

Having first entered the States in 1978 for a small acquisition in Utah, CRH spent the next four to five years slowly spreading its empire over the west coast, spilling into several states and eventually the Rocky Mountains. CRH was doing $150 million in turnover by the mid-eighties.

"The first big move for CRH came when it acquired Callanan back on the east coast. It brought it back into what was closer to the Irish core business of quarrying. The move doubled the size of CRH in the States – so really it was the first transformative move.

"From 1986 to 1991 we continued to grow at a measured pace. But the big bang for CRH in the States probably came in the 1990s recovery after the recession in 1992. We grew the business from hundreds of millions to $6bn sales by the end of the nineties. So it was really a dramatic move, but it wasn't one big deal. It was a series of deals gradually getting better, but spread around the US and supported by the local network rather than just done from head office."

CRH entered the western European market in the 1970s. Establishing itself in Holland originally, growth was steady but not dramatic. Two decades later, it was. "The 1990s brought very significant growth [in western Europe] because CRH went into the quarrying and cement side in Europe for the first time, in Poland initially, and followed in Finland, Switzerland and countries like that. They built out very successful businesses there.

"So both sides of the group were growing in parallel. But the US went from being a group to being over 50% of the business in the mid-1990s – and has more or less stayed there, plus or minus a percent." While the pressure of managing 50% of an Irish business on US shores may sound daunting, he credits the CRH management for developing his skills.

O'Mahony had been recruited by Don Godson. "I went to the States then to work for Don in the eighties, early nineties," he recalls. "I came back to Ireland for two years in the nineties to run the Irish and UK operations working for Tony Barry, and then went back to the States for six years. Don was CEO at this stage, so I worked for him.

"I came back to Ireland in 2000 as CEO and I was chairman of the board with Tony Barry. Subsequently, Tony retired and Pat Molloy became chairman. So I was very much bound with Don and Tony, and learned an enormous amount from them. And that was very much the CRH way. Rather than going out looking for a superstar, we tried to develop our own inside."

"Back then you were given an opportunity. Someone kept an eye on you, and you were expected to step up, take responsibility and work with the team with someone keeping an eye on you so you didn't go off and do something stupid. When you were in place, you had to groom people underneath you to be your successor – but they were groomed through real responsibility rather than 'we'll put him here for six months, we'll put him there for six months'. It was real jobs and you either cut it or you didn't."

From 1999 to 2008, O'Mahony notes that despite periods of substantial growth and strong performance, the company also faced a downcycle from 2001 to 2002. CRH also faced a sudden downturn that started seeping into profits in late 2007, where "the wheels began to come off". "From the middle of 2007 we didn't see the crisis any earlier than anyone else, but we saw it probably at the earlier end. We started into cutbacks and they went on for a number of years afterwards."

While people may believe that CRH's secret to success lay in its growth, O'Mahony argues that a focus on analysing the company's strengths accounts for its continued success. "People talk about CRH as being a growth story, but CRH first and foremost was about performance. So the sort of thing you thought about when you got out of bed in the morning wasn't 'which company are we going to buy this week?', it was 'how are the existing businesses performing?' Because without that there wasn't a basis for growth.

"If there was one characteristic I would think about in CRH it wasn't restlessness for growth. That was there, and was fantastic and we grew it. There was a relentless focus on performance, performance, performance – and that's actually what created the platform and the cashflow for growth. That wasn't instilled by me: that came in the early days."

Entering China

One of CRH's massive success stories is its conquest of China. Initially the company began its quest into Asia in the 1990s, but it was the 2000s that saw CRH getting ready to mobilise plans. There were the obvious cultural barriers.

"You had a central government in Beijing with a communist party, but you'd also a government at the province level, at a city level and a town level. You had a government at four different levels and each one of those could be the person you're trying to buy a company from, the person you're trying to partner with, your customer or your regulator. You had to find your way; to tread your way to find something that made sense for you, and people hadn't experienced that before.

"In fact, to buy any company at the time there were limits on foreign ownership so in a way partnership was essential. Trying to pick the right partner and find a way into it was very important. We did a lot of ground research before we got involved – before we did anything – and then we got involved in a modest way in the north east of the country." Setting up base in the city of Harbin, close to the North Korean border, CRH adopted a long-term strategy. Rather than chasing the emerging business exploits down along the coast, which was experiencing rapid growth, the company followed its previous expansion model.

"Our experience in Europe and the US would have said that some of the non-sexy growth areas were the best places to build business and get superior long-term returns. We started out up there, and I think the bulk of the investment is still there. It broadened out and then we invested in the neighbouring province."

The challenge for a foreign company going into China, in addition to learning how the government and regulation worked, was to work with the partner company to develop a short- and medium-term solution. O'Mahony points to a major difficulty foreign companies faced in the Chinese market: the long-term investment requires a short-term return on investment to keep all parties interested.

"I think that's been the difficulty for companies going to China. It can suck in an enormous amount of cash if you're not careful. Just trying to balance getting some sort of short-term return out of it with big amounts of cash behind it for the long-run can be a stressful situation. In our mind, we had a proportion of group assets. We weren't going to exceed going to these areas and we were going to take it at a very measured pace. We used to joke, in my time when I was CEO, about our geographical strategy being 50% in Europe, 50% in the US, and the final 20% in emerging markets.

"That was my way of saying we weren't going to take the eye off the major existing markets we were in, but there'd be a proportion going to emerging markets. It might be 10 or 15% over time, but it wasn't going to be 50%."

Moving on

Taking his experience of global strategy and staged growth, O'Mahony moved on to join the board of Smurfit Kappa Group in 2007, before taking on the role of chairman in 2008. He highlights a difference between the two corporations and the successful expansion into Europe and the US: it was the prudent financing of CRH that helped the company withstand the economic crisis, while Smurfit Kappa was close to its maximum exposure on leverage, which forced tough action. "We [Smurfit] IPO-ed in 2007 at €16.50, and went up to €21. I became chairman in the end of 2008 and the world was in full crisis mode at that stage. The share price went down to the €1s some time thereafter and then a long, long recovery and back up to €26."

With a slumping share price, the board devised a clear plan of action: conserve cash, drive the debt down, get the leverage in good shape and get the rating where it should be. The underlying mission was to drive performance and get to a position whereby the group could grow and move forward when the economy had recovered.

The plan meant that O'Mahony's first act as chairman in 2008 was to cut the dividend. "When I say cut the dividend, I mean we dropped it completely. Now, I had come from a company where we'd grown the dividend every year for something like 25 years, so this was utterly alien to every fibre of my body – but it was a deliberate strategy."

The move received a mixed reaction from shareholders, but when the company stabilised the dividend was reinstated – with a promise to deliver it on a progressive basis from then on. It was a commitment that the group has since been able to deliver.

O'Mahony is open-minded when the subject of governance comes into play. While he acknowledges that the concepts of governance and independence are vital within a business, the reality is that a stifled board structure puts the business at risk of being too far removed from its marketplace. "I think one of the dangers is that you build too many structures and become too bureaucratic and actually become removed from the business. I think what regulation and society have to do is say: how does this strike the best balance between adequate regulation, adequate oversight but leave the business free to get on with what it is about? Which is generating business, creating jobs, making returns.

"Yes, done properly in accordance with the law, but recognising you're out in the risk-taking area. The whole question of how do you reward risk-taking: how do you reward executives who take risk? I don't think it's about building a whole pile of new structures on top of everything. I think that becomes a disaster, to be honest."

Chairing the IDA

One structure that O'Mahony does fully support is the ongoing work of the IDA. Appointed as chairman of the government body in February 2010, the Tipperary native was there during the biggest economic downturn in the history of the State. Despite the devastating effect that the economic downturn had on unemployment rates, the IDA managed to secure a wealth of opportunities by attracting foreign investment to Irish shores. O'Mahony is in high praise of his predecessors – a generation of Irish managers who built on early success at the IDA to bring in more companies to the country.

"I was really impressed, when I became chairman of the board, by a large number of things – but [among] the things that impressed me was the culture in the IDA. It was a public entity, run as kind of a semi-state, but had a strong entrepreneurial culture in the organisation close to the private sector concept.

"The IDA had a very good culture; a strong sense of leadership. I think that's the great testament to the IDA: that under many, many CEOs over the years it has kept up the momentum for the future generations."

Cutbacks and resource constraints were a particular hindrance, as he recalls. "The frustrating thing was that the country was in the eye of the storm at the time, and of course out of necessity there were cutbacks at government level. I mean, that's what you do in business and I pay credit to the various politicians that took the necessary steps to keep the country alive and afloat. Irish government bonds were selling at 16/17% interest rates – cutbacks meant there was a fairly uniform one-size-fits-all approach to funding."

Another area of great concern for the IDA was creating opportunity across Ireland. Marketing rural areas proved unsuccessful for the government agency, which risked losing foreign investment if it proposed the wrong opportunity at a time of high unemployment. While there was support from government to attract jobs for cross-region support, O'Mahony concedes that the primary aim was securing jobs for Ireland full-stop. While there was an effort to promote all areas, there was ultimately a greater interest in the major 'magnets' of Dublin, Cork and Galway.

"It wasn't because of any lack of effort by the IDA to move them on elsewhere and encourage them to go elsewhere, but the clients were saying 'we want to go to Dublin, there's a cluster in Dublin, that's where we can recruit people, keep people, we don't want to even think of going some place else, that's where we have to be'.

"What do you do in that case? Do you say you can't come, we don't want you? That'd be crazy." O'Mahony instead believes that the shortfall in attracting regional investment from foreign industries is a shared re-sponsibility between the IDA and local communities. "It's very much a partnership thing, a bit more self-help and self-reliance. The solution is very much in the local interest groups, the private sector business, private institutions and local authorities working closer together.

"Then putting pressure on the IDA to work with them, to make it happen and the IDA then having a leadership role in trying to attract the people in and bringing the roadshows."

The Irish at home and abroad

Reflecting on his own career path, O'Mahony sees a strong benefit in trusting the Irish diaspora network to pave the way for Irish enterprise abroad and drive investment back into the economy.

The ability to influence the future entrepreneurs and investors in the Irish economy is a skill that O'Mahony associates with the natural demeanour of Irish people. "Going in with that sense of Irishness, the ability to shake hands, say hello and talk to people. Once they hear you're from Ireland, if they have a knowledge of Ireland that's generally a positive impression so it does help to open the door. As a country we're non-threatening; our image of the world is generally good, as a force for good.

"We haven't been imperialist, haven't taken over people. We've sent out missionaries, we've tried to educate people, we've emigrated and populated countries, so there is an openness to Irishness. Now you just have to be careful that you don't assume that that equals success. It just opens the door then you've got to go and deliver."

O'Mahony recognises Tony O'Reilly as being an inspiration for others, with his Heinz career particularly influential. "Tony O'Reilly's leadership position was at a time when we weren't really a business-oriented country and certainly didn't have an international presence. What I really respect him for is becoming CEO of a Fortune 500 company; that's just an incredible achievement – one of the first overseas guys or non-US guys to do it."

Despite a string of accolades, CEO positions, chairmanships and directorships, O'Mahony's personal career highlight was to break the mould in a family of schoolteachers. Entering business and travelling the world, but being fortunate enough to remain tied to an Irish company, has been his greatest achievement.

"To me it's just fantastic that I had the opportunity to join CRH. Maybe I was lucky to be born 40 years earlier than today. It's all about, first of all, being fortunate enough to get on that team, fortunate enough to have mentors who looked over my shoulder when I was getting a chance to get on and get responsibility, and dust me down once or twice when I might have screwed up. You weren't encouraged to screw up too often in CRH, so I learned fairly quickly. But I had that support and then, in time, to get the chance to move up the ranks and have a board that had the ambition to go out and grow... It was a unique time; it was fantastic."

O'Mahony believes that Ireland could become more successful with the right attitude. "Ireland is actually a wonderful place to live, there's a vibrancy in Ireland, there's a sense of informality in Ireland, there's an ability to get on and do things when you want to get on and do it. If you want to you can find obstacles, plenty of obstacles; but if you want to get on and do things you can do it."

Successes like CRH and Smurfit Kappa prove the point, he says. "If we can only go out and stick our chests out a little bit and build on those successes and talk about them, recognise that business is not a dirty word – the banking collapse notwithstanding.

"Business is what ultimately creates wealth and jobs and employment and the future. It really is, and we have the successes here. But somehow society sometimes gets this negative view – and you see it in political discourse, and that's bad and wrong. We're not a Greece, we're actually a successful country and we've so much to build on."

CHAPTER 38

Interview: Richard Burrows

In conversation with Ian Hyland

FORMER IRISH DISTILLERS CHIEF RICHARD BURROWS DISCUSSES THE BUSINESS LANDSCAPE, HIS WIDE-RANGING CAREER, AND THE IRISH WHISKEY RENAISSANCE IN WHICH HE PLAYED A LARGE ROLE.

The year was 1963. US President John F Kennedy arrived in Dublin to a raucous reception, Shelbourne had won the FAI Cup for the third time and, less known to history, the small firm that would later form part of global corporation KPMG then went under the moniker of Stokes Kennedy Crowley. Among a number of fresh faces at the firm that year was one Richard Burrows, whose ascent among the global business community would mirror that of his employers.

Those were times of great excitement for anyone with a stake in the Irish economy. A period of economic expansion began when Seán Lemass was appointed Taoiseach in 1959, with the introduction of tax breaks and grants for foreign direct investment and increased capital expenditure, in a move away from the protectionist policies introduced by Éamon de Valera during the 1930s.

The new programme paved the way for increased industrialisation and free trade: the Anglo-Irish Free Trade Agreement was signed on December 14th 1965, dismantling existing trade barriers between Ireland and Britain. Less than ten years later the Irish public would vote to join the EEC, and Ireland became a full member in 1973.

"Looking back, there was a lot of excitement about the Anglo Irish Free Trade Agreement; there was a lot of excitement about the EEC as it was then, and what it could become and whether we should or shouldn't join it," Burrows explains. "And of course you had a completely changed Seán Lemass pursuing a very sensible commercial policy to try to get business to react, and aided at the time by Ken Whitaker.

"I was lucky enough to work in Stokes at the time, and because of the nature of the practice I got to see a wide variety of business, unlike unfortunate articled clerks who go into accountancy firms and get pigeonholed today. In those days you worked across a broad span of different businesses, and that brought me primarily into contact with the drinks industry, and the shape of the constituent firms that finally came together to form United Distillers of Ireland [later Irish Distillers]. But I was involved in everything from stockbrokers to clubs and farms."

This exposure to such a broad range of businesses would prove fruitful, and Burrows quickly gained a keen appreciation that "scale outside of Ireland was something that was going to be critically important, as and when the protective trade barriers would be swept away".

During the time that Burrows received his first introduction to the Irish drinks industry at Stokes, the distilleries were struggling from decades of blows: by 1970 Irish Distillers was the sole survivor, incorporating Jameson, Paddy, Powers and Bushmills (which joined in 1972) under its umbrella.

There were a number of reasons behind this steady decline. Irish whiskey had once been a force to be reckoned with on the global market, particularly in the USA, though the industry failed to move with the times. "They failed to embrace the invention of grain whiskey, which meant that blended whiskeys were far more palatable to the drinker than a pure pot still whiskey – even though it was invented by an Irishman called Angus Coffey in Bow Street Distillery in Dublin," says Burrows.

Coffey would go on to sell his patent to distillers in Scotland, a move that largely prompted a surge in scotch whisky sales across the globe, threatening their Irish counterparts. But Burrows also notes that they lost their foothold in important markets through a lack of innovation, alongside world events outside of their control. "They were shut out of a lot of markets during the

Second World War, when the government decided that whiskey should be kept at home for revenue purposes rather than exported. Independence didn't help either because a lot of the colonial world decided to go the scotch route rather than the Irish route," he adds.

There was something of a resurgence in Irish whiskey during the 1960s, however. In 1966 the founding families of Irish whiskey decided to come together and form a single force within the Irish market in a bid to protect their trade in Ireland and build a strong export market. Kevin McCourt, the former director general of RTÉ, took up the post of managing director at Irish Distillers in 1968, spearheading modernisation efforts as he moved all production to a single site in Midleton in a bid to combat the scotch threat and reverse the trend of decline.

"That really prompted an era of magnificent development which hasn't been equalled in the world yet, whereby Kevin McCourt came in and employed the best flavourists and scientists in the world, and essentially created a new blend of Irish whiskey which became known as Jameson North American blend," Burrows explains. "The rest then is a 50-year story of growth, but it was pretty difficult from the early days."

Rising force

As Irish whiskey was beginning to find its feet again during the 1960s, Burrows was itching to complete his accountancy exams and dive into the business world. Clearly he displayed potential, and he was offered a partnership with Stokes before he completed his finals. On reflection, however, he turned it down.

Following a suggestion that he travel to London to study the emergent management consulting business, an aspect which was just beginning to be embraced by accounting firms, Burrows joined Peat Marwick Mitchell – another future pillar of KMPG, and Stokes' "London correspondent firm" as he describes it. This proved to be an interesting experience for the young accountant, delving into topics such as efficiency-type studies, cost savings, and the overall endeavour to develop new ways of operating in a more efficient manner – all of which would be of benefit to him in the not so distant future.

Burrows' time in London, however, was interrupted by the proposed four-way merger of Irish Distillers with PJ Carroll, Waterford Glass and Irish

Glass Bottle in 1968. With a large body of experience working with and within the distilling industry he was quickly headhunted by Kevin McCourt, who had fears about what might happen to the industry should a conglomerate form, and hastened to put together a plan of defence. Those early preparations would pay off.

"I was whistled back from London to work on the defence planning for United Irish Distillers against that merger, which ultimately fell apart because we could justify remaining independent on the basis that it would be far better for shareholders of United Irish Distillers than sinking their lot into a mixed bag of businesses, as it turned out," Burrows recalls.

Burrows had found his niche. What followed was a move to import company Edward Dillon, which was majority-owned by Irish Distillers, where he served as an assistant to the managing director. After his arrival, the firm quickly took over wine importers Fitzgerald and Company, with Burrows overseeing its integration into Edward Dillon as managing director between 1971 and 1972. Then, in the midst of proposals by Seagram Company Ltd to acquire Bushmills from brewing company Bass Charrington (in order to sell it to Irish Distillers in exchange for a chunk of the latter's business), Burrows took another step up the ladder, taking on the role of chief executive with Bushmills in 1972. "That was really my proper entry into the distilling business," he reflects.

A premium proposition

In today's business world the concept of operating without a clear and well-devised marketing strategy seems a strange one. Not so 40 years ago, to the extent that Burrows can recall when Irish Distillers employed their first marketers – and the reaction to these individuals with their strange new ideas.

"I can remember the first two brand managers [who came] into Irish Distillers back in 1975. These guys arrived in and people thought they had horns; they were extraordinary people. They came in with fancy salary packages and company cars and expense accounts, and they were quite unlike any of the rest of the people around," he says. "The fact that neither of them survived for very long I suppose tells you the difficulty of grafting on that new resource onto a very traditional company." While those first two marketing pioneers may have failed, their successors certainly succeeded in building the company's marketing expertise and prowess, ensuring that lessons arising from the failure to innovate in years past were learned. "But it took a long time," Burrows adds. "The first person who actually made a difference was Michael Cummins. He was recruited in from Guinness and was really a marketer to his fingertips; he was the guy who was most responsible for building the current Jameson brand into the shape in which you see it."

In 1978 Burrows was appointed chief executive of Irish Distillers, a mere ten years after he had first joined the group. By 1980, despite their best efforts Irish Distillers had failed to make a breakthrough. Burrows brought in global management consulting firm McKinsey and Company to assess the state of play. The prognosis wasn't good.

"They concluded that the best thing we could do is sell the business, that we hadn't a hope," says Burrows. They did, however, advise that if selling the business wasn't an option, taking the premium route was the only other alternative – developing the brand as a superior proposition in the mind of the consumer when compared to scotch whisky. "Those words really formed the basis of the strategy for the next 30 years: the premium alternative to scotch, three times distilled against the double-distilled scotch whiskey. So the packaging had to be right; the labelling had to be right."

Most importantly, the price had to be right too. Selling a premium brand at a discounted price can be a recipe for failure, despite slower sales progression when a premium price tag is employed. Ultimately it proved to be a successful move.

The period from the late 1970s to the early 1990s was one of misery for Ireland's public finances, and for many of its citizens: though the recession at that time was a global one, Ireland was one of the countries hit hardest. Despite temporarily strong economic performance during the late 1970s a number of factors, including the fiscal policy of the Fianna Fáil government elected to power in 1977, resulted in record deficits.

Expansionary measures backfired, instead leading to increased inflation and a reduction in gross national income per capita. The national debt, unemployment and emigration began to soar. One year after Bob Geldof's Live Aid in 1985, which aimed to raise funds in support of Ethiopian famine victims, Bono and a host of other Irish and honorary Irish musicians took to the stage in Dublin for Self Aid in a bid to raise awareness of Ireland's chronic unemployment problem: almost 250,000 people were out of work.

In a *Today Tonight* report on Wexford town in March 1981, reporter Joe Little described how the dole queue in the once thriving town had "rocketed to 1,800 last year alone. The train out of town holds little promise; the national dole queue is growing as well. So the social problems of large-scale unemployment now threaten to set in."

A lack of opportunity forced thousands of Ireland's best and brightest to emigrate in a significant brain drain. A 2009 article in the *Irish Independent* quoted a Higher Education Authority report from 1987 that showed that 50% of engineering students and 70% of architecture graduates left the country in the six months after completing their studies. Unskilled and semi-skilled workers were also leaving for greener fields in large numbers. That trend peaked in 1989, which saw just over 70,000 people leave the country in search of better prospects.

Irish businesses suffered too. Restaurants experienced decline as the cash-strapped population slowed or simply stopped eating out. New car registrations dropped dramatically, sending the industry into a slump – former Ford main dealer Bill Cullen acquired the Renault franchise in 1986 for £1. The market for Irish whiskey was no exception to the trend.

"Like most things, the spirits market was in decline, duties were on the increase and consumers were pressed. So there wasn't any profit growth at home, and to try and take profit growth... building business on a measured basis in export markets meant that profitability was challenged," says Burrows.

Such trying times meant that Irish Distillers became an acquisition target at a time when the industry was in consolidation mode. Concerns over differential pricing within the EEC led to a situation whereby major players within the European market began to acquire their distribution arms in overseas markets. For Irish Distillers, a small organisation compared to their much larger competitors, it meant losing their independent distributors and finding it increasingly difficult to plot a route to market. That meant that some form of a liaison with a major international group was going to be necessary if they were to not only survive, but thrive.

"We were looking at different options. Because of the difficulty that existed at home from the point of view of profitability, the company didn't have the market cap or capacity to become an aggressive buyer of businesses abroad. So we were left with the situation of seeing what was around and how we could link to someone else," says Burrows.

Irish Distillers' plans soon became known in the trade and it found itself on the receiving end of a hostile bid from three companies: Guinness, GrandMet and Allied-Lyons. The defence was long and arduous. Echoing fears previously expressed by Kevin McCourt in the 1960s, Burrows and Irish Distillers took their case to the Competition Commission in Brussels – and won. The consortium was dismembered, though GrandMet (now part of Diageo) was allowed to go it alone. Irish Distillers, however, had lined up a potential suitor in the meantime: French conglomerate Pernod Ricard, a company with which Burrows had become quite familiar. They were interested – but, like several other potential buyers, they were holding off on any potential deal until they could identify a clear route. Eventually they were persuaded to make a competing bid, which was ultimately successful in June 1988.

"That was transformative and the principal reason for that is it opened a route to market. Pernod Ricard had already established its own distribution network in key markets, and so suddenly the portfolio of Irish Distillers was slotted into that distribution network," says Burrows. "And I suppose, maybe because of the enthusiasm within Pernod Ricard having won this epic battle for Irish Distillers... everybody wanted to be involved, so that meant it was all hands to the pump."

That move would lead to the revitalisation of Irish whiskey across the globe, particularly the Jameson brand: in 1990 Jameson had 2% market share of the world whiskey market, a figure that is approaching 4% according to Burrows. "[That] may sound very little, but actually it's quite a transforma-tive thing. A lot of other brands are proliferating today and there may well be an opportunity for them all to grow. But the fact of the matter is brands make categories; categories don't make brands," Burrows states. "And so Jameson has created the Irish whiskey category, and others can piggyback on that – but you need one really strong brand to be developing consumer awareness around the category in order for the business to grow."

Modern playing field

Burrows' time at the helm of Irish Distillers came to an end in 2008, having witnessed the industry's renaissance sparked by – among a number of factors – Pernod Ricard's investment in Irish Distillers, alongside the establishment of the Cooley Distillery in Co Louth in 1987. According to Drinks Industry Ireland, Irish whiskey was the fastest-growing spirit on the planet between 2009 and 2014. Exports are expanding, and new distilleries are opening around the country – including the Teeling sons' new hotspot in Dublin's Liberties and Walsh Whiskey's endeavour in Co Carlow, a €25m investment in a distillery that has the capacity to produce 8m bottles of whiskey per annum.

Since leaving Irish Distillers Burrows has been busy, and he could be described as the definition of a man with fingers in many pies. Now serving as chair of British American Tobacco, he also spent a number of years as Bank of Ireland's governor, and the head of IBEC between 1998 and 2000, alongside roles as a director with organisations including CityJet, Long Mountain Wines and Cork University Foundation.

A past recipient of the Chevalier of the Légion d'Honneur in France, Burrows is also a member of the Trilateral Commission, a non-partisan organisation that was founded by David Rockefeller in 1973 to develop cooperation and business interests between Europe, North America and Japan. As such, it's fair to say that he has a firm handle on the business landscape globally and on home shores alike, and says that the latter has begun to emerge from the choppy waters of the global recession.

"I think Irish business is in terrific shape today. I [recently] met John Lyons, who was head of the IDA in the US, and he was telling me about attracting Google to Ireland. In their first iteration, Google came and employed 20 people in Ireland... how they have transformed into the operation that they are – that speaks for the health and welfare of Irish business," he asserts. "Irish business is terrifically good, and why is it so good? I think we have a number of natural advantages that are often talked about: the fact that we speak English as our mother tongue, the fact that we have such proximity to the UK and the EU – but the fact that we have this appeal in America is something I think is hugely important. We cross divides, we have a rather unique position as an island country, and business certainly can prosper from that."

Much of that success can be explained by the development of the Irish brand, which Burrows describes as a practical brand employed by a principled nation, something reflected in our business reputation and our willingness to spread our wings beyond Ireland's borders. Ireland's position is also bolstered by a population with a great entrepreneurial spirit, it's fair to say, and Burrows highlights a number of those individuals who have impressed him throughout the years – such as Michael Killeen, a charismatic individual who was appointed head of the IDA in 1970. "I think Michael was a real visionary in terms of how he developed the IDA's contacts around the world. I think we really owe a great debt to him," Burrows says.

Michael Smurfit also features on that list, as does Michael O'Leary – despite Burrows not being a major fan of travelling Ryanair. "There are many other examples. I think the real nation-builders were people like Seán Lemass, people like Ken Whitaker... Ray MacSharry, who came in with a clear idea of what he wanted to do," he adds.

So does Burrows have a positive outlook for Ireland Inc as it searches for a brighter future while emerging from the clutches of recession? "I am hopeful. I think the government has done a very good job in managing us out of what were very dangerous times. I think that being consistent and being unswerving in the strategy that they followed... I think we're on a path to recovery," he muses. "Currency probably didn't help for a while but it is now helping. I think the success of attracting inward investment, our tourism product – which has sustained us right through this – and agriculture is there and really remains to be properly exploited."

Despite the fact that our growth rate statistics have been influenced by a number of multinational companies and their presence here, other indicators such as improving public finances and declining debt levels make for positive reading. Burrows is singing from the same hymnsheet, and believes that it is only a matter of time before Ireland experiences an overdue resurgence.

"I think that if some things that have gone against us outside of Ireland had gone the other way, we'd be a long way further ahead. For example, if we had seen some kind of recovery in Europe, which just hasn't happened yet," he says. "There's a big dividend to come to Ireland when that happens, and it will happen."

CHAPTER 39

Interview: Wilbur Ross
In conversation with Ian Hyland

WHY INVEST IN IRISH BANKS IN THE MIDDLE OF THE COUNTRY'S WORST-EVER
BANKING CRISIS? WILBUR ROSS, WHO WOULD BECOME US SECRETARY OF
COMMERCE SHORTLY AFTER THIS INTERVIEW, DID JUST THAT.

It is no exaggeration to say that Wilbur Ross probably knows more about bankruptcy and distressed assets than anyone else in the world. He certainly knows about the opportunities afforded by businesses facing into such financial straits, with *The New York Times* once describing him as "a dean of vulture investing".

Born in New Jersey and educated at Yale and Harvard, Donald Trump's future secretary of commerce spent much of his career turning the unprofitable and undesirable businesses of the world into high-performing, high-return assets. Ross got his start in the mid-1970s, when he began working as a bankruptcy adviser for the American wing of the Rothschild Group, a Chicago-based investment bank. He spent 24 years at the company. By the end of his time at Rothschild he was also running its private equity fund, which he bought out in 2000 to launch the New York-based WL Ross and Co.

The decision to strike out on his own has, like so many of Ross's risky decisions, paid off handsomely. WL Ross and Co now has about $9 billion under management, and Ross himself is listed by *Forbes* as having a net worth of $3 billion. Most of Ross's fortune has been earned through the acquisition and subsequent sale of distressed assets across a diverse range of industries.

In 2001 he sent shockwaves through the financial world with his investment in the US steel industry, an uncompetitive sector that was generally considered to be in crisis, with its potential for profit hamstrung by foreign competitors and legacy labour costs – high union wages and fully funded pensions for a huge number of retirees. Over 30 American steel companies had filed for bankruptcy in the three years preceding Ross's investments. Undeterred, Ross bought collapsed giants LTV and Bethlehem Steel for $325m and $1.1bn respectively, turned them into ISG (International Steel Group), and became responsible for roughly 20% of steel production in the US. A contemporary article about him in *Bloomberg* magazine ran with the headline 'Is Wilbur Ross Crazy?' – they weren't the only ones asking the question.

Ross shortly proved the doubters wrong, radically altering working and manufacturing processes in the factories, turning the companies around, and promptly selling ISG to ArcelorMittal, now the world's largest steel company, for $4.5bn in 2005. WL Ross and Co made $2.5bn from the deal, while Ross himself reportedly took home $300 million.

Bank of Ireland

Ross has made similar investments across a range of industries, from textiles to coal to automotive components, but he is perhaps best known in Ireland for his connection to banking. At the height of the euro crisis in 2011 – shortly after the EU/IMF bailout, when Ireland's credit rating had been demoted to junk status – a group of private investors purchased a 34.9% stake in Bank of Ireland for just €1.1bn, keeping the bank from full nationalisation in the process.

Ross took control of around 9% of the bank, buying in at just 10c a share. Three years later he sold all his holdings in the bank for between 26c and 33c a share, and tripled his initial investment. Despite the state of Irish finance at the time he got involved, Ross says he could always see a way forward for the bank and for the country, but only if the two could work together.

"Buying into a big bank in a small country is really buying a warrant on the whole economy," he says. "If the economy doesn't flourish neither can the bank, and in a curious way if the bank doesn't flourish neither does the economy – they are symbiotic in that sort of sense."

The most important thing for Ross was that the underlying fundamentals of the business, and the country, were strong. Were the bailout and what preceded it a terminal disease, or a temporary bump in the road?

"The first thing we had to convince ourselves of was the fundamentals of Ireland Inc," he says. "Prior to the banks getting the same real estate disease that the American banks got and a lot of the European banks got – prior to that, the Irish economy was very well run. Debt was 26% of GDP, fully funded national pension fund, very hospitable community to inbound FDI, practically a wholly owned subsidiary of the US – $116bn of US investment, more than the BRIC [Brazil, Russia, India and China] countries. Those were the fundamentals, and a favourable trade balance.

"Those fundamentals didn't change when the crisis came. All that happened was an enormous financial burden that got created to straighten out the banks. They had the misfortune of being early in the cycle, and therefore the EU was much stricter on them than it was, for example, on Greece. So the country had this big debt problem but you knew once they worked through it things would be good again. Nothing had fundamentally changed, just this one horrible interruption that came in."

Ross was also sure that the attitude of the Irish government was supportive of what they were trying to do, with both the Taoiseach, Enda Kenny, and the minister for finance, Michael Noonan, making it clear that they understood the commercial reality of the bank – in which they too had a significant stake.

"It was clear the finance minister supported things and understood it; it was clear the Taoiseach supported it and understood it, and probably understood better than any American president during the same period what was happening here," he says. "Sure there were bumps and grinds along the way, but they were supportive and they did what they needed to do. The final piece of the puzzle was the nature of the Irish public, the population, and we were convinced, as proved to be true, that they were not going to react in the same way southern Europeans did, with strikes and carbombings and all sorts of misbehaviour. We were convinced as painful as it would be and was, the Irish public would grit their teeth and grind their way through it.

"So you had all these things lined up: a good government history, good fundamentals to the economy, good nature to the population itself. You had a temporary problem."

Reading the signals

Ross's focus on sound fundamentals has been his guiding light throughout his career in business. Figuring out the structure of a business and learning how to improve and take advantage of that structure is always more important than passing trends. This was a huge factor in drawing Ross to Ireland.

"We figured out a long time ago that you can't micromanage your way out of the wrong macro factors," he says. "If the macro factors are right you're halfway home in getting the micros. So we felt quite convinced that the macros were good. In retrospect what's sad is that if the Troika had been a little more lenient with Ireland I think the economy would have recovered even sooner. I think the EU owes Ireland something because they proved to be better at rewarding bad behaviour than they have been good behaviour – because Ireland has been the poster-child of the bailout."

Ross says that the Irish government's line on corporate tax – their decision not to raise it when under pressure from the EU to do so – was a strong signal for the international financial community. "Ireland held the mark on that and that took a lot of courage, because they desperately needed the funding," he says. "They were right to do it, because that symbolised to people outside that the pro-business nature of Ireland was not going to change regardless of the economic situation that developed."

The economic situation today is obviously quite different from the scene that Ross entered upon in 2011. Property values have largely recovered, and many of the key economic indicators – GDP, exports, inward investment – are improving year on year. Ross's time with Bank of Ireland has directly led to more connections with Irish markets, particularly the real estate investments of Invesco, WL Ross and Co's parent company. Ross chairs several of the funds that Invesco manages, and he says that they are expanding their representation in Europe generally – but particularly in Ireland.

"Banks nowadays lend between 50-60% of the value of the property – and if it's a NAMA property, then NAMA will probably take back 50-60% – and there's a huge amount of equity coming in from overseas, and also some domestic investors," he says. "We're trying to fill the gap from the 50-60% up to 70-75% or even 80%, so there's a tranche of debt on which you can make a pretty decent interest rate and get some sort of equity kicker and yet it enhances the return to the ultimate equity owner. It's a niche that needs to be filled.

"So that's a good thing for the country: that will help real estate values. Real estate values need two things: they need inbound migration – during the crisis there was outbound migration – and you need debt. You need leverage, because real estate is a commodity that needs leverage. So by putting some extra leverage I think we're helping facilitate the turnaround of the real estate part of the economy."

The rising fortunes of Ireland's banks, with AIB and Permanent TSB both returning to profit, indicates a positive future for Irish business, freeing up money for investment in the Irish economy through property and SME loans. Ross says that the government's decision to bail out the banks is now paying off.

"I think it's constructive: you have to get the banks back to normalcy," he says. "It's better for the country to do that and as they re-privatise these things it will help pay down the debts of the country. Bank of Ireland has repaid over €6bn and the government still has a good size stake in it – and at some point I assume they'll liquefy that. So it's not only good to have a strong banking system from the economy point of view, it's also very good from the sovereign debt point of view. There have been times recently where Irish debt has traded at a lower yield than US government debt – during the crisis you'd have never imagined that this would be possible. But it's great; it's letting them refinance, which is helping quite a bit."

Human links

Beyond the financial side of things, Ross says that there are strong personal and cultural reasons for people like him, and other American investors, to want to come to Ireland and develop their businesses here. Alongside key facets such as infrastructure and the lack of a language barrier, the importance of the social connection, the generations of Irish-Americans who have made careers for themselves in corporate America, and the connection they feel to Ireland cannot be overestimated. These connections create a real value for people coming to Ireland.

"I think the first time I ever heard of a racetrack was somebody in the family buying Irish sweepstakes tickets," he says. "That's a trivial thing, but the point is there's always been some give and take between Ireland and the US. There's obviously lots of Irish-Americans, my wife included. There is a comfort level in dealing with people who have a commonality in background, there is a commonality of religious background, even though within Ireland you have the two that don't always get on as well as they might, but still, it's very much a western heritage. The language is obviously the same, a lot of the customs are the same and there is inflection back and forth. I think that is one of the many reasons why so many US companies have continued to invest there right through the crisis. You have a young, very well-educated labour force, and there are three ingredients you don't always find: there's very good telecom infrastructure, very good transport infrastructure, good geography. And it's the only English-speaking country using the euro."

With so many different views in Ireland and elsewhere about the European project, many tensions have arisen around sovereignty, policy and planning within the EU in recent years. The stresses the union has found itself under since 2008, with multiple bailouts and crises, represent the greatest challenge facing the European community since its formation. Ross, while somewhat sceptical of seeing Europe as a whole, has little doubt that many individual states are in great shape and have many reasons to be optimistic about the future – they've faced the worst of they'll have to face, and are coming out the other side.

"To me, Europe is in some ways a figment of the imagination in that no person has ever introduced themselves as a European," he says. "I think when you talk about Europe you have to talk country by country.

"The one I worry about is France. France has been a very wealthy country but the attitude of the government towards business is awful. They seem to think even though a company is shareholder-owned, the government should really have the main voice in it, so that makes it very difficult to invest there. They are having a terrible brain drain, because a lot of young professionals are leaving over tax issues, and a lot of wealthy people are leaving. Somebody told me that London is now the third-largest French city in the world – and Brussels has a lot too.

"By and large those people aren't going to move back. So there's been a permanent migration out of France of wealthy people, and of young professionals. And that's damaging to a country."

CHAPTER 40

Interview: Tommy Breen
In conversation with Ian Hyland

THE FORMER DCC CHIEF EXECUTIVE DISCUSSES GROWTH, SCALE, ENTREPRENEURSHIP – AND WHY STABILITY AND RETURN ON CAPITAL HAVE BEEN DCC HALLMARKS THROUGHOUT ITS SUBSTANTIAL EVOLUTION.

The story of Tommy Breen is inseparable from that of the company he has worked with for 31 years – DCC. What started as a basic venture capital fund called Development Capital Corporation Limited in 1976 has since grown into a multi-divisional industrial holding group active in markets across Ireland, the UK and continental Europe.

Having managed several divisions within the group, Breen was appointed chief operating officer of DCC in March 2006 and became group managing director in July 2007. He was appointed chief executive in May 2008, only the second CEO in the company's history. By the time he announced his retirement in April 2017 the group employed over 10,000 people and was one of only five Irish companies listed on the FTSE100 as Donal Murphy took over the helm.

When Breen in 1985, DCC was still largely focused on – as its name suggested – providing development capital. Its founder, Jim Flavin, had started the company after heading up AIB's venture capital operation, with initial funding for DCC coming from 11 Irish institutions each providing £1m. By the time Breen joined the team they were attracting other key investors and providing some very significant returns. "The early investors were the Aer Lingus pension fund, the Guinness pension fund, the Trinity College pension fund and a number of life offices," Breen says. "We set up as a limited company, not structured as a fund, and made lots of investments. Some worked and some didn't work. It wasn't all success, but it grew from those small beginnings in the period between 1976 and 1990. By 1990 we had a balance sheet, having raised some more money, and the returns had been strong, of £100m. The compound return for every pound invested in DCC from 1976 up to 1990 was 23%."

Things began to change around 1990. Having reached a significant scale in Ireland, DCC was finding it difficult to identify opportunities that would continue to reap those impressive returns. Moving into the UK venture capital market was the next logical step. But what worked in Ireland did not necessarily work elsewhere – and with many bigger fish in a much bigger pond, useful opportunities were thin on the ground. The experience was important nonetheless: it helped Breen and DCC to see where they could be truly effective, and formed the roots of what the group would become.

"In London we were pretty small and we were struggling to get opportunities in large enough businesses," he says. "We also felt that there were some of our businesses that we'd already invested in that, if we had control of them, we could push them on. So a decision was taken in 1990, a pretty fundamental decision — and we haven't actually come across a parallel anywhere for it — where we decided that we were going to change direction and move away from venture development capital into what in those days I suppose was termed an industrial holding company. Some of what DCC is today actually has its genesis in some of those venture capital opportunities in London that we invested in."

This kind of transition was not without difficulties, requiring divestment from some businesses that were identified as being outside of the new core interest. It took time, but by the middle of the decade the group was moving in a direction with which Breen and his partners were comfortable.

"A lot changed," says Breen. "We went from being investors in those businesses to taking operational responsibility for them. It's tough for businesses when they have to fundamentally change strategy because it is a time of risk. We have always had this clear strategic objective of what we want to do. We want cash-generative businesses, producing high returns on capital and affording us opportunities to reinvest with cash coming out of those businesses with high returns. And that's a very financially-driven strategy and we need business strategies, as well as energy and healthcare and technology, to feed into that. But we've been pretty consistent. We've had that mantra there since then and I suppose it has been brick upon brick since 1994."

Return on capital

That methodical approach has yielded rich dividends for all involved in DCC, and Breen embodies it more than most. The group has four main divisions, with the Energy Division being the major player. It's followed by a Health Product Division, a technology distribution business and an environmental business, which deals mostly with recycling and resource recovery. Each division is relatively autonomous, with Breen and the rest of the Dublin-based head office simply ensuring that they're managed as well as they can be, without worrying too much about an overall synergy between the different strands. It's an old-school approach, but it works.

"The thing that drives us is return on capital," says Breen. "We are a public company, we want to grow profits, we want to pay dividends, and we want to do all of that. But fundamentally we have this view that the way we will add real value in the business is if we're re-investing the cash flow that is coming out of the business at a high rate of return. So return on capital employed is the first thing we look at. We think about that not just when we're making that initial investment – but you know, in anything we do, we analyse our business. If you take the various aspects of our energy business or technology distribution business, we're analysing quite small parts of those businesses, looking at what's the return on the capital we've tied up in that business. So that's what drives us."

Stability is a watchword for Breen and the rest of the team at DCC. He has been there for over three decades, but most of the senior management have been with the group for comparable lengths of time. When they hire someone, they tend to keep them. Of course, Breen recognises that such stability can lead to stagnation, and he says that keeping a balance between the old and the new, the experienced and the youthful, is particularly important. Attracting young talent and giving them the chance to prove themselves is a key part of their management strategy. "We have been fortunate that we have a team that have been together for a long period of time," he says. "I think that's terribly important in a business that's growing and developing. I think the challenge in that, then, is making sure that you have opportunities. We can all get very stale. Are Tommy Breen and [chief financial officer] Fergal O'Dwyer going to come up with fresh ideas? It's very important to bring young people in. Young people are attracted to a growth story, and to being part of something that is growing, and growing internationally as well. It provides opportunity. That's one thing people have not been stuck for. We've been able to keep people, give them opportunities to grow and develop and, at the same time, bring young people in."

Breen has always encouraged his teams to be entrepreneurial in their approach, perhaps more so than might usually be expected in a company like DCC. He says he operates an open-door policy in the office, and invites the younger members of staff to make suggestions, to bring ideas, and to show ambition. It's important, he says, that people with such ambitions know that the senior management is behind them, and can support them financially. This requires a cautious approach to capital management, and making sure that there's always money there to pounce on an opportunity when it arises.

"We've never had a situation here where we have two guys coming forward and saying 'I want to make an acquisition' at the one time, and us saying 'Well, you know, we don't have enough capital to do both of those so we've got to make a choice'," he says. "We've never had that situation. That can be scary because it means we've had enough capital to make all the mistakes we want. But the thing that we say – and it's kind of ingrained in here – is that we will invest in any of those businesses. They all are driven to grow their businesses as long as we believe, and we don't always get it right, that the capital investment is going to drive higher returns."

A significant aspect of Breen's tenure as chief executive has been the expansion of DCC's presence in continental Europe. Before he took charge, almost all their business was in Ireland and the UK. Now over a third is spread across Europe, with key investments in France, Belgium, Denmark and elsewhere. Much like their initial move into the UK market back in 1990, this new expansion has been driven by a need for scale. As many Irish businesses have found, there's only so big you can get at home. "One of the challenges in growing a business in Ireland is that we've a very small domestic market and you know, very often businesses don't have scale," he says. "If you're operating in the UK or you're operating in France or Germany, you can build a pretty big business in your own domestic market before you have to think about the challenges of going cross-border. In Ireland, you don't have to get very big — you can have a big market share in whatever sector you are in.

"The businesses we moved into the UK, culturally and language-wise, it's a very easy market. But we've been driven more or less by trying to get scale in the markets we're in. If you go back seven years or so, we'd no business outside the UK and Ireland. Today the business is growing to where we have about 35% of the business in continental Europe, about 60% or so in the UK, and about 5 or 6% in Ireland. That's not because we made a decision to not invest in Ireland, that's because in the businesses we're in we've pretty big market shares."

Seen it all

Given his long career, Breen has basically seen it all when it comes to Irish business. He's seen the ups and downs more than once, and how others have weathered the storms. Even though so many people have come and gone, and so much has changed in Irish business during his time, he still looks up to his old mentor Jim Flavin.

"Jim left the bank, raised some money, took some big risks along the way, took a business and brought it from venture development capital to where it went to," he says. "I just admire people who take risks and have the drive, courage and determination to get on with it, and Jim did. I also worked, albeit not very closely, with the CRH story, which is a similar thing. It's a bigger business and a much older business than us."

Breen particularly recalls a meeting in 1995, when CRH chairman Tony Barry was on the board of DCC and offered food for thought. "I wasn't on the board of DCC but I was in making a presentation, recommending an investment in a technology distribution business. It was a small business but it was growing exponentially. I presented this business and why we should buy it, and it was going to grow forever and Tony put his hand up and said: 'Tommy, what's the cash payback on this?' I thought 'Are you mad? This business doesn't pay you back cash, this business wants more business to grow.' And, of course, he was right. I should have thought about that. He just had this perspective, so I admire Tony greatly. I think they are the people I admire."

CHAPTER 41

Interview: Deirdre Somers
In conversation with Ruraidh Conlon O'Reilly

THE IRISH STOCK EXCHANGE CEO DISCUSSES THE PAST, PRESENT AND FUTURE
OF THE DUBLIN-BASED INSTITUTION AND TALKS IPOs, TECHNOLOGY AND IRELAND'S
MOST VISIONARY BUSINESS LEADERS.

Depending on one's perspective the Irish Stock Exchange can appear in some ways colourful, in other ways staid. Founded in 1793, it has functioned right through the gamut of Ireland's eventful 19th and 20th century upheavals, and played a key role in its commercial and infrastructural development. The Grand and Royal Canals, the Bank of Ireland, the building of railways, the Guinness story and the expensive business of state-building all come to life through its prism.

And yet it has never been the most glamorous of institutions, even within a rather buttoned-down business culture: its Anglesea Street premises in Temple Bar has always been a quieter place than the hustle and bustle of the City of London, New York or Frankfurt, and Ireland's more ostentatious businesspeople have tended to be builders or investors rather than stockbrokers.

Few people have observed and experienced the Irish Stock Exchange's workings as closely as Deirdre Somers. Entering the business world as a chartered accountant in 1987, she joined the ISE in 1995 and rose through the ranks to become its CEO in 2007. Needless to say, the institution – and indeed the Irish business environment – have changed enormously since she joined.

"When I joined the exchange it was only a couple of months after it de-merged from the London Stock Exchange, so in 1995 it was a very small company with under 20 people with a building on Anglesea Street and pretty much nothing else," she recalls. "It was mutual. It was limited by guarantee from its owners. So I suppose where we started from in 1995 was pretty small, probably quite inward-looking, very much geared towards facilitating the membership base like all mutuals, and that was really what it was.

"Now it is demutualised, it is still owned by stockbrokers but it is a private company with shares like any normal company, it is very commercial, it is profitable. About 70% of its business is international, it has created world-leading positions in niche areas and it is objectively a successful business that has managed to diversify against a backdrop of hugely challenging trends for the industry – and those trends are very relentless consolidation that was brought about because exchanges moved away from being people-based practices to technology-based enabled trading."

Technology was a profound change for stock exchanges worldwide, and along with improvements in speed and service forced a very different business model. The 'Big Bang' of financial market deregulation and com- puterisation kicked off a relentless pursuit of speed and interoperability of connectivity, which required investment and research. Then came years of European financial integration that broke down many of the franchises, en- titlements and monopolies that might have existed in the past.

"All of that financial integration favoured the much larger geographies with the larger ecosystems and deeper pockets, so commercially and busi- ness-wise the exchange has managed to create a reality for itself despite all of those counter trends, and it is now sitting in a situation where we have a very good business."

The other major change, says Somers, is cultural. "You look back to '87 when I joined the business world and I think exchanges would have been seen as pretty parochial clubs, very entitled, patriarchal. Now I see it as an organi- sation that is very internationalised, very open, very transparent, 50% female at all levels and one of the best places to work in Ireland, as proven by the Best Place to Work survey, which is from our staff... I think culturally that has been a pretty monumental change. I think it has been all good really."

Technological revolution

The physical experience of all stock exchanges has been revolutionised thanks to the computer. Stock exchanges were originally a venue in a building; now people get together on technological platforms rather than trading floors. Ask Somers just how important technology is and one might as well have asked previous generations how important the building was. The ISE connects to and clears through Eurex, one of the best clearing systems in the world, and connects and maintains that connection itself through Euroclear for settlement.

"Without that underpinning the exchange wouldn't exist. Within our niche businesses, we've gone from a paper-heavy review process, which had documents being couriered away and sent back in envelopes – and that was the world I joined in 1995 – to now effectively paperless offices where everything is now on screen, everything can be audited back and traced. And that is our own technology we built ourself to underscore what we do, so everything that we do is technologically enabled.

"The old idea of people in funny jackets screaming at each other on a floor is completely gone in cash equity; it is going in pretty much all other types of assets in the exchange world. Notwithstanding the nostalgia that people still have for the old trading floors and see them as the quintessential trading floors... you still see them in NYSE and the opening bell; you see people bustling around but they are not actually trading any more. These are media outlets, they are a PR business, because everything happens on technology nowadays. For people who don't believe me, I like to say equity trading happens in splits of nanoseconds now and there is no room for a man in a funny coat in a nanosecond. So technology is everything.

"As much as you want to be nostalgic about taking the humanity out of trading – and there is that aspect of it; I think people will write psychology papers about it in the future – you can't put that genie back in the bottle. The new world wants to be able to trade in splits; in tiny microseconds."

It's often tempting to see stock exchanges as independent, above-business institutions – forgetting that they are themselves commercial entities. The world in which the ISE operates is a highly competitive one, Somers acknowledges.

"Your greatest challenge is always your greatest strength and when we set up as a standalone company in '95 with the mother of all competitors, the London Stock Exchange, next door to us... We were effectively connected in every possible way from an ecosystem perspective and finding ways to compete in '95 with that reality was very challenging. Before any of our peers in Europe we had to step up and do things a little differently.

"When [EU harmonisation directive] Mifid 1 came we were probably best positioned of all the exchanges in Europe to deal with the opening of competition in the European market because we always had it. We had always competed directly with the London Stock Exchange. Whereas my peers in Europe would have greeted that competitive force with horror and to some extent rejection, it was nothing new for us. In the cash equity space we have always competed head-to-head with London and we continue to do so, and we've continued to win that battle in a large part because we have the majority of liquidity in Irish cash equity shares and that's against the backdrop of a pretty formidable competitor.

"The 70% business that we have is a niche business and I have consistently said that being consolidated into a larger exchange is not a strategy. What is a strategy is doing a corporate action, whatever that might be: to do something you believe you can't do on your own. And in the absence of that box being ticked, I see no merit in being subsumed into a larger entity just because that is the trend. I don't see a value for the business of the exchange to do that on balance and until I see that value I don't believe it is an appropriate thing for us to do."

Supply and demand

Just as technology and culture change, so too does the type of shares being supplied and demanded. Themes and trends come and go. "I think there are some very significant changes happening in the cash equity market at the moment and probably the most dominant one is the move to passive investment," Somers says. "It favours much larger companies, which I think is going to be a challenge for all exchanges. If we move from passive, technology is always going to be a trend as people will always believe there is some great growth trajectory in technology stocks whether it be nanotechnology, biotechnology and I'm sure we'll see artificial intelligence coming in fairly soon.

"So there is always going to be a trend in exchanges. I've been here for 22 years; I joined when exploration was the trend. It moved from there into technology in its original newbie internet days; we're now moving into more granular and more diverse technology and I don't think that trend is going to change any time soon. I would love to see a more comprehensive trend towards solid dividend-earnings stock with good predictable growth trajectories that aren't going to deliver tenfold returns in two years but will give you a dividend over and above and a fixed yield over and above anything that you will get in other asset types. I don't quite understand why that hasn't happened, quite frankly. But the markets will always decide what is trendy at any given time."

At the time of writing, a politically rocky world and jumpy global market doesn't encourage companies to take the plunge and list. "The trend for IPOs within the western world is very poor; the US and Europe together are 50% down on what they would have been in the 1990s and we're no different. As much as I would love to, we can't buck an international trend that is: western-based companies are not IPOing at the rate at which they used to and there are many in the US and Europe trying to examine the reasons for that and how we can address that.

"Having said that, I think we would be optimistic that we will have a few IPOs in the next 18 months but whether or not those will manifest will really depend on market conditions, and I believe Brexit will have a big influence on that – and how the market assimilates Brexit into how much volatility that's going to bring to market conditions."

As a key figure at the centre of the Irish business scene, Somers observes its movers and shakers at close range. Asked if there is one she particularly admires, Tony Ryan comes immediately to mind.

"I think Tony Ryan was that very rare combination of entrepreneurship and deep managerial capability and resilience – and you know lots of people see clever niches and clever trends, but very few have the capacity to take those and turn them into significant businesses, which is what he did in aircraft leasing. Although ultimately where that went with GPA is not what he would have expected, he did revolutionise the aircraft leasing industry internationally and it still has his footprints all over it.

"I think secondly he had the capacity to see talent and enable talent – and you see that in Ryanair, which on every possible level was a fragile business. He had the intelligence and the strength to put a very strong person behind there and stand behind that person with very difficult decisions that were culturally probably very difficult for him to go with, but he did that and we now have a world-leading airline based in Ireland and managed in Ireland. If you look at trends internationally, that is an extraordinary outcome for a small island. An extraordinary outcome. That could have never been achieved without the talents of Tony Ryan.

"I think pretty much anyone who managed Kerry Group... it goes back to Denis Brosnan at the very beginning. This is a company that understands its DNA, understands at a very deep level, and I would say the same for Glanbia. They may have removed themselves from the cooperative type of structure but they still have a deep understanding of that culture that makes them great – and they have built from that culture without losing that sense of grounding and foundation, and I think that those are two extraordinary companies that I think we should be immensely proud of as Irish people. And I think the leadership of those two companies, without exception, has always had this subtlety of understanding that culture as well as that quiet but relentless ambition for the next stage for their companies' growth, and I think Ireland has benefited immensely from both of those companies as a result."

Somers has also noticed distinctive characteristics of Irish business, its people and their style over the years – almost to her surprise. "It's something I've learned a lot about since I took over as president of the Federation of European Stock Exchanges because I totally underestimated it before I had that role. The role involves a lot of advocacy at a senior level in Europe and within the Commission and within the Parliament, and I think I completely underestimated before I took that role the capacity that Irish people have for the human – the emotional intelligence I suppose – that people bring to business... the interest they have in the human being that they are doing business with, the ease of connection that they make in business, where people do business with people, and I think there is a natural empathy within the Irish condition for that sort of human relationship which is not as obvious as I thought it was outside of Ireland.

"So I think that is quite unique: I think we have a warmth, an empathy and a curiosity of people that naturally draws people in and means we get a disproportionate amount of face-time to our size. So that's the first."

The second is that because we live on an island we probably have the most international outlook for business and financial services aside from the City of London. "We look at financial services in a far more internationalised way than any of our European peers; than much larger countries that are far more inward-looking, that are far more protective and naturally so, and understandably so, but lose that internationalised dimension – but we as a small island on the periphery of Europe are constantly challenging ourselves as to what we believe we can do in the context of what is happening internationally. We don't have the comfort of our larger European colleagues of a larger economy, and I think that has given us a resilience and a capability for change that many other countries do not have."

CHAPTER 42

Interview: Tony O'Reilly Jr

In conversation with Ian Hyland

THE PROVIDENCE RESOURCES CEO TALKS ABOUT HIS CAREER, THE EXPLORATION INDUSTRY, THE QUEST FOR OIL AND GAS OFF THE IRISH COAST, AND HIS FATHER'S ILLUSTRIOUS EXAMPLE.

The O'Reilly name is one of the most prominent in Irish business, established through the endeavours of Sir Anthony O'Reilly at Heinz, Independent News and Media, Waterford Wedgwood, Atlantic Resources, ARCON, Fitzwilton, and many other companies – and not forgetting his international rugby career and any number of other adventures in an action-packed life.

Sons Cameron and Gavin followed him into the business world, as did Tony Jr, whose knowledge of business was of course already at an unusually high level when he began his working life.

"After working at Coopers and Lybrand in New York for two years, I came home in 1992 to work at ARCON, but of course my awareness of Irish business goes back to the mid-seventies when I was old enough to understand what my father was doing in all his various businesses in Ireland," he recalls. "In our house, business and family life were intertwined. And I guess that the view that I had at that stage was that there were a select few people who were really making waves in Ireland. Yes, there was the old order that existed, but then you had the new challengers if you will: the Tony Ryans, the Michael Smurfits, the various 'beef barons', the John Magniers, and of course my father – people like that – but it seemed like a very small, select group."

O'Reilly recalls a very different Irish economy back then, before European structural funds led to an upgrade in its infrastructure and before the lower 12.5% tax base had brought in substantial foreign investment: it was a "tough, tough operating environment", he says, as he recalls from when he started working at ARCON's mining operations in Co Kilkenny.

"When I was involved in ARCON back in 1992, we were about to start constructing a zinc mine in Kilkenny. You've got to remember that it was still a country that was crying out for employment, crying out for opportunities, and there wasn't necessarily joined-up thinking in terms of how to make that happen. Through the nineties it obviously all changed, with the IDA having built a strong platform in the eighties. And then it started to really come home to roost when the first big tranche of funds from the European Union permeated through the economy... and with good management of this 'windfall' allowing for the underwriting of a new tax base, suddenly Ireland became a go-to place, and so you started to see a lot mor, 473e investment – but the investment was very much geared at that time to foreign multinational manufacturers coming into Ireland.

"I would have said at that stage that it was still tough for Irish companies to get help and investment." O'Reilly remembers receiving no assistance in developing Galmoy's zinc resources. "In fact we were embroiled in long legal and planning processes which cost us tens of millions, which at that time was a significant amount of money, trying to create something that ultimately would be sustainable for the Irish economy. And then, even when we got the go-ahead, we still had to pay to bring electricity to our mine, upgrade the road infrastructure and put in a piped water system – all with no financial assistance from the government.

"One can clearly say that Ireland successfully leveraged its greatest resource wealth, its people, by bringing in the foreign multinationals who also were able to avail of the lower corporation tax – but when it came to developing our 'other' natural resources, oil and gas and mining, we had an inconsistent philosophy and approach. Developing our natural resources – oil, gas and mining – should have been the cornerstone of every national development plan. And although it was given lip service in the past, there really wasn't bite behind it to actually make it come to pass."

Natural resources mindset

The difficulties that he experienced at Galmoy can be attributed, he says, to long-standing and inherited – and sometimes misguided – attitudes. "My general macro view is that we, as a nation, treated differently the development of our natural resources – and maybe it goes back in our history to being tenants of British landlords – so when we finally got ownership of our land in 1922, everyone felt they owned "our" natural resources; everyone had a bit of a take on it.

"As such, entrepreneurs in the oil, gas and mining industry would be confronted with the notion from commentators that the State would be giving away 'our natural resources', and that view definitely played out in terms of mining developments in the seventies and eighties – but also in the offshore sector – and the result of this was that different rules were applied to the development of our natural resources and this was best demonstrated by the setting of a tax rate twice the corporate tax rate."

As such, O'Reilly thinks this was somewhat counterproductive in terms of developing our natural resources, and as a result they didn't develop as quickly as other industries did – and that's because there was no joined up thinking. It didn't help that there was no IDA-led initiative for the development of natural resources, which could have helped, he says. Since natural resources have a much longer lead-time than pharmaceuticals or the IFSC-based financial services firms it was, says O'Reilly, a missed opportunity.

Again, it comes down to a historically inherited view. "I go back to our history: there is an emotional link with our land. Even though they are not putting in the huge amounts of capital, certain people believe that there is some extra benefit that should accrue from the land to them, and as a result, that the State would be giving away our natural resources. And my argument – and indeed my father's, and many others in the natural resource sector – has always been that we are not giving away our natural resources; what we are actually trying to do is to find and develop our natural resources and bring in the significant capital that is required to really develop an incremental industry for Ireland."

Tara Mines and Silvermines, along with O'Reilly's ARCON-owned Galmoy and Anglo American's Lisheen mines, did ultimately succeed in exploiting natural resources, he recalls, creating large employment and big tax revenue. "But you know, that was really more down to the sheer determination of the promoters behind it to push the opportunity to develop our natural resources.

"With natural resources, there's also luck involved – I mean yes, you also have to have technology but chance is still a major element… it is a risky business. But go back to the mindset: when I did my Leaving Cert, we were told Ireland really had no natural resources. The mindset that 'we don't have it, so it's not really an industry that's worthwhile promoting' didn't help – and then there's the other view that if there is an opportunity, sure then they'll come anyway." But what many people failed to realise was that because of the huge capital costs involved, one still needed to go the extra mile to entice people to come in, invest and stay, O'Reilly says.

"So I think past government policies could have been a little more proactive in trying to promote Ireland as a destination to explore, especially as it was a sector where there was no certainty of success. Investing in natural resources, be it onshore or offshore, is a numbers game – you have to make the investment, you have to explore, and there'll be failures along the way, but ultimately if you stick with it as we have, you will get success in the end."

Trailblazers

O'Reilly encountered plenty of trailblazers throughout his time in an industry known for them. "Well, in the Tara Mines days, Pat Hughes at Northgate Exploration was notable. He was a true pioneer in Irish mining. I would also say that other people such as Michael Whelan from Aran Energy, Richard Conroy, and my father (who started Atlantic Resources in 1981) all played pivotal roles in the early days." When one talks about Ireland within the Irish natural resources space, Tullow always gets mentioned. "Aidan Heavey has been phenomenal in what he has done in building Tullow. Though he didn't actually have any assets here, to his real credit, he based a lot of his team here in Ireland allowing them to then go off and do things further afield."

O'Reilly again recalls his formative years, and becoming aware of the likes of Paddy McGrath, Seamus Purcell, Tony Ryan, Michael Smurfit and PV Doyle – figures he describes as "omnipresent". "It was a much smaller universe." Asked how did they interact with government, O'Reilly says that "I think there was a little more entrepreneurial spirit with the government, in a sense that as a nation, we didn't have much – everyone was really trying to figure out how they'd get investment into Ireland. So you'd have these great ambassadors flying the flag with their various business interests.

"And yes, I do think that there was more joined-up thinking between government and business, albeit excepting what I said about natural resources, which was a separate issue. The general view was: 'lads, let's get jobs to Ireland, what do we need to do?' – and all those people that I mentioned, and many more, played a role in doing that.

"I think as it went through the nineties, the work of these pioneers and indeed the IDA started to create its own momentum; then as you got into this millennium one saw the über-growth of Ireland, the property boom, all that sort of stuff – and yes, government probably became a little bit more structured by nature of there being inevitably more processes and controls – some of that entrepreneurial spirit probably went away and one probably saw more barriers being put up.

"More walls, more structures and processes and controls; the natural evolution if you will. And there was always a cynical view from certain quarters that these guys doing business were always a 'how are ya fixed, let's get something on the side' – but I don't think that that was actually ever the case with the Michael Smurfits or my father or the Tony Ryans. Inevitably there would have been some general scepticism that some industry leaders were getting sweetheart deals from the government – but on balance, I don't think that they were. They were going off blazing ahead, making things happen."

The Irish abroad

Diaspora networks, Irish America and institutions such as the Ireland Funds played important roles in the story of Irish business, he says, resulting from the waves of emigration in the 1950s and 1980s. "So many of those people who emigrated availed of the opportunities and worked their way into organisations and up the tree are now in leadership positions where they can help define future investment back into Ireland, which they all do.

"One strength of the Irish is that we are generally very good communicators – we've gone out into the world and worked ourselves into societies. Perhaps this is because we didn't have a colonial empire, so we didn't come with any baggage. So we could be pathfinders and trailblazers going out, and there wasn't that resistance to us. And there's something special about the Irish diaspora and that is that there is still that desire to come back and give back to Ireland." The diaspora element, initiatives such as Ireland INC and emigrant networks have given people business connections back to their home country, and these are followed up.

O'Reilly believes that throughout the banking crisis, economic collapse and thereafter, this strong diaspora showed a willingness to return, sort out issues, network, create opportunities and try to solve problems. Without that, the Irish experience would have been more like that of Greece or Spain.

His father's son

Needless to say, O'Reilly has been a close observer of his father's career. He followed him into business, and into natural resources: a labour of love, he agrees. "He was a businessman, he had a Rolodex that was pretty exceptional in the United States and he looked at the basic geography of Ireland and England and said, well, 'Jaysus, England can't have all the oil'. And he wasn't just referring to the North Sea: if you just go 50 kilometres across the Irish Sea to Liverpool Bay, that's an area that has produced two billion barrels of oil and gas over the last 40 years, so it's right on our doorstep.

"His view was actually based on the fact that there had already been some notable success: in the 1970s, Marathon discovered and developed the Kinsale gas field, which has supplied most of Ireland's gas for the past 30 years. He knew Ireland had natural resources, but what was needed was going out and doing more investigation – but because Ireland didn't have the capital then, you would need to bring in third-party capital.

"His model for his company was to get licences offshore, do some initial work, and then leverage in partners by working through his Rolodex – and no-one should be apologetic about that: use it; bring the companies in. Back in the eighties, he ventured with a host of companies including Getty, BP, Hess, Philips, Mobil and Gulf in drilling, and then it's really a numbers game of drilling as many wells as you can – and of course, Lady Luck needs to be there as well.

"That's the history of how we got involved in natural resources. Yes, it was a commercial enterprise in the sense that if it comes in, you can make a lot of money – but I think in my father's particular case, he also felt that if there was anything that could transform the Irish economy at the time, it was really harnessing its natural resource wealth.

"And he put a huge amount of money in: if I think about the 70-odd million he put into oil and gas, or the 70 or 80 million that he put into mining and consider what if he had put that sort of money into other businesses in the US where he was working his day job, I think that he might have had a different financial outcome. But that was his wont, his patriotism – and it's not just oil and gas, but if you look at the investments that he made over the decades in Ireland, it was clearly a labour of love, or nationalistic pride – whether it was Independent News and Media, whether it was Wellworth's supermarkets in Northern Ireland, whether it was Fitzwilton doing all the various businesses north and south, or whether it was Waterford Wedgwood capturing the US market, there was that extra bit of Irish passion involved.

"It wasn't just all business; he wanted to create Irish businesses and make them world-beaters – like Independent used to be, like Waterford Wedgwood in the millennium and, obviously, in natural resources with Atlantic Resources, ARCON and Providence" – the latter described by O'Reilly as being at a very exciting time of its development.

The search continues

A work in progress, yes, but O'Reilly is optimistic that the development of the oil and gas industry will finally reach its expectations. "If you think about it, for most of the past we have imported 100% of our oil and before Corrib came online, some 95% of our gas – so demand is not an issue... supply is, and as I said earlier, it really is a numbers game and it's all about getting more wells drilled by getting more international companies to deploy their capital in Ireland.

"Obviously, the benefit that we have today, which maybe my father and various colleagues who worked in the sector didn't have years ago, is that we now have significant technological advances. And we now have an economy that would consume anything that is discovered, because in the seventies and eighties Ireland was largely an agriculture-based economy and it didn't have the same requirements for energy. Today, we also have a far better tax structure than in the seventies or eighties – albeit at a base rate of 25% that can increase to 55%, it is still out of equilibrium with the 12.5% corporation tax paid by foreign multinationals – and yet ironically a great deal of investment being made today offshore is being done by foreign companies."

We have the right ingredients – market demand and technological advances, O'Reilly says. "It's really about getting more wells drilled, and historically this has been a problem because we still haven't had a lot of wells drilled – and that's where Providence comes in. We drilled a well in 2012, we drilled a well in 2013, and we'll be drilling again this year – but an industry average of one well per year is simply not enough. We need a lot more, and obviously any success will promote further investment. Allied to what the industry is doing, what we need to do is to ensure that we have government policies that continue to streamline regulations and make it an attractive investment area.

"Whilst the last two years have seen a significant increase in interest by the industry, I would still call for an IDA-led initiative to further facilitate and promote the development of our natural resources both onshore and offshore, as well as streamlining the planning processes, because the level of investment required for natural resources dwarfs any other investment that you would have for other sectors, and so a great deal of that capital has got to come in from overseas – and capital by its nature is opportunistic, so it will go where it believes it will get the best return. Not only are you dealing with geology, which is the big unknown, but actually the timeline to make things happen... government should try to do whatever they can; make it as easy as possible to make things happen.

"That being said, I'm a great believer that you should also let private capital work; so excepting any promotional role, and of course appropriate regulations, I don't think there should be a public-private partnership for natural resource development. Some people used to talk about national oil companies or national mining companies – I mean, if people want to take the Irish economy and basically gamble State funds, that's what they'd be doing if they were to get involved. As I said earlier, natural resources is, by its very nature, a risky business.

"So I'm not a believer in State enterprise coming in. I think the State should get their appropriate return by the successful development of oil and gas fields or mines, as well as the tax income, the jobs, and the multiplier economic effect that comes from all of that."

A changing industry

The key metric in the industry is the oil price. Industry commentators suggest that anything sub-$30 makes exploration more difficult, but O'Reilly notes that costs in the industry have fallen through the floor too. "This is a fantastically good time to be investing, and we're seeing, for example, rig rates 50% to 75% of what they were three years ago." He anticipates more consolidation in the industry.

Meanwhile, the oil and gas industry is under pressure from new industries, new people and new competitors – such as Tesla, the electric car, and hybrid fuel-efficient models being pursued by so many of the major manufacturers. Tesla's Elon Musk is the leading, charismatic figure among this zeitgeist.

"Well you know, electric cars are definitely a new element for the resource industry and I understand his driver – and I think he is truly unique in opening up, not copyrighting things, and sharing the knowledge to create a bigger and better industry," O'Reilly says of Musk.

"But, as it relates to the oil and gas industry, hydrocarbons are going to still be the mainstay: even for electric cars, you still need energy to generate the electricity for the cars. So I think oil and gas are here to stay – yes, I think there will be a lot more environmental awareness of how you can further reduce emissions and that's already happening with technology, but unless there's some truly new disruptive technology, a carbon-based energy platform is here to stay."

Past, present, future

As for the future, what does it hold for O'Reilly, Providence and the industry? "Success for us looks like a continuation of what we're doing, which is trying to drill as many basins of Ireland and get developments going and having an economic interest in a number of producing fields five to ten years from now. That's our model, while we still continue to look for more opportunities.

"Our business is 100% focused on Ireland: we've historically been in the Gulf of Mexico, in England, in Nigeria and places like this, but we've decided that our knowledge of the Irish offshore is second to none and it's an area that is still too early to tell just how big it could be – there are certainly going to be more fields to be found offshore Ireland; the real question is how quickly it is going to be done. And obviously Providence intends to be the company leading the charge."

O'Reilly cites two career highlights in his time in the resource sector. "One would be the Galmoy zinc mine: bringing that production with all the issues of planning, legal challenges, Supreme Court challenges, local planning issues, financing issues... it was five years of incredibly intense work, with really not much help from anybody, obviously besides our board and our shareholders.

"And I think the Dunquin well that was drilled in 2013 by ExxonMobil and in which Providence participated, having originally generated the prospect opportunity in 2004, was a key well for Ireland." Although that well wasn't deemed commercial, it did prove the presence of oil in the Porcupine Basin and this was a major catalyst for the international industry in looking at Ireland anew.

Ultimately, it led to the most successful licensing round in the history of the Irish State with new Porcupine Basin licences being offered in 2016 to a range of leading international companies including the likes of ExxonMobil, Statoil, CNOOC, Woodside, Cairn, Eni and BP, says O'Reilly.

And here again, Providence took a leadership role and invested more. "Our key decision was in early 2014 when we agreed to underwrite a major 3D seismic survey – most companies would have probably not had the courage to invest immediately after the Dunquin well, but our board had the foresight to say 'let's build on this new knowledge'."

Following the analysis of the acquired 3D data, including a major collaborative project with Schlumberger, Providence is now back to the drilling phase. And it is bringing others with them: indeed, March 2017 saw O'Reilly and Providence announce a significant deal with Cairn Energy, which will now take a 30% working interest in Providence's Porcupine Basin well. More recently, it just announced major deals with "super-major" Total, bringing them into the Irish offshore for the first time.

O'Reilly still views the Irish offshore as unfinished business – "but I think our activities offshore Ireland have materially changed the perception of the Irish offshore in the context that Ireland has been historically looked at as a gas-prone area, and yet we have an oil project off the south coast (Barryroe) and now clearly the Porcupine Basin is viewed in a completely different light." As O'Reilly reiterates – "it's all about investment, and happily that is now happening".

Looking back, having encountered a multitude of prominent figures throughout his life, there was no shortage of business inspiration to draw upon. Who stands out? "Obviously, besides my father, who I think is quite unique, I think that of the older generation one has to highlight Tony Ryan and Michael Smurfit." Today, though, there are so many dynamic business leaders in Ireland it is hard to single any one person out.

As both observer and participant, Tony O'Reilly Jr has a unique perspective on Irish business – past, present and future.

CHAPTER 43

Interview: Anne Heraty

In conversation with Ruraidh Conlon O'Reilly

THE CPL FOUNDER REVEALS A UNIQUE PERSPECTIVE ON RECRUITMENT, TECHNOLOGY, ENTREPRENEURSHIP AND THE LONG-RUNNING THEME OF WOMEN IN BUSINESS.

As the 1980s were drawing to a close, recruiter Anne Heraty faced a choice. She wanted to focus on one sector as a specialist rather than a generalist, and she identified the technology sector as her aim, having taken an interest at UCD.

"I felt that I wanted to build a deep knowledge of one sector – because that was the best way that I could advise both my clients and those people who were looking for jobs in terms of the best opportunities, or even the best way to advance their career," she recalls. Her boss refused. Fast-forward to the present day and CPL Resources, which she left to found, is publicly listed, has revenues of half a billion euros and has offices in nine countries.

"That was the end of 1989. I decided I was going to set up on my own, specialising in tech, and then a friend of mine said that they would back me. And that's how I got started.

"It was tough going at first, because when I set up at the end of '89 or beginning of 1990 unemployment was running at about 15.5%," she recalls. Low-value manufacturing industry was going or gone and a new wave of companies had not yet started to come in. The first two to three years were a grind. "We would have had companies like Hyster, the big multinational companies... Data Products; Moss Technologies were quite a big company at the time. Of course you'd have companies like Quinnsworth, which was a big company. Digital Equipment would have been a big client of ours before they became Compaq." Even so, FDI companies like Microsoft and Pfizer were already in place – a sign of things to come, perhaps.

"The big milestones for us were the early client wins – we had to work really hard; you really do, particularly when you set up a business in a recession. You work really hard to win your business. We focused on the kind of service we could deliver for those clients and that was the important thing. Then, as the tech sector started to grow in the early nineties that was obviously significant for us.

"We saw people coming back into Ireland. I did my degree in 1984 and a lot of my class would have left Ireland right through the mid-eighties to the end of the eighties. Then I set up at the end of the eighties coming into the nineties, and we started to see, into the early nineties when industry really started to grow here, a lot of the multinationals coming into Ireland. And then we started to see people who had left in that brain drain of the eighties coming right back. That was really positive for us. It was really great to see: people who had gone abroad, got really good experience and were now coming back home to really good jobs."

The specialist recruitment field was sparse back then, and CPL had found its niche in technology. "A lot of the companies who were our competitors then are no longer around: companies like Marlborough... there were a number of companies at that time who would have been our competitors. The industry was naturally much smaller then than it is now. The number of people employed in the country was obviously significantly less – so it was very different to how it is today.

"The industry now is much more vibrant, though I would still say that in a lot of ways the fundamentals remain the same. It's still very much about people, their potential, their skillsets and their capability, and our ability to assess that potential in particular."

Working with the FDI companies that experienced so much growth throughout the nineties was instructive, Heraty says. "Their thinking was different: it was more global, first of all. For us, in an island economy, that was important. They were very export-oriented. A lot of the time there was a big focus on learning and development, in terms of the quality and capability of their people.

"I'm not saying that Irish companies didn't have that too," she says: some Irish companies were particularly renowned for training and upskilling. "For those of us who worked with them as partners they were supportive and demanding: they expected us to be thought leaders in terms of our own particular disciplines."

Rocky waters

But niche, specialist work came with its own risks, and when the dotcom bubble burst CPL, having grown through the nineties as the specialist recruiters into the tech sector, took a substantial hit. "We went public in 1999, and at that time tech was the place to be. Then, of course, it led into Y2K, and the whole dotcom bubble. It's very interesting: in that period of time, between 2001 and 2003, say: unemployment went up but unemployment within the tech sector was significantly higher.

"It was a particularly difficult time. We had people here with phenomenal skills who were suddenly finding themselves out of work, and I think it had quite an impact on the sector for the next couple of years. It's only in the last eight to ten years that we've really started to see people go back into technical disciplines in college in the kinds of numbers that you'd expect."

In a few years there was another economic crisis: in banking, rather than technology, but this one dragged down every sector. "We took a significant hit again," Heraty says. "At that time, in terms of CPL we were a much more diversified business at that stage. We were in a number of specialist sectors – and certainly it was a significant blow, but we recovered relatively quickly: three to four years."

Recovered, and flourished. Dublin's tech and startup scene is busy and CPL's revenues grew 10% in 2016. "It's a very exciting time, I would think, in the tech sector here in Ireland at the moment," says Heraty, "both within the indigenous tech sector and also within the multinational sector. There's a phenomenal startup ecosystem and I think it's fantastic to see things like TechIreland and Startup Dublin and Startup Ireland... that whole excitement around building businesses within the tech sector.

"The other thing that really strikes me about our young Irish graduates and entrepreneurs coming through is that they're thinking global on day one now. They're not thinking about a home market here, or whatever. They're thinking about developing products for the global stage. I think it's fantastic to see that. The combination of the global companies and the local indigenous entrepreneurial startup mindset here, and the skills and capabilities, is creating something quite special."

As a recruiter, Heraty has a unique perspective on the skills and requirements demanded by companies, and supplied by candidates. "I think our education system is right up there," she argues. "I think the quality of Irish graduates is really strong. There's always things we can do better – there's no question about that.

"But I think you've only got to look at the destination of Irish graduates, both locally here and globally, and you'll see how successful we are. Take the engineering disciplines: the number of Irish-born people who have led international or global companies... In even more recent times, how well Irish people have done within some of the big global companies like Google and Facebook and Amazon and so on. I think the quality of our graduates is good and strong."

Women's representation in boardrooms and companies has been a very long-running theme within Irish business. When she started out, was Heraty aware that there were so few female entrepreneurs on the Irish business scene? "It never occurred to me. It really didn't! It wasn't something that crossed my mind at all – only when people pointed it out to me. Mind you, subsequently in the years that followed... I had grown up in a family business; my mother had been quite a driver of that business so I suppose I had a good role model early on and I just never thought it would be any different.

"Like anyone, in the early years of growing the business I was just very focused on building our own team and building our client relationships and all that – so I didn't have much time to think about much else: just focused on the business. But as the business grew and developed it's something that I became much more aware of, and indeed as I was growing my own team – the need for diversity within our own teams. That's really when it came into focus for me. I do quite a lot of work with women entrepreneurs and am very supportive, but also for women in corporate life, in terms of climbing the corporate ladder as well."

Did she encounter any sexism as she drove CPL from success to success? "No, I can't really say that I did in fact. Maybe I have been fortunate that the world was starting to change and how people think about work and how people think about their teams and all that; the diversity and so on... I think that was starting to change as I was growing the business. It was mostly a very positive reaction in terms of support from clients and right across the business environment."

The technology sector nowadays is somewhat more gender-diverse and culturally diverse in Ireland compared to the early 1990s – an interesting and positive development in Dublin and Ireland. "I do think it's still a real concern that there's not enough young females taking the STEM subjects," she cautions. "That's definitely something that we need to continue to work on.

"One of the things that I really liked about the tech sector, and one of the reasons why I wanted to specialise in tech, is that I always felt it was a real meritocracy. When we talk about the tech sector I also think that we need to broaden out our horizons around the kind of jobs that are available in tech. It's not all just about purely developers and engineers. It can be a finance person within the tech sector; sales, HR... there's a whole plethora of roles across the sector. So I think we need to broaden out our thinking around it."

Asked to name some of the standout Irish businesses of her time, Heraty mentions, for example, Kerry Group, Ryanair and Digicel. "There have been some phenomenal Irish success stories," she says. Indeed, she founded one of them.

CHAPTER 44

Interview: Donald Keough
In conversation with Ian Hyland

SHORTLY BEFORE HIS DEATH IN 2015, DON KEOUGH DISCUSSED HIS CAREER AT COCA-COLA, IRISH AMERICA, AND THE IRISH DIASPORA IN WHICH HE MADE A LEADING CONTRIBUTION.

Serving as president, chief operating officer and director of the Coca-Cola Company, Donald Keough enjoyed a remarkable career. Following his retirement from Coca-Cola in April 1993, he became chairman of the board of Allen & Company, an investment banking firm based in New York.

Throughout this extraordinary corporate success, Keough has paid tribute to his Irish heritage. His great-grandfather, Michael Keough, left Co Wexford in the 1840s to settle in the US. In recent times, Keough publicly called for Ireland to have a diaspora minister, as he believes it would transform relations between Ireland and its emigrants. "It was just a thought," he says. Diaspora as a word needs deep meaning, he believes, and in order for this to be realised, it must be viewed in Ireland as an enormously important word.

"Irish diaspora is an important part of the history, and literally, the present of Ireland," he says. The diaspora should not be a mere compilation of historical data: instead, it must be treated as something very much alive.

Linking Ireland and Notre Dame together via a football game was special, he recalls. With at least 35,000 people visiting Ireland, more Americans came to see the college football game in Ireland than went to the 2012 Olympics in London. Many of these visitors spent a week touring Ireland with cash-laden wallets, and enjoyed themselves immensely.

"The Taoiseach and the entire cabinet participated in various meetings we had. There were at least ten or 15 special meetings about culture, business, history," Keough says: it was a hugely successful event. "They used it very well to make it not just a game, but to make it an important time to be in Ireland." It also showcased the connection that Ireland brings to people who have a special place for Ireland in their lives and their own ancestral history.

Of the 77 million people who have been considered Irish diaspora, around 44 million of those are in the United States. Keough points to the fact that the first people who left Ireland did so under very unhappy circumstances. "The first generation of Irish here didn't go home. Looking back or thinking about Ireland was sad," he says.

His own family is just such an example. "My own father; he didn't go to Ireland until it was late in his life and he was always kind of afraid to think of it. When he went he was sorry it had taken so long to get there."

Now, Keough says, the Irish are everywhere: in Canada, Argentina, Australia and so on. "My point is, you have to give them reasons other than an advertisement to return home." Over the past 40 years, in Donald Keough's eyes, Irish America became much more alive – but it's crucial to keep that connection going. The advent of *Irish America* magazine brought something new for those who had a deep affinity for Ireland. "When *Irish America* magazine came out that provided a vehicle for people who had Irish in their blood to begin to have a communication device through which they could become reconnected," he says.

Coca-Cola

From his work at the Coca-Cola Company, Donald Keough came to believe that the IDA is a wonderful group. "They went out to seek business opportunities for Ireland and they came to Atlanta," he recalls, and the State agency informed Coca-Cola of the educated workforce that Ireland possessed. The IDA came to Atlanta at a perfect time. "They were willing to do anything to find land if you needed it to build facilities. They came with a set of proposals that made it hard not to take a look at," he adds.

He credits Kieran McGowan of the IDA for Coca-Cola's first investment in Drogheda. "This guy was tough to turn down," he says. Following success in Drogheda, they made a second investment in Ballina and another sizeable investment in Wexford. The Coca-Cola Company also has an office in Dublin. While the investment that Coca-Cola made in Ireland serves as an example, many more companies follow – by Keough's count, some 750 companies have made an investment in Ireland. So why Ireland? "The Irish made it easy to pick Ireland," he says.

With Irish companies prospering in North America, Keough points to Michael Smurfit as an example of such success. "Michael Smurfit did a superb job in building that great company, which is a big-functioning company in the US right now." Coca-Cola's headquarters are in Atlanta, Georgia, and the south-east of the US is a region ignored by Ireland until recently, Keough says. "You don't have to go back many years, in terms of contacting the Irish government in the US… it was really restricted to the eastern borders, to New York and Boston." A vast amount of business has been developed between Ireland and the south-east of the US; the linkage between both, Keough says, is of tremendous value.

Born in 1926, Donald Keough is proud of leading Irish businesspeople. He mentions those who have had important input into the Ireland Funds, such as Pat Fitzpatrick. Keough also looks to younger business people, such as Martin Naughton's son Fergal, who serves as a trustee of Notre Dame. Fergal Naughton brought a group of young Irish people to the US to meet with top executives in Chicago and at Notre Dame.

In his own words, one of the best things that ever happened to Donald Keough was meeting Martin Naughton. Together they established the Keough-Naughton Institute of Irish Studies in the 1990s. Hosting over 10,000 students since then, the institute offers Irish language courses to American students.

"We have students going back and forth to Ireland. They attend Trinity and UCD," Keough explains. He and Martin Naughton gave O'Connell House in Dublin to Notre Dame. "It is the centre of our business there," he adds. "They come back and their lives have been changed. They love Ireland, and for the rest of their lives they will be linking back and forth to Ireland." That, he says, keeps the diaspora alive.

Don Keough died in February 2015, heaving behind a legacy of executive achievement in corporate America – and a name that lives on in Irish-American life.

Above: Martin
Shanahan, CEO of
IDA Ireland since 2014.
Below left: Anne Heraty
established recruitment
giant CPL in 1989. Below right:
Shaun Murphy, elected
managing partner of
KPMG Ireland in
2012.

Above: Aviation pioneer Tony Ryan in 2005, two years before his death. **Below:** former UN general secretary Kofi Annan, *Business & Finance* publisher Ian Hyland and former president Mary Robinson upon her recognition with the Outstanding Contribution to Ireland Award.

Above: Julie
Sinnamon, CEO
of Enterprise Ireland.
Above right: Aidan
Heavey, founder of Tullow
Oil. **Below:** Bank of Ireland
rescuer and later US
secretary of commerce
Wilbur Ross rings the
NYSE bell in 2013.

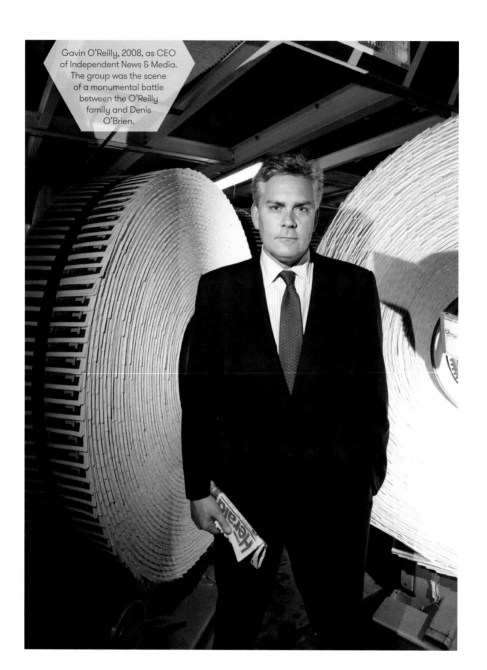

Gavin O'Reilly, 2008, as CEO of Independent News & Media. The group was the scene of a monumental battle between the O'Reilly family and Denis O'Brien.

Above: Tony O'Reilly Jr, 2006. His Providence Resources continues the search for oil and gas off Ireland's coast.
Below: Denis O'Brien ally Leslie Buckley would become chairman of INM as the O'Reilly family lost control.

Above: Liam O'Mahony steered concrete giant CRH for a decade, going on to chair Smurfit Kappa. **Left:** Simon Boucher, CEO of the Irish Management Institute. Founded in 1952, its influence has been keenly felt.

Above and right: Taoiseach Enda Kenny on an Enterprise Ireland trade mission duties to Abu Dhabi in 2014, and at the IMI conference in 2016.

Bill Clinton, honoured for his contribution to Ireland at the Business & Finance Awards in 2010.

Above: Paul Marchant, who succeeded Arthur Ryan as CEO of Primark in 2009.
Below: Minister for Finance Brian Lenihan and TK Whitaker at the 50th anniversary of the Economic and Social Research Institute, 2010.

Above: Louise Phelan of PayPal is one of the most senior Irish executives in a US multinational. **Below:** Tommy Breen's leadership of DCC turned it into a major player on the global energy market.

Right: Sean Dorgan, former CEO of the IDA and Richard Burrows as governor of the Bank of Ireland, later chairman of British American Tobacco. **Below:** Niall FitzGerald, former CEO and chairman of Unilever, is one of Ireland's most senior global executives.

Above: Banker Wilbur Ross invested in Bank of Ireland after the economic collapse and would serve in the Trump administration. **Left:** Brian Cowen, minister for finance from 2004 to 2008 and Taoiseach from 2008-2011, meets the Enterprise Ireland management team.

Above: Willie Walsh served as CEO of Aer Lingus – and returned to buy the company as head of International Airlines Group.
Right: Paul Coulson of packaging group Ardagh as the company floats on the NYSE, 2017.

Deirdre Somers, CEO of the Irish Stock Exchange since 2007. The 18th-century ISE is now a modern, global high-tech player with four main markets.

Right: Paschal Donohue, Minister for Finance. **Below left:** Siobhán Talbot of Glanbia, another major success in the global agri-food sector. **Below right:** Danny McCoy, CEO of employers' lobby IBEC.

Above: Ian Hyland, Mike Bloomberg and Denis O'Brien, 2011. **Right:** GPA alumnus Dómhnal Slattery, founder and CEO of aircraft leasing giant Avolon, has kept Ireland at the forefront of an enormous and ever-growing international leasing scene.

CHAPTER 45

Interview: John Fitzpatrick
In conversation with Ian Hyland

THE TRANSATLANTIC HOTELIER REMEMBERS HIS PIONEERING FATHER PADDY, INDUSTRY LEGEND PV DOYLE, THE HOTEL AND TOURISM INDUSTRIES, AND HIS EXPERIENCE OF IRISH AMERICA.

The phrase 'Irish-American hotelier', today, brings to mind one name: Fitzpatrick. But before opening the Fitzpatrick Manhattan hotel in the early 1990s, John Fitzpatrick had a trade to learn. His father was another icon of the industry, Paddy, and John's first memory of work in the hotel sector was in the Killiney Castle Hotel in the seventies, when the Troubles were making an impression.

"I wouldn't have known the day-to-day business yet because I was still too young, but every Friday night the car park would fill up with yellow number plates – and even then, I knew those plates were from Northern Ireland," he remembers. "They'd all come to us to get a break from it all. We became hugely popular in Northern Ireland, and that was even before the M50 – so to get to Killiney Castle from Belfast it took another hour after you got to Dublin... still, they came.

"I remember that times were tough. I was too young to know the economy; I just know that my father worked every hour he was given. I was telling someone recently that the only time we saw Dad was in the evenings between six and eight when he came home to change and he'd be gone again because we were at school. And then on Sunday. Dad spent Sunday with you, but you really spent Sunday with Dad."

Paddy worked for the legendary hotelier PV Doyle, and Sundays consisted of getting into the car and hitting the Tara Towers and the Montrose, before lunch at the Green Isle. Working for Doyle, Paddy had to check every hotel, every Sunday.

"Those are little things that flash back. We grew up in the business, as Dad's whole life was his hotels. Maybe he took Saturday afternoon off, and then Sunday morning he'd be up at Killiney Golf Club for a quick round with Seán Barrett, Frank Conroy or David Austin... that was the limit of his downtime."

That devotion, or obsession, led inevitably to America. "You see, Dad loved the States – and later on, that was why we came to be here in New York. He knew that Americans had a great amount of disposable income at that time, and a love for Ireland, so they would be a good source of business. The Irish were our base and our core, but the cream on the cake came from him going out and getting the American tour operators to bring business in to us.

"Dad was a great networker," remembers John, "and his ability to bring in American tourists helped get us through the Troubles. That type of business came in very strong from May until September: it was serious stuff." That clientele became even more important when Paddy bought the Shannon Shamrock Hotel in Co Clare in the 1970s.

Even so, it was his son who made the greatest inroads into North America, a move that required him to go at things his own way. "My dad always had a dream of opening a hotel in the States. He was always an optimist, which was important, but sometimes he went overboard. His real dream was to have a Fitzpatrick hotel in every major American city. Well if I could talk to my dad now, I'd say 'More power to you, Paddy, but trying to keep two going in one city is hard enough'. But that was his dream.

"For me, things really evolved when I finished training. I loved the States... Dad brought me on a couple of sales trips there, and then he sent me to the University of Nevada in Las Vegas.

"That's where I got the bug – I got the taste of America. After completing the programme, I went back home and worked for a year or so. Then I got itchy to go out on my own and return to the States. Truthfully, I also wanted to work for someone else besides my father, because frankly he was very tough to work for. Nothing you ever did was really good enough and that's typical between fathers and sons; you feel like you can never be good enough.

"I wanted to work for someone else and learn something new." John spent a year working in Chicago and it gave him the degree of independence he needed. He then went back home and helped to run the hotels in Ireland.

Paddy then wanted to enter the US market and secured funding from NCB, then run by Dermot Desmond. It was tough going at first, as the Fitzpatrick Hotels name could only go so far in the States.

"If you think of it, the whole of Ireland is the same size as the state of Nevada, so when we got here they did not know us and couldn't even get our name right. We were called Fitzgerald, Fitzwilliam – everything but Fitzpatrick. I remember being on sales calls and people would ask 'why I should I stay with you when we have Hilton, Sheraton and Marriott?' I came to realise that the Americans were very brand-driven, and it was a big shock to me.

"Dad's idea, and it was a good one, was: there's popular Irish bars all over New York, but there's no Irish hotels and there should be if we could capture the right spirit. We had to create a place where people felt a warm welcome. That was his model. Breaking into the branded market was the hardest thing."

How did they break in? "Grafting," John recalls. "I can remember that in the first two months we had no sales whatsoever; I was very worried. AIB were our bankers up on Park Avenue and they were getting very nervous.

"I can remember calling our sales and marketing director back in Ireland, Phil O'Regan, and asking her to help me put a plan together. We sat down, did some research together and agreed that there was enough business within ten blocks of the Fitzpatrick Manhattan Hotel to fill 100 rooms: enough business that there was no need to go to Washington or Chicago; we just had to get out there with a local focus.

"In those days before 9/11 changed security practices you could just walk into buildings, check all the companies listed on the lobby directory and make a list of companies to target. The first time we did this, we found ten companies in one building and I can remember giving the list to our general manager. He looked at me and said 'how am I going to do these calls – who's going to look after the hotel?' And I said 'there's nobody in the hotel to look after, so go out and do your calls, please.'

"We called this local networking approach 'grafting', and we've kind of kept this model to this day. Dad was very astute, and held onto some very basic sales guidelines that continue to hold true: on Monday nobody wants to see you, so set your week up carefully. On Tuesday, Wednesday and Thursday you better be out on sales calls. On Friday nobody is around, so that's when you do your research and follow-up.

"This basic approach led us to our first major account, the large law firm Skadden, Arps. This was an important milestone, and then we started winning corporate accounts that provided a solid basis for growth. It always starts with just one."

Irish America

The Irish America that John Fitzptarick entered was very different from the Irish society that he knew back home, he recalls. "Back home, people are certainly friendly, and may wish each other well, but the Irish Americans over here... really stick together, and help each other. And when I say help, I mean contacts or whatever it is. Maybe it's because we are all strangers in a strange land.

"When I first came here I can remember Niall O'Dowd walking in the front door of my hotel. I didn't know who he was, and he said 'you're welcome; anything I can do for you...' other people walked in and did the same. You just wouldn't get that in Ireland; that's what we do out here. When you come here, you have to realise that you can't do it all on your own and you do need help. It's more of a club, and they were a great help to me."

Within a few months of opening, Gregory Peck came to stay. He was put in the penthouse and all was in hand. "The day he arrived, the request comes that he wants a direct line. I let him know that we had dedicated private lines through our switchboard, but he says no, he wants his own direct line: his own line with his own number. Now what the hell am I going to do?

"My office at this stage was in room 203, which was in a hollow of my U-shaped building on the second floor. I had 15 floors between my office and the penthouse, at an average of 10 feet per floor. I went around to Radio Shack and bought all the telephone cables I could, and connected my private line to the penthouse by going to the penthouse, throwing the phoneline out of a window and connecting to the phone in my office, 15 floors below.

"I also had to ring a few friends like David O'Halloran and Tony O'Reilly Jr and tell them not to ring my number for a few days. They all asked 'why', and I had to explain that 'Gregory Peck might pick up the phone'. We had a good laugh with it – that was the Irish-American spirit of the time."

Fitzpatrick hit another milestone when he joined bidding for the contract to run British Airways' hotel in New York. He had noticed the building and enquired about what BA were doing with it. "They said 'we're making a crew hotel but the problem is it's the first crew hotel in the world, and the crews don't want to move into it because they think it's going to be a dormitory'. It was a great opportunity so I put my name as one of the management companies to tender." Asking who the other tenderers were, Fitzpatrick learned that they were Sheraton and Trusthouse Forte.

"And I remember I went home at Christmas. This was before the Good Friday Agreement, and I told my father that I had thrown my name in the ring for the BA hotel. 'That's good,' he said, but then asked: 'A British company, John?'

"'Yeah', I said, and then he asked 'Who are you up against?' And I said Trusthouse Forte. Then he said: 'So you, a Paddy, think you're going to go in and get a management contract on a hotel that is owned by British Airways and up against Trusthouse Forte? Well, good luck there', he says.

"I reminded him: 'Dad, you're always the one who says if you don't ask you never get.' Well...they went for it, and in a time of strong union power the British Airways unions were in the driving seat for final approval. The last question their union rep asked me was: 'If you get the contract, will all your staff be Irish?'

"Now as this was before the Good Friday Agreement I didn't know where he was going with that, but I replied very quickly that while not all of my staff will be Irish, most of it will – it is who we are.' He looked up at me and he said 'Well that's ok – my wife is Irish'. This is further proof that it is always good to be honest."

Expansion

Further expansion beckoned. John had strong interest in both Chicago and Washington DC, but Boston didn't appeal to him. "Why should I come 3,000 miles to open a hotel in a city that's no bigger than Dublin? That's the way I looked at it – Chicago was bigger, as was Washington, which also made many political connections available to us.

"So we picked Chicago, but as it turned out we probably couldn't have picked a worse time." It opened just before 9/11, and the industry went into immediate crisis thereafter.

"It was tough for the next few years. I wasn't sure what was going to happen, but anyway, thank god, in those days you had banks that stayed with you. I remember going to meet my banks in Dublin – Bank of Scotland and ICC – and I was worrying going into the meeting because when you're asked to have lunch with the bank up in the boardroom, it's either a very good message or a very bad message.

"We had already lost my father at that stage; he had been diagnosed with cancer and then passed following eight or nine months of struggle. So I kind of felt on my own, and I remember walking in there wondering what I was going to do. I decided to be very open and honest about our challenges.

"Well, the banks put me at ease very quickly when one of them said 'John, we appreciate your candour. We know that we are not in the hotel business. So we've all agreed that if you can't get us out of it, we know we won't be able to do it ourselves, so we're sticking with you'.

"This gave me great confidence, and I will be forever grateful to those bankers – Joe O'Reilly and Gerry Quigley of Bank of Scotland and ICC –

CHAPTER 45 - INTERVIEW: JOHN FITZPATRICK

for their support. I was worried going in that day, and the times themselves had me questioning things too.

"The Celtic Tiger was booming in Ireland and I felt that everyone there was doing so well and I was barely scraping by over here, trying to get things on track. It was a down-time, but thank god the banks stuck with me.

"Chicago came back, thank god, much quicker than I thought it would. Then New York came back and things started booming. Later, a huge offer for Chicago came from out of the blue. I really wasn't looking to sell. I mean, when things were tough at one stage I was looking at converting them into apartments, but things came back and the hotel was making money. I only had one director on the board, Brendan Gilmore – a great guy. I remember getting a phonecall from Brendan. My family were 50% owners at that stage, and he said 'I heard you got an offer. Wouldn't it have been nice to let your director know that you got an offer?'

"I probably had a cheeky answer for him, and also said that I wasn't selling so there was no point ringing. He said 'Can I ask you a question?' And I said 'What, Brendan?' He said: 'I just want to say you're now a 50% owner of three hotels'. I am, yeah, because the family own 50%. 'And if you get another one, you'll still only be 50% owner.'

"So he asked: 'What if you were to sell Chicago and become 100% owner of two hotels?'

It was the best advice I ever got, and I acted on it. When I sold Chicago I came back to New York, bought the family out and was then able to freely steer my course. So it was a rough five years after 9/11 but then it turned out very well."

The Irish tourism experience

Needless to say, Fitzpatrick has a distinctive outlook on tourism to Ireland. He remembers Deutsche Bank bringing golfers over in the middle of the Celtic Tiger. "A guy said to me: 'I'm bringing four guys over and its costing me €1,500 a day to play golf. John, it's not Monte Carlo, it's not Saint Tropez, it's Ireland.

"For a little while, we lost clear sight of ourselves. I think we got it back over the last few years though. Because of the bad economy you were seeing those five-star hotels and beautiful golf courses at half nothing. That's where Tourism Ireland did a good job of using that opportunity to get people back." Before the crash Irish tourism had overpriced and lost the run of itself. Now it's back where it should be.

Ireland remains a great experience, despite Irish complaints about the weather, he says. "When we ask most Americans about their visits to Ireland, the first thing we usually ask about is weather. They tend to take no notice – they are not there for the weather, they are there for the experience.

"I think Ireland is more welcoming now. I think in those days it was hard to get good people to work in hotels during the Celtic Tiger. They were above it, and it was very hard to get the right staff. Now people realise normalcy is back. And you have to look at the bright side of what had become a bad situation: because a lot of money was spent during the Celtic Tiger, there's some great hotels there that offer great value. It helps bring people in."

Travel and global experience were obviously important to the hotelier as a young man. "If I didn't travel when I was younger, I wouldn't have gotten the experience I did," he recalls. "Maybe I wouldn't have had the courage to come out here in the 1990s: if I hadn't spent time in the States training, it might have been too intimidating or even unfamiliar to me.

"Every year we bring graduates over from the Irish colleges with hospitality programmes every year... in our industry, it's the greatest way to get experience. They come out here so excited to have the opportunity to work in the States. They get a visa through us that lets them work for a year. We often try to bring the very best back.

"One thing I am sure of is that the secret to a good hotel is to have a good team in place. When I get compliments about the hotel from people who say they love the hotel, they almost always mention 'your employees are great' – that's the key. And that commitment to good service has to start with me.

"I have to walk the walk, as the Americans say. It goes back to what my father always said: "No matter what hotel you have, or how big you get, don't forget you're an innkeeper. You've got to remember that. People want that.'"

A global Irish perspective is important, Fitzpatrick says, "because over here the Irish get so much attention for such a small country... Just look: every week of St Patrick's Day each March, we go down to the White House in Washington. Every year, the US president meets the Irish delegation, and the next day the vice president holds a breakfast for the Taoiseach. We've earned so much respect out here, and I think it's very, very important."

Plans and schemes

As for Fitzpatrick Hotels, is further expansion on the cards? "Of course I'd like to expand. However, things have changed in the business world especially with how banks lend, so we'd have to be very careful. It would have to be a great deal. I know the risks I took 30 years ago... and I don't know if you could take them now.

"So what I'm saying is that while I want to expand, we're all being restricted a bit more than we used to. Banks won't lend as much. And we're being careful. We've considered things in Ireland, too. Ireland is a great place to invest. Hotel rates in Dublin are often higher than those in New York at this point – the city can use a few more hotels, so you never know."

Fitzpatrick's focus in recent years has changed to encompass some other things that are very important to him besides his hotel group. He chaired the Hotel Association of New York City for eight years before serving a term as chairman of the American Hotel and Lodging Association. He remains on the boards of both organisations today.

Philanthropy has become an important part of his life. He started the Eithne and Paddy Fitzpatrick Memorial Foundation to support worthy causes in memory of his late parents. As he notes, "when I was in Ireland you never thought about getting involved in the world, you didn't know what philanthropy was, you always thought it was for people who had millions and they just had to find a way of giving away money.

"Well, here in the States philanthropy is not just for ones who have a lot of money. Philanthropy is part of the American value system; it's like it is part of your genetic profile here, and that's a great thing about this culture."

When it came time for his foundation to select worthy causes to support, Fitzpatrick turned to the Ireland Funds for direction. This was the beginning of what became an incredibly important affiliation to John Fitzpatrick.

After working with the Ireland Funds for a few years, Fitzpatrick became an active member. A short time later he joined their board. At the time of writing he is in his second term as chairman.

"I know that Sir Tony O'Reilly and the late Dan Rooney set the fund up to help improves things in all of Ireland, especially up North.... we have been so proud to support causes like Integrated Education, the Corrymeela Communities, the US's Music Generation, Barretstown Children's Camp, and several great initiatives tied to the peace process in Northern Ireland." In America the presumption is that the peace process is completed, but Fitzpatrick and those clued in know otherwise. "There is still so much to be done there," he says.

Asked about the stand-out Irish business leaders over the years, Fitzpatrick thinks back. "In the early days we'd always hear our parents talk about Dr Smurfit or Tony O'Reilly, and we learned so much from watching how they did things. Today, I admire the way the likes of Denis O'Brien does things. He runs his company well, and he features philanthropy prominently as part of his corporate culture. Michael O'Leary also stands out to me."

As for a career highlight, that's a question to ponder. "I think I've had some highlights, and some lowlights as well, but I think where I really came into my own in terms of both my career and myself was when I moved to the States. I became independent in every sense by being here.

"I love my family dearly, but working in a family business can present some unique challenges, and I find that our family has gotten on better since we all went out on our own; we're a closer family now being separated than we were together.

"On top of that, I've been able to grow a business my way and experience some incredible things, like my deep involvement with the Ireland Funds. None of this would have happened had I stayed home in Ireland."

John Fitzpatrick is only the second generation of an Irish hotel dynasty, but he has carved out a distinctive journey to the peak of his industry – becoming a leading voice of Irish-American business in the process.

PART

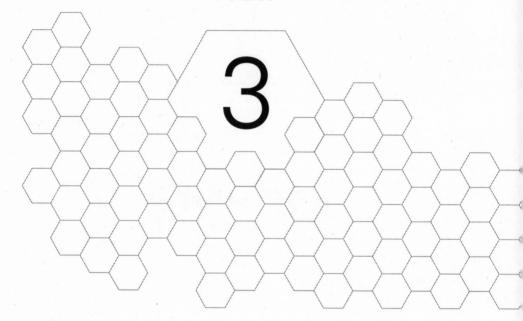

3

ARCHIVES

CHAPTER 46

Interview: Tony Ryan
By Gabi Thesing

TONY RYAN FOUNDED TWO COMPANIES IN IRELAND THAT BECAME WORLD-CLASS PLAYERS. THROUGH HIS ACADEMY AND ROSTER OF TALENT, HE HAS BUILT A PROFOUND LEGACY. FROM BUSINESS & FINANCE, OCTOBER 20TH 2005.

There is a smell of fried fish wafting through the house. Somehow it is not what you would expect when being shown around a stately home owned by one of Ireland's wealthiest men.

While you may not expect it, it is strangely comforting. In a country where people tend to refer to their abode as mere "property", Tony Ryan's Lyons Demesne is a home.

Just outside Newcastle in Co Kildare at the bottom of the Hill of Lyons, the mansion was in a state of near-ruin when Ryan bought it in 1996. He has done a fine job restoring it to its original splendour – it is warm and inviting. There are fresh flowers everywhere and Kenneth Turner-scented candles keep it fragrant.

Family photographs and lots of fluffy toys show there is new life in the old structure dating from 1797. Those working with Ryan on the estate say his grandchildren are frequent visitors.

Tony Ryan is something of an enigma. Intensely private, he has shaped modern corporate Ireland like no other entrepreneur. With aircraft leasing company Guinness Peat Aviation (GPA) he was the first in Ireland to scale the dizzy heights of founding and running a world-class company from these shores. When the company's flotation was pulled in

1992, it was the closest corporate Ireland had come to meltdown. What was supposed to be a bigger IPO than Smurfit's – then the benchmark for all of Ireland Inc's corporate activity – didn't come off. It shook many to the core and the repercussions resonated for years after.

It came up again five years later when former Ryan protégé Denis O'Brien first started talking about floating his then loss-making telecoms venture Esat Telecom. Journalists were asking if this was heading for a GPA-like disaster. Incidentally, it wasn't and, as history has shown, the float made O'Brien and many who worked with him very wealthy.

By the same token, GPA did come out well the other end and so did Tony Ryan. As founder of Europe's most successful airline, Ryanair (which also bears his name), in business he more than rehabilitated himself from the perceived failure of the GPA float. In his office, a model aircraft of his latest venture, Singapore-based low-fares carrier Tiger Airways, shows he is more than prepared to do it all again.

Tony Ryan's lasting legacy, though, is the breadth of entrepreneurial managers now running many of Ireland's most successful companies. Denis O'Brien calls him the "Vincent O'Brien of picking managers".

"He could pick talent the same way Vincent O'Brien would pick successful racehorses. He instilled a sense of urgency into their business dealings and kept telling them that 'doesn't matter that we are an Irish company'," he recalls.

Ryan may not believe that the State has any business running airlines, airports and trains, yet a considerable number of his former GPA lieutenants now sit on the boards of the three airport authorities and Aer Lingus.

Former GPA CEO Patrick Blaney and general counsel Rose Hynes have been appointed to the Shannon Airport Authority. Colm Barrington, who used to head up GPA Capital, has been appointed to the Dublin Airport Authority. John Sharman developed financing resources for the expanding GPA in the early 1980s, and helped steer Aer Lingus through its most recent crisis as chairman of the State carrier.

His former personal assistant, Michael O'Leary, is Europe's best-known airline chief, while O'Leary's predecessor, Denis O'Brien, is the multimillionaire owner of telecoms and broadcasting assets worldwide. Furthermore, Ireland now ranks as one of the top two or three world centres for aviation leasing. It is estimated that between Dublin and Shannon there are over 20 Irish and multinational companies working in this highly specialised field of asset management. Many of these were founded or are led by former GPA executives.

Track record

This is not a bad track record for a man whose first job after school was at the sugar factory in Thurles, determining the grades of sweetness in the beet. He grew up in south Tipperary during the 1930s and 1940s and despite the economic bleakness in Ireland at the time, he says his upbringing was not of the *Angela's Ashes* ilk.

"I don't have any angry stories like that," he says. Emigration was the order of the day, but not something that Ryan says he was overly conscious of. "One-third of my class became priests so emigration wasn't on their mind."

In 1954 he joined Aer Lingus at Shannon Airport. The State carrier was small and only serviced continental European routes. Transatlantic services had been suspended during the war and had not been reinstated at that stage. In 1966 he went to New York as assistant station manager at the airport and then moved on to Chicago. He remembers his time with Aer Lingus in the US as very dynamic.

In 1972, though, he went back to base at Aer Lingus in Dublin. "I had a good job, but I came back to a civil service structure at Aer Lingus. It was a big monopoly and seen as one of the jewels in the Irish semi-state sector. It was profitable, but not profitable every year."

This was still a decade away from the establishment of lower fares and Ryanair. Did he then have a sense that the Aer Lingus monopoly could be broken? "No, but there was a lot of frustration on the part of the passengers, because flying was very expensive and the ferries were still transporting the bulk of people to and from the island."

Ryan says he has good memories of Aer Lingus. However, he says it is time that the government got out of Aer Lingus, privatised it and didn't retain a stake in the airline. He does not believe that Aer Lingus as a State airline is of strategic importance. "If there is a market where people want to fly, there will be airlines flying in and out of Ireland."

He is not interested in buying Aer Lingus because he says it is not profitable enough. Furthermore, Ryan expects Aer Lingus to be bought by a larger carrier, as it is too small to go it alone in the midst of anticipated consolidation among Europe's state carriers.

At the time of Ryan's return to Aer Lingus in the early 1970s, state carriers were the only game in town. They owned their aircraft, they were designed to their own specifications and when they weren't needed they were grounded, clocking up handsome depreciation charges while not earning any money.

Aer Lingus had just ordered two Boeing 747s in anticipation of a burgeoning tourist market but the Troubles in the North put a kibosh on those calculations.

Ryan was head of aircraft leasing at Aer Lingus, 'wet leased' the aircraft to Air Siam, and spent two years in Thailand with the aircraft and the crew. "At that time, airlines didn't loan each other aircraft and while the concept of the wet lease may not have been radical, it was certainly unusual."

Prior to departing for Thailand, Ryan had approached Aer Lingus with the concept of an aircraft leasing company as a standalone business. Aer Lingus investment bankers Guinness and Mahon turned down the proposal. Back in Ireland in 1975, Ryan again approached Aer Lingus with a proposal to set up GPA and the airline's dynamic new chief executive didn't need much persuasion. "He saw an opportunity," Ryan says.

At the time, Aer Lingus had an 8% stake in London merchant bank Guinness Peat Group, which also came on board. Aer Lingus and Guinness Peat took a 45% stake each in the newly formed Guinness Peat Aviation.

Ryan put in £5,000 for his 10% stake and, with just £50,000 in capital, established his aircraft broking business in Shannon because of its 0% tax base.

In the first year GPA had profits of £138. In the space of 15 years it became the most valuable Irish company ever. At its peak it was capitalised at close to $4bn and in 1991, Ryan's last year as chief executive, GPA recorded profits of $260m.

At the time, GPA was seen as the best company in Ireland to work for and Ryan had his pick of the brightest. He worked them hard and gave them huge responsibility at a young age.

"You had a lot of people in their 20s doing major aircraft transactions; you would have never got that experience elsewhere, ever. You developed a strong entrepreneurial spirit and work ethic. Also people got paid well.

"People got to see you work hard and you got rewarded," remembers Tom McAleese, managing director of Barclays Bank Ireland, also a former GPA executive.

Ryan is much more sanguine about the perceived "youth" of his troupe. "Napoleon's generals were 19, Onassis had his first ship when he was 21. Young people can hack it.

"We were very fortunate that we benefited from Ireland's educational build-up in the sixties. It is something that personally I am very conscious of. These guys were well-educated, hungry to work and hungry to stay on in Ireland."

High-flying GPA came crashing down in 1992 after an aborted stock market flotation, triggered by US institutions' lack of interest in the issue. The company went into a tailspin on the back of $4bn in debt and $17bn worth of aircraft under order or optioned. Eventually GE Capital came to the rescue and the business was restructured. The renamed AerFi, which was profitable again, was sold in 2000 to the aircraft financing arm of the DaimlerChrysler Group for $750m.

Cleared for take-off

By the time GPA went down, Ryan's other major project gained altitude. Ryanair flew its first route between Waterford and London Gatwick with a 15-seater Bandeirante aircraft in July 1985. It took a few years and approximately £25m investment by Ryan to keep the airline afloat.

It is now Europe's largest low-fares airline, carrying 35 million passengers, operating from 15 bases in Europe and servicing 266 routes to 21 countries. Last year the airline recorded pre-tax profits of €269m on revenues of €1.37bn.

Ryanair chief Michael O'Leary worked as Ryan's personal assistant in the late 1980s and on more than one occasion told Ryan to close the loss-making airline.

69-year-old Ryan has done well financially out of the airline and, over the years, reduced his shareholding to approximately 0.75%.

The family, through its investment vehicle Irlandia Investments, is now backing Shanghai-based Tiger Airways, which tries to replicate the low-fares model in the Far East. The airline has been in operation for a year and flies to ten cities in six countries. The airline has just purchased eight new Airbus aircraft and will take delivery of them between March 2006 and summer 2007, bringing the fleet to 12.

He shows very little sign of slowing down and divides his time between Lyons Demesne, the US, London and Monte Carlo. He was once described as being happiest when he steps on or off a plane. He has four stud farms in Ireland and Kentucky and is currently in the process of restoring an old village on the Lyons Demesne estate.

Another project finally coming to fruition is the TA Ryan Academy for Entrepreneurship, located at Citywest and developed by Dublin City University. The academy will be officially opened by Taoiseach Bertie Ahern in the coming weeks.

"For a long time I was of the view that you couldn't teach entrepreneurship. I would have been convinced that if you wanted to make an entrepreneur you'd go to a certain part of Dublin, get a man who was selling cabbages and buy him a van," Ryan says.

"However, I spent some time at MIT (Massachusetts Institute of Technology), which convinced me that you may not be able to make entrepreneurs but that you could create a week-long boot-camp style course where people would learn to network, and be introduced to role models and international banks. It was actually my sons' idea to establish the academy."

The Ryan family will have invested close to €4m in the project. The academy's plaque will read 'Better to wear away than rust away', which Ryan says was his father's motto.

It appears that Ryan has taken it to heart as well.

CHAPTER 47

Interview: Sir Anthony O'Reilly
By Constantin Gurdgiev

FOLLOWING THE SALE OF EIRCOM, SIR ANTHONY O'REILLY STEPPED DOWN
AS CHAIRMAN IN AUGUST 2006 AND DISCUSSED A WIDE RANGE OF TOPICS IN
BUSINESS & FINANCE, SEPTEMBER 7TH AND 21ST 2006.

CONSTANTIN GURDGIEV (CG): Sir Anthony, your legacy here in Ireland will inevitably be associated with your chairmanship of Eircom. Following the sale of Eircom to Babcock and Brown (B&B), and the delisting of Eircom, the overall record of the company in opening markets and unrolling broadband came under renewed scrutiny. In your view, was Eircom's privatisation a long-term success story for shareholders, the exchequer and customers?

SIR ANTHONY O'REILLY (TOR): From the point of view of the shareholders and consumers, the privatisation of Eircom, in the end, was a success. In Ireland, telephone bills today are substantially below the levels seen prior to privatisation. We have access to quality service on a far greater scale than before. Competition has been good for the telecommunications industry. I think it is indisputable and from that point of view you can say that the Eircom [privatisation] has been a success.

Look at any other service, or range of goods available in Ireland. Since the 1990s, all of these increased hugely in cost. Probably the only two cases of clear reductions in the cost of services along with improvement of quality are in telecommunications and airlines. These are the only two sectors and the credit there goes to Ryanair and Eircom.

CG: In fact broadband appears to be the magic word for anyone looking at criticising Eircom during the whole post-privatisation period. It is the area where Eircom is being increasingly pressured by the Government and ComReg.

TOR: I can ask you in return – in your own experience is there a single country where the telecom company is popular? Were AT&T or BT or Ma Bell ever popular? Whenever anyone wants to bitch about something, it's the telephone company that first comes to mind. Telecom Éireann – with all its posts and wires – was fairly unpopular. When your line went down or you couldn't get a phone connection or you had a bad call, you blamed the company. Telecoms were always beat-me-up boys everywhere, not just in Ireland.

CG: On the other hand, Eircom was oversold by the government, wasn't it?

TOR: The primary beneficiary of the privatisation of Eircom was in fact the State – it got £8bn which, with some serendipity, the government put into a pension fund. At least a large share of it. So not all of it was lost to the Irish people, although admittedly a very specific group of Irish people. But given the whole environment of, first, the dotcom revolution, then its collapse – Eircom was bound to run into disfavour. I mean, here is the most over-marketed stock in the history of this country, starting with the fact that the public do not particularly like telephone companies in any event and then the stock falls. What do you expect? Do you remember that famous AGM when some 2,000 people showed up at the RDS? It went on for eight hours. From that unpromising start Eircom decided to sell its mobile unit, which it did rather well.

When you compare with the condition they were in and if you look at Vodafone today – it was a terrific deal. The board of Ray MacSharry rescued what was a very unpromising situation: an unpopular and over-marketed telephone company. They got 220p per share at the time, some £4bn. If you actually had shares of Vodafone on that day, you would have got something around the same valuation.

Today, with all that Vodafone achieved around the world, the enormous deal with Mannesmann, expansion in Japan, the globalisation of Vodafone, the shares are worth only 113p... So Eircom was left with the fixed-line business and that business is declining everywhere around the world. The real question then is at what rate is it going down? In point of fact, in Ireland the number of new connections is not declining.

The mobile market went up dramatically since the late 1990s, but Irish fixed-line business remains pretty much the same today because our population has gone up dramatically. This performance stands in contrast with, say, France or Germany where the fixed-line business has fallen some 5% per year over the last six years.

CG: Following the sale of the mobile division, Eircom had an auction between E-Island and Valentia. It was one of the most fiercely contested auctions in the history of this country.

TOR: Yes, starting off at 110 – E-Island's original offer. The price finally got to 137.5 but was defeated. In fact, *Business & Finance* broke the story. Certainly the market thought that we in Valentia paid too much for the company.

CG: After the auction, HSBC stated: "It is hard to imagine that Valentia is not overpaying for Eircom. It remains to be seen if O'Reilly's bid represents a misplaced nationalism or the over-heated bidding process." So, in August 2001, the public image of the company remained less than favourable. Do you think that there is a part of our psyche that still views Eircom as some sort of a State or public asset, rather than just a company?

TOR: Well, now, turning to that misplaced nationalism... I think this is a good quote to start the whole story of the Eircom privatisation. You are right about the public perception of Eircom. In fact, in the public view, Eircom has "a responsibility to the common people of Ireland to deliver to them that which is most desired". And today this, of course, is broadband – instant broadband. With on-demand video. You name it and it is their responsibility to deliver it.

There's an attitude in Ireland which I would describe as an entitlement attitude. Remember – we were quite a socialised society in the past. We felt that the government owed us telephone services, proper water, roads. When we talked about economic issues we talked about the government and it was an entirely different Ireland from what we have today. That is changing and today we have a society where everyone fundamentally now understands that goods and services have to be paid for by the consumer.

Broadband vs narrowband

CG: And yet this spirit of self-reliance does not exactly hold when it comes to things like broadband. In broadband, the government tries to fundamentally alter the way the private sector operates by setting centrally planned targets for coverage and quality. These are based on what one may call artificial spatial development objectives, whereby the State sees certain services, such as telecommunications and broadband, as a necessity to be delivered to every home. This now forms an effective State-set benchmark for Eircom. But what does this mean for the future of the company?

TOR: Broadband is the issue which is not fully understood. First of all, very few people can define what broadband really is and subsequently what Eircom is supposed to deliver. I can go to the Dáil and ask all of the TDs what they mean by the term broadband and what is the cost that you would expect to pay for it. There will be no single answer. There are huge questions that remain unanswered and we had no proper discussion as to what it is that the State expects us to deliver and at what speed and cost. There is this wonderful myth that goes something like this: "The people of Ireland will not achieve the optimal rates of economic growth if they do not have broadband."

Now, the people of Northern Ireland do have broadband with almost 100% coverage and they have almost no capital investment going into their economy, while we have one of the highest rates of capital inflows in the world. So allegedly having limited broadband we still have dramatic capital investment but are now being told that if we don't achieve 100% coverage of broadband services we will not achieve optimal economic growth. There has to be something wrong with this proposition.

In reality, what happened in Ireland is that we put in place a flat-rate narrow-band dial-up service that supplies access to the internet at the cheapest price possible – €9.99 per month, less than half, I repeat, less than half of the average European price. This allows you access to your e-mails and allows you buy airline tickets etc. Tens of thousands of households in Ireland are happy to subscribe to it. It was a brilliant move by Dermot Ahern [minister for communications, marine and natural resources at the time]. It was based on fixed-line connections and Eircom was required to provide this.

This made broadband marginally less attractive to many households that required access to the internet for the services I have described above. So giving a consumer an elective choice – broadband or narrow-band – many consumers opted for the cheapest service. We now have 400,000 customers using narrowband access for as little as a few euro per month. Compare this with broadband that will cost you €30 per month.

So many consumers made this choice and Eircom has roughly 75% of this market. But we also have an excellent broadband product at excellent speeds and it appears to be growing at a rate of 100,000 new users every six to eight months."

CG: But there is more to the story of broadband versus narrowband in Ireland. In fact, the cable delivery is a good example of how we can get policy wrong despite setting broadband targets.

TOR: Going back in history, Independent News and Media was a part-owner of the American cable provider Chorus. In the US, cable provides 40% of broadband. In Ireland until recently, cable supplied next to zero primarily because the regulator decided to make no price increases available to Chorus or NTL for a period of four years for the basic TV service. As a result, we got out of the market for broadband by cable.

NTL will probably never be a major broadband provider in this country and the regulator, in this case, killed off a potential source of broadband competition. Of course, the advantage of cable delivery is that it can supply all three services simultaneously – telephony, broadband and TV. With Eircom the story is similar – Eircom went for the very sophisticated broadband solutions around 2000 and what they needed to justify that was a broadcasting licence to allow delivery of a triple play of telephony, broadband and TV at the same time.

The government did not make a broadcasting licence available – so the government effectively said no to competition with cable providers. This meant that the very sophisticated equipment in which Eircom invested was left idle. So technology is there but it is not being used.

The incredible situation is that the original Eircom tried to get into the game of delivering comprehensive broadband and then a combination of the flat-rate narrow-band services and lack of competition in the cable business meant that the new Eircom had to reduce its ambitions. Now this became an issue even though today we have better coverage of broadband than you'll find in the USA, equal to the European average and at a growth rate higher than the European average. With this momentum, the reality is that broadband coverage will not be an issue in two to three years.

Consumer choice or sacred cows

CG: You've touched upon a couple of interesting issues rarely discussed in the media. First is the role of consumer choice in setting demand for services such as broadband. The second is whether we really need 100% broadband coverage in this country. Why are our policymakers appearing to be unwilling to simply recognise the reality of the markets? We have competition, we have technological solutions that are not dependent on Eircom, so if there is real demand for broadband, someone surely will come in and offer the supply of this service? Does this point to our policymakers continuing to view some projects as some sort of a sacred cow that must be protected at any cost?

TOR: Absolutely. When it comes to certain projects, broadband being one, "we must have this" seems to be the response from the policy circles. These are the infamous objectives of the State. Go back and look at the original ones: the re-unification of Ireland, restoration of the Irish language and the draining of the Shannon – all three were never achieved. Happily, broadband in all its variety has achieved its objective and, as I have said, will not be an issue in two to three years' time.

CG: There is a theory with some practical implications that when a capital-intensive business like a telecom faces potentially heavy regulation, one strategy to protect the company from regulatory overreach is to convert shareholders' equity into debt liabilities. This allows companies to plead high costs of regulation and effectively reduce regulatory burden. Some analysts suggest that recent takeover activities in the global telecoms business are driven by similar considerations. In the case of Eircom, delisting following the B&B purchase was done on a heavily leveraged basis – is this simply coincident with the global trend or is this an opportunity recognised and capitalised on by B&B?

TOR: I cannot really answer this for B&B but they certainly have substantial debt on their hands – around $4bn (€3.1bn). On the other hand, they got a very good company to work with. They got an excellent mobile division with Meteor – the Ryanair of mobile telecommunications. It's the area where Vodafone and O2 don't particularly want to go and Meteor will be, in my view, a great success story in the next few years.

Second, Eircom has now established a critical mass in broadband. Whether we both are right in the sense of being sceptical about the real profitability of the broadband market, Eircom remains supremely competitive in it.

An individualistic island

CG: You've mentioned ComReg. Some would say that so far, ComReg has been mostly a conduit for EU regulation implementation in Ireland rather than an original player in the marketplace. What is your feeling about this spread of Brussels' remit over local regulation?

TOR: There are very few regulators who would go 100% against what Brussels wants. There is a degree of flexibility in the overall remit from Brussels that can be interpreted at the regional level by individual regulators, but I think all of them are moving in the same direction, and I think ComReg latterly has done a good job for the industry and the consumer against this criterion.

Fundamentally, the word that dominated Irish political thinking for many years has been sovereignty – the abstract idea that ruled our State for some 70 years. But what does it mean?

In relation to Brussels we substantially reduced our sovereignty to act uni-laterally. That has been the price that we've paid, so that now 70% of all laws and regulations are not being set by the Dáil, they are made by Europe. When we joined Europe, I don't think we fully understood what this menu really contained, nor do we fully understand it today. But because our joining of the EU was lubricated by substantial transfers of assets and money, we are prepared to accept it almost categorically.

There is certainly a case for questioning this – and I am sure in time there will be a party in Ireland that will do so. There is a view that the European Union was launched on the basis of a number of ideas, among them that it will be able to control economic activity and that French farmers, for example, would never be exposed to world competition.

The CAP was set up basically to favour French farmers' interests and it will continue to be shaped along these lines. All international trade movements, the World Trade Organisation (WTO) and the rest of the market reforms will collide with the rock of the agricultural subsidies in Europe. Globalisation will affect everything that is industrial, but it will not change agriculture substantially.

CG: There is a third dimension of trade – trade in services – that also crashed at the walls of Europe. The initial rejection of the Services Directive and subsequent watering down of its provisions – this was also driven by France.

TOR: Well, the French are very clever, very centralist. They will always look after their own interest. I always believed that Europe will be run in the German image, but it will be Franco-centric in its policies – de Gaulle's famous 'Europe Des Patrie'. This is fair – we know who we are playing against and what the rules of the game are, and our civil servants in Dublin and Brussels are very astute, but Brussels is not a collection of jolly people sitting around the table and thinking 'how can we integrate with the world economically?' It is a collection of jolly people sitting around the table and thinking 'how can we protect France' or 'how can we improve Germany?'

Yet I still think that despite these problems, there are many areas where the main thrust of Brussels is positive. And we are the beneficiaries of it in Ireland.

Flight path for Aer Lingus

CG: You spoke earlier about capital mobility and the threats this presents if we were to fail to assure fair return on imported capital. Are you optimistic about the possibility for the successful sale of Aer Lingus, given the conditions of partial privatisation – the share retained by the unions and the State?

TOR: The Employee Share Ownership Trust played a pivotal – and under the leadership of Con Scanlon a very constructive – part in the Eircom story, and the Esot will play a very important part in the attractiveness of Aer Lingus going to market. I am conscious that there are enormously important intrusions by some governments in the process of private ownership of companies. Take South Africa, where the government now demands that 25% of all companies must be owned by black investors or employees. While socially laudable, this does have an effect on foreign investment there.

In the case of Aer Lingus, people will look at the prospectus and they will ask themselves what rate of return on capital can they get over the next 10 years by investing in an Irish airline and what kind of risks do these returns contain.

Ryanair probably will give them a sense of encouragement because it was able to do something that no-one else could in Irish private capitalism, and they have done a remarkable job and I think Michael O'Leary is a remarkable leader. So I feel that people will look at Aer Lingus from a pure return-on-capital point of view, risk-adjusted for the share ownership structure and for the growth prospects of the airline.

The unions are not the key to everything. When you look at foreign investment in Ireland, multinational companies sidelined the issue of the unions and built on this.

In the case of Eircom, the injection of money into Esot did help us to reduce the size of the workforce from around 10,700 to some 7,000 employees.

We paid a big price for this, but I believe that this is yet another form of risk that one has to deal with.

International capital lessons

CG: Going back to the Eircom story – after the IPO you stayed on as chairman, even though you were neither a majority shareholder nor were you earning an exceptional salary from this. If investing in State-owned enterprises is all about return on the capital, why did you choose to make such a decision?

TOR: I felt a strong sense of responsibility to the new board of directors and the incoming shareholders. I had made money out of Eircom through my investment in the Valentia consortium and there was, at the time, talk about venture capitalists coming in, making money and getting out, with the accusation that they somehow left an underfunded and a weakened company behind.

This was not so – just look at the subsequent stock performance relative to the broader telecom markets. I think it was very important that there was an orderly return of Eircom to the market and it was equally important that as chairman I should act as an entirely impartial party.

At Valentia the challenge was allocating resources, and all of the partners – Providence Capital, George Soros and Goldman Sachs – brought precise discipline to the whole process of capital allocation and cost management. And I think we proved our point – we satisfied the demands of the shareholders, built a leaner and more efficient company and refloated it, and the people who bought it from us recently sold on to Babcock and Brown and made 62% in 18 months. And as I said two weeks ago, only airlines – Ryanair and I might add Aer Lingus – have reduced their prices over the last seven years. Everything else – gas, electricity, road tolls, food, et cetera – has gone up in price during that period.

So it was not the case of venture capitalists deciding to take everything out of the company and squeeze the assets.

It has been a really successful process for both consumers and the investors. But most importantly, it's been a progressive process for the watching international financial community who now have that little bit more confidence in investing in Irish assets than they had some years ago.

Competitive advantage

CG: In your view, then, Eircom is part of the story of the important drivers of Irish growth – privatisations, development of the markets, inflow of capital and improvements in the way global financial markets view Ireland. Taxation is yet another factor. After years of success, with other countries – most significantly those of eastern Europe – moving fast into our space, do we still hold a competitive edge?

TOR: I think our competitive advantage is seriously threatened today and I feel that Ireland must be made aware that the current prosperity can obscure for us the fact that everyone in the new Europe has woken up to the anatomy of the Irish miracle.

These new countries set out to replicate our success and they know full well that it was largely founded on the basis of low taxes. I am trying to articulate the need for reproducing the low-tax regime found in the Republic of Ireland and bringing it to Northern Ireland. I recently met Gordon Brown to advance this argument and said that the introduction of a standard rate of tax across the island at 12.5% would make investment on this island location-indifferent.

In fact every party in Northern Ireland agrees on this point – a low-tax regime in Northern Ireland can bring about a huge spurt of economic activity. So the answer is that it is going to get tougher and tougher for Ireland because new European countries are going to strive for lower tax rates than us.

Again, if you can make a product, say Dell computers, and you are indifferent in your business to things like the language spoken by the workers, then look at Estonia – it gives you productive young workers at no tax at all. There will be pressure on the companies operating in Ireland today to go east. But an additional problem is that with the rising cost of doing business here and shortages of labour, we are actually losing our competitiveness vis-à-vis the old European states.

Models for growth?

CG: There is a penchant in Ireland to compare ourselves to the two main models – the Nordic and the US. Yet another model that is almost never mentioned in Ireland is that of Hong Kong. Like Ireland it is a small, open economy adjoining a giant one. From your point of view, would you rather see Ireland moving closer to Hong Kong or to Stockholm?

TOR: I think if you visit Hong Kong you must be excited by how energetic the place really is. You cannot but notice also how just beyond the perimeter, there is that great country called China. There is a pulsating appetite from the mainland for everything produced in Hong Kong. On the other hand there are many social problems, such as uncontrolled immigration and the fact that it is a somewhat artificial world, along the lines of Malaysia and Singapore. I don't think that these are viable models for us – they lack the same sense of individualism that we have, they are more centralised, and the state – ideologically, not welfare-wise – plays a far more central role there. Ireland is a very individualistic country, we take a more competitive approach to running our business and we are more personal in the way we run our own lives. Chinese and Asian cultures in general are more docile, so a 'strong man' approach to management can work there on a larger scale than it can in Ireland.

I do like the Swedish model in terms of the welfare it provides, but I dislike it in terms of taxation. I think it is very interesting to see that the big Swedish companies now primarily operate outside Sweden, and the country's growth must inevitably have been impacted over recent years.

What is important is that Ireland should not take its new prosperity for granted, for it might become a very short-term thing unless we find new, innovative ways to support it. The only way we really can galvanise the economy for the next 25 years is to attract more and more international capital – both human and financial – into Ireland. That is why I think the issues of immigration and capital should be central to how we think about the future of this country.

Immigration

CG: On immigration, just few weeks ago Labour Party leader Pat Rabbitte repeated his comments about the danger of an 'open doors' immigration policy toward eastern European workers. Do you share his concerns?

TOR: Ask yourself: what made America grow? Immigration is the answer. The skills of the world came to America, seized new opportunities and even today the debate about Mexican workers recognises this. It is unavoidable that we are going to have immigration as long as we have new physical and financial capital coming into the country. This is the main benefit of being a member of the common market. So what Pat Rabbitte is really saying is that the unions are hugely challenged by this; by events like the Irish Ferries dispute.

We can slam shut the doors on immigration the way the French did with their Polish plumber campaign. There are certain countries in Europe that do hold a different view of immigration than we do. But your question is whether we can sustain our open-door policy. My view is that yes, we should be able to sustain our policy on immigration. But this does not apply to everyone. For example, where do secularism and religion come into it? It is an entirely new debate, which Ireland, inevitably, will have to face.

CG: Yet the Irish Ferries dispute taught us also about the lack of proper policy debate in Ireland. In the majority of western democracies the debate is quite often being driven by business leaders, openly speaking about their views on government policies, as well as by intellectuals. In Ireland it is virtually unheard of that a businessperson would stimulate a debate about policies. We seem to be more comfortable with sponsoring festivals and golf events than with sponsoring research into social policies and promoting alternative views and ideas. Do you feel that as we become more comfortable with our newly acquired wealth we will see the emergence of more policy-conscious and more proactive business leaders?

Think tanks

TOR: When you asked the question about why I stayed at Eircom, I answered it by saying that I wanted to be a champion of the capacity of Ireland to build real public ownership of companies through the marketplace. This was a statement of my belief in that debate and certainly the wider audience, the City of London or US capital markets for example, will have no doubt now that it is possible to get a fair deal in Ireland.

Of course in the US, for example, you have the Brookings Institution, the American Enterprise Institute, the Hoover Institute and many other think tanks that span the whole political spectrum. These are very important catalysts for the way the American political system works. We don't have these here. We should have them. I think the ESRI is a fine starting point.

We need centres for catalysing the debate – not just the employers or IBEC's views or the unions' views, but think tanks and our business schools expressing trenchant views of our society and structures. So far we have a rather simplistic adversarial relationship between, say, the trade unions and the employers. Yet when you ask Irish people 'What do you class yourself as?', the vast majority of the people believe that they are 'middle class'. I often wonder who represents them at the partnership table.

CHAPTER 48

Interview: Fran Rooney
By Tom McEnaney

TOM MCENANEY LOOKS AT THE RISE AND RISE OF BALTIMORE TECHNOLOGIES' FRAN ROONEY, BUSINESS PERSON OF THE YEAR. FROM BUSINESS & FINANCE, MARCH 30TH 2000.

Fran Rooney looked a comfortable figure as he settled into his office in the basement of the IFSC at 8.30 last Monday morning. Not for the first time he was explaining to a reporter what Baltimore was about. Not just what they do, you understand, but how in heaven's name did he grow a company which he purchased for less than £500,000 four years ago to the stage where it was worth £4bn.

That's what Baltimore was valued at on the London Stock Exchange at the beginning of the interview. Three hours later, the interview complete, Baltimore was valued at £4.3bn and Rooney's personal wealth had increased by £10m.

To see how far the rise of Baltimore is from what most of us consider to be reality, the increase in the value of the company in part of one morning earlier this week was greater than the total value of each of 32 separate companies listed on the Dublin exchange.

Rooney seems entirely unfazed by the movement. Indeed, he seems entirely unfazed by the whole phenomenon. A former employee of the P&T – for younger readers the forerunner of Eircom and An Post – his personal wealth is now in the nine-figure category, at least on paper. But Rooney behaves as if he created billion-pound companies every day. At one point we break for coffee and, as Rooney heads for the kitchen, he explains that he doesn't like the idea of having secretaries around to make coffee when he's perfectly capable of doing it for himself.

This is not just an act. He does know where the sugar is kept. Meet the man and you come away with the impression that the wealth and success have certainly not gone to his head. His only nod in the direction of indulgence since the success of Baltimore was to buy a slightly larger house in Castleknock for his family "and a few nice holidays".

Because the phenomenal rise of Baltimore is related to the phenomenal rise of internet stocks it is easy to think of the success of the company as being no more than part of a wider trend. But the truth is considerably different.

Although hit by the volatility of the technology sector over the past few weeks, Baltimore's rise has been steady, if spectacular. Internet companies will come and go but as the leader in securing electronic transactions in Europe and South-East Asia, Baltimore is likely to succeed no matter who tends to survive the shake-up when it comes.

The company has only recently targeted the US market where it is already one of the major players. At the end of last year the US accounted for 5% of Baltimore revenues. This year that percentage is expected to grow to 20%. Two companies, Entrust and Verisign have a greater share of the US market but, according to Rooney, neither of these has been on the shortlist for most of the contracts Baltimore has won. "Of the 250 contracts we have bid for so far, 75 have been decided and we have won 50 of these," he said.

Baltimore is not a profitable company but that is because it has decided to grow quickly and not because it is incapable of making a profit. In fact, the company was profitable every month for 14 months until August 1998. That's when Rooney decided the company needed to get big quickly, and that's exactly what it has done.

At the end of that year it reversed into the larger British company Zergo, which among other things gave it a listing on the London exchange, where its shares were valued at stg£3.50 in January of last year. By the end of October the shares were trading at £15, which grew to £36 by Christmas. In January Baltimore shares were trading at £47. By the middle of last month they were valued at £80 and earlier this week they were changing hands for £96.

It is hardly surprising to say that Baltimore's success has been greater than its chief executive envisioned, but to see how much greater you need to look into the mind of the 29-year-old Rooney. He has always believed in having clear goals and at 29 his goals were very clear indeed. By the age of 40 he wanted to be heading a company, by 45 he wanted to have his mortgage paid off, and by 50 he wanted to be in a position to retire. Rooney is now 43.

The story of how Rooney came to be the head of Baltimore has been told more than once. Having joined the Department of Posts and Telegraphs out of school in 1974, he spent 16 years improving and educating himself part-time. He qualified as a chartered accountant, as well as earning qualifications in public administration and computer technology. Rooney moved to NIB for a few years and later set up a company called Meridian VAT Processing International.

His ability to set this company up quickly attracted the attention of financier Dermot Desmond, who recruited Rooney to help build Quay Financial Software. After QFS was sold off in 1995, Rooney developed the business plan for Baltimore. Desmond agreed to back it and an electronic security phenomenon was born.

So far so good. Having good experience, good qualifications, good backing and a good idea, it is not difficult to see how the ambitious Rooney made a success of the company. But the secret element which turned a successful company into a phenomenally successful company, which after only four years qualified for entry into the FTSE list of Britain's 100 largest companies, can be described in one word – vision, Rooney's vision.

Let's go back to that merger with Zergo, which was the first major milestone in the life of what was still a young company. According to one person who knows Rooney well, he decided around August 1998 that the company would be worth $50m by the end of the year.

Zergo was a company in a similar business, which had a software and a hardware division. It had a listing on the London exchange and had annual revenues of $24m. At the time the deal was being negotiated Baltimore revenues amounted to only about $5m. Nonetheless, Rooney managed to negotiate a deal where the much smaller Irish company was valued at half the market cap of Zergo. And of course shortly afterwards the new company was renamed Baltimore and Rooney became the chief executive.

There were two very clever elements to that deal. It was negotiated on the basis of the number of shares which would accrue to the original Baltimore shareholders. When the deal was announced on December 16th 1998, those shares were worth $45m. By the time the deal was closed, on January 11th 1999, the same shares were worth $84m.

But Rooney had said that he wanted Baltimore to be worth $50m by the end of 1998 and a $45m valuation was $5m short.

The Zergo board, on the other hand, refused to give the Baltimore shareholders more than one-third of the new company. So Rooney negotiated a deal which included $5m in convertible and redeemable loan notes for the original Baltimore shareholders. That meant Rooney was able to achieve his target.

"It's very important to have a clear vision of what you want to achieve," said Rooney, when asked what advice he would give to other Irish business people. "Then you have to map out what the time frame is for getting there. Then the approach is to fill in what you need to get there."

Rooney's vision so impressed the Zergo board that they were willing to be taken over by the smaller board on what were very favourable terms for the original Baltimore shareholders. At the time Dermot Desmond owned about 57% of the company and Rooney had about 13%. And as for the $5m convertible loan note, it can be cashed in May and, based on Baltimore's current share price, is valued at about $80m. Vision.

The second major corporate milestone for Rooney was the acquisition of GTE Cybertrust Solutions, which was closed earlier this week. While the Baltimore boys negotiated the Zergo deal based on the number of shares they would receive, the Cybertrust deal was negotiated based on the value of shares Baltimore would give up. The advantages for a company whose share price is growing at such a fast pace is obvious. The result was that Baltimore managed to purchase a company with revenues equivalent to half Baltimore revenues for a price equivalent to only one twentieth of Baltimore's market cap. Vision.

Of course it's about more than putting together clever deals. In order to be big, Rooney realised early on that he had to look big. There is a well-travelled story that at a data security conference in California in 1998, Rooney put 10 of his 15 staff on the stand in order to look bigger than he was. He then threw a party in a hotel suite. What customers in attendance did not know was that all of the drink had been purchased in duty-free by each of the staff members on the way over.

But in perception terms, Rooney's greatest coup was to persuade the US president, Bill Clinton, and the Taoiseach, Bertie Ahern, to sign an electronic commerce communiqué in front of the world's media using Baltimore encryption software.

When he talks about his employees, Rooney returns to the concept of trust. "People are very important. It's about creating an environment where people trust each other and have respect for each other." It should also be borne in mind that 15% of the company has been set aside for staff at the company.

Rooney learned how to manage people at a young age. At 15 he realised there was enough talent in his native Cabra to start up a soccer team. He started the team and then managed it. Later he went on to play with Shamrock Rovers when Johnny Giles was player/manager at the club and he has also played with Bohemians, Home Farm and St Patrick's Athletic.

Although Baltimore has received a huge amount of publicity, it does not use the services of a PR consultancy firm and, in the words of Rooney, "has never spent a penny on advertising".

If Rooney is an egotistical man he hides it well, and he is not quick to venture opinions on subjects not related to his business. When pushed on the state of the country, his analysis is such that he might be talking about a company in need of a new computer system. "We have made huge improvements but the pace at which we are moving is far too slow. There are far too many legacy issues around. The administrative culture could be completely changed. IBEC, the unions and the civil service, they all need co be re-evaluated."

That re-evaluation should not, he said, stop there, but should also apply to the government. Rooney favours a more presidential-style government which would be free to run the country without having to worry about having a majority in the house. Perhaps then we could go from being a very successful economy to being a phenomenally successful economy.

Baltimore and security in focus

Baltimore is a company oft talked about but seldom understood. Even well informed business people tend to satisfy themselves with the notion that the company has something to do with internet security. There is also a widely-held perception that it secures credit card transactions over the web.

First, let's dispel the misinformation. Baltimore is not about making financial transactions secure; it is about making all communications between companies, organisations or individuals using its system, secure. Those communications could include financial transactions, but they could also be email, or internal mail.

In explaining what his company does, Rooney makes considerable use of the word "trust". It is important, he says, that people can trust that their online transactions are secure. Indeed, it is only when this trust is there that many transactions can take place. Trust across the internet is a clearly defined concept with four elements: confidentiality (ensuring nobody else reads your message), integrity (ensuring your message has not been changed), authentification (ensuring the message is from the person it claims to be from) and non-repudiation (ensuring the message carries the weight of a legal document).

The latter element is obviously in the hands of national governments and, according to Rooney, Ireland, the US and Italy are among countries currently changing their legislation to give legal weight to correspondence sent electronically.

Internationally-adopted standards have set the way in which these goals are to be attained. The system is known as public key infrastructure.

The system is not so much complicated as demanding of a different way of thinking about security. It involves what are known as 'keys', which are used to encrypt and decipher messages.

There are different levels of encryption. Baltimore uses 124-bit encryption, which put simply means it would take a very smart person using a very powerful computer millennia to break the code.

Every individual using the system has two keys: a private key, to which only he has access, and a public key, which is kept in a directory to which everybody or a select group of people have access.

Let's say John wants to send a secure message to Mary. As it happens, he's asking her out for a pint, but the content of the message is unimportant for the purposes of our exercise.

The software which John is using will access Mary's 'public key' and will use this to encrypt the message. John then sends the message. The only software which can decipher that message is the software with access to Mary's 'private key' and the only person with Mary's private key is, of course, Mary. The private key itself could be related to a person's thumb-print or a smart-card which they carry.

Mary's elation at receiving an invite from the fair John will be marred by doubt were she not sure that it could not have come from the office prankster. She needs to know that it could only have come from John. This is why we have what is called a 'check sum'. Put very simply, John's computer assigns a value to every character in the message and adds these values together to get one number, which is individual to that message. If the message is changed in any way the check sum will not match the body of the message.

John's computer now uses his private key to encrypt the 'check sum'. And, as the smart people at the front of the class will already have guessed, only John's public key can be used to decipher that sum. Because her computer has to use John's public key in this way Mary knows the message came from John.

This is not just about a piece of software. This is about a whole infra-structure and Baltimore provides that infrastructure. The infrastructure has to be able to communicate with a company's existing systems. Selling and installing the toolkits which facilitate this accounts for about 30% of Baltimore revenues. According to Rooney, even where a company has chosen a rival's security platform, Baltimore is often called in to integrate that platform with the company's existing computer system.

CHAPTER 49

Interview: Tom Roche
By David O'Sullivan

CRH CO-FOUNDER AND MAN OF THE YEAR TOM ROCHE TALKS ABOUT HIS RISE
TO THE TOP OF IRISH INDUSTRY AND WHY HE STILL HAS MUCH TO CONTRIBUTE.
FROM BUSINESS & FINANCE, JANUARY 3RD, 1974.

With his traditional aversion to personal publicity he has been described as Ireland's Howard Hughes. He is one of the most powerful and influential figures on the Irish industrial scene, heading up as he does Cement-Roadstone Holdings, the Republic's largest industrial enterprise.

Tom Roche, in his 57th year, has just completed one of his most successful years as a businessman. Not only has he steered CRH to yet again higher profits but he has also broadened the European base of the company with the relatively recent incursions into the French and Dutch construction sectors. In a private capacity he retains his interests in the Irish Hydro-Carbon Company, which intends to build an oil refinery in Co Kerry, and in the controversial Bula with its interests in the lead-zinc orebody at Navan. He has a quiet, retiring personality and yet evokes the most passionately loyal emotions in many of his employees. In this, one of the rare interviews he has given to the media, he talks to David O'Sullivan about himself, his background, his business philosophy and his aspirations.

When he was 14 years of age Tom Roche lost his father in an accident. By the age of 16 he was working and, unknown to himself at that time, had embarked on a long road that would eventually wind toward his management of the largest industrial enterprise in the land. The transition from schoolboy to workman was as dramatic as it was sudden – "I was at Blackrock College one day and I had a shovel in my hand the next. It was as quick as that." He and his brother Donal teamed up and bought a small sand and coal business. He readily admits that this was an entirely new scene for him, but "as I was always interested in doing things with my hands – I was very fond of carpentry – this appealed to me more than going to school." The early business days for him were the difficult times of the 1930s with the trade war at its height and the economy gripped in the twin teeth of the huge world depression and the then-popular theory of each country being self-sufficient. "In that time of 1932 I personally had a great element of fear, because we simply had to work or we didn't have very much to eat."

The business grew slowly up to the war. "We began with a staff of three people including my brother and myself. We bought more trucks and continued to make concrete blocks. Generally we were connected with the building industry. We knew very little about sophisticated business methods, but we could see that we could make a living out of hauling sand and selling concrete blocks."

One of his biggest problems in those early days was to get good aggregate, in the form of gravel and sand, for making concrete blocks. "During the war, when things were fairly quiet in Ireland, we had plenty of time to think both about transport and the supply of good aggregate." The small transport fleet – he started off with one Model 'T' one-ton truck – had to be kept going during the trying times of the early forties and some ingenious methods were devised to this end, for example using gas balloons from producers fired by anthracite or charcoal.

"We visited plants in Cork where they had already washing and crushing facilities. We thought – 'well, this is the thing to go into as soon as the war ends.' With that in view, then, we formed a small company – the Castle Sand Company – and with a capital of £5,000 we began work."

Around 1948 he had been very friendly with Con Creedon, his next-door neighbour, who had just floated Gypsum Industries on the Irish Stock Exchange. By this time considerable experience had been gained in the sand and gravel business. The company bought its own washing and crushing plant and the transport fleet was augmented by purchasing ex-US Army trucks. Further pits were started and an engineering shop was established to overhaul the company's growing inventory of equipment. The company was growing quickly and by 1950 it had entered the quarrying business, mainly to supply roadworking materials to county councils.

Roche went to the same solicitor Con Creedon had used for floating Gypsum, Plunkett Dillon, and Roadstone Ltd emerged as a public company. "Suddenly we were in the bigger league. The business grew because we seemed to come into it when there was a much bigger expenditure on roads and building." Despite a serious recession around 1957 the growth of the company was accelerating year by year. From the start-up stage, with three people employed, to the present day the rate of expansion is reflected adequately in the 3,500 people now working in the Roadstone section of the Cement-Roadstone Group.

It has been said of Tom Roche by one of his employees: "The boss is a doer. He gets away with the unconventional – he's a great man for shovels and diggers. He gets mortally upset with planning." With a wry smile on his face he agrees broadly and explains. "From the time the British were here the emphasis on education seems to be more on the professions and not on manufacturing industry. In the time I grew up not many well-educated people took their coats off having become qualified and got back into the grime of industry. This has been a great loss to the country."

He offers the additional observation that "the system of awards in this country does not favour the practical people enough. For one reason or another the people on the shop-floor or on the quarry-floor are neither looked upon nor rewarded as much as accountants or lawyers or the other professions that have to do with business."

He advances the observation humorously: "It's nicer for the wife to say her husband is either an architect or a lawyer rather than being a works manager. In my view the works manager is the fellow who really creates the wealth. The other fellows dispose of it afterwards." It is his philosophy that the manufactured article be produced to the best design and at the lowest cost. He generalises the point finally: "the people responsible for doing that, in my view, are not rewarded sufficiently in this country."

Roche is not an organisation man. He confides that his temperament does not allow him to be. A senior executive of Roadstone has commented that "he doesn't like meetings – he suffers them". Again he agrees but defends himself by saying that he finds he "can talk best to one person at a time".

With a lot of reason he argues that only through profits can extra meaningful employment be generated. He argues that Irish industry must become more competitive through increased efficiency. Although he adds that personally he is more interested in constructing factories, for example, than making money for himself for money's sake.

He holds strong views on the unequal distribution of wealth in capitalist economies and feels that the huge speculative profits which have been made over the years by some people with the expenditure of very little effort is the cause of a great deal of justified social unrest and bitter feelings. He does not dwell upon the point but adds that in a curious way, he wished the Russian economic system had worked and would like to see the evolution of a better system here... "I think there is a lot to be said for everyone in society to drive around in Renault Fours."

Tom Roche has always been associated with a nationalist approach toward Irish business. Asked whether it was this imputed nationalism which prompted his company's move to take over Cement Ltd he explains: "It is true that I have always identified myself with Ireland. My grand-father, although I never knew the gentleman very well, was an MP. He duly did his stint in Galway Gaol." He feels a sense of camaraderie toward fellow Irishmen. "I feel a great pride when people, whether from America, or Britain or Europe, come over to Ireland and see the progress we have made and the things we have done ourselves." He quotes the example of Nitrigin Éireann and Jack Hynes – "a man who has shown that Irishmen can make the grade".

He gazes out the window momentarily and thinks. He turns around in his chair and begins again. He gently insists that his motivation in making the moves to take over Cement was not inspired by jingoism or a sense of extreme nationalism. It was a logical and long-considered move. His primary motivation, he says, was a deep sense of frustration at the continuing labour problems there. Not much short of 25% of Cement's total output went to

Roche's company and when Cement's employees went on the 1970 six-month marathon strike he decided to make a move.

On two counts he admits a certain regret about the formation of CRH – "part of the company must sell to its competitors and the whole company has become a target of criticisms on monopoly grounds". He adds finally: "I did not create Cement Ltd."

He disagrees that mistakes have been made in the expansion of the cement-manufacturing capacity at Platin "more and more we realise that Gunnar Larsen's vision was the correct one". He does agree that the beginning of the merger was quite difficult: "we were, in a sense, the mavericks, they were the establishment." He feels that the expansion of the company into the continent of Europe will provide the entire group with a firm base for continued growth. The Van Neerbos purchase, he says, came about quite by accident. For some years the Van Neerbos brothers had been Dutch agents for Roadstone products. On one of his many trips to the continent Roche mentioned to them that if ever they considered selling their interests in the company they should contact him first. And they did.

His decision to steer the group into the offshore exploration business may not reflect itself in the company's trading ever. But then with the risk elements in the offshore exploration game if commercially exploitable finds are ever made the benefits to the group could be enormous.

It is not only through Cement-Roadstone that Roche has developed his entrepreneurial flair. His establishment of Bula marked one of the most amazing developments in Irish business for some time. He refuses to be drawn on the issue, pointing to the sub-judice rule.

He comments, however, that at the time he became involved in Bula the government had just slapped an extra 8% onto the Corporation Profits Tax Bill. He saw the opportunity in the then tax-free metal mining field and took it. He is silent for a moment and adds cautiously that Bula does not rank among his prouder personal achievements. He is not at ease talking on this issue, so we talk about oil refining.

His involvement with the Irish Hydro-Carbon Company, which is expecting a decision on a detailed planning application for the construction of an oil refinery in Bantry Bay, reflects even more accurately his enterprise.

The subject is changed again. Has he any advice for young people starting out in the adult world? He pauses and wipes his brow. Then he articulates at length on how short one life can be. "We spend most of our lives striving for things. And not that the striving is not enjoyable. In the end we have only one life. And it's a short one."

He has often felt that he should write a book about himself. He had the title for the book before he ever thought what he could write in it: "The man who had everything." He goes on to explain that as the company became more successful he found himself with "a wonderful wife and family and a beautiful house". And yet, he adds, material wealth cannot bring enduring happiness. His best advice to any young person would be "to do whatever gives them most satisfaction – whether that be building a skyscraper or travelling to foreign lands with a rucksack on your back". He concludes by saying it is the advice he has given his four children.

He sincerely regrets having lost contact with a lot of his employees. He used to live in Inchicore and for many years worked side by side with his employees. He feels a great sympathy with the Irish working man – "he was damn badly treated up to the war". He agrees wholeheartedly with the necessity for the trade union movement and adds that "we should have inherited the dignity and worth of labour. But we didn't." Emphasising that he would not wish to seem patronising he admits that, even today, in many places in Ireland workers are treated without respect. He shares an ambition that one day he will see a statue erected at the Roadstone quarry at Belgard which would symbolise in stone the rise of the Irish worker.

He appears to be highly regarded by many of his employees, particularly long-serving ones. His attitudes towards his staff have always been practical, understanding, but above all, down-to-earth ones. Yet another executive said of him: "He likes guys who make a b--ls of things and admit it!"

His leisure activities are few. He likes golf and fishing but finds that most of his evenings are spent at home with his family. "We don't go out a great deal." He also likes motoring holidays and reading.

And when the statue is erected he feels that more than anything else it will articulate the feeling that whatever we have done in Ireland "we have done it ourselves".

Has he any intention of retiring? He doesn't labour the reply but simply says: "I feel I have a lot of leadership and ideas to contribute yet."

CHAPTER 50

Interview: Bernie Cahill
By Dan White

BUSINESS & FINANCE PROFILES MAN OF THE YEAR BERNIE CAHILL, WHO INNOVATED AT EXPRESS DAIRIES AND TURNED AROUND IRISH SUGAR, LATER CHAIRING AER LINGUS. FROM BUSINESS & FINANCE, JANUARY 11TH 1990.

*B*ernie Cahill has built Express Dairies into a quiet giant of Irish industry. *The Cork-based subsidiary of multinational Grand Metropolitan has an outstanding record in developing new products and its pioneering whey treatment process is copied across the world. As chairman of Irish Sugar, Cahill has also presided over a remarkable resurgence in the company's fortunes, and faced down fierce political opposition to the closure of the uneconomic Tuam and Thurles plants, closures which have transformed the group's outlook.*

As the great milk price boom of the 1980s fades into memory, things are going to get a lot tougher in the dairy business. For the 1990s, added-value is going to be the name of the game. At Express Dairies Bernie Cahill has a headstart on most of his competitors. Express turns whey into alcohol and cream into Baileys base. Along the way he has found the time to preside over Irish Sugar's return to rude health.

Express Dairies is the quiet giant of the Irish dairy industry. Its 1988 turnover was £210m and the group has 522 employees. It owns 80% of Carbery Milk Products, the biggest cheese plant in Ireland, at Ballineen in Co Cork. Carbery turns 70m gallons of milk into 16,000 tonnes of cheddar annually. On the side it turns out 6m litres of pure alcohol. In the north east its Virginia Milk Products supplies the cream base to Baileys. Both the Virginia plant and the Killeshandra-based MacCormac Milk Products also process skim milk.

Last year Express stepped uncharacteristically into the limelight when it teamed up with Waterford Foods to acquire Premier Tir Laighean (PTL), which supplies 70% of the Dublin liquid milk market, for £46.5m. Express processes in the region of 158m gallons of milk annually. This puts it just ahead of Avonmore at the top of the milk league table. It also has extensive interests in Northern Ireland.

Cahill is a 33-year veteran of Express, now a subsidiary of British conglomerate GrandMet. After qualifying as a dairy scientist from UCC in 1954 he spent two years in Clare and North Tipperary with the old Dairy Disposal Board. In 1956 he went to the UK and spent a year with the Milk Marketing Board before joining Express.

In 1965 he returned to Ireland and virtually single-handedly set up an Irish offshoot for Express. First item on the agenda was Carbery. At the time Cahill was managing an Express factory in the UK and there was a shortage of product. He was commissioned to carry out a survey of the Irish dairy industry. He found that his native West Cork was the only area which was not served by a major processing plant.

It was then a question of securing milk supplies from the local co-ops. At about the same time Kraft was also seeking to set up an operation in West Cork. However, Kraft wanted year-round milk supplies. The Bere Island-born Cahill had a better understanding of the realities of doing business with West Cork farmers. As a sweetener he brought in the four local co-ops – Bandon, Drinagh, Barryroe and Lisavaird, collectively known as the West Cork Federation – as 20% minority shareholders in Carbery.

When Cahill came back to his native county in 1965 it was originally on a two-year contract. "Something happened to that," he jokes.

In 1966, when Carbery started production, it was manufacturing only cheese. The problem with cheese, as any dairy man will tell you, is the by-products.

"If you produce cheese you also produce large quantities of whey," explains Cahill. Up to the mid-1970s Carbery, like everyone else in the business, dried the whey. The 1973 oil crisis suddenly made this a very expensive proposition. The whey consists of proteins which can be used to make baby food and lactose or milk sugar.

While it had long been known that it was possible to convert lactose into alcohol, it had never before been done on a commercial basis. Enter Cahill. Undaunted by the challenge, he and his colleagues spent a year seeking the strain of yeast which would make alcohol production a paying proposition. The first alcohol flowed in June 1978 and the Ballineen plant now produces 6m litres of pure alcohol annually. For the arithmetically-minded that is the equivalent of 21m bottles or 1.75m cases. In other words, Express is not only one of the biggest players in the Irish dairy industry, it is also, after Irish Distillers, the second biggest producer of potable alcohol.

Carbery now buys in whey from other processors and it handles three times as much whey as was originally planned in 1978. Most of the alcohol used in Baileys, produced by fellow-GrandMet subsidiary Gilbeys of Ireland, is supplied by the Ballineen plant.

Ballineen was the first plant of its kind in the world. It very quickly attracted the attention of the New Zealanders. As large dairy producers and cheese manufacturers they too had the problem of disposing of the resulting whey. At the same time they were importing a million gallons of alcohol a year from Australia. The Ballineen technology was franchised: there are now two such plants in New Zealand and it has become a net exporter of alcohol.

New Zealand was not the only country to see the merits of Cahill's innovation. The biggest cheese plant in the world was completed recently at Corona near Los Angeles. It produces 41,000 tonnes of cheese a year. The resulting pool of whey is correspondingly huge. It is also using Carbery's know-how to produce industrial alcohol for the pharmaceutical industry and for use in the alcohol-based fuel 'gasohol'.

So far Ballineen remains the only plant of its kind in Ireland. An attempt was made to repeat the trick in partnership with Golden Vale. A joint venture called Deelvale was based in Newcastle West. "We wanted to develop it into another Carbery," Cahill recalls.

It was not to be. Successive milk wars between the co-ops ensured that Deelvale never got the regular uninterrupted supplies of milk which were vital if it were to function efficiently. Eventually Express sold its shareholding to Golden Vale. Its disappointment with Deelvale did not retard Express's expansion elsewhere in Ireland. In 1972 it bought the dairy division of Bovril. At the time it had a small plant in Virginia in Cavan, which was renamed Virginia Milk Products. It was buying in skim milk from the local co-ops and shipping it across the Border. Express immediately installed dryers to do the job on the spot. In addition to Virginia there was also a cheese plant in Northern Ireland. This now helps to keep Carbery supplied with whey.

Express has a considerable north-eastern presence. Every year Virginia processes about 36m gallons of milk to produce the cream base that goes into Baileys. The skim milk remaining is processed into fat-filled milk powder, which Express markets under the Millac brand name. The Virginia plant processes a total of over 70m gallons annually. In recent years Virginia has acquired MacCormack Milk Products in nearby Killeshandra. It processes 15m gallons of milk into various products such as calf milk replacer.

Irish Sugar

Bernie Cahill's progress at Express has been relatively low-key; the same could not be said about his chairmanship of Irish Sugar. Since his appointment in 1985 the one-time lame duck has made an apparently miraculous recovery.

From after-tax losses of £15m over 1985 and 1986, the company has been thoroughly turned around. In 1987 pre-tax profits were £9.5m and in 1988 they reached £13.5m. For the six months to March 1989 profits climbed another 40% to £8.6m. The soon-to-be-announced full-year 1989 results will include a £10m extraordinary item due to the controversial closure of the Thurles Sugar Factory. Partially offsetting this will be the £10m which the company raised through selling its Dublin headquarters.

Having spurned the attentions of Larry Goodman among others, Irish Sugar is now being spoken of as a candidate for a stock exchange flotation. Its recent £17.6m purchase of 50% of the Odlum flour milling business points firmly in that direction.

What is Cahill's view on privatising Irish Sugar? He points out that any decision on the matter will have to be taken by the Government. When it is put to him whether he favours floating off the company he replies: "Personally I do."

If it comes, flotation may resemble some of the co-op shares issue. The employees and the growers are likely to be first in the queue of those eligible for shares. Only then will the institutions be invited to participate.

Like the dairy industry, sugar is subject to an EC quota regime. Ireland is limited to a 200,000 tonne production quota. This quota is currently vested with Irish Sugar. But the company would be unwise to base its future plans on the assumption that this will continue indefinitely, and therein lurks a danger for the group.

Ireland is not a low-cost beet producer. Several European countries can grow the crop more cheaply. Were the EC to decide at some stage to transfer the quotas to the individual growers, it is entirely possible that Irish quotas could be sold to overseas producers. This is not a prospect Cahill views with relish.

"One of the things we have got to do is to protect this company for Ireland. Any future decision must ensure that the beet quota stays in Ireland."

The key to this will be maintaining good relations with the growers. Irish Sugar has been relatively successful in this regard down the years. Privatising the company and giving the beet growers a stake in its future is one way of keeping everyone happy.

Perhaps the most remarkable achievement of Cahill's tenure at Irish Sugar was the closure of the two uneconomic plants at Tuam and Thurles. The Thurles closure in the constituency of the then-agriculture minister was managed at the most sensitive time – the run-up to the year's general election. But Irish Sugar stuck to its guns, and in doing so has transformed the outlook for the company. How does Cahill feel now about the controversy the closures caused?

"I was sad it created such uproar at the time. When we made the decisions we worked very hard to find alternatives. When I came in in 1985 our directive from the State, which was given to all State companies, was to operate on a commercial basis. When you are given that directive, then you operate on that basis until the shareholder tells you otherwise."

Irish Sugar is now a showcase example of what a State company can achieve with the right management and without government interference in its day-to-day affairs, even though for much of the early 1980s its very survival was in doubt. "If we had not done what we have done then Irish Sugar would not have been a survivor in a few years," says Cahill bluntly.

If sugar now appears to have a bright future, the outlook for the dairy sector is less clear. After more than a decade and a half of surface calm, the industry is in for a series of changes the like of which have not been seen since Ireland first joined the EC in 1973. Falling milk prices will accelerate the change. The acquisition of Bailieboro and Westmeath by Larry Goodman's Food Industries, and Express and Waterford Foods' purchase of Premier Tir Laighean, are merely the beginning of a process which will transform the industry.

Cahill himself is convinced of the need for further takeovers and amalgamations to reduce the number of groups in the dairy industry: "I would see the numbers reducing. In ten years' time there will be only two or three major players. It is our intention to be one of those."

He stresses that merely creating a smaller number of larger companies in the dairy industry is not enough. Such a process only makes sense if costs are reduced as a result. "People talk an awful lot about amalgamation. They forget that the most important thing is rationalisation. That is where the cost benefits of amalgamation will come from."

Express/Waterford Foods will have to wring plenty of savings out of PTL if they are to justify the price paid (£46.5m for a company which lost £2m in 1988 and had net assets of only £1.8m). "We paid too much for it. There is no doubt about it" is Cahill's candid opinion.

A sceptic might argue that the Express interest in PTL had less to do with any cost savings that could be achieved than with its determination to prevent Food Industries securing control of the 66m gallon PTL milk pool. Over half of that, 36m gallons, is supplied to Virginia for Baileys. Gilbeys' 1989 profits were £46m. The Express profits are not disclosed. According to Cahill they are "very commercial".

Cahill concedes that Express was "particularly interested in [PTL's] surplus milk", but stresses that this was only one of a number of reasons for the buy. "We are not very strong in Ireland in consumer products. Waterford Foods are very strong in this area and in liquid milk operations. We felt that this was a perfect match for the two companies."

An interesting feature of the Express expansion in Ireland has been the way in which it has tended to operate either through or in partnership with co-ops. To this day it has very few direct suppliers. Both Carbery and its north-eastern operations rely primarily on the local co-ops for supplies of milk. Even before the joint PTL acquisition, Express already owned an effective 40% of PTL's Dublin liquid milk operation Premier Dairies.

With Food Industries now attempting to unite the north-eastern co-ops in a shotgun marriage, will Express step in and once more deny Food Industries the prize? Cahill is giving very little away.

"We have a policy. If co-ops are interested in working with us there are many ways of developing that relationship. There is Carbery, Premier. There may be others. We are flexible in what we have to do."

After 24 years at the helm Cahill turned over the day-to-day running of Express to managing director John Barry last November. This will give him more time to pursue his sailing hobby, but don't be deluded into thinking that he is about to slide into sedate retirement. At Express he retains responsibility for dealing with major customers, agencies and trade. This takes up most of his week. He spreads two or three days a month on Irish Sugar business, and more when required.

Cahill goes out of his way to stress his reliance on the management teams at Express and Irish Sugar. At Irish Sugar he was appointed chairman. He is also anxious that Express's other senior executives should not be ignored: "One of the strong points about Express in Ireland is that it has operated to a central theme. We have developed a very strong commercially orientated management."

That theme is the same for both Irish Sugar and Express: "If you have the right products and produce them efficiently, then you will stay in the market. If you don't, then you don't deserve to be in the market."

For his relentless pursuit of a commercial and innovative Irish dairy sector and his tough-minded guidance of Irish Sugar, Bernie Cahill is a worthy Man of the Year.

CHAPTER 51

Interview: Ray MacSharry
By Aileen O'Toole

RECENTLY DEPARTED MINISTER FOR FINANCE RAY MACSHARRY'S REFORMS AND CUTBACKS MADE THE NEW EU AGRICULTURE COMMISSIONER MAN OF THE YEAR IN 1989. FROM BUSINESS & FINANCE, JANUARY 5TH, 1989.

As Minister for Finance Ray MacSharry was admired by civil servants, economists, businesspeople, his fellow members of Fianna Fáil and, privately, by like-minded members of opposition parties. He may have been the instigator of unpopular policies yet, unlike Richie Ryan in the mid-1970s, his political image did not suffer unduly, beyond being branded Mac the Knife (it is a name, incidentally, which he does not mind at all. "It's a great name. Did you know there's a song called 'Mac the Knife'?" he asks.)

Ray MacSharry this week begins a new career as European commissioner for agriculture; he leaves a considerable legacy not just at the Department of Finance but one which touches every branch of the Irish economy.

There are those who will argue that his ministerial term was so distinguished, and his achievements so great, because an absence of effective opposition in the Dáil made it easier to push through unpalatable measures. Or they will suggest that he had the advantage of a united cabinet behind him, unlike his predecessor who had the trauma of trying to get approval from a coalition grouping with widely differing economic views. Or they will say that MacSharry had luck on his side, that some of the key indicators (like inflation) would have come right anyway and that an unexpected result from the tax amnesty has helped to put a better gloss on this year's figures.

There is a measure of truth in each of those arguments, but independent economists are convinced that we would not have seen the progress we have witnessed in the last couple of years without a committed government and an able minister for finance. "In his department he commanded respect. He got things done. He accepted the advice he was given, went to the cabinet and got it accepted," comments one.

"He was held in high regard," notes another. "He was decisive and his personal style was to delegate. But the big difference was that the government was serious." The fact that this devotion to fiscal rectitude is newly founded does not overly concern them. "With Fianna Fáil the problem was convincing them of the right thing to do. Once they are convinced they are committed. With the previous government, they claimed to know what the right thing was but did nothing about it. To me, that was more worrying," one says.

To Ray MacSharry, attempting to put order on the national finances was not an entirely new experience. He was the minister for finance in the short-lived Fianna Fáil government of 1982 and introduced a supplementary budget, expressing sentiments akin to those made in his two subsequent budget speeches: "It is time to give a new sense of direction to the economy and to harness more effectively the resources that are available to us," he began his budget address shortly after the minority Fianna Fáil government assumed power in March 1987. The broad thrust of the budget he introduced was the one which Fine Gael had proposed but which its coalition partner had rejected, causing the government to collapse.

"When I left Finance in December 1982 we owed £12bn and when we came into government in 1987 we were facing a debt of £24bn," MacSharry recaps. "It had more than doubled in four and a quarter years."

The economic picture was grim – Ireland had hopped on a debt rollercoaster which kept going faster and faster. The external debt had risen from £500m in 1974 to more than £10bn by the end of 1986, sapping the economy through high interest payments, some of which had to be borrowed, and which were exported to foreign banks. The entire public sector debt represented an astonishing 165% of GNP, one of the highest ratios within the OECD. Translating the figures into more meaningful terms, we owed £21,000 for every employed person, around double the average industrial salary. The cost of servicing the debt absorbed virtually all income from PAYE.

Added to that, national output in 1986 was lower than it had been in 1980, when other economies had shown steady growth; unemployment had reached 18% of the workforce and looked set to continue rising; there was no export growth in 1986, caused in the main by international factors; there was a 4.5% drop in construction activity; investment fell by 2.5% while interest rates were on the way up again.

Faced with this depressing scene, what did Ray MacSharry do following his appointment? "One does not get too much time to sit back and relax – you have to get on with the job. The immediate priority with a minority government was to prepare a budget that would sufficiently reduce expenditure to show some downward trend in the exchequer borrowing requirement... we had to more or less ignore the possibility of a defeat in the Dáil, we had to just go and do what needed to be done to get the EBR under control."

Twenty-one days after his appointment he introduced his budget with its twin priorities to try to control the debt and curb public spending. He set a target of reducing the EBR to 10.7% of GNP, compared with 13% the previous year, and thus went further than what Fine Gael suggested in its proposed budget; it wanted to cut the EBR to 11.7%. The second target was to trim the current budget deficit from 8.5% of GNP in 1986 to 6.9%. Both targets were comfortably met, the EBR coming in at 10.3% and the current budget deficit at 6.7%.

Another round of ambitious targets was set by MacSharry in his 1988 budget, with EBR targeted to come down to 8.2%, making it the lowest since 1974/1975, and the current budget deficit coming in at 6.3%. A number of factors, but primarily more buoyant tax receipts, have conspired to make for a better than expected outturn from 1988. "I would leave the tax amnesty out of the reckoning completely because it is a once-off,"

MacSharry says of the £500m windfall. "Without the amnesty we have come from an EBR of 13.2% to probably 7% in two budgets. No other economy in the world has done so well."

Ministers for finance, he argues, have little room for manoeuvre on budget day: "We spend around £10bn, £2bn is gone immediately on servicing the national debt, £2.5bn goes on social welfare, around the same again on public service pay. If you add to that £1.3bn for health services and £1.2bn for education and the other 14 or 15 government departments are left with very little money to run the show, yet they are the motivators of the economy."

Budget days are now very different: "Fifteen or 20 years ago budget day normally meant who gets what. In the last couple of years it's who do we take what from. We're walking a tightrope – you can't get away from the fact that servicing the debt costs £2bn a year."

Away from the dry economic statistics, the approach to managing the economy has taken a number of forms. There has been the pruning of spending in government departments and State agencies; the word from the top has been to scrutinise each and every budget with a view to seeing where savings can be made.

In the 1987 budget, £63m was lopped off what the coalition had allocated for current spending and the outturn represented an increase of 2% over 1986, when inflation was running at 4%; on the capital side there was a cut of £13m or 1.3%. In 1988 there were cuts of £240m on current spending and £201m on capital expenditure while for 1989 the government has said that the effective cut will be £311m.

The brakes were put on public service recruitment and attractive terms were offered for voluntary redundancies – 8,700 have left the 218,000-strong public service since the beginning of 1987 under the redundancy programme. Then there was the agreement with the trade unions and employers which maps out a programme of economic reform up to the year 1990; one of the more immediate benefits of the Programme for National Recovery was the three-year pay deal, giving employers an ability to plan ahead and giving the government better hope of industrial peace and the general support from the unions on the economic goals which were set.

While the budgetary strategy has met with support from industry and economists, there has been a negative reaction to the cuts in health and education. MacSharry is philosophical: "There is pressure on for every pound. Nobody is going to tell you that you are going to save a pound, they always want another one to spend. Where savings have been identified they will be made next year and the year afterwards, because we have this huge umbrella of debt hanging over us. We have to pay that as will the next generation. No place has been left untouched and no place will. Notwith-standing the great progress we have made, we have to continue to save every 50p we can in every department. It is not a question of saving every pound any more."

Less than two years after this new approach began, there are tangible results. Inflation is running at just 2%, less than half the UK rate and below the forecast 3.5% rate for all OECD countries in 1988. The prime lending rate is 8%, six percentage points below the equivalent UK rate. Exports achieved another all-time high in 1988, reaching £12bn compared with the previous year's total of £10.7m. Based on the trade figures which have already been published, Ireland is on course to break another record for our balance of trade surplus, with economists predicting over £2bn compared with last year's £1.5bn.

The economy is set to show growth of 2% in 1988, with 5% being recorded the previous year. This has confounded the economists who had been predicting that the budgetary measures would have a negative effect on the economy. "After the 1987 budget we were told by the economists that with these savings we were making we were deflating the economy. The economy grew by more than it ever did for a number of years because we got the confidence back and people started to spend their own money again. We did not need the exchequer to motivate the economy. The same thing was said in January 1988 – they said that it was a deflationary budget, that there would be no growth. It's positive and it's going to be more positive than any of us expected."

Some economists have criticised the 1989 estimates, which they feel represent a softening of the government's resolve because many of the cuts are not as real as they first appear. It is a criticism which MacSharry rejects.

"Last May or June we were told by people that there was no need for the government to reduce expenditure whatsoever for 1989. We said no, that we would continue to make savings. We did that and as soon as we did people are saying that we did not cut enough. Which way do people want it? I wish they would make up their minds. The trouble is that they do not have to, they can back, each way, any particular bet any particular day but the minister for finance has to make his decisions and stand by them."

Does he bother therefore with any economic forecasts? "I always pay attention to them but when you get conflicting ones from the same sources it is very difficult."

The one economic indicator that has not come right is unemployment, standing at 240,000 in 1988 with emigration running at around 30,000 a year. Some consolation was taken from the annual employment survey which showed an increase of 6,000 in the year to April and the first sizeable increase since 1980. "It is unfortunate but the last element that comes in the cycle is employment. It is beginning to turn up but we have a long way to go," MacSharry suggests.

"Over the last year when people have been talking about the amnesty money, or the improvements in the economy there is an assumption that we must begin to spend it straight away. Each of the opposition parties in the Dáil have produced plans with anything from £400m to £600m in tax giveaways. We do not have that kind of money. If that kind of money did become available to us, it must be used to try and get some of the 240,000 people who are not at work to work so that they can contribute more to the creation of wealth in the economy and reduce the costs to the exchequer. Also, we must continue to reduce the EBR. We always have to strike a balance – looking after the less well off, reducing the debt and motivating greater activity in the economy." What about tax? "It is a balance between the lot. Tax concessions can help to motivate the economy."

He is bullish about the prospects for 1989, and concurs with predictions for growth of between 2.8% and 3%: "Barring major accidents that is the way it should be, notwithstanding the fact that we are still pulling money out of the system in the savings we have made for 1989. I think we can look forward with greater confidence than we could a year ago. I think we have made massive progress in 1987 and 1988 and will do so again in 1989. It is beginning to gain its own momentum already and that must continue. You cannot change your philosophy because if you do you stop creating the momentum out there, which is massively helping to solve your problems."

He resigned from the cabinet in November to become Ireland's European commissioner, but so far there is no evidence that the pattern which he helped set on economic matters will be broken. The Taoiseach's adjournment speech in the Dáil before Christmas spells out clearly a message which Ray MacSharry delivered very often as minister for finance – there is some considerable distance to go before our economic troubles are solved.

"The limited margin of manoeuvre that we have won must be consolidated and extended, not squandered," stated Charles Haughey. "The total national debt is still in the region of £25bn. It costs us approximately £2bn every year to pay the interest on that debt. This huge annual interest payment is equivalent to nearly £2,500 annually per taxpayer... in 1987 the national debt amounted to approximately 133% of gross national product and this basic position is relatively unchanged."

What Ray MacSharry has done is to help begin a process to stop the debt growing faster than the country's resources. The direction he has shown will have an impact on every company in the country.

"I have done a good bit of what needs to be done"

Ray MacSharry has no formal educational qualifications. He failed his Intermediate Certificate in the days when it was necessary to pass Irish to pass the entire examination. He got three honours but only a 38% mark in Irish. He admits he had no interest in school – Summerhill College, Sligo – where he was once suspended for smoking. He left before the Leaving Certificate.

His lack of qualifications was never a handicap, even when it came to the task of managing the nation's finances. "I am happy to have been blessed with reasonable common sense and judgement and that is probably more important than having 45 letters after your name, not that I disrespect anybody who has," he says.

After school, MacSharry went to work for an uncle in the meat trade but soon struck out on his own, acquiring a truck and becoming a haulier for local businesses in his native Sligo. He became active in politics in 1967, with his election to Sligo Co Council and took a Dáil seat in the Sligo/Leitrim constituency in the 1969 General Election. He wound up the haulage business soon after his election win and has been a full-time politician ever since.

It is a political career that has been distinguished and not without controversy. He was junior minister at the Department of Finance between 1977 and 1979, when he became minister for agriculture until Fianna Fáil lost the 1981 general election. He was tánaiste and minister for finance in the short-lived Fianna Fáil government of 1982. He was a member of the European Parliament for three years in the mid-1980s. "I went to pay my bills and made no secret of it," he says. He has six children and the cost of their education was one of the main reasons for opting for a career in Strasbourg.

That European election result represented a big personal triumph – he topped the poll in Sligo/Leitrim and showed that no damage had been caused to his political reputation by the revelation that he taped a conversation with Martin O'Donoghue. That was probably the lowpoint of his career – he argued that he acted in good faith but nonetheless offered his resignation from the Fianna Fáil front bench.

His term as minister for finance was a political comeback of a kind not usually witnessed. The events of 1982 have been wiped from the public mind and MacSharry's standing as an astute politician has been enhanced during his term at the Department of Finance.

Like most politicians he is thick-skinned and continues to be about the subject of the spending of National Lottery money. Much capital has been made out of how Sligo has benefited disproportionately from the lottery. MacSharry says: "Sligo is getting money not because I live there but because it is the centre of a region. Money is going to be spent on the major centres and I make no apologies for that."

Next stop is Brussels and taking charge of the agricultural brief, which consumes 60% of the £35bn Community budget. He quit as minister for finance because he had "done a good bit of what needs to be done. It's a question of keeping a truck on the middle of the road and there are plenty of people capable of doing that." He took the commissioner's job because he sees "further challenges and opportunities in the EEC".

He totally dismisses accusations that he is going for personal financial gain – he will earn £120,000 a year.

"I do not have to concern myself about that (monetary gain). My family are mostly reared and I resent the kind of things that have been said... I resent also and totally reject what has been said about individuals (the Taoiseach and fellow cabinet members) not wanting me to go. They might have liked me to stay but they were the people who nominated me to go."

Crowley, Joe 192
Cullen, Bill 444
Culliton, Jim 124
Culliton Report 293
Curley, Ian 377
Cummins, Michael 443
Curragh, The 188, 190
Curran, Maurice 117
Curran, Noel 85
Dáil Eireann 6, 54, 56, 71, 72, 87, 98, 111,
  112, 114, 115, 117, 153, 518, 521, 553,
  555, 558, 559, 560
Daily Telegraph, The 65
DaimlerChrysler Group 511
Dairy Disposal Company 212, 546
Dairygold 103, 213
Dakota 105
Dallas, 201, 247
Daly, Vincent 381
Dand, David 381
Danske Bank 178
Dargan, Michael 261, 262
Darling, Alistair 365
Data Products 483
Davidson, Norris 200
Davy, Brian 23, 26
Davy, Eugene 23
Davy, James 23
Davy, Joe 23
Davy Stockbrokers 23, 24, 25, 76, 83, 107
DCC 237, 457-461
DCU Ryan Academy 512
Debenhams 256
Deelvale 547, 548
De Gaulle, General Charles 19, 50, 65, 522
Deloitte Haskins 75, 106, 253
Delors, Jacques 59, 120, 121
Dell 102, 108, 279, 525
Delors, Jacques 97, 119, 348
Delves, Colm 392
Dempsey, Jeremiah 262
Deng Xiaoping 90, 127
Denmark 2, 7, 16, 17, 18, 47, 51, 105, 122,
  156, 288, 408, 460
Dennis, Dick 23
Department of Agriculture 216

Department of Communications 125
Department of Economic Planning and
  Development 310
Department of Education 389, 390
Department of Finance 3, 4, 5, 7, 8, 11, 14,
  17, 18, 20, 21, 29, 30, 50, 54, 62, 86, 97,
  118, 303, 304, 310, 313, 314, 398,411, 414,
  553, 560
Department of Foreign Affairs 19, 41, 46,
  54, 392
Department of Health 412
Department of Industry and Commerce 3,
  4, 5, 8, 18, 53, 55, 113, 272, 273, 414
Department of Jobs, Enterprise and
  Innovation, 282
Department of Labour 112
Department of Local Government 307
Department of Posts and Telegraphs 160,
  529, 530
Department of the Taoiseach 85, 86, 307,
  401
Derry, 58, 202
Desmond, Dermot 24, 113, 313, 381, 392,
  395-403, 495, 531, 532
Dettori, Frankie 190
Deutsche Bank 499
De Valera, Éamon 8, 12, 49, 52, 53, 157,
  196, 199, 304, 439
Diageo 445
Digby, Dillon 262
Digicel 357, 358, 359, 383, 387, 392, 487
Digiserve 238
Digital Corporation 123, 124, 265, 484
Dillon & Co 24
Dillon & Waldron 24
Dineen, Pat 355
Director of Public Prosecutions 118
Disney 255
Distilled Media 206
Division, 201
Dixon, Tim 98
Dockrells 32
Doherty, Colm 181
Doherty, Moya 135
Doherty, Seán 111
Dolan, Joe 286

Photo credits:
Bertie Ahern/Shane Ross
Liam Cosgrave
Dublin Docklands (George's Dock)
Dublin Docklands (Point Depot and Port)
Garret Fitzgerald dissolving the Dáil
Seán Lemass/Éamon de Valera
Jack Lynch and TK Whitaker
Tony O'Reilly/Albert Reynolds
Feargal Quinn/Charles Haughey/Peter Sutherland
Michael Smurfit at AGM:
Part of the Independent News and Media/ NLI Collection.

Richard Burrows/Patrick Ricard/Leo Crawford
John Magnier/Dermot Desmond
Brian Lenihan/TK Whitaker
Charlie McCreevy/Dermot Desmond
Charlie McCreevy/Peter Sutherland
Denis O'Brien on rooftop
Frances Ruane/Mary Harney:
Images courtesy of Independent News and Media

Leslie Buckley at AGM: by Mark Condren for Independent News and Media.
Bill Clinton, Business & Finance Awards 2010: David Cantwell.
Conference of Free State Chambers of Commerce/first meeting of the Federation of Saorstát Industries: Chambers Ireland.
Paul Connolly: Eamonn Farrell/Photocall Ireland.
Paul Coulson: Geoffrey Hauschild.
Bill Cullen: Nicole Browne/Photocall Ireland.
Dermot Desmond/JP McManus: David Cantwell.
Dermot Desmond with briefcase: Eamonn Farrell/Photocall Ireland.
Ben Dunne; Anne Heraty: Leon Farrell/ Photocall Ireland.
Esat Digifone licence application: Fennell Photography.
Niall Fitzgerald: Jim Winslet.

Margaret Heffernan: National University of Ireland/Lensmen.
Herb Kelleher: NYSE/Valerie Caviness.
Enda Kenny at conference/IMI campus: Irish Management Institute.
Oonah Keogh: Irish Stock Exchange.
Seán Lemass at IMI conference: Irish Management Institute.
John Major/Ian Hyland: John T Ohle.
George Mitchell onstage: John T Ohle.
Paddy Moriarty: ESB.
Pádraig O hUiginn: John T Ohle.
Liam O'Mahony: Aidan Crawley.
Gavin O'Reilly: Jason Clarke Photography.
Tony O'Reilly and horses: Camera Press/ Terence Spencer and Camera Press/Jonathan Player.
Tony Ryan, 2005: Aidan Crawley.
George Sisk: John Reid.
Domhnal Slattery: Peter Houlihan.
Deirdre Somers: David Levenson/Bloomberg.
Siobhán Talbot: Eugene Langan Photography.
Greg Turley: Crispin Rodwell.

Although every attempt has been made to identify photographers, due to the passage of time it has not always been possible to do so throughout the extensive Business & Finance archives. The publishers will be grateful to acknowledge them in future editions of this volume.

In loving memory of
Brian O'Reilly,
1951-2016
-RCOR